Butting Out

ANANYA CHATTERJEA

Butting Out

Reading Resistive Choreographies
Through Works by Jawole Willa Jo Zollar
and Chandralekha

WESLEYAN UNIVERSITY PRESS

MIDDLETOWN, CONNECTICUT

Published by Wesleyan University Press, Middletown, CT 06459

© 2004 by Ananya Chatterjea

Printed in in the United States of America

5   4   3   2   1

LIBRARY OF CONGRESS CATALOGING-IN-PUBLICATION DATA

Chatterjea, Ananya.
   Butting out : reading resistive choreographies through works by Jawole
Willa Jo Zollar and Chandralekha / Ananya Chatterjea.—1st ed.
       p. cm.
   Includes bibliographical references and index.
   ISBN 0–8195–6732–9 (cloth) — ISBN 0–8195–6733–7 (pbk. : alk. paper)
       1. Dance—Social aspects.   2. Feminism and the arts.   3. Choreography—
Study and teaching.   4. Chandralekha.   5. Zollar, Willa Jo.   I. Title.
   GV1588.6.C53 2004
   792.8'2—dc22   2004019055

TO ARTISTS WHO BELIEVE IN THEIR POWER TO INSPIRE CHANGE

But first,

To my incredible parents Chitra and Deb Prasad Chatterjee,
whose unconditional love has shored me up always.

And to Srija, whose beautiful spirit flows through all of my creative work.

Contents

Acknowledgments

The publication of this book marks the end of one phase of a journey that begun several years ago, a journey that has been marked with explorations, recurring questions, eurekas, moments of total resonance, and much growth. Along the way I have been nurtured and supported by many friends and colleagues without whom I might never have arrived at this point. To all of them my grateful thanks.

First of all to my advisers, with whom I began work on this project in its first and distant incarnation as my doctoral dissertation: Dr. Brenda Dixon-Gottschild, Dr. Cindy Patton, Dr. Edrie Ferdun. From each of you I learned, and continue to learn, invaluable research and life skills. Specifically, to Brenda, for bringing me to an area of study that I might never have appreciated to this extent, and for continuously encouraging me to find new directions in my research; to Cindy for insisting that I not shy away from discourse and instilling me with some faith in my theorizing; and to Edrie for opening me to the power of integration, a continuous dancing and thinking. Thanks also to Dr. Sarah Hilsendager for guiding me in finding funds that supported this initial phase of research and to the Graduate School, Temple University, for the Russell Conwell Fellowship and the Dissertation Completion Fellowship, which made the initial part of this research project possible.

At the University of Minnesota, where I began the rigorous process of overhauling the dissertation and rewriting it as a book, I want to thank first of all my colleagues, particularly Marge Maddux, Lance Brockman, and Michal Kobialka, whose continuous guidance and support has been invaluable. The Office of Multicultural Affairs at the University of Minnesota also supported this project generously with a multiyear grant. Importantly, to my students in the Department of Theater Arts and Dance I owe deep gratitude: they pushed me to think further and deeper with their many questions and arguments from different perspectives, while continuously surprising me with their belief in my projects. In particular, I want to thank Nora Jenneman and Melissa Kennedy, who supported the research on this project through the University of Minnesota's Undergraduate Research Opportunities Program.

Colleagues have been invaluable in this journey, reading my writing with keen attention despite incredibly busy schedules, and offering vital comments and critique. For this gift of time and thought, for the endless hours of debate and dialogue, and readings and rereadings, I thank Tommy DeFrantz, Rod Fergusson, Vinay Gidwani, Anna Scott, and, of course, Jigna Desai.

I have had the opportunity to publish some versions of some chapters in forums that offered valuable editorial guidance. Some versions of chapters 6, Subversive Dancing, Womb Wars, and Sri, have been published in the journals *Discourses in Dance* (Spring 2004), *Theater Journal* (October 2003), and *Dance Research Journal* (Spring 1998 and Fall 2001).

Lastly, I want to express my gratitude to those closest to me without whose faith and encouragement—and patience, during the long hours of work—this project would have taken much longer to complete. Meena Natarajan, Dipankar Mukherji, and Divya Karan have always been at the forefront of this support system, reading, discussing, pushing, and always encouraging. My partner in more ways than one, Darren Johnson, has also been there continuously, insisting on that commitment to excellence we always talked about, and putting up with all that that search entailed. I would never have believed that children could be such pillars of strength and encouragement had I not experienced how my daughter, Srija, stood by me, reminding me daily how much we could do once this was done. The research for this project began before she was born and is finally coming to one cycle of completion when she is seven. Srija's patience has been historic.

My deepest gratitude to Jawole Willa Jo Zollar and Chandralekha, who received me and my project with openness and shared so much with me. For their gifts of time, energy, thought, knowledge, and love, I cannot express enough thanks. My gratefulness to Sadanand Menon, without whose active support many parts of this project would have remained incomplete, and to the administrative staff in Urban Bush Women Offices, in particular Amy Cassello, Vanessa Manley, Nel Shelby, whose assistance in different ways has been crucial for this project. Finally, deep appreciation and thanks to Bette Marshall, Cylla von Tiedemann, Dona Ann McAdams, Dashrath Patel, and Sadanand Menon, for their generosity and their passion for the dance—their images run through the book, bringing alive the works I talk about. I am thankful for their kindness with these pictures that enrich my work in many ways.

Preface

As a South Asian "contemporary" choreographer, trained primarily in classical dance in India, and now living and working in the West, I am still trying to figure how to explain what I do without sounding exasperated at the repetitiveness of the entire procedure, to individuals who are quite puzzled when I describe my work. Of course this should not be surprising in a society where the extensive commodification of artifacts from "other" cultures has only served to further reify their "tradition-bound"-ness versus the high modernity of the West. In India, on the other hand, the masking of the choreographic process, within the constantly evolving neoclassical forms in order to foreground the continuity of a rich tradition, makes for an equally difficult situation. And between the high valorization of the classical tradition and the superficial, slavish imitations of some notion of "Western" movement—that is, of jazz-oriented Broadway-style moves—that usurps the name of "contemporary" in the current dance scene in India, the negotiation of a category of "contemporary" dance, based on indigenous cultural practices, moved by a progressive politics and philosophy, is a slippery task.

Also, in the case of contemporary Indian dance, there is double jeopardy. There is a particular non-resident Indian (NRI) phenomenon, which once again feeds into the cultural politics at "home" and makes for a particular kind of confusion. And while this is particularly true of Indian dance, it is in fact a scenario that affects South Asian communities generally because of the way Bollywood, as Bombay's Hindi film industry is aptly known, lionizes media attention in South Asia and in neighboring areas. So much so that one of the first smuggled goods to enter Afghanistan from India, after the fall of the Taliban government, was supposedly pirated copies of the Hindi movie, *Lagaan*. Specifically, in NRI communities, Hindi film dances, which draw from various dance genres, particularly folk, often rip-offs of MTV music videos, with all their glamour of rhythm, sexual excitement, revealing costumes, and copies of the latest "moves" from Hollywood, come to stand in for "Indian culture." This phenomenon, which reflects processes of globalization (that is, availability in international markets) and the domestication of plastic reality of contemporary Bollywood culture (available for private ownership through products like videos and DVDs), creates a dangerous uniformity of misperception that masquerades as "culture." It is particularly problematic because the field of dance is overly populated by female dancing bodies, and Hindi film dances invariably spectacularize the female body as sexual object. Indeed, it would be no exaggeration to say that Hindi film dances always aim at titillation, for the seduction comes to stand in for the consummation, since the Indian censors refuse to allow filming of the latter. While they no doubt constitute an interesting phenomenon and are a vital part of the emerging "Indy-pop" genre, they also cause endless frustration to teachers of classical dance whose students have begun to request that they be taught some "Hindi film dances," which are much more exciting and offer instant gratification as opposed to the long years of rigorous training necessary for learning the classical forms. They also mess with the rhetoric of "purity" that the classical forms are enmeshed in. On the other hand, their positioning as the obverse of the classical, leads, in popular imagination, to their conflation with "contemporary" Indian dance. This is frustrating for choreographers like me, whose work, in the absence of a fully theorized contemporary genre, sometimes gets lumped together with Hindi film dance, which is most often politically extremely problematic, if not directly antifeminist.

Lately of course, there is another peril. One realizes that the images of the Odissi dancer in Michael Jackson's music video and Madonna's *mehendi* (henna)-mania, were only the tip of a chilling iceberg. Watching the chorus line in *Moulin Rouge* dancing to the Hindi film number *Chamma Chamma*, and the terrible pastiche of exotica from "other" cultures, I have struggled to find a space where I can claim elements of South Asian-ness without immediately falling into the exotic trip. In particular, lately, I have wrestled with a colleague who has repeatedly told me that the moment he sees me in a sari, he immediately reads me as "exotic," such is the context, and can I not "deconstruct the sari on my body?" Apparently, as long as I did not, there was no way to read the radicalness of my work.

Initially these conversations frustrated me because I felt hemmed in by an external gaze, but I have to recognize audience expectations and conditions. These encounters led to deeper questions in my work: about what it meant for me to be located in the West, where it seemed the woman in a sari always already reads as a variation on the constant theme of unmoving "tradition." It apparently didn't really matter to these audiences that the dance sari is always short, to facilitate movement of the legs, and hence does not drape over the entire body as "regular" saris do, and is very simple in design. The differences between the regular sari and the dance sari were apparently "too subtle . . . we just don't see it."

Obviously there are many individuals for whom this is not true, and who read these differences quite well. I had to acknowledge, however, that there are probably many more for whom the woman-in-sari is perceived to be just too "different" to allow for distinctions within the genre. But for me the sari was a starting point in aesthetic exploration; it was something I grew up dancing in, and it situated me within the artistic frame I wanted to work in. I was neither willing nor interested in "deconstructing the sari on my body": it felt like an assigned project for the education of others. Besides, the dance movement was already deconstructing an aesthetic, but then again, without an adequate grounding in the "traditional" aesthetic, there was hardly a way to evaluate that. With subsequent conversations, I began to wonder if the only way I could be seen as doing "contemporary performance" was by putting on the black dress or the loose pants and tank top, and conforming to the specific definition of the "downtown" aesthetic. This felt like the tyranny of the West, its aesthetic imperative.

Anyways, as an artist then, I remained with a problem, one I was going to have to continue to grapple with if I chose to remain in the West. I could choose either to take into consideration the needs of the audience for my work, who often did not have enough of a background to "read" the codes of the performances, or I could choose to create for my artistic pleasure and be honest about the aims of the performance, and hope that the program notes and post-performance discussions, besides the aesthetic structure itself, would do the job. For the sake of my aesthetic fulfillment I have chosen to go with the latter course of action, but I recognize that the question is not a closed one. And over the years I have recognized the connectedness of the world and the reach of Western dominance, such that these same issues feed into and circulate in India as well—with different outcomes of course. So, though the emerging field of contemporary choreography is populated by artists such as Chandralekha, Manjusri Chaki-Sircar, Daksha Seth, Maya Rao and others, who work with genres, images, and inspirations that are indigenous, conflations of "contemporary" with superficial and commodified notions of "Western" dance are increasingly dominant.

Recurrent experiences such as this have made me think deeply about the ways in which choreographers from non-white and non-Western contexts are often misread by critics and audiences here. The issue is even more urgent when the choreographers are working in ways that deviate from "traditional" practice. In these situations it is more vital that critics are able to contextualize the pieces with sensitivity, because their words carry a great deal of weight. This might seem a really simple point, but one would be surprised at how often misreadings are perpetuated in and by the media. It is also vital for scholars to "read" such work with understanding of context, such that we are able to document and demonstrate the kinds of interventions effected by cultural production, particularly dancing bodies. I believe I came to write this book because I wanted to insist on a hearing of my readings of other contemporary choreographers. But more importantly, I have written this book to tether my readings to a history of ideas, to suggest that racial and cultural difference are matters neither personal nor ontological, but of construction, and need to be understood through critical engagement.

Generally my research focuses on the works of choreographers of color, the politics of whose work challenges establishment and questions our thinking. I am fascinated by the multilayered commentaries on sociocultural and political conditions that emerge from such work and I read the dancing bodies in their choreographies to foreground and theorize the vital interventions performed by them, which often have significant ramifications for other disciplines. For this particular project, I have studied the works of two women choreographers: one of them, Jawole Willa Jo Zollar, artistic director of the Urban Bush Women Company, based in New York, a company of black diasporic dancers, primarily women; the other, Chandralekha, a contemporary choreographer working with South Asian dancers and martial artists in Chennai, India. Both of these choreographers, in their own ways, have radicalized the cultural production in their communities, weaving the aesthetic and the political in powerful signification. I offer my readings of their works as instances of my thesis that, often despite lack of acknowledgment as such, artists of color and from the third world are creating some of the most radical images in the global community. These are works that redefine notions of beauty and empowerment and offer to us visions for a future we can work toward. These are images that, through their complexity, resist commodification even as they pass through the global circuits of capital, and refuse marketing as exotic entertainment even as they travel across the world. This also means that while I claim that these are exceptionally talented artists, I also place them in a range of artists working creatively in non-white, non-Western communities across the world in contemporary times. They are not exceptions that prove the rule of "traditional" cultures, but part of a continuum.

Working with these choreographers, following them around, participating in classes, rehearsals, and workshops, nationally and internationally, observing different audience reactions, analyzing media coverage, have highlighted for me what I already knew but now recognize as an urgent problem: the categories and paradigms that dominate the field of cultural production, while overdetermining the possibilities of the reception of such work, also reveal themselves as terribly inadequate to set any kind of context. Working to emphasize context and cultural specificity in analysis and interpretation of choreography, I ultimately came to theorize alternative concepts of local postmoderns, cutting-edge feminisms, and radical aesthetics. The articulation and discussion of these concepts in relation to the work of these choreographers comprises the substantial part of this book. For leading me to work and rework these concepts by creating work that confronted me with new challenges every-day, I thank these artists and others like them. This book, like their work, is suffused with the hope that the multiple dimensions, the power and the poetry, of such performance ultimately come to be recognized in their fullness.

Butting Out

Chandralekha observing rehearsal, Tramway Theater, Glasgow. Photo © Dashrath Patel.

Premises and Locations

Historical Complaints

Typical of the historiography responding to the western project of modernity, historical narratives written about the development of dance in the
modern and postmodern genres in Europe and America are primarily constructed through tracing the innovations and contributions of individuals
whose work appears to have been phenomenal in the cultural arena of the
times. A perception that strikes any reader of these histories is that these
narratives, despite some recent scholarly interventions, are remarkably
focused on retaining a focus both on the ways in which white artists have
shaped cultural development in the West, and on constructing this narrative self-referentially, such that it seems indubitable that the genius of these
individuals blossoms in a self-contained and narrowly defined context.
Causality and change are skewed in this vision, sometimes mismatched,
and their relationship often rendered opaque. Indeed, one of the methodological and operational goals of my project is a flipping-over of this perspective so that these relationships come to be seen from another lens, or,
that another set of relationings become visible. Let me give an example. In
the 2001 Conference of the Congress of Research on Dance, African American scholar Carl Paris, talking about the limited black presence in the early
postmodern scene, referred to Sally Banes's observation that postmodern
dance comes to mean differently in its later phases, accommodating some
of the very features that the Judsonites had rejected as antithetical to postmodernism. This then, coming to revert the earlier rejection of musicality,
for instance, made way for some black artists to enter the work. Paris
reverses the picture to suggest that it was in fact the influence of black
artists working in innovative ways that brought about these changes in the
postmodern aesthetic, and this reconceptualization in turn allowed for their
work to be considered postmodern.

Conceptions and myths about the "other," as much as real influences
and inspirations, have, of course, been part of the performative imagination
in the West since early times, notable as much in the geographical and cultural gobbledygook marking the conceptualization of the "Orient" in the
sari-and-pointe-shoe-clad figure of the heroine of *La Bayadere*, as in later

somewhat more sophisticated incarnations of the same. For instance, Nijinsky's role as the Hindu god Krishna in Ballet Russe's *Le Dieu Blue* or as the
golden slave in *Scheherazade*, Ruth St. Denis's *Dance of the Red and Gold
Sari*, Yvonne Rainer's discursive meditations upon the expression of emotion and the place of meaning in dance in her *India Journal*, and the range
of social dances that traveled from the Harlem ballrooms to downtown
clubs. Notable also in the multiple renderings of the story of Salome, the
Oriental virgin-whore: Loie Fuller in 1905, Maud Allan in 1907, Ruth St.
Denis in 1931, to name a few. At the same time of course, these dominant
genres of concert dance, apparently marked and named with reference to
culturally specific contexts of the white West, gain distinction and definition only through an oppositional relationship to the "other." Here the
double erasure: though influences from the "other" might be at the very
core of these "newly" formulated genres—modern, postmodern—these
former must be distanced from the latter and in fact be marked as their
very antithesis.

The work of cultural theorists like Homi Bhabha, Paul Gilroy, and
others in pointing out such basic disjunctions in the Western formulations
of the modern has made significant interventions in this regard. I invoke
these ideas primarily in order to articulate them in terms of dance and performance histories. I also want to emphasize that concepts of modern and
postmodern then, into which are inevitably built notions of progress and
radical inventiveness, operate in discussions of global cultures primarily to
reify "difference" and fix ideas of what is radical, avant-garde, cutting-edge
as the prerogative of the white West. This in turn means that the cutting-
edge work of artists from "other" cultural contexts can barely be acknowledged as such in the writings of critics and scholars, and the appreciation
of audiences in the Euro-American West. The way in which this prerogative
functions is primarily to question non-white, non-Western choreographers'
descriptions of their works as "contemporary" or "radical." However, *if* that
categorization is granted, then it almost seems a corollary that such "modernization" is a result of influence from the West, and these two categories
are regularly collapsed via a seemingly inevitable and exclusive relationship.
I will pick up this complaint again after the following notes.

I need to reflect briefly on my use of terminology before I go on. For
while there is no doubt that broad binarized categories, East/West, first/
third world, reify the picture, it seems to me that to do away with these
descriptors completely results in a flattening of differences which distorts
the picture equally. Despite certain upsets in the traditional alignment of
powers, the proliferation of a seemingly uniform commodity culture in
urban centres, and the burgeoning of diasporic communities and hybrid
identities, there are irreducible differences, between first and third worlds

for instance. In fact, it is impossible to deny that fault lines exist—perhaps in ways all the more dangerous for their decode, between, for instance, what is designated as "first" and what "third" world, and along lines of race, among other differentials. These re/mark (on) the discrepancies in political and economic power of nation states, of "worlds" we inhabit and whose passports make us inherit different policies as we travel across a world made apparently accessible to all who have the money to accommodate the exchange rate. At any rate, I am fully cognizant of the dangers of compartmentalized readings and want to clarify that I am using these terms as referring more to politics, ideologies, and aesthetics than to geographies and surfaces. In the following section, I intend to qualify and delimit my use of these terms and specify the context and politics of such usage.

Note-able sections

Note 1: My usage of typically binarized terms such as West and non-West reflects the symbolic capital that has accrued to the signifier "West" through historical, economic, and political processes, and the understanding that the West has come to signify, for "others," less a location and more a set of relationships woven through unequally positioned histories. My initial hesitations about referring to diverse groups of peoples of color through a negative—non-Western—were overturned by its current usage in these communities where in fact it has been reclaimed. While the term indicates effectively the broad, racist sweep of Eurocentric politics that has often relegated all that is "different" into one general category, brushing over the diversities among these, it has also come to signify a practice of marking one's difference from what is "the West," a strategy of resistive identifications. Clearly, however, this is not to deny either that these categories do not indicate uniform populations, or that they are intersected by internal hierarchies.

I have tended to use the terms "West" or "Euro-American" to refer to an unproblematized location in institutionalized white hegemony, and to a mental habit of impatience or imperviousness towards critiques of unearned privilege. I am aware that, in continuing to use these loaded terms, I can be charged with persisting in reifying an increasingly heterogeneous world. Such distinctions, however, are ubiquitous in the popular imaginary, particularly in the West, and dominant stereotypes color local understandings of racial and cultural differences. In this context, without disregarding the differential locationings instituted by gender, class, and sexuality, I want to insist that the discrepant power relations effected by racial and national differences are crucial and to deprioritize or flatten these would be nothing less than hazardous.

Similarly, the concepts of "first" and "third" worlds are complicated by the current heterogeneity of populations globally, by the increasingly hectic race for placement in the global circuits of capitalist commodification, and the complex collusions of internal/national and external/ multinational hierarchies created by the workings of a dubious globalization. Locked into a struggle to follow western standards of progress and modernity, third world nations are seemingly competing to live down the category of "underdeveloped" or "developing" ascribed to them—a trajectory that, through industrial and technological takeovers, has paved the way for first world neo-colonialism. The connotations and denotations of these terms have changed constantly and vitally from their initial conception at the 1955 Bandung Conference of recently decolonized and independent Asian and African nations— where these nations positioned themselves as constituting a non-aligned third world, in between the Capitalist first world and the Socialist second world—to a very typical use in contemporary times, a supplier of cheap labor for large first world–controlled corporations. That such binaries still continue to hold significance and make their mark on global politics, despite the irrevocable mixed-up-ness of exclusive and contradictory organizing categories, is highly indicative of the incisive capitalism and multinational-driven politics of our times, signaling the ultimate domination of the EuroWest.

These hierarchies weigh heavily in the personal histories of both choreographers, not just in terms of producers and sponsors for their work, but particularly during the extensive traveling they do with their companies. While Zollar talks about often having met with hostility within national borders, Chandralekha emphasizes in particular the differential treatment she and her company often receive as they travel internationally with their Indian passports, reflecting the suspicion and distrust that travelers from the third world often meet with.[1] While the sponsors of performances abroad or organizers of festivals, and other choreographers and dancers who have participated in the same engagements are appreciative of the work and of the artists themselves, immigration officials at airports remind them repeatedly of the difference between passports from first- and third-world countries. Of course one must be attentive to the peculiar contextual complexity marking the functioning of these terms: while African Americans are located, literally, in one of the most powerful first-world countries, the abject racism that permeates their lives and the collusion of race and class suggest endangered life conditions that suspend many of the "privileges" that come with that passport. Yet, as I have suggested before, despite the flattening process of corporate globalization, basic

life conditions remain vitally different and refuse the blurring of
boundaries between geographically differentiated "first" and "third"
worlds, between "developed" and "developing" nations: remarkable
differences remain and insist on marking their "differance."

Note 2: One is also conscious of rising complaints about the excess and
overcompensation that seems to mark the cultural and artistic work of
people of color: there are "too many" performances about the Middle
Passage, though it seems quite natural that the *Nutcracker* be produced
every year, for instance. This also reflects the narrow notion of diversity
allowed by mainstream politics, where there is little space for difference.[2] In the lip service to a "multicultural" agenda, a select few are celebrated to serve as the ticket to liberalism, representatives of "color" or
their entire race, to the detriment and erasure of many others who are
vitally different.

This perception of "too much" also extends to the presence of color in
other fields of endeavor, as Jacqui Alexander pointed out in a keynote
address at a conference on Third World Women:[3] there are too many
South Asian women in academia, for instance, though national statis-
tics will cause us to wonder how, and against what paradigm of quantitative normativity, one reaches this conclusion. In relation to these
issues and recent outrages over "reverse racisms" that diffuse the focus
on the cosmetic nature of the measures by the establishment to somehow settle claims for a more equitable society, I want to re-emphasize
that it is dangerous not to inspect the range and changing forms and
dimensions of Western or Euro-American domination. Obviously it
continues to impact contemporary cultural politics globally and main-
tains the skewed power structure with minimal adjustments to changing situations—issues that are addressed with complexity and
brilliance by scholars of postcolonial, race, and cultural studies for
instance.

Note 3: Vigilant to the possible problems in conflating "black" with "third
world" or "color" particularly in the American context, and a resultant
diminishing of the specificity of the black American experience, I have
kept these nomenclatures separate. However, this project yearns
toward a politics that might be described as "black" as the term is currently used in particular diasporic communities of color. In several
Europe-based diasporas, certainly in the United Kingdom and somewhat in Canada too, communities of color have picked up on the older
colonial usage of the term, indicating all non-white populations, to
resignify it in keeping with their politics. Here "black" is not an ontological category, but a political one, marked not just racially but
specifically by the politics of resistance to a hegemonically regulated

sociopolitical system, and is taken on by individuals across different non-white groups to signal a solidarity of radical politics along lines of race, gender, class, and sexuality. This politics of coalition among communities of color is exciting to me; it spells hope. Specifically, it reminds me of Cornel West's prophetic articulation, a decade ago, about the "new cultural politics of difference" that "affirms the perennial quest for the precious ideals of individuality and democracy by digging deep into the depths of human particularities and social specificities in order to construct new kinds of connections, affinities and communities across empire, nation, region, race, gender, age, and sexual orientation . . . This connectedness does not signal a homogeneous unity or a monolithic totality but rather a contingent, fragile coalition building in an effort to pursue common radical libertarian and democratic goals that overlap."[4] West's concept works through a balance of individual endeavour and community reinforcement, a politics of self-determination and coalition, very differently from the success stories of hardened individualism propagated by capitalism.

Note 4: On the other hand, I have preferred to use the descriptor black, unless I am referring specifically to African American contexts. This is in order to recognize the diversity and diasporic nature of the black communities in America, of peoples of African heritage whose nationalities and cultures are different, reflecting both the cultural specificities and differences of immigrant African communities, Nigerian, Senegalese, Ghanaian; as well as the reformulations of these specificities in diaspora: Afro-Caribbean cultural practices have inflected Africanist traditions differently from Afro-Brazilian or African American ones. Distancing myself from essentializing notions of blackness, I have used the term Africanist, not to indicate an overarching pan-Africanness, but rather the shared roots of cultural practices, even if mutated in journeys across different seas. I am inspired by Brenda Dixon Gottschild's notion that a theory of Africanisms is close to a "theory of intertextuality, which seeks to deal with the how or the process-phenomenon of the living text, rather than the text as product."[5] Like Dixon-Gottschild, I conceive of Africanisms as a range of aesthetic and philosophic approaches, and like her I distinguish the term from a more essentialized notion of Afrocentricity. And, following her, I read Africanisms as resonances interwoven into the innovative work of specific "black" artists, or as overt citations that reformulate the whole, and always as a presence or modality that is in constant interaction with a given textuality in the negotiation of meaning.

Note 5: I want to emphasize the multiple layered import of the concept of "mainstream." Primarily, I use the term to refer to the dominant genres of Euro-American concert dance, but more specifically, my reference is to the dominant forms in the context of American dance. I am aware that, while there are some general trends that run across Euro-American cultural contexts, the historical relationship of different communities of color to the dominant groups and ensuing cultural policy make for scenarios in Britain and Canada that are rather different from the United States for instance. Moreover, there are also those genres or kinds of work that, produced in "minority" communities in keeping with an official mandate, get signed on by mainstream Western culture as acceptable markers of "ethnic"/"non-Western" cultures. Such work can safely be used to fulfill the limited slots in the showcase of a "multicultural" or "diversity agenda," and very often remains embedded in hierarchical premises that confirm the status quo. Importantly again, the mainstream is located in a relationship of some degree of comfort with the establishment, and productive of a kind of awkwardness or lack in those who do not or cannot participate in it. And then there are those forms, such as Bharatanatyam in India, that are cast as enjoying national acclaim within their specific cultural scenarios, and, supported by government cultural policies, *seem* to be directly representative of that community's preferred aesthetics. Without denying the historical importance and weight of such forms, I want to suggest that once forms and styles are accepted within some notion of the "official" culture, problematic hierarchies are created. Hegemonic notions of "Tradition" are formulated, which tend to even out differences among local practices and create a hierarchical cultural scene. In an uncanny echoing of the local in the global, such practices constitute another kind of mainstream, mobilizing an exclusive route of legitimization through invocations of "tradition" and "culture." All of the varying distinctions I have outlined in these notes are productive of hierarchies that rend the broad field of "culture" and are important to take into account in any discussion about cultural production.

To return to my introductory reflections then, any discussions of "Dance History" that do not immediately negotiate differential understandings of organizing concepts and genres such that they do not only reinforce Eurocentric hierarchies, tend to repeat the Orientalist move Edward Said talks about. The way in which European modernity comes to be constructed suggests that only in Europe and America can dance be said to have reached pinnacles of "development," having passed through the classi-

cal and the modern to the postmodern eras with near-Weberian inevitability. Such is this understanding of the modern that one cannot be modern
without implicating an other in "primitive," an operation that effectively
encompasses the global even while seemingly only describing current local
developments.[6] Thus in contrast, non-Western cultures, supposedly marking the realm of "tradition," are seemingly stuck in antiquity, glorious
often, but impervious, despite encounters with colonization, to the rational
march of developmental logic that apparently characterizes Western modernity.[7] Here, other modes of conceptualizing changes in cultural processes
are eclipsed by this teleological model.

In the cultural field, the containment conferred by this self-referential-
ity in discussions of modern and postmodern white/Western dance is all
the more problematic because both genres have been deeply influenced
both formatively and in terms of content by non-Western, non-white dance
forms, against which they have sought to define themselves. And, while the
influences of *thematic* material from the East—China (*White Jade*), India
(*Radha*), Egypt (*Dance of Rebirth*)—on Ruth St. Denis; of Asian dance
forms—the spiral, the yogic influence in the fourth position on the floor in
the Graham technique; and of Native American rituals on *structure*—as in
Graham's *Primitive Mysteries*, have been acknowledged, still others have
gone unaccredited. However, while these acknowledgments have made for
a more complex discussion of the aesthetic and philosophical bases of
"modern" dance, they have not still led to a questioning of what it might
mean to name as "modern" that which refers repeatedly to the "primitive"
others. This is even less the case with postmodern dance in the West. It is
instructive to pause momentarily and register the upset that this idea of the
long history of hybridity of Euro-American dance causes, forcing for one, a
re-examination of the ideas of the singularity, individualism, and purity of
cultural production here.

Here I want to briefly revisit Brenda Dixon-Gottschild's thesis that
black performance and art forms have been a constant presence in American culture, entering the mainstream through subterranean influences as
well as conscious borrowings, mostly unacknowledged, from the choreography of Balanchine, the Cubism of Picasso, to the "cool" attitude of postmodern choreographers. Dixon-Gottschild raises vital questions about the
problem of naming, wherein the politics of recognizing/denying access and
inspiration are played out. She asks for instance, how cultural hierarchies
might have been affected, had Cubism, admittedly inspired by the lines of
Congo masks, been named such that there was an overt acknowledgment,
locating its foundational muse in African culture.[8] In fact, examinations of
moments such as these, where the genius of an individual whose innovative work apparently changes the course of artistic development in the

West, often make unarguably clear the subterranean presence of the "other." This is not to take away from the brilliance of these individuals who are in fact able to recognize in the forms and structures of "other" aesthetic practices, potential energies for revitalizing their artistic arena. It is, however, to remind that what is often read in the history of Western culture as the frame-breaking innovation of individuals, might often be traced back to inspirations from other contexts. As it stands then, the monolithic construction of a historical narrative of Western dance, particularly of modern and postmodern dance, as anything less than an intercultural study, must be fraught with denials about what lies at the base of these outbursts of creative activity, such key moments of breakaway from tradition.

Interestingly, this disavowal of what often lies at the core is repeatedly paralleled by assertions that it is inspiration from the white West that has enabled artists from "other" cultures to create contemporary or radical work. I want to refer briefly to an article by Deborah Jowitt in the *Village Voice* titled "Rich and Strange: Three Women Ignite Asian Traditions," where she combined a preview of Chandralekha's *Raga* (1998) with reviews of Yin Mei's *Empty Tradition* and Margarita Guergue's *De Flor*.[9] The bolded "strange" in the title inevitably catches one's eye: is it the igniting of "Asian traditions" that are strange, because they are supposed to represent some kind of still center? At any rate, while she clearly understands Chandralekha's manipulation of traditional movement material, her alteration of "context and performance style" in choreography, and respects her search into "tradition," Jowitt still ends up with a problematic reification in her writing. She says, for instance, "If artists of her caliber borrow from the West, they borrow primarily the credo of freedom and personal expression," which once again implicates the non-West in a dark and oppressive zone of un-freedom, never mind the structured improvisation that is innate in a dance form like Kathak, and that is the hallmark of several African and Africanist dance styles.[10] It further hierarchizes Western individualism, also aligned with the grand trajectory of modernity, as an ultimate and indubitable value. In all fairness, in talking about the work of the third choreographer, Guergue, Jowitt refers to her study of Butoh and its influence on her choreography, and says "The West has a tradition of borrowing from the East."[11] But these two quoted statements do not quite work as parallels, of course, because she doesn't clearly specify in the second case what exactly is borrowed. And while we can assume that she is referring to the training in a specific physical discipline, she explicitly talks about Butoh as an "oblique yet potent *influence*" only (italics mine) on the piece.[12]

I want to contest that general but untheorized assumption that postmodernism, which seems to be inevitably associated with a radical philosophy and practice, belongs to white Euro-American cultural production, and as the exception that proves the rule, to Japan by way of Butoh and capitalist success. In making this claim I am no doubt strongly motivated by the conflation that seems to mark general as well as specialized usage of the postmodern with that which is avant-garde, cutting-edge, the articulation of a radical aesthetics. This of course, particularly true of dance, makes of the postmodern much more than a chronological category, wrapping it in layers of desire and excitement. At any rate, I want to suggest that if the discourse and markers of postmodernism are constituted with specific reference to the cultural contexts in which they are articulated, then postmodernism, as it comes to figure in cultures of color, constantly changes shape and form, and re/marks itself anew repeatedly. This conceptualization of alternative postmoderns is inspired by studying the groundbreaking and exciting interventions in the work of two choreographers whose artistic careers I have followed for a while now: Chandralekha, a contemporary choreographer from India, and Jawole Willa Jo Zollar, an African American choreographer. I will work through readings of dancing bodies in their works to suggest the very different possibilities these choreographers create to address issues that complicate questions of representation in the particular cultural contexts they work in. I will also discuss how notions of postmodernism in dance, feminist performance, and radical aesthetics come to be marked by refigurative insistence in accordance with cultural specificities, and thus come to have greater currency in transnational, cross-cultural dialogues and political formations.

Brief Introductions

Chandralekha, a choreographer working out of Chennai, India, was initially trained in Bharatanatyam, but, disillusioned by its current commercialized marketing, moved away from performing it in order to examine its form and philosophical base. She began to choreograph on her own in 1960 and is now an internationally recognized choreographer, working with the classical dance form Bharatanatyam, the martial art form Kalarippayattu, and the physical discipline Yoga, to create evening-length pieces that have been instrumental in the global recognition of a "contemporary" genre of Indian dance. Chandralekha's choreography is performed by the Chandralekha group, with different dancers being recruited for different projects, but more often than not dominated by women dancers.

Jawole Willa Jo Zollar began dancing as a child, imbibing vernacular dance forms from her environment and her family, but her experience of dance in college pushed her to create her own work. Here she recognized the disjunctive relationships between the community dance traditions and cultural forms she grew up with, her training in black dance traditions, and the more institutionalized modes of dance training, ballet and modern dance. She established her company, the Urban Bush Women, in 1984 in New York City. Today it is a substantially large company with a packed touring schedule including national and international engagements, comprising mostly women dancers. Zollar is currently also Professor of Dance in the University of Florida at Tallahassee. Both choreographers have been occasional performers in their own choreography.

Though these choreographers are not at all interested in creating work that is marked by separatist impulses, much of their work is clearly dominated by the use of women dancers. This is more consistently the case with Zollar, whose company is primarily female, while the rotating composition of Chandralekha's group has made for more or less male performers at different times. At any rate, there is no doubt that the choreography, for both artists, is women-centered, and that the work moves from a recognition of the institutionalized oppressions of women and a commitment to resist them through the articulation of the artistic vision. The performance of critiques of patriarchy and embodiment of radical female consciousnesses are particularly significant in the historical contexts from which these works emerge. Both in the contexts of the British colonization of India, the movement for independence and to establish the Indian nation-state, and in the politics of slavery in America, subsequent freedom struggles, and Black Nationalism, issues of gender and sexuality were wrapped up in several layers of silencing. Laboring under the typical politics marking the sociocultural arena in communities under siege and in the politics of reclamation or recuperation, the female body often became the site upon which these contestations were played out, and gendered and sexual politics were often subsumed under "larger" political movements. In both contexts too, the concert stage became an arena where, in the aftermath of charged political struggles, women rushed in to eke out spaces for articulating complex and "new," also marked as "modern," subjectivities. These are legacies that have continued to haunt the fraught issues of representation and are continuously played out in the creation and reception of cultural production. It is in the light of these specific histories that the resistive and radical interventions and the aesthetic innovations in the work of choreographers such as Zollar and Chandralekha are best understood.

Though they are both important figures in the international circuit of touring companies, and though the reception of their performance obviously differs in different locations, I am framing much of my argument about the work of Chandralekha and Zollar in the dominant terms of the field as I see it from here, in the United States. This is because their work—as is the work of most artists, certainly those of color—tends to be categorized in terms of descriptors generated from and in terms of Euro-American culture and it is against and in relation to these formulations that

I make my argument. Further, while for Zollar this is "home" ground, forums here have different valence for Chandralekha. There is little doubt that North America has the unique cultural and financial capital to present artists from different cultures and countries, particularly now when the push to fulfill a multicultural agenda creates unique sanctions, and that often this kind of "validation"—since presentation in American institutions is inevitably marked as prestigious at "home" and elsewhere—has immense effects on artists' reputations. As Bhabha points out in discussing the Third Cinema Conference in Edinburgh that events such as these "never fail[s] to reveal the disproportionate influence of the West as cultural forum, in all three senses of that word: as place of public exhibition and discussion, as place of judgment, and as market-place."[13]

On Togetherness

One of the most common questions I have received with regard to this project concerns the decision to study the works of Zollar and Chandralekha together. My project works against the structure of a typical cross-cultural study attempting to locate "similarities" among the works of these very distinct choreographers. Nor is this a comparative study working through superficial notions of multiculturalism, bringing together these choreographers in a more or less undifferentiated category of "women of color." My search has been, rather, to show how, despite different histories, and cultural and aesthetic contexts, the commitment to a generally understood progressive politics and embodiment of ideas resonate in the works of these choreographers, while of course they are manifested differently and must be read as such. The larger argument that my project seeks to think through, moreover, emphasizes the specificity of the cultural and political context in which these choreographers are located in order to articulate theoretical constructs about cultural production here. Indeed, working with the broad rubric of resistant dancing bodies, I have traced common concerns and recurrent questions in the particular sociocultural histories in these contexts, issues that are played out in particularly marked ways despite the apparently flattening effects of "postmodern" life conditions and the far-flung reaches of "globalization." Such shared yet different thematics are the focus of Chapter 2, while the series of shorter chapters that make up the last section of the book analyze and theorize specific pieces created by these choreographers. No doubt these "readings" of their works also make a larger suggestion about the richly creative and radical energies that seem to infuse the artistic production of some women artists of color, and those located in the third world in contemporary times. Obviously, this is not an entirely "new" phenomenon, for resistive work has continuously been produced in these communities. However, what is striking is that the artistic edge of the times, with specific reference to the general field of performing arts, seems to be marked largely by such women artists. I offer my study of their work as instances of this observation.

I am also impatient to work through what I often describe as "the great distraction of Whiteness" and write from an awareness of differences marked horizontally and internally—across non-white, non-Western cultures—in a way that moves us to a more complex theorization of racial and cultural difference.[14] Most of the time the conversations around these issues are formulated in strictly bichromatic terms: white versus the rest, a tendency that only reifies the picture and prevents vital dialogues across populations of color. It is important not to write about artists of color only reactively, only in terms of an over-arching racism where one dominant culture dictates the terms of dialogue between all other cultures. Ultimately, this creates a reductive picture where the only conversation of race relations is one where the struggle is always to assert one's identity against the dominance of whiteness. Instead, I want to write from a complex location where racial and cultural differences are understood not simplistically and only vertically, but more as a complex network of relationships where the commitment to a similar politics of resistance does not still demand uniformity of aesthetic or discursive formations. Thus Chapter 5, tracing the different histories and sociocultural contexts of the two choreographers, still shows how legacies of oppressions parallel each other as much as they ask for context-specific understanding. It is my hope that negotiating spaces for these individual-yet-together readings will allow for a stronger theorization of the emergent yet immediately shifting edges of local postmoderns.

On Marginalities

In general, I perceive the location of these two artists on the edges of the cultural context in which they work, having opted out of the dominant modes of artistic production therein. Committed to a continuous articulation of critiques of the status quo and hegemonized establishmentarism, pushing the boundaries of a vaguely "liberal" policy, artists like Chandralekha and Zollar often remind us of bell hooks's exhortation to choose the "margin as a space of radical openness" and "a site of resistance."[15] It is indeed true that after many long years of struggle, both of these artists have succeeded in creating a niche for themselves in the artistic arena, and in that sense can hardly be described as "marginal": Zollar's company, for instance, was the first dance company to be awarded the Capezio Award ($10,000) for Outstanding Achievement in Dance in 1994, and Chandralekha was the first South Asian artist to be produced by BAM (1998). Both of these artists are in fact widely recognized in dance circles internationally. Yet, it is also true that lack of funding has recently plagued the

Urban Bush Women and has forced a series of restructuring and downsizing operations, and Chandralekha has no state support for her work at all. Certainly, they are far from being part of the "mainstream"—understood in its multiple senses—both in terms of their audiences, their funding, and the number and kind of bookings they get.

The processes that have led to their resounding success—by which I mean international recognition as well as high visibility in the communities where they work—are diverse, but it would be remiss of us to forget both the enormous amount of reaction they have had to work through, the continuity of the struggle to survive and persist in creating and producing work. Moreover, the wider context of the phenomenon of this "success" has to be considered. It might be instructive to consider for instance: on what terms was the success gained? Was it the window of opportunity offered by the governmental policy of multicultural support that made it possible for Zollar to get general operating support to set up her company and Chandralekha to be produced at larger institutions like BAM and the Queens Museum? Also, given the subversive nature of the work, is the success based on some misreading, or some non-reading of the strongly resistive premise of the work? What tweakings of a philosophy of liberalism, which runs through the mission statements of most of these institutions, have been affected, in order to allow for such staging? I suggest that there are some of these and other factors worked into genuine appreciation of the powerful and thought-provoking work.

However, one crucial question that begs attention is whether it is possible to retain the resistive potential of cultural production once it is framed in productions by large-scale institutions? After serious and long debates, it seems to me that it is first of all important to qualify that question so that the institutions that produced these choreographers in the United States are self-admittedly left-leaning spaces—whether smaller-scale institutions such as Danspace at St. Mark's Church or Dance Theater Workshop (both institutions claiming some commitment to "diversity") or larger spaces such as Brooklyn Academy of Music (with its international "New Wave" festival), Jacob's Pillow ("an internationally celebrated center for dance"), and more recently, the midtown Joyce Theater (admittedly "New York's home for dance"), whose self-proclaimed reputation as liberal, and reach as international, are also furthered by such programming.[16] At any rate, it is important to remember that artists, however active in their locationing as marginal, desire and need production conditions that offer aesthetic fulfillment through access to good performance conditions: sprung floors, possibilities of lighting and scenography that enhance the performance, availability of rehearsal space, and such. This is true even though neither of these artists work regularly with heavy technical necessities. I have learned from my own experience in working with community-based spaces and organizers who can afford no more than a barebones technical rehearsal, that while such performances are important in terms of the audiences they serve and reach, and in how they locate art, the lack of resources to fill out the details of artistic vision occasionally becomes draining. However, this does not mean that they do not engage in grassroots or community-based work. Zollar is well known for her community workshops, projects and performances and Chandralekha often stages her work in village locations, and is known to premiere much of her work in Skills, the small open-air stage attached to her house, for the local community. In fact, it is the ability of these artists to make work that is rooted in the issues of the "community" at large, and yet demand top production value when working with large producing houses, their ability to move across these seemingly oppositional categories, that signals transgression in terms of a reified mainstream.

Given this, a more interesting question to consider in this situation is, how their work transforms the spaces in which they are produced. For instance, the marketing and outreach efforts of publicity personnel have to adopt new strategies, and the look of audiences changes considerably when for instance, the Joyce Theater in midtown Manhattan runs a season of the Urban Bush Women (1999), or when the Ordway Theater in St. Paul produces a dance drama of the Chorus Repertory Theater from Manipur, India (2000), directed by Ratan Thiyyam. These productions, I would argue, refigure the way in which these spaces are perceived in the minds of audiences, even if it is to effect a slight shift from being understood as a more or less traditional space, producing recognized, mainstream companies with proven professional viability, to being seen as a more "liberal" space taking moderate risks with producing experimental work, whose artistic excellence is already proven in foreign or "other" contexts, but is new to this audience.

Such large-scale productions, historically attended by critics from major papers, also heighten the pressure for articulating different paradigms in dance criticism, if only by pointing out the inadequacies of existing dominant frames of writing about performance. Indeed, on several separate occasions, both Chandralekha and Zollar have urged the need to set in motion a different critical mode with different sets of priorities and lines of interrogation such that it could respond adequately to and comment upon the work of radical artists from cultures of color. While Chandralekha emphasized the refocusing of the critical lens from the exoticized conception of the danseuse whose bejeweled and adorned beauty seduces the audience's vision away from a more direct attention to questions of form and the embodiment of concepts, Zollar emphasized the importance of a perspective that will bridge the gaps between aesthetics and social awareness, and the critic's perception of performers as cultural activists.

Where am I? The Location of the Authorial Voice
in Relationship to These Choreographers

Obviously, given our legacy of identity politics—which though definitely
useful in certain contexts, is now rightly critiqued as essentialist and problematic—the question about how a South Asian researcher, whose first
meaningful encounter with African American dance outside of Hollywood
portrayals happened only a little more than a decade ago upon arriving in
the United States, writes about African American dance, is unavoidable.
Admittedly as a dancer and choreographer trained in Indian movement and
performance forms, and having grown up in India, my initial knowledge of
the complex development of black dance, in America and elsewhere, was
obviously limited. However, while subsequent research and kinesthetic
experiencing have created in-depth understanding of the context, and while
I have insisted on sensitive and context-specific research, I want to challenge essentializing claims of cultural ownership, that only a member of a
"community"—constructed through a narrow understanding of race as an
ontological category, and however fraught with other "differences" that
would, if considered, destabilize that very unitary notion of community—
can conduct research about it without distorting the analytical framework.

It is valuable to recall Trinh T. Minh-ha's critique of the general
assumptions in ethnographic practices whereby correct cultural practice
implies that only "Africans show Africa, Asians Asia, and Euro-Americans,
the world."[17] Trinh also talks, in the same context, about a revisioning of the
notion of difference, which is distinguished from separatism: "Many of us
still hold onto the concept of difference not as a tool of creativity to question
multiple forms of repression and dominance, but as a tool of segregation,
to exert power on the basis of racial and sexual essences."[18] Her notion of
difference, which allows for the imagination of community primarily on
the basis of shared politics as in the works of Jawole Willa Jo Zollar and
Chandralekha, even when the manifestation of these politics differ in terms
of logistical choices, is at the core of the conception of my project. Her
ideas recall Bhabha's critique of the way in which the endorsement of
cultural diversity has made way for a suppression of "difference," and his
contention that while the notion of cultural diversity is upheld by most
democratic societies as a necessary good, the potential of "unequal, uneven,
multiple, and potentially antagonistic political identities" emerging from
the articulation of cultural difference is effectively contained.[19] In writing
about these choreographers from different communities and contexts,
working with different aesthetics and issues but sharing some political resonances, I want to invoke that notion of difference elaborated by Bhabha: "a
position of liminality, in that productive sense of the construction of culture
as difference, in the spirit of alterity or otherness" in opposition to the

showcasing of different cultural practices in a valorization of an official cultural liberalism.[20]

At the same time, I want to be vigilant about simplifying issues of access. As an Indian woman who has grown in India for the major part of her life, writing about black artists working in the United States, I have constantly been aware of the in-depth, sensitive, and multipronged research needed to claim any kind of understanding of and location in black culture. Moreover, I do not dismiss the tensions and misgivings, along with common concerns and shared dreams, with which race relations between different Asian and black communities are fraught, both here in the United States and elsewhere. I realize that these communities are also racialized differently in the United States than in other European and North American countries, and necessarily cast in a "pecking" hierarchical order in a sociopolitical structure that is predicated upon a pernicious racism. Further, relations between artists from different communities of color here are mediated by safety-valve multi-culti policies that more often than not intensify competitiveness and internal tensions. Moreover, these communities are trying to negotiate through different histories of colonization and slavery and internalized concepts of white superiority and self-distrust, all of which play into the cultural politics discussed in Chapter 5. It is my strong belief that while it is important to be sensitive to the host of existent hostilities and prejudices that might jeopardize intercultural research here, it is equally important not to let them paralyze such projects.

In reflecting on the location of the authorial voice, I am drawn to recognition of how in fact my engagement with the subjects and the writing of my research has come to be layered with reflections from different perspectives through time. I was initially attracted to the work of these choreographers probably because of my own artistic work where I seek to create political theatre, primarily dance and movement-based pieces about issues in the lives of women of color, particularly South Asian women. Growing up in Calcutta, India, disturbed by the split between the ideologies imbibed from the classical forms I was learning and performing, and life conditions in postcolonial "modernizing" India, I had long been interested in Chandralekha's work that seemed to grow out of these very questions. Excited as I was by the suggestion of new possibilities when she presented *Angika* in 1985, creating headlines, I was unable at that point due to financial and family constraints to go to Chennai where she was based and work with her. I continued my choreographic explorations on my own, but I followed Chandralekha's work over the years, hoping all the time for an opportunity to work with her.

I arrived in the United States in 1989, much inspired by reading about Martha Graham and other modern pioneers, eager to experience "different" dance forms and to understand in what other terms the dancing body could be imagined. However, my expectations and my experience proved to be greatly different from each other. I encountered resistance repeatedly in composition and choreography classes. My interest lay in intersecting some elements of "traditional" Indian dance, such as narrative and the rich vocabulary of gestural and facial expression, in deconstructive ways, with contemporary movement modes and politics, to reflect my own conflicted consciousness. But for my fellow students and instructors, my manipulation of the traditional elements was either too "westernized" or too "culture-specific" for comfortable viewing. Finally, one of my teachers, from whom I no doubt learned a lot, sighed and said, "Well, I guess you're just not what we want to see." The remark was revelatory of the struggle we were locked into, particularly over my refusal to represent the classical and the traditional images that confirmed me in the desired image of my "ethnicity." Through the years, I was reminded constantly that artists of color, and certainly women choreographers of color, have to be vigilant about the different expectations that are constantly laid upon them, and that the implication of resisting these expectations is often devaluation of such work. Ultimately, I was convinced that the choreographies of women of color, particularly resistive work, warrant a clearly differentiated framework of analysis and interpretation: my search for a theoretical context that would frame these aesthetics began from that point.

I encountered Jawole Willa Jo Zollar's choreography later, through performances in New York City, and was immediately struck by the aesthetic and political richness of her work. I was drawn to examine her work in more depth when she came to Temple University, where I was doing my doctoral work, as part of the Distinguished Speaker Series in 1993. Zollar addressed issues of silences around racial and cultural specificities, of naming and self-definition, and a politics of resistance. She talked specifically about the necessity of "minority" cultures writing about their dances and about the particular norms that constitute excellence in these traditions. She pointed out the typical misreadings and exoticizations that continue to attend mainstream critics' writing about movement based on Africanist forms: what still gets attention are the haunting rhythms and colorful costumes, while the nuances of technique, dramatic elements, choreographic structure, and aesthetics are seldom discussed in detail.

On this occasion, Zollar also spoke about the name she had given her company, "Urban Bush Women," and explained that she had deliberately embraced a term used derogatorily by colonizers of Africa, to subvert that economy of exchange and imbue it with positive meaning. Also, she highlighted the metaphoric value of the name: like a bush that grows despite receiving no nurture from the outside, African American cultural forms will continue to blossom in spite of the efforts to put them down. Finally, for her, the name invoked women's pubic growth, and is associated, for her, with a celebration of black female sexuality. The three-pronged subversive embedded in the name of her company is threatening enough for many. But in spite of facing difficulty from presenters she has refused to opt for a "safer" name.

As I became increasingly familiar with these choreographers and their work, I began to see resonances, contexted as they were in their cultural traditions, and I understood why they too were interested in each other's work. I also realized that reviews and other writings about them often veiled their work in exoticized notions of diversity and seldom discussed either the subtle aspects of the cultural politics in their works, or the kinds of interventions their works were making. It is both my conviction of the power of this work as well as failed recognitions of its alterity, that have moved me to theorize contexted "readings" of these pieces. However, this research also made me realize that I could not write a book *about* these two choreographers and that this would be far from a biographical or ethnological project. Again, while my readings theorize the resistive potential of these works, I realized that in order to effect a paradigm shift in the way these categories are conceptualized, I would have to first map my critique of the field and show that only a reading against the grain of popular notions of such work could pave the way for the kind of full-bodied engagement with them that I felt they commanded. In fact the questions and concerns that their works raised lead to theoretical constructs, analyses, deconstructions, and rehistoricizations that are now in fact the center of my book, and the works of these two choreographers are ways in which these ideas become palpable. I have placed the actual readings of the pieces choreographed by these artists in the last section of the book because I feel that the discursive trail that Chapters 3, 4, and 5 journey through are in fact necessary work that scholars of dance and performance studies, cultural studies, and other fields with some investment in theorizing cultural production, must undertake in order to open up the field for a necessary shift of the conceptual and critical frame. Some of the issues that problematize the field currently are introduced in this chapter and resonate throughout the text, while the biggest arguments and historical refigurings are dealt with in Chapters 4 and 5.

Butting Out!! Disrupting linear neatness and spinal containment, a personal take on resistive aesthetics, and pleasure in physicality. A graphic metaphor for alternative aesthetics: in the works of both these choreographers, and in the dance and several life practices of Indian, African American, and several peoples of color, the deep flexion of the hip socket is more often than not balanced by a releasing out of the hip and the butt. This, of course, is an unacceptable posture in the plie of European dance, where the pelvis is ideally kept in strict vertical alignment with the straight spine. I realized the differences in aesthetic preferences while taking one of my first classes at the Graham studio in New York City in 1989. Not surprisingly, I was the only brown woman in class and I happened to be standing next to the only black woman there. Suddenly the teacher came up to the two of us, pointed to our butts and exclaimed: "That is so rude, to have it sticking out like that! Yours sticks out because of body type (pointing to the black woman) and yours sticks out because of your training (pointing to me)! Come on now, align yourselves properly!" I had just arrived in the United States and was not very savvy about racial politics—it took me a while to get the full import of her comments and her sweeping categorizations.

Framing Issues: The Fraught Question of "Tradition"

It is interesting that most of the better-known writing about women artists of color have emphasized their contribution to reviving or bringing to light different unacknowledged traditions, and how their work, whether choreographic or performance or both, has been significant in struggles against shameful exclusions. In this, the work of non-white Western women artists, particularly in postcolonial contexts, have been scripted in "tradition" and entrusted with the responsibility with embodying cultural continuity, that are in danger of being eclipsed by Western dominance. This precludes examinations of how in fact they have mediated their relationship to "tradition" even while resisting the values of a super-imposed dominant paradigm, often creating significant commentary. Despite significant recent interventions, much of the scholarship in this field stays within the boundaries of a "liberal" philosophy, veering away from probing further into the radical potential of such work except in rather general terms, and from seeking to understand the kinds of questions such work may have raised. And while the work of several such artists is indeed significant because of their role in giving fresh life to threatened traditions, the work of some others asks for different readings. My project is inspired by the recognition of the multiple valences that are embodied in the works of such choreographers: performances of evidence, memory, presence, and pleasure where dancing bodies are powerful signifiers, rewriting histories, commenting on present politics, invoking an unprescribed future that is energized by many struggles against injustice.

The Postmodern Claim

One of the important questions relates to the difficulty of locating the works of Zollar and Chandralekha in the genres that are used to categorize cultural performances: their works are resistant yet reaffirm deep roots in long-standing cultural practices; "postmodern" in relation to their contexts and defiant of traditional constructions of femininity and of gender roles, yet their stagings have little correspondence with the Europeanist paradigms that have regularly hijacked such agendas. These claims and local formulations of postmodern that form the core of my discursive framework are discussed in detail in Chapter 4. Here, I want to insist briefly that the revisioning of traditional cultural practices that mark their work is as much a critique of a problematic and uncritical nostalgia for an "unadulterated" past, as it is a critique of what in that "tradition" is problematic in the light of contemporary politics. It is a remolding of inherited cultural practices in terms of daily logistics, not at all a "revival." The way in which history is reckoned with in the formulation of such postmoderns, as contested narrative, intersected with often conflicting interpretations of the past, such that the choreography becomes a mode whereby history can be imagined or interpreted yet again through the interstices of the present enactments, revealing the complex politics and subtle negotiations in the passage of "tradition" are discussed in Chapters 4 and 5. As subjects of history, actively reshaping, commenting upon, reclaiming, and repeatedly going beyond that past, these women artists distance themselves from a conception of themselves as objects of history and tradition, passive recipients of a past knowable only through the interpretations and tellings of others. I want to characterize this particular kind of political reflexivity and the critical politics informing the nuanced rearticulation of received artistic form, as "postmodern."

Readings of the work of Chandralekha and Jawole Willa Jo Zollar, then, seem to stretch the genre categorizations that dominate much of our understandings of dance. Critics and audiences often react with questions about the root influences of what they have just seen. Their puzzlement exposes the facile and inadequate categories that circulate and the stereotyped characteristics and images that are associated with a particular dance genre or style. The interventions in their work are indeed in their manipulation of movement practices that are part of the embodied "traditions" in their cultural contexts, the revisioned understandings of history, the drawing on everyday sayings, practices, life forms to transform the contexts of artistic activity. This reminds me of Homi Bhabha's notion of a "beyondness" that characterized much of the cultural production of the concluding years of the last century, poised at the edge of a much hyped-up moment of a change in time.

The "beyond" is neither a new horizon, nor a leaving behind of the past . . . Beginnings and endings may be the sustaining myths of the middle years; but in the fin de siecle we find ourselves in the moment of transit where space and time cross to produce complex figures of difference and identity, past and present, inside and outside, inclusion and exclusion. For there is a sense of disorientation, a disturbance of direction, in the "beyond: an exploratory, restless movement caught so well in the French rendition of the words au-dela—here and there, on all sides, fort/da, hither and thither, back and forth.[21]

Bhabha talks about this notion of "beyondness" in his introductory essay to *The Location of Culture*, where he relocates the project of Western modernity in order to intersect it with perspectives from postcolonial histories. In this particular essay, he draws attention to the way in which essentialized cultural identities and ideas of homogenous national traditions are being challenged, such that the mobile zone of the "beyond" becomes a site for redefinition and reinscription of past, present, and future. Totalizing theories of experience, history, and tradition are destabilized here where the past is refigured to intervene in the performance in the present. The works of artists such as Chandralekha and Zollar invoke just such conceptual realms marked by continuous negotiations of meaning and relevance, in order to energize aesthetic and political ideas that deploy and simultaneously deconstruct received wisdom and restructure given modes of understanding and meaning-making.

Of Gazes

The other framing issue that is imperative to address, especially when working with female choreographers of color, concerns questions of representation and the ways in which dancing bodies of color are often spectacularized and held in the objectifying "gaze" of the dominant cultural framework. Female bodies of color, especially in postcolonial contexts, are loaded historically and their appearance in fields of representation is immediately fraught with dilemmas and issues of producing visibility and access. For artists working with non-white Western bodies in an international frame, dealing with issues of gender and sexuality, and fracturing the visual contract and stereotypical imagery that dominate such representation generally, the issues are even more complex. Talking in another context, art historian Darcy Grigsby draws attention to the ethics of such representation:

> For the feminist artist representing female bodies, one dilemma is the role of visibility itself. After all, the history of women's visibility is predominantly the history of women's objectification and oppression. To produce images of women, to perform female, is, therefore, to take responsibility for what it is to make bodies visible.[22]

The responsibility of producing images of female bodies . . . Yvonne Rainer, postmodern choreographer and one of the most innovative artists in the field of dance, when faced with these questions, felt there was no way to avoid the objectification of the female body, and she created one kind of answer by opting out of the situation, giving up dance and choosing to work instead with film. Yet, even in *The Man Who Envied Women,* for instance, she refused to bring the central female character into sight, but traced her presence constantly through her voice and through allusions to her by other characters.

Both Zollar and Chandralekha are located in historical contexts where women's rearticulations of indigenous cultural practices on the concert stage have come after much struggle against erasures and exclusions. Such "invisibility" is not a valid option for them and they seek instead to foreground resistive practices in the idiomatic and choreographic structures and through the staging of what might be described as overwhelming presence. They repeatedly create images of women that question and subvert the stereotypical images of black and brown women of color that proliferate in the media, while insisting on cultural specificity. Again, to intervene in the typical audience-performer relationship and foster a kind of visibility-resistant-to-objectification, Zollar often brings the typical black call-and-response modality into mainstream performance spaces to encourage a sense of engaged spectatorship, diminishing the distance between audience and performer. She also sometimes speaks directly to audiences, asking them to reply to her questions, exhorting them to be active participants in creating a performance event. For Chandralekha, one of the most effective devices is that of returning the gaze, whereby, for instance, the entire group of five women may huddle close together in a corner of the stage and then simultaneously direct their gaze at some point in the audience, forcing a moment of direct encounter and holding it briefly, before they move into another sequence.

Body Knowledges

The above discussion highlights one of the basic premises of my argument: the political valence of the body, particularly of the performing body. It is by now well theorized that cultural constructions play a vital role in formulating bodies and their performances (in the Butlerian sense) of raced, gendered, classed, and sexed identities, which subsequently become "naturalized." Yet, performance also offers possibilities of using bodies in certain ways to either reaffirm sociocultural expectations or to subvert them in the context of such expectations. This latter is exactly the kind of interventionary practice the two choreographers engage in. As one of the basic processes in the training of her dancers, Chandralekha works towards the "unlearning" of learned, and subsequently internalized, ways of holding and controlling the body in "classical" styles, and then relearning its articulation through an intersection of movement systems. For Zollar, the training in formalized dance styles must be balanced by practicing knowledge of some "street" styles, and by an interactive relationship among these styles in performance. Theirs is a deliberate intervention into notions of "technique" of the trained dancer, contrary to the not-so-rare assumption among mainstream critics that they "don't know any better."[23]

Though this is something I will elaborate on in Chapter 3, I want to stake out the intellectual territory for my argument by introducing my claim about the specific intelligence of the body here. The concept of kinesthetic intelligence, which means that the body works through a certain mode of knowing and knowledge-making distinct from other forms of intellection, is central to my work. Philosopher Noel Carroll, describing the aerial performance technique of Batya Zamir, refers to this kind of embodied intelligence:

> This knowledge is of a special sort: it is a performance intelligence that responds, without intellectualization, to the object worked with. This facility is analogous to the carpenter who, feeling a board cracking under his hammering, immediately, without deliberation, changes the tempo and force of his blows. Zamir's work celebrates this judgment—the intelligent action that comes from practice with materials than from contemplation or deliberation.[24]

Unfortunately, even while drawing attention to it, Carroll's statement reinforces the binary. I would suggest instead that it is not that the body responds *without* deliberation, but that it works through its own mode of considering options, and decision making, which may not be recognized as such in terms of the categories of intellectual activity. However, it is also true, as Carroll indicates, that such fine judgment can only arise from sustained study, and I believe that this apparent lack of conscious decision making is also the result of a certain naturalization of "other" thinking processes: a habituation of a specific set of skills so complete that it often leads to a problematic erasure of the processes of acquisition of such knowledge in discursive and general thinking.

Education theorist Howard Gardner, talking about the multiple intelligences human beings are endowed with, describes the bodily kinesthetic intelligence as being characterized by "the ability to use one's body in highly differentiated and skilled ways, for expressive as well as goal-directed purposes," treating "these two capacities—control of one's bodily motions and capacity to handle objects skillfully—as the cores of bodily intelligence."[25] Gardner's delineation is interesting and I want to ponder its specific operational mode in the context of my arguments in this book. The finely chiseled kinesthetic intelligence of a performer, while refining technique as defined in particular training systems, also inflects the same movement with the particular "nuance" that is as much individual stylization as the stuff of cultural specificity. I think of transitions in the work of these artists: sliding from a balletic rond de jomb to a grounded and turning kick influenced by Capoeira; from a floored spinal stretch from yoga into a quick step footwork pattern from Bharatnatyam; often embodying them simultaneously, the body negotiating through different energies and centers. I also want to mark the kinesthetic intelligence in these choreographers' conceptualizations of highly articulate bodies, of how bodies must be configured and movements arranged in order to subvert traditional hierarchies, of how dancing bodies can signify such that ideas and politics become incarnate and uniquely mobilized. It is also this intelligence at work that creates resonance around certain images in our—the audience's—perception, layered with different levels of recognition or questioning, or through invoking visceral reactions to movement. These moments of reverberation are, I propose, crucial to the task of "reading" dance.

In highlighting choreographic choices and how they resonate with sociopolitical commentary, I want to insist on perceiving the body as *intelligent and multivalent*, which subverts the traditional distrust of the body in much of European or Western discourse. I also want to assert the body's proactive role in political and cultural commentary, locate intellect within the body, and recognize how the articulations of the intelligent body are chiseled through the fine and intense training modes used by these choreographers. This in turn deflates continued associations of whiteness with superior intellect, and of others with inferior intellect, but "natural" rhythm or grace, evident in performing bodies, and the age-old binarized association of men with intellect and women with sensation. While some of these prejudices may seem too simplistic to warrant mention in discourse, casual observations of pop or public culture—sports commentary on Venus and Serena Williams's "natural game," for instance—will reveal how these myths continue to haunt the lives particularly of women of color.

"Reading"

While Chapter 3 traces the discursive history of reading dancing bodies in Dance Studies and other related fields, I want to briefly introduce the ideas that position this discursive practice for me. Susan Foster has insisted, in the context of performance, on recognizing the body's "placement within a system of power relations and its concomitant role as a locus of ideological commentary."[26] Remembering this statement in the context of "reading" dance, I want to extend the Foucaultian location of the body in a grid of power relations, as well as Foster's belief that the body is always "endowed with a symbolic significance that permeates its very existence" by pointing to the ways in which performers (in all senses of the term) manipulate, resist, or subvert these significances and power-effects that accrue to the body.[27] Such interpretive "reading" foregrounds and theorizes the political-aesthetic commentary and the interventions into given power relations in various fields that the choreographies of Zollar and Chandralekha perform. The stuff of reading comes from images, motifs, phrases, movement quality, and predominant thematic and aesthetic modalities of a piece that create our overall "impression" of it. And while meaning does not exist in actions as such, movements are hardly performed or perceived divorced from their history of culturally specific usage. Hence it is also imperative that "reading" is context-sensitive, attentive to the conditions of the imagining and production of choreography and its reception, and the processes at work in the construction of "meaning" in that framework.

I also want to draw attention to the visual immediacy of dance, which I believe heightens its political profile, and also often provides strong indication about the politics of the choreographer. For performance, unlike other art forms, is anchored in the materiality of dancing bodies that tethers it to an immediate recognition of the race, gender, and other physical markers of identity of those who have been chosen to embody it. However "abstract" the theme, the relationship of aesthetic choices—made palpable through evidence of company composition, casting choices, technical inflections, and other factors predicated in the quality of "liveness"—to the politics of the choreographer make for direct reckoning. My comments about the hypervisibility of the dancing body and the particular kind of recognition it compels in terms of the already racialized and gendered syntax of perception in place, while clearly not aimed at a simplistic and narrow equationing, are intended to draw attention to the particularity of analytical and interpretive frameworks that the process of "reading" dance calls for. This is especially significant in the context of the overwhelming presence that I have said characterizes the work of choreographers like Zollar and Chandralekha. Let us listen for a moment to Hortense Spillers as she talks about the fissure that the enslaved body always signals in "regular" modes of expression:

> The captive body, then, brings into focus a gathering of social realities as well as a metaphor for value so thoroughly interwoven in their literal and figurative emphases that distinctions between them are virtually useless. Even though the captive flesh or body has been "liberated" . . . dominant symbolic activity, the ruling episteme that releases the dynamics of

naming and valuation, remains grounded in the originating metaphors of captivity and mutilation, so that it is as if neither time nor history, nor historiography and its topics, shows movement, as if the human subject is "murdered" over and over again by the passions of a bloodless and anonymous archaism, showing itself in endless disguise.[28]

Similarly, since the founding paradigms for "seeing" are mediated through pre-existing grammars, organized hierarchically, live performance calls for acknowledgment of performing bodies and their symbolic valence in those very terms. This in turn moves us to reflect on how the choreographer has played into or subverted such grammars—for instance, in the plethora of dancing bodies available who the choreographer has chosen to signify what and how—and what that immediately tells us about the politics of the decision maker here. This has important implications for the project of "reading" dance: especially when the body being foregrounded and represented is one that has traditionally been "othered" in several modes of deployments of the dominant grammar, then part of the project of reading is both to interpret the signifying processes at work in the choreography and also to examine how such work intervenes in the dominant visual and symbolic economy, and how, in fact, these are altered in that interaction.

No Unperspired Naturalness Here

Extending the idea of kinesthetic intelligence, I am convinced about the importance of writing so as to emphasize the intention—aesthetic and political—in the works of these choreographers, contesting the dominant paradigms of representing "tradition" and innovating "instinctively." In either of these cases, the dancing body of color is most often a mute or passive body—either a vehicle of cultural preservation, or a clean slate upon which un-theorized instincts play themselves out—which are then credited for the artwork. These are ideologies that characteristically diminish and invisibilize the creative and political labor of artists of color and the complex processes in which they engage in working out the conceptual framework for choreography. This has only reinforced that relegation of non-white dance forms to that zone of passivity, where there is no space for artistic intention, a clearly deliberated and articulated politics, a consciously crafted aesthetic.

I am reminded once more of Homi Bhabha who critiques the way in which cultural difference is opened up by Eurocentric theory only to foreclose the possibility of active articulation of that "other" itself. In this "closed circle of interpretation" there is no space for the "other' to theorize an oppositional discourse from its own perspective, but must be content to remain a "docile body of difference" that marks the horizons of a progressive discourse in the West, now able to theorize "cultural difference," albeit from its own viewpoint only. As Bhabha asks:

> What is at stake in the naming of critical theory as "Western"? It is, obviously, a designation of institutional power and ideological Eurocentricity. Critical theory often engages with texts within the familiar traditions and conditions of colonial anthropology either to universalize their meaning within its own cultural and academic discourse, or to sharpen its internal critique of Western logocentric sign, the idealist subject, or indeed the illusions and delusions of civil society . . . In order to be institutionally effective as a discipline, the knowledge of cultural difference must be made to foreclose on the Other; difference and otherness thus become the fantasy of a certain cultural space or, indeed, the certainty of a form of theoretical knowledge that deconstructs the epistemological "edge" of the West.[29]

In terms of dance and performance studies then, this argument operates with redoubled force because within the typical claiming of the radical discursive and performative edge as Western or Euro-American, there is also the hierarchy of associating the "other" with a "simple" body.

However, in the post-Foucaultian death-of-the-author moment, we are acutely aware of the impossibility of knowing the "intention" of the author through a text: rather, our "readings" of the work, interpreting it from varied perspectives, interact with it, and create intertextual understandings. There are conceptual difficulties in using analytical frameworks that are developed in terms of a specific field of inquiry in another vitally different: for instance, choreographies are not "texts" and in fact, have no existence as such independent of the performing body.[30] But also, the discursive needs and concerns in the field of Dance Studies at this point urge us to consider the question of intent from different angles. In a discipline with ephemerality at its core, readings, which help anchor the work in discussions of cultural production, are important. Yet the discursive field of Dance Studies is just developing, and critical reviews of work are often rent with mis-understandings of context, a historic frustration of choreographers and dancers of color. While my readings of the pieces are not reportings of the choreographers' avowed "intention," as known through their "testimonies," they are influenced by my knowledge of the cultural politics in their work. My emphasis on intention is not to assign to the choreographers some kind of sovereign subjectivity that transcends those historical circumstances that constitute conditions of possibility for the choices they make. Rather, it is meant to mark their choreography as resulting from actively theorized choices, aesthetic and political, about the form, content, and structure of their artistic work, all of which reflect specific positionalities in the contexts in which they live and work. No doubt my reading of their work is one interpretive direction only in a wider realm of possibilities, open to contestation or enrichment by others. Ultimately what I am asking for is a recognition that we need to study, discuss, and debate the work of artists of color with much greater complexity than has seemed to be the norm: as the work of talented individuals, who have been influenced by and draw on their cultural legacies and traditions, but who have labored to craft their aesthetics and politics, which now enrich our worlds.

About Writing

In writing about the resistive practices of these two choreographers, I am drawn to think about Trinh T. Minh-ha's concept of a writing from within:

> A writing *for* the people, *by* the people, and *from* the people is, literally, a multipolar reflecting reflection that remains free from the conditions of subjectivity and objectivity and yet reveals them both. I write to show myself showing people who show me my own showing. I-You: not one, not two. In this unwonted spectacle made of reality and fiction, where redoubled images form and reform, neither I, nor you come first. No primary core of irradiation can be caught hold of, no hierarchical first, second, or third exists except as mere illusion. All is empty when one is plural.[31]

It seems to me that artists in the field are often irritated by the work of scholars who write about their work but do so from a distance, without necessarily understanding the embodied center of their work. It is likely that performers have been at the receiving end of some arrogant theorizing on the part of academics who might not have paid attention to the specific modes and concerns at work in this field. Yet this dismissal produces a problematic anti-intellectualism that often voids the critical commentary embodied in some performance, something that is of even more vital significance in current times. Recognizing that I am ending up staking a claim for specialized reading of dance that is after all produced for general public viewing, I still want to invoke a privileged "insider" positioning in my analysis in order to bring the perspective of the body into the writing. For I do believe that my intimacy with the practice of movement, my experienced understanding of bodily disciplines and techniques, allow me—or any dance practitioner within that field—a certain kind of reflexivity that balances "outside" (perceiving and responding to the work from a distance) and "inside" (inside the work itself, taking on the realization and interpretation of a vision) perspectives. This modality is linked to the mode of writing in this project: I want to foreground a kind of writing about performance that is oriented differently from newspaper reviews, not toward an evaluation of the "success" of the work, but more toward a consideration of what kind of sociocultural commentaries are offered by such work, what kind of political interventions it does or can make in specific contexts, and how the reformulation of the aesthetic framework affects the broader cultural field. This is part of my larger goal of situating dance and choreographic work in the larger frame of cultural production as a potent source of information, analysis, and critique, linked intimately to the processes of sociocultural and political change.

One more aspect of racial politics inspires me in my writing: it reinforces Trinh's exhortation to third-world women to write about themselves and their work. Black cultural scholar Henry Louis Gates, Jr., talking about the emergence of the black literary tradition in America, writes, "Making the book speak, then, constituted a motivated and political engagement with and condemnation of Europe's fundamental sign of domination, the commodity of writing, the text and technology of reason."[32] This intertwining of literacy and literature with rationality is misleading and specifically Eurocentric, however, and Gates goes on to wonder "if the sort of subjectivity which these writers seek through the act of writing can be realized through a process which is so very ironic from the outset: how can the black subject posit a full and sufficient self in a language in which blackness is a sign of absence?"[33] The question is not dissimilar to one asked by the French feminist writers, in a different context, about signification by absence: how can what is by definition the "other" be brought within the expressive capacities of language that is based upon its very exclusion? The question also reminds us of one asked by female performers about the problematics of representation, about visibility-without-objectification.

While thinkers like Gates remind us of the irony and the difficulties the process of writing in academic or formal English is fraught with, artists like Toni Morrison remind us that the separatism proposed by the French feminists at a certain point is, in fact, not a practical solution at all, marking as it does an incommunicable difference. Instead, in her seminal essay "Unspeakable Things Unspoken," Morrison talks about the different strategies she has used in her writing to highlight the presence of African American overtones in American literature.[34] This both ruptures the notion of an untouched dominant expressive mode, and reminds us that artists constantly create devices that transform that mode itself. I want to refer back to Spiller's notion of the subverted symbolic order and to the politics of resistant visibility that seeks to disrupt audience expectations in performance, and suggest that the work of choreographers such as these remind us of the possibilities of subverting or manipulating established forms even while working with them.

Methodological Concerns

My research methodology, and the way in which language is wielded to talk about the body, is guided by concerns about bringing the weight and materiality of the dancing body to bear upon discursive developments, differently from several scholars in other fields who refer to bodily processes as part of the process of intellectual inquiry, but do not necessarily register the terms of such engagement. Feminist and Performance Studies scholar Peggy Phelan marks an interesting difference:

> With a broad stroke it can be said that for feminist theorists concerned primarily with theatrical performance the living performing body is the center of semiotic crossings, which allows one to perceive, interpret and document the performance event; while, for feminists interested in the discursive performance, the acts of signifying systems themselves (language and the codes of textuality) are the center of interpretive analyses.[35]

Phelan takes care to qualify this "broad stroke," however, which is not necessarily a complete and invariable pronouncement, and warns against the possible false assumption that the "living performing body" is outside of signifying systems. Reminding us that signifying systems are themselves always already incorporated, embodied, she underlines the inevitable interactive existence of bodies and systems of signification. This inevitable implication in the very systems one is resisting, and the notion of resisting from the inside, have been useful in theorizing alternative models of subversive choreography.

My research methodology was based on an interweaving of the observation-participation model of postmodern anthropology and an interpretive theorizing mode drawing on insights from current discursive trends in cultural studies, performance studies, gender studies, race studies, postcolonial and subaltern studies. Data for close description of movement sequences was gathered from notes taken during performances, workshops conducted by these choreographers, rehearsals, classes, and training sessions directed by them. Notes taken during observing and participating in rehearsals and training sessions are complemented with interviews and conversations with both choreographers and their company members. My earlier comments on the specificity of embodied knowledge feed into my rationale for engaging in participatory fieldwork, and with coupling observation with participation. The project was fueled and enriched by the process of intersecting intellectual with kinesthetic understanding, observations of performances with conversations with those who embodied the performance, observations during workshops with an in-body sensing of the movement by participation in training sessions, and my reflections on doing and seeing such movement with the choreographers' verbally described images that inspire the movement.

I have been deeply influenced by Patti Lather's concept of research as praxis in my work.[36] Taking off from Gramscian and Frierean ideologies, Lather argues that no research is neutral or bias-free and urges a research method that is explicitly committed to critiquing the status quo and to building a more just society. Disciplines implicated in corresponding activisms, such as feminist, neo-Marxist critical ethnography, and Frierean "empowering" participatory methodologies, are instances. Many of her ideas are implicit in my envisioning of this book and in the structure of my research, focused as it is upon the practice of artists and upon suggesting ways of "looking" that might make a difference in the ways in which such work is viewed. Again, I have sought to implement in my process what she describes as hallmarks of such methodology: reciprocity as a data-gathering device, where the research process is based on the evolution of the relationship between researcher and researched from stranger to friend, and about the mutual negotiation of meaning and power, and data and theory. She also emphasizes the dialogic nature of the research process and the stance of dialectical theory-building which characterizes the researcher's attitude versus the mode of theoretical imposition.

While these ideas may not be obvious in the text itself, they have continued to be integral to my investigative and reflective processes: over the years of my research, I established a close working relationship with both Zollar and Chandralekha and their dancers and constantly engaged in conversations with them to ensure an exchange of ideas and perceptions. I have also shared with them what I have written about them. In fact, while I have approached my reading of their work through the ideological constructs of academic discourse, I am aware that my research is enriched by the deeply personal relationships that I have developed with these two women and with many of the women in their company. Traveling with them and their companies, taking class with them, learning some of their choreographies, eating and socializing with them, have drawn this relationship closer and have offered many opportunities to dialogue with them about the issues in creating and readings work. The emotional and close interaction with them has enabled a more sensitive and intense inquiry into and understanding of their choreographic process.

Lastly, I find Lather's concept of "epistemological breaks" repeatedly embodied in the signifying practices of these choreographers and I have read the choreographies with specific attention to the important interventions in the ideological realms of cultural production.[37] Lather describes this phenomenon as a rupture in the established way of conceptualizing an issue that essentially inverts meaning. The very premise upon which this book is postulated—the signifying practices and political affect of the dancing body—is part of such an epistemological shift that we are beginning to see in performance and dance studies. My project joins the move towards effecting that shift, whose genealogy I will trace in the next chapter, and which in fact, effects another shift within that move by focusing on the work of women of color.

Audiences

I have tried to write to an eclectic group of audiences in this book: dance scholars, especially those interested in analyzing issues of race and class in and through performance, scholars of women's studies, race studies, and cultural studies. It is also my hope that this book will interest scholars working in such fields as postcolonial and subaltern studies, fields, in other words, with an investment in theorizing the politics of cultural production in relation to a larger scheme of power relations. I am aware that distinct groups of scholars might respond with greater or lesser interest to the different sections of the book: for instance, the first half of Chapter 3 might present certain methodological questions to scholars of women's studies and postcolonial studies with its challenge of thinking through the body, while the latter half of the chapter, tracing a genealogy of the project of "reading dance," is addressed to the very specific group of dance scholars. Chapter 5, on the other hand, clearly works through discourses that have evolved in the South Asian subaltern studies group of scholars, and thinks through these arguments in the service of constructing a more useful dance history. Here the audiences are both scholars in different fields and in broadly different contexts, including differences in geographical location and all its attendant discrepancies, often writing in different languages. This shifting focus and location of the authorial voice has been necessitated largely because of the necessarily interdisciplinary nature of this project, itself a corollary of the multiple significatory layers of the dancing body and because I have found it imperative to draw on arguments from different disciplinary frameworks in order to support the claims I am making. Also, as the instance from Chapter 5 pointed out, the engaging of disciplinary foci developed in different parts of the world has been a indispensable part of this project: this shifting voice has become necessary in order to break the Americanization that has dominated any racialized discourse in academia, and understanding racial and cultural categories through other kinds of histories and historiographies. Elsewhere these shifts are partially a result of the emerging status of dance studies, where the corpus of discursive and terminological literature is relatively small. This means also that in working through arguments from different disciplines in the area of Dance Studies, one has to engage with the terminology and modality of these disciplines. This might have created a certain variability of tone and unevenness of address. For this, I apologize, but realize it has resulted from the particular process and structure of this project, reflecting the shifts in distinct audiences and arguments being invoked, and the kind of theoretical alliances I seek to make in this book.

CHAPTER 2   **By Way of Introductions**

In this chapter, by way of further introducing and locating the choreographers, I want to don my anthropological hat momentarily and share perceptions about some of the paradigms through which I have read their work. In particular, I will talk about their conceptualization of "technique," how they situate their artistic work, how their artistic work relates to other aspects of their lives, and some other paradigmatic concerns in their work. The tenor of this chapter is somewhat different: it is more informational than conceptual, though the former is in the service of the latter. It is my hope that these details will make concrete the context and the choreography I will discuss, and will illuminate the previous theorization of alternative postmoderns. Moreover, I have not attempted to exactly balance discussions of the two bodies of work in relation to these concerns, but have, rather, adapted them to the nature of the work of these artists. For instance, in the discussion on Chandralekha's technique I have examined the specific deconstruction of classicisms and "tradition" that is the particular point of departure and resistance in her work. On the other hand, in the discussion on Zollar's technique, it is much more the deployment and intersections of techniques in choreography that demand analytical analysis, and here I have worked more through discussions of her pieces.

Artist as Cultural Activist

The commitment to forging an aesthetic from lived realities is central to the work of both Chandralekha and Zollar, and it is characterized by their choreographed articulation of complex critiques of hegemonic sociopolitical phenomena marking the contexts in which they live and work. While all cultural production happens in a specific context that directly or indirectly impinges upon it, what is special about these artists is the depth of the sociopolitical critique and commentary embodied in their work, the multiple ways in which these are reflected in their artistic choices, and the urgency of the critique their works stage. Their radical politics in fact shapes the particular formal and structural choices and interventions in their works and permeates their thematic concerns, and are integrally connected to the general aesthetic framework of their work.

How Chandralekha came to move away from her budding career as an exponent of classical Bharatanatyam is telling in this regard. This anecdote seems to be almost a moment of epiphany in her life: when, isolated from and unresponsive to the life conditions that form its context, the concretized classical dance struck her as being a deadening and insular practice. The sense of the split between the art and life conditions hit her powerfully during her *arangetram*, her first public performance as a classical dancer.[1] Performing for a show organized by the Rayalaseema Drought Relief Fund, Chandralekha began her recital with a piece entitled *Mathura Nagarilo*, which depicts the river Yamuna and the water-play of young women in the flowing river. However, as she performed the "sensuality, the luxuriance and abundance of water," she was stunned by the paradoxical situation in which she was implicated: "Suddenly, I froze, with the realization that I was portraying all this profusion of water in the context of a drought. I remembered photographs in the newspapers of cracked earth, of long winding queues of people waiting for water with little tins in hand."[2] The conflicted juxtaposition—of the reality of the lack and the images of drought in her mind, with her embodiment of rolling waves and Guru Ellapa's compelling singing of *Mathura Nagarilo* in the background— undercut forever the possibility of unreflecting pleasure in the idealized world of the classical dance. After this experience, she eschewed considerations of a career as a classical performer. Yet this did not translate into a move toward realism, the realistic depiction of life conditions. Nor did it entail a simplistic and total rejection of those dance forms, but instead initiated a search to negotiate their continued relevance in lived situations, extending the typical metaphoric mode of classical *abhinaya*. Moreover, it fueled her concept of dreams: dreams imagined as visions that reconceive the organization of sociopolitical structures and facilitate awareness and change.

Her rigorous examination of context and relevance, and the reworking of technique and embodied articulation from that perspective, situate Chandralekha's work in the larger context of the women's resistance movements in India. Talking about her interaction with feminist groups and the work she has been doing with women, Chandralekha had long indicated the significance of such work for her artistic practice.

> I have been doing body workshops for them, carrying the basics of dance to women to help them understand their bodies especially at the level of generating energy. Something that will help them strengthen their spine, which means confidence; something that will make them aware of their own energy centers, their physicality, their sensuality; something that will help them maintain their dignity and cope with the social attacks they face

everyday. Doing this is more relevant to me than coming to the city and putting on a dance spectacle.[3]

It is this work that is reflected in the images she creates, this search for self-empowerment, self-confidence, wholeness, and energy, that becomes the inspiration repeatedly for her choreography. And it is in reminding Indian women about an ancient core of ideas in their indigenous cultural context—about the power of feminine energy, about the vital spiritual centers located in their spines, and the energies available to them in their own bodies—that Chandralekha taps the past to mobilize it in the present. These ideas, that have come to be obscured by myths generated by patriarchal normativity, are invoked in different contexts to inspire self-esteem and urge self-realization for women whose space for self is at risk, often abused or violated; principles of movement from dance are deployed in a context of unspecialized knowledge of movement, to generate a revaluation of physicality and sexuality. Also, through this transformation, dance is reconceptualized as a practice that generates a particularly powerful awareness of bodies and how they come to be produced. This is one of the markers of the radical in Chandralekha's work: the relatively "modern" idea of a women's *movement* is revitalized through rearticulating ideas drawn from older, traditional, and indigenous thought-systems and cultural practices. This alignment immediately challenges the reactive and reactionary "modernity" of contemporary critiques that, ignoring historic evidence, align notions of women's rights and demands for gender equality with Westernization, and uphold notions of tradition that cancel the possibility of resistive and progressive thought in past times.

Radical Feminisms

The visions, images, values, and desires that remain in my imagination after seeing their work and the analyses they inspire lead me to describe the feminist agendas of Zollar and Chandralekha as radical. Obviously, I am not using the term "radical" as it operates in the categorization of the feminist movement in the United States, where radical feminism, working through a base of biological difference, is distinguished from liberal and Marxist feminisms. As I use it, and in the contexts and histories from which their works emerge, the term "radical" here refers more to a vision that challenges histories of silences and erasures enforced through multiple co-operative hierarchies, and that reaches toward an aesthetic that "seeks to uncover and restore links between art and revolutionary politics . . . while offering an expansive critical foundation for aesthetic evaluation."[4] This articulation is central to the way in which the creative productions of these artists function as acts of cultural activism. For example, in

1987, Chandralekha was invited to collaborate in a theatrical project with eminent theater personalities, Rustom Barucha and Manuel Lutgenhorst, to act as the central character in this monodrama, *Request Concert*, a dramatized critique of an oppressively mechanized world that increasingly erases space for individuation and self-determination. Initially, Chandralekha worked as directed, performing the series of gestures simulating eating, drinking, sleeping, listening to the radio, watching television, with utter disconnection between the actions and her engagement in completing them. In the original text by Franz Xavier Kroetz, the woman, after preparing for the next day's work and going to bed, abruptly but still in a matter-of-fact way, gets up and commits suicide. Here was a critical moment for Chandralekha. Though her suicide may have been for the character a way of breaking through the sheer mechanization and boredom of her routine, of regaining agency in an apparently over-determined situation, Chandralekha, filtering the more "general" critique of mechanization through her specifically gendered lens, insisted that it amounted to an "anti-life statement." What kind of agency and choice is signaled through this woman's negation of life?

In subsequent conversations Chandralekha argued that, as she concieved it, the woman in Kroetz's play was imprisoned most strongly within the walls of her mind, and instead of choosing freedom through death, she wanted her to choose life, resisting through humanizing the mechanization. Her embodiment of this section through movement alone is described thus by Barucha who was present through the rehearsals and performances:

> Chandra's opting for a very heightened representation of the woman's suffering . . . was represented through a slow and tortured roll on the ground with the hands flailing outward, which would occasionally culminate in freezes where the body would be locked into disembodied shapes. These spasms of movement, which almost resembled death-throes, would continue till Chandra would gradually rise from the ground with her back to the audience and press herself against the back wall of the theater. Against this expanse, she would rise on her toes stretching her hands upwards so that it would almost seem as if she had hanged herself. Then, very gradually she would turn and "free herself from the wall," raising her hands upwards in a tentative gesture of rebellion.[5]

This abstract representation of the struggle against internalized routines that thereafter gnaw away at creative powers and strength, points both to her complex analysis of oppression and to her sensitive awareness of gendered difference. That systems of oppression are supported and perpetuated by the internalization and naturalization of their operational procedures is an understanding that is both Foucaultian and reminiscent of Marxist notions of false consciousness. Despite her recognition of the pervasive networks created by these ideological systems, Chandralekha's refusal to foreclose the possibility of agency and her insistence on reaching toward some possibility of self-determination is a choice that emphasizes her radical feminist creative agenda.

The strong connection between art and life emphasized in the work of both artists directly impacts their creative process as well. Neither of them work through realism, however, but try to find ways to metaphorize issues and comment through more abstract, but richly layered imagery. Chandralekha, for instance, talks about a newspaper headline that disturbed her immensely: "Woman throws herself in well." As if this is quotidian, nothing unusual. Reporting the suicide, the newspapers listed all the details that constituted the apparent reality of the incident. For Chandralekha however, despite all the information concerning the "case," vital questions remained unanswered and unanswerable, and were in fact obscured by the kind of journalistic information and prosaic reporting that couched our knowledge about the incident. From this incident has come a returning unanswered question: "A woman has killed herself by throwing herself inside the well. How can we poeticize this?"[6] Her search has been to personalize the incident, to humanize her response and distinguish it from the impersonal, dry, factual reporting of the media. Her understanding of the suicide is thus mediated through her reflections on the total hopelessness, despair, and negation of life and energy the woman must have experienced, finally arriving at a decision to carry this life-negating energy to its logical conclusion, very different from women who have *been* killed. These ideas are articulated through powerful poetry and visuals in her handmade book, inspired also by that same incident, *One More News*. The images in this book evoke a terror-ridden world where cries for help resound through vacant spaces, for the world has gone deaf and blind. That suicide can exist as an option, a solution to difficult situations, especially for women suffering from domestic abuse and other manifestations of an abject patriarchy, is obviously deeply painful for Chandralekha. She interprets this choice as an espousal of negativity, and she has repeatedly urged women's movements to focus on redirecting internalized destructive energies, and on modes of resistance that will reinforce, not destabilize, life energies, which are inevitably invoked and celebrated in her works.

> Taking one's life seems to be the one and only time a woman exercises her
> right of decision making . . . If women become aware that their dying will
> not change other women's destinies but, on the other hand, will reinforce

their oppression, will they not opt instead of death, for life, however difficult, rough, harsh, cruel. Would they not give their energy to change rather than to the maintenance of oppression, the status quo? Would they not give their energy to their sisters, rather than to their oppressors?[7]

The Politics of Defiant Hope

The concept of a radical feminist aesthetic and the insistence on life-energies brings me to one of Zollar's older and much celebrated pieces *Anarchy, Wild Women, and Dinah* (1986). Reflecting on the relative silence about female trickster figures in African American folk tales where male tricksters abound, Zollar conducted in-depth research to discover the figure of Dinah, a female trickster figure from African American folklore. However, while songs and stories about the strong-willed Dinah abounded, they were not organized to comprise a single corpus as stories of male trickster figures such as High John the Conqueror had. Gathering together these tales about Dinah's uncompromising recalcitrance, Zollar combined them in this piece with her imaginings about the mischief she brews in contemporary times in which conventions and acknowledged rules of performance are broken with vibrant energy. In fact, even as Zollar invokes this figure—Dinah, who is "part of what I would call the wild women's tradition, women who did what they wanted to do, when they wanted to do, how they wanted to do, despite any Supreme Court rulings, and who they wanted to do it with"—she exits the stage picking her teeth. Zollar structures the piece in double-time frames such that the irrepressible spirit of Dinah, the archetypal character, meshes finely with the current resistance politics of these black women who are well aware of the recurrent failure of the legal system to deliver justice. So the Urban Bush Women can engage in a robust celebration of that spirit of resistance through their energetic singing and dancing in sections such as *Dinah* and *Wild Women Don't Get the Blues*, which are replete with fast and intricate footwork delineating complex rhythms, swiveling hips, circling shoulders, plunging arms, and kicking legs, as well as enjoy a short repast on stage, sitting comfortably with their legs open, backs loose, and eating as noisily as they can. At the same time, however, they recognize that this spirit is not one of unrealistic freedom but is undercut by the adversities and afflictions of everyday life. The women have to grapple with the blues that overcome them in specific sections of the piece in order to arrive at the possibility of celebration.

Celebration in the face of, and in fact as a survival strategy against, life conditions that are difficult, working with a vibrant sense of community: I cannot but mention briefly Zollar's unique *I Don't know, But I Been Told, If You Keep Dancin' You'll Never Grow Old* (1989). The title is telling: even though there is no sure knowledge about a "solution"—*I Don't Know*—but

Urban Bush Women, Zollar's *I Don't Know, But I Been Told*. . . . Photo by Cylla Von Tiedemann.

the commitment is to reaching toward a desired ideal despite the arduous
journey. This piece takes off from the frustrating arguments Zollar has had
over the years with funders and presenters, who insist on compartmentaliz-
ing dance into "high art" and "low art," categories that ultimately coincide
with race and class hierarchies, and assign hierarchical standing to them by
yardsticks that are at best, arbitrary. Away from the classicism of ballet and
modern dance, away from the nonchalant pedestrian styles of the early
American postmodern, Zollar's *I Don't Know* . . . defies this dichotomiza-
tion of art, and insists on creating concert dance from black street forms,
intersecting them with game structures and community building practices,
and on celebrating Zollar's belief that "dance is about people dancing."[8] In
this piece, Zollar builds the choreography on references to handclapping
games, jump rope, double dutch, word games, cheerleading, ring games,
step dancing, playground chants, vogueing, soul train lines, and social
dances, and celebrates these street vocal and movement forms that have
continuously vitalized the creative legacy of black performance. This multiplicity of references and the absence of pyrotechnics of presentation distance the piece from the commodified versions of "hip-hop" that are
currently often seen on the concert stage. These forms come to be refigured
in Zollar's choreography, through a complex interweaving of movement,
rhythm, song, and words, where street and concert stage repeatedly reflect

and segue into each other. In her refusal to work only with acceptable dance genres in creating "high art" concert dance, she reminds us of the post-modern choreographers of the Judson era, except that besides pedestrian movement, she brings into focus black popular performance traditions, vernacular practices that are testament to the continuity and richness of black creative work in America. Moreover, she shows up the gaps in the postmodern movement that broke with hierarchies of high and low art, but left many other barriers intact.

This commitment to hope, without ever bypassing or romanticizing the struggle of resistance movements, what I call a politics of defiant hope, is characteristic of the work of these two choreographers. This is also the spiritual force in their work and leads to repeated affirmations of life force in their work. Their hope is defiant precisely because it acknowledges that it works through given conditions, reinvents lived and imperfect worlds in terms of a hopeful real that lies beyond the horizon of realization. This hope, which sustains the work of these choreographers, is defiant because it refuses its own demise, eked out painstakingly when not only larger ideals of religion, law, democracy, but also local resistance movements apparently committed to critiques of unilateral workings of power and control, continuously evidence themselves as co-opted by political powerplays and bankrupt of possibilities of delivering justice. This hope is also constantly negotiated through the creative labor of artists such as these when possibilities of progressive resistance movements are increasingly jeopardized by the diminishing choices in a world dominated by overpowering oppositionalities such as Talibanesque hegemonies and American super-powerism.

I am reminded of Cornel West in thinking about a politics of defiant hope and the unfinished project of a postmodern revolution in the West. West argues that some of the resistive practices assigned to Euro-American postmodern practice were always already cultural modes among African American peoples, "emerging out of an acknowledgment of a reality they cannot *not know*—the ragged edges of the real, of necessity; a reality historically constructed by white supremacist practices in North America during the age of Europe."[9] This resistance, forged in the face of relentless efforts to dehumanize and crush, has been continuously irradiated with a hope that is also defiant in that it challenges current realities, and dares it to show its limits. The alternative postmodern of these choreographers of color, in ways very different from the Euro-American postmodern, is driven by such defiant hope, dancing as if to will change into being.

Such hope and an unwavering faith in artistic work as a strong force of social change vitalizes Zollar's intertwined artistic-political agenda, such that community-based artwork becomes a necessary corollary of her artistic work with her company. She involves herself and her company in community issues not just through the artistic work she creates, but also overtly, through arts-in-education projects, financial remuneration for which can sometimes be meager or nothing at all. The company does several workshops, lecture demonstrations, and performances for school audiences through the year as part of fulfilling the mission of the company. This constitutes an essential and meaningful part of the company's engagements for Zollar who realized early that even if her life had to be "moving from one hotel room to another," it had to allow for fulfillment beyond her own artistic pursuits. [10] In the words of Lloyd Daniel, education consultant for the Urban Bush Women, a primary goal of the company is to create "a new dancer for a new society," an "artist/athlete/thinker/ healer/organizer committed to the liberation of women, people of color, and all those who have nothing other than their labor to sell. As we learn, grow, and create beauty we hope to help in the building of a more sane and just society."[11]

The 1992 trip of the UBW to New Orleans, where they were initially contracted for five performances but ended up being involved in more than ten educational and community-oriented programs as well, is a clear instance of this commitment. These programs were further taken on after serious preparation that included discussion, study, and workshop sessions conducted by Daniel, which resulted in the creation of the community engagement curriculum. The following listing of the several projects taken on by UBW during that tour demonstrates the multiple prongs of the program, the several issues addressed. The company, headed by Zollar, worked on the following projects on a daily basis: a sociopolitical commentary wall mural in collaboration with Pieces of Power, a teen visual arts group; a teen mothers program at a public high school; a program for the development of math skills through basketball and movement games with teenagers at the Tambourine and Fan Center; a pregnancy prevention program in collaboration with the Kujichagulia Center, using drumming, dancing, and singing workshops; a literacy workshop at the Community Book Center; cultural and self-development programs in collaboration with And Still I Rise, a welfare rights organization; a program for the collection of oral histories, and for the development of movement and vocal skills at the Voice from the Deep Puppet Theater; creative thinking and writing for radio projects at the community radio station; creative writing, reading and liberation hip-hop projects with writer Kalamu Ya Salaam; programs for the development of critical thinking in teens at the Peoples Institute for Survival and Beyond. Another pathbreaking project, the Dixwell Community Project, was undertaken in the summer of 2001. In this remarkably successful engagement, Zollar worked with members of the largely black communities in this working-class area of Connecticut, near Yale University, to improvise together and create a presentation, to be performed by several children and youths from the community as well as company members, at the prestigious Festival of Arts and Ideas.[12]

Refiguring the Body-In-Movement: Ideologies of Training[13]

The conceptualization of the dancing body in keeping with a specific politics, aesthetic, and ideas of representation, is obvious in the particularization of technique and idiom in the work of these choreographers. While maintaining an emphasis on technical excellence, in fact, both choreographers insist that dancers be acutely aware of the ways technical training produces bodies, as well as naturalizes notions of aesthetics, line, excellence, technique, and such. Thus, the training and choreographic processes used by both choreographers generally begin with a re-examination of "technique," often involving a mode of "untraining" or at least of undoing some of the "affect" of the dancers' technical training. Moreover, both choreographers work with a distinct aesthetic that deftly interweaves references to different styles and genres, and thus requires a fine internal negotiation between centers and images of the body, as well as a finely tuned deployment of energy circuits. And because the choreographers work with an aesthetic sensibility that challenges the "classical" or aesthetic norm, they insist that dancers training in these techniques are very strong, such that the interventions into the classical lines read clearly through deliberately marked and re-marked lines.

Disillusioned with the commercialization marking the currently practiced forms of Bharatnatyam, Chandralekha chose to deconstruct the idiom to its bases and work with them, combining them with movement forms like yoga and martial art forms like Kalarippayattu. She drew simple movements from the daily repertoire of gestures, the lifting of a hand, the quick turning of a head, the slackening of a tired back, and incorporated them into the classical base of this idiom as and when she has needed to expand the movement base in her explorations of thematic and formal elements. Clearly then, in refiguring this movement base, Chandralekha has had to work through a complex relationship with "tradition." While she has rejected the "diabolical smiles" on the "vacant" faces of contemporary classical dancers and the prescriptiveness that the classical dance has become laden with, all in the name of "tradition," Chandralekha has also insisted that she is "an uncompromising traditionalist."[14] For her, however, tradition here refers not to hierarchical and legitimating systems, but to continual indigenous cultural practices, and the above claim is as much a statement about a conscious and deliberate location in the movement systems that are part of her context as it is a reaction to the conflation of contemporary choreography with "Westernization."

Working to chisel this highly charged metaphoric movement vocabulary, she has arrived at an idiom powerful in its minimalism. Her turning away from the high aesthetic elaboration of Indian classical dance, the intricate adornment of *mudras* and virtuous footwork that mark the *nritta* or "pure dance" sections of most classical dance forms, her rejection of the detailed facial expressions that mark the *angika abhinaya* of classical performance, are connected to her exploration of the context and location of the dancing body in contemporary India. Moreover, the abstract structuring of her work, releasing of the organizational logic of a piece from the need either to communicate a narrative or to adhere to the direction spelled out by the *nattuvanar*, as the enunicator of syllabic accompaniments and percussionist for Bharatanatyam is called, who is also in control of the tempo of the piece, marks a practice that goes against the grain of established conventions and audience expectations and allows for other possibilities. This articulation of a contemporary aesthetic through the abstract unfoldings of the moving body, while remaining moored in cultural specificities, rejecting what passes for "tradition," is still based, as *Angika* makes clear, on some notion of recuperation. Indeed in a talk opening *The Other Festival*, a forum presenting the work of "alternative" performing artists in Chennai, she said,

> I realized how body and its sensuality had been entirely sublimated and negated in deference to the notion of the decorative. Where was the body? It struck me that "recovery of the body" could be a specific project in the Indian dance context—Bharatanatyam . . . An open quest for a more open body language, the need to see pared down to its basics, divested of trinkets—all that mask the face and form and camouflage the energy sources of the body. In the process, it was inevitable that more open body-language meant integrating the principles of multiple physical disciplines, aspects of abstraction, minimalism, time and space frames like the *vilambita* mode and the multicentered space mode. It also meant . . . going beyond mere technique and virtuosity—to a world of imagination—a world of geometry of space, geometry of the body.[15]

This quest for "recovery" is, I believe, best understood as a process of resituating the dance in an aesthetic-spiritual-political realm different from and critical of the commercialism that has come to shape classical dance in current times, while remaining seeped in long-standing cultural and aesthetic practices. *Angika*, which I will "read" in detail subsequently, marks the concretization of this quest. At any rate, in the terms in which it is couched, it also reads as a modernist critique of the grandiose rhetoric of the neo-classical modern that mythologizes the dance and obscures the reconstruction of the "classical" dance. Interestingly of course, the images of dancing bodies that Chandralekha sculpts thereafter seem to invite analysis as postmodern, as I have elaborated earlier.

The process of "recovery" has entailed fine and detailed investigation and study of basic elements of the form. Thus, for her, the basic position of Bharatnatyam, and of several other styles of Indian classical dance, the *mandala* is a manifestation of the cosmic location of the body and the relationship of bodily processes to those at work in the universe at large.

> In terms of the body, *mandala* is a holistic concept integrating the human body with itself, with the community and with the environment. It generates a centered, tensile, and complex visual form. It is a principle of power, of stability, of balance, of holding the earth . . . of squaring and circularizing the body and of breaking the tension and rigidity of the vertical line by a curve.
>
> This inward/outward dynamic of the *mandala*—one spatial movement curving inward and another flowing outward, radiating into expanding circles while intensely held by the *bindu*—is its basic strength.[16]

In her unique exposition of the *mandala*, Chandralekha reveals the dynamism and potential power of this starting point of dance, something that is often understood in limited ways as a shape or body position. With ultimate regard for its classically prescribed dimensions, which provides the starting point for her explorations, we see that Chandralekha's choreography deploys it as anything but a flat or fixed position—she upturns it, the feet thrusting up toward the sky; she makes it unstationary, weaving it into skipping sequences, drawn from the structure of children's games, a way of traveling through space; she abstracts the principle of opposed but balanced energies, one reaching down through the pelvis, the other reaching up through the spine, and emphasizes it in the many ways in which the *mandala* is embodied.

Similarly, the three basic elements of classical choreography besides the *mandala*, the *bhramari* (turns), the *chaari* (walks), and the *utplavana* (jumps) are explored and rearticulated to form Chandralekha's technical base. *Bhramaris* are aerialized, for instance, *chaaris* are floored with the body parallel to the ground, floor positions are inserted into *utplavanas*. Hand gestures, which comprise an entire vocabulary in Indian classical performance, are explored more in their capacities to enhance and dynamize forms, to extend the lines of the body in this embodiment of an abstract and minimal aesthetics. Into the classically defined repertoire of *mudras*, otherwise known primarily for their role in weaving complex narratives, are introduced hand gestures from ritual practices, such as the *yoni mudra*. In this way, Chandralekha reconceptualizes the principles and technical hallmarks of *abhinaya*—the technique of generalization through depersonalization, the use of a detailed repertoire of eye gestures, for instance—and resituates them in an abstract context not to serve narrative functions, but to explore realms of ideas, to question or resignify existing symbolic codes. These strategies work together to radicalize the typical concept of the Indian, particularly female, dancing body, disrupting the romanticism governing ideas of such bodies with a minimalist and focused exploration of energies, what she has referred to as her search of the geometry of the body.

In formulating her typical movement idiom through critical deconstruction of the classical and neoclassical practices through a painstakingly theorized politics, there is no search for "newness." Instead, the search is to understand the possible relevancies of these legacies of the body in contemporary times, how they come to be figured in today's world. Here, where the radical, the avant-garde, is based on a recycling and revisioning of older cultural practices, past history and present creation coalesce and comment upon each other. For instance, Chandralekha draws on the ancient tantric and yogic precept that the spine, along which the *chakra*s (energy centers) are located, is the source of the body's strength, to comment on the contemporary degradation of women in Indian society: the loss of self-confidence of the women in *Sri* is imaged through the walk with the "broken" spine, which I will describe in the chapter on that piece. The comment contains its own looping critique: the image of contemporary women with broken spines in their labored walk challenges the silences in the very past from which she has drawn about the suffering women must have endured even then, about the patriarchal hegemonies with which that past is ridden. The movement sources used by her are thus critiqued, discarded, or expanded, and ultimately reborn in the embodiment of her work.

It is in this mode of reinterpreting the very traditions within which she claims her location, intersecting them with her critiques and politics, thus radicalizing the ways in which they signify, that the subversive power of Chandralekha's work is generated. In particular, it is even through her adherence to the exact dimensions and contexts of the tenets of classical performance, understood through her own vision, that Chandralekha reconceptualizes the female body against the produced narratives of a statist and patriarchal cultural history, troubling the predictable, safe, and hegemonic representations that dominate the current cultural mainstream. I am repeating Chandralekha's own emphasis on working with and through local traditions, cultural practices indigenous to the Indian context, because of the implications that come to accrue to contemporary choreography in Indian dance, and to further contextualize the rhetoric of the project of recovery. I have already talked about how innovation and contemporaneity in dance seem to result inevitably from western influence. In this context, it is important to register Chandralekha's insistence on her location in cultural specificity coupled with her resistance to having concepts from Euro-American modern dance foisted upon her work: "The East, in order to be 'contemporary' in its expression, need not have the burden of using the West as a crutch or ready reference. To me, to be 'contemporary' would mean to understand and express the East in its own terms."[17]

Thus it is that a concept such as *rasa*, the mood energizing performance, a central concept in classical performance, comes to be understood in its own terms in a contemporary context. Distancing *rasa* from esoteric and mystical concepts, Chandralekha talks about it instead as "a harmonious integration of the individual with himself, with his society and nature" which, in an "epoch of social fracture, is to enter the realm of human liberation."[18] In its translation from the framework of aesthetic theory written between the third and fifth century, in the treatises of performance scholars such as Bharata, to the context of contemporary performance, *rasa* then comes to be understood as aspirations for relationality and for a concrete sense of the location of individual-in-community. Also, in shifting the lens through which the dancing body is viewed, she refuses the image of the dancer that proliferates the commercialized market of current classical dance, the bejewelled, semi-divine, "nayika" or heroine dancing of idealized or divine love, and works instead with dancers who have discarded the jewels, flowers, and silks and prefer to explore choreographies of sensual-spiritual journeys. Past the conviction of Euro-American modern dance in the "truth" of the body, past the postmodern choreographer's attempts to find the "natural" body and movement, past the agendas that governed the "recovery" of neoclassical Bharatnatyam, Chandralekha's work is marked by her search for articulations of a complex politics and philosophy of the body.

Obviously then, the dancers who want to work with Chandralekha, generally highly trained in classical Bharatnatyam which, like all classical forms, produces and naturalizes a specific kind of dancing body, are open to examining their training. In fact, for Chandralekha what is most important in training her dancers is that they successfully "unlearn" the social conventions that have come to be naturalized in their embodiment, get past the presentational "projection" of forms they have learned as part of their dance training. Indeed, the search in her movement seems to be for an aesthetic that exceeds the codified "affect" of the trained body. If, as Martha Graham insisted, the body does not lie, it does indeed equivocate: beyond signaling behaviors "learned" or imbibed through socialization, it naturalizes extended systems of training. For instance, Chandralekha talks about having to remind her dancers repeatedly to do away with the empty and synthetic smiles that classical dancers automatically wear when they perform unless exploring specifically different emotions—a post-proscenium development. Thus dancers she works with, usually highly trained in Bharatnatyam, undergo some training in Kalarippayattu and, or, yoga, basically nonperformance-oriented movement forms that have a very different focus and orientation from concert dance forms. Because of her particular aesthetic preference and her definition of what constitutes "dance" movement, she also works with performers who have had little if any training in dance specifically, but are highly skilled in Kalarippayuttu and, or, yoga. At any rate, all of her performers participate in various kinds of movement and theater workshops conducted by artists from around the world for her company. They also engage in dialogue with her and other colleagues, constantly questioning what they are dancing and why.

The Hybrid Moving of Zollar

Dancers who come to audition for the Urban Bush Women are required to have formal dance training, preferably in modern or jazz styles and some form of African-based dance, which complements practice in some form of non-mainstream, non-concert dance, such as street or social dance forms. What is important about this stipulation is the body attitude that the dancers bring to their movement—not a strict, unidimensional sense about line and "technique," but an awareness of the varied ways in which these ideas can be understood and the multiple aesthetics that can inform movement. The way in which street movement forms intersect, comment upon, and sometimes undercut the aesthetic preferences of specific established styles of Western concert dance requires that dancers be ready to "unlearn" specificities of "technique," much in a similar way as Chandralekha's dancers. They must also be ready to sing, act, and speak on stage, though heightened proficiency in vocalizing and theatrical techniques is acquired through training with the company. According to Zollar, it takes an already trained dancer at least two years, working intensively with movement, trust exercises (since the intense nature of the work requires emotional preparation), vocal processes, theatrical and performance techniques (aimed at sharpening performers' reflexes to make instantaneous decisions and react intelligently to unforeseen situations on stage), to reach the level of technical excellence and body-mind integration that the company has come to be known for.

Classes and rehearsals conducted by Zollar work through a double focus on process and product. Dancers must be ready to work holistically, with all the varied elements that may be required for that day's work. Because the work is intense, requiring full concentration, all sessions begin with a check-in circle time, where dancers can share issues they are currently dealing with, with the others. This takes away from working time, but it encourages both the sense of a supportive community and a full commitment to the work on the part of each individual. Sessions end with similar check-out times, where any disturbances experienced during the day can be brought up and dealt with, instead of letting them fester. Zollar believes that such measures are essential in order to access the kind of sensitivity, finesse, and emotional giving she demands of her performers.

Zollar's own movement style and range are based on her early apprenticeship in black non-mainstream performance genres, social dances, and on the dancing she learned as a child from her Dunham-trained teacher, Joseph Stevenson, with whom she performed in clubs and vaudeville acts. After spending years re-educating her body in terms of "proper" dance training and "technique," which seemed to her to annihilate the special features of individual movement in the drive to approximate a rigid conception of the dancerly body, she returned to her early training which was "all about style and personality."[19] It is important, thus, that the company has no "uniform" look: Zollar has always insisted that, in this company comprising primarily African American women, there be a variety of skin tone, body type, basic training, and cultural background. Dancers in the company have included black performers from the Caribbean, Africa, and Britain as well, all of whom bring to their performing distinctive training backgrounds as well as culturally and personally specific movement styles, reflecting the complex ways in which issues of diasporic African identities are conceptualized in the company and the work. In training her dancers, Zollar seeks to draw out the individual talents she works with: "I don't make judgments on my dancers. I work with who they are."[20] Further, for Zollar, a particular conception of a "dancerly" body, loaded with issues of weight and particularities of anatomical measurement, is anathema. She speaks with disappointment about the training she received in college: here, for the first time, she received "information" about the supposedly ideal dancer's body, and about how her own body did not quite measure up to those precepts. For her, judgments of right and wrong about the body and movement really uphold arbitrary presuppositions and obscure the range and diversity of movement available to different bodies.

Moreover, the multicenteredness in different aspects of the movement, integral to the aesthetics and philosophy of her work, and held together by the spiritual and political passion that characterizes her work, evolve from a holistic mode of training and working interweaving various modalities and styles, rather than the kind of eclecticism that Sally Banes describes as typical of the late postmodern. Zollar: "I try to train my company to have the feeling of African dance, in terms of the approach to movement and the body and the dynamics—but with more of the gestural and spatial range and focus of modern dance."[21] So her dancers work with the typical features of Africanist movement, such as polyrhythms and polycentricity, where different rhythms and tempi must mark the movement emanating from different centers of the body, the head, the chest, the pelvis. Such isolations of body parts are complemented with a strong conception of the "center" of modern dance and ballet, to enable difficult balances inspired by these movement aesthetics. Again, while features of Africanist rhythmicity, such as call-and-response, preserving and suspending the beat, sensing and marking the "break" with the percussionist, must be perfected in movement as well as in vocalization, Zollar will sometimes introduce her dancers to the unmarked, breath rhythms of T'ai chi or yoga-inspired movement. Further, while Zollar herself, or a company member, most often teaches class, different guest teachers, from different movement genres and styles, are frequently invited to conduct company classes. Again, class might one day begin with a total focus on training the voice, since a cappella singing is so much part of the work, with dancers making up lyrics on the spur of the moment and creating new songs under the direction of the vocal trainer. Another day might begin with focusing on theater, working with a dramaturge to search for and conjure up internal motivation for gesture and dialogue.

Though she recognizes that most African American choreographers have kept away from this genre largely because of histories of prejudices and exclusions, Zollar also works intensely with contact improvisation, which, for her, is very much about sensing internal rhythm, one's own as well as that of others in the space. In this abstract understanding in terms of the relationship of self-and-other, which is the way Zollar thinks about it, the genre is sympathetic to Africanist aesthetics. She also feels that contact offers vital training in the giving and sharing of weight and modes of supporting: here contact helps to increase dancers' alertness and sensitivity to each others' energy fields and thus fine tune those sections where improvisation melds into choreographed structure. This is a vital skill for the repertoire is filled with pieces where improvisation must interweave, without jarring breaks, into set movement. Moreover, in working with such intense emotional and thematic content, in the heightened performative state, unexpected, unrehearsed, things happen, and those on stage must sense the need of the moment and improvise to get the piece back on track. Apart from contact improvisation, Zollar also works with her dancers to refine their energy management through different exercises in kinesthetic awareness, varying timing skills, injury prevention systems, and internal strengthening exercises drawn from the Pilates and floor-barre systems.

I will briefly describe an exercise that Zollar uses to explore this theme of the giving and taking of weight to emphasize the multiple points on which dancers need to concentrate. On this particular day, the class taught by Zollar explored the themes of weight and release in movement. After the initial warm-up, most of the day was devoted to a continued exploration of these ideas. Dancers first worked in pairs, sensing each other's breath rhythms to establish some degree of mutuality in a simple exercise of sinking to the floor and coming up together. As one of the pair, and then the other, began to let go of her weight more and more, depending on her partner to keep her from falling over as they went down and came up, Zollar instructed them to sense, kinesthetically, what it was about the supporter that made the person being supported feel insecure, which fingers needed to give more pressure, which part of the torso held rigid. With this sense of what was needed to make a person who had let go of her weight feel more secure, dancers were told to all work together as a group of six.

Having worked with her dancers in an ideal situation where two were working intensely, concentrating specifically on the sharing of each other's weight, Zollar now moved on to a performative mode, where such exclusive concentration might not always be available. One person in the group was told to go into "a state of suspended falling," as if she is wounded. The others, who were engaged in their own movements prior to her falling, needed to sense immediately where, or under which part of her body, she needed support, and take on their share of the responsibility for the going down and coming up. Zollar pointed out that, in fact, the falling person might never really be able to let go of her weight completely though it must look like she has, but must retain some central, deep point of control. She also needed to help the others by giving some information about how and when she wanted to be lifted, for instance by lifting her hips slightly, or signaling through her breath that she was ready to be helped up. Clearly, her dancers must be comfortable with inhabiting this precarious point between having control and losing it, and with risking going over the edge. Mental and emotional readiness for such work is important training in this work, and procedures for this state of preparedness are built into the way rehearsals are structured: through the "check-in" and "check-out" times that begin and end the sessions, as well as through the intense discussions that are interspersed throughout the choreographic process. These skills of readiness are also heightened, in the typically holisitic way of working, through game structures. The "zip-zap-boing game," for instance, is a group game demanding close and sustained attention and mental and physical presence, quickening the dancers into a state of constant alertness through the concentration required for staying "in" the game, even as they are caught up in the fun.

Here, training in technique becomes a way to build community, often a resistive one, deeply aware of political connotations of artistic practice. The training process prepares dancers to constantly test the limits of their movement abilities in rehearsal, so that they are still safe performing difficult and complex phrases even when they have entered a heightened emotional state in performance. As Ntozake Shange says of the risk-taking built into the movement of a piece like *Shelter,* "Every dancer is at risk: to be dropped, to fall, to go too far. But it is an unspoken knowing that saves them."[22] This "knowing" is not some mystical gift: it is an achieved kines-thetic skill, which the dancers have to work long to acquire. Typical to this group of women, it is a skill that necessarily works as much as part of indi-vidual technique, as one completed in relationing, watching out for each other on stage, peripheral sensing of each others' energies even when totally focused on one's own performance. It is my hope that this discus-sion of training processes both emphasizes the depth and range of skills Zollar insists that her dancers be equipped with, and also challenges stereo-typical naturalizing of performance skills for black dancers. Both this pres-ent discussion and the following one exploring the deployment of this training in choreography are inspired by my own experience with the com-pany: having participated in training sessions with Zollar's dancers several times, I have repeatedly been amazed at the level of technical excellence and range the dancers come to acquire.

Here again, artistic excellence is a given, if shifting, norm: Eurocentric norms of body and line are broken down, and what is practiced instead is a more complex and nuanced ideal of technical manipulation, where the dancing body, moving between different aesthetic frameworks, works with a greatly expanded repertoire of movement. This is particularly in relation to the concept of "line," often misread by critics. Look at this phrase from the middle section of *Nyabinghi Dreamtime,* for instance. As the rest of the dancers dance in a loose cluster in center stage, Treva Offut, spins out from the group and launches herself into a circle around the others. Hopping forward on one foot, she propels herself on with the other leg, which is flexed behind from the knee and flung out behind her on every step. Her body is jostled on each step to open her torso out and fling her arms wide, returning to a slight forward tilted chest on the down moment. For Debo-rah Jowitt, reviewing this piece for the *Village Voice,* this is an interesting moment certainly, but one where, typical of this company in her opinion, line and technique are held in disregard. Here, though apparently positively reviewed, the performance is measured against parameters that make the review quite offensive.

> As is usually the case with UBW, the artifice of choreography is disguised
> by impetuous, rough-edged performing. The movement isn't "authentic,"

Urban Bush Women, Zollar's *Nyabinghi Dreamtime*. Photo by Dona Ann McAdams.

but neither does it display inappropriate finesse or a European-American concept of virtuosity. Watch skinny Offut propel herself in a hop around the stage, one leg thrusting out behind her like a rocket booster. She's totally inside the action and how it gets her where she's going, line be damned.[23]

What does "rough-edged" mean? If the performance were indeed "impetuous," the dancers would have to be literally superhuman to be able to display such technical refinement, moving between two very different aesthetics and keeping on top of the demanding choreography of leaps, jumps, balances, mixed with low and grounded Africanist movement. What is "authentic" and what "inappropriate?" Who decides? And in fact, line isn't damned in Offut's movement, nor is her approach to the movement purely functional: a certain notion of "line" is revised, deliberately played with, angularized, differently from dominant aesthetic trends and in keeping with "other" aesthetics. Moreover, what might have been obvious to Jowitt, had she not chosen to speak from her positioning in a Euro-American aesthetic, is the remarkable exercise of balance whereby the dancer must remain, perhaps as much "inside" as on top of the movement, so that even in those moments that look off-balance, emphasized by the off-vertical spine shifting back and forth from the center line while thrusting forward, she is entirely in control of her body. Besides, that hop isn't the only movement Offut performs. How does this "othering," which seems to be the criterion for approval here, hold when Offut or other dancers perform immaculate grand jetés in quick succession or promenade with one leg in attitude, or perform a difficult balance in adagio? There's not much comment on that. It might seem that the call for a paradigm shift in reviewing dance is dated, but such reviews from such seasoned critics and writers remind us that obviously much work remains to be done.

Look at the complexity of technique in this other section in the same piece—a solo, danced by the priestess figure. As the group gathers to sit huddled together in upstage left corner, the priestess whips herself up with a high kick, foot flexed, in center stage. The moment of landing is obscured as she slides easily into a split on the floor, and scrambles up immediately, butt raised up. On her feet but still bent over, she lifts herself into a jump, limbs flinging out in different directions. One more time, the moment of reaching the floor is eclipsed as she steps onto a turned out foot and leans her torso forward, the other leg extending slowly in a long and steady arabesque line, rising even above her head. The moment of perfect stillness is ruffled as the leg brushes forward and initiates a pattern of footsteps, the back curving in and out on alternate steps, punctuated by a series of toe turns, the hips and shoulders turning in and out rapidly, swinging the arms and legs with them. For me, this entire section is exemplary of the particularly difficult virtuosity that Zollar's choreography demands of her dancers' bodies: they must constantly alternate between different centers, shift their centers of gravity, be in charge of their bodies when they give the impression of having given up control of them, regain verticality when it seems impossible, and ease into a difficult balance when drawing the body out of a rapidly moving, rhythmic step pattern. Moreover, technique here acquires remarkable transparency: we are moved to ask, for instance, what it means to create a "priestess" character in terms of agility, negotiation, balance, and flexibility. I think it dramatizes her role as mediator between divine and human, but also creates an inspiring image of a female leader for communities-in-resistance.

Empowered, interweaving shifts are a dominating presence in Zollar's idiomatic base, conveying both the multiple strengths and centers of the dancers and the intersected and intersecting aesthetic framework of the technique. Long extended lines of the body, reaching back into space, one arm elongating the line of the spine, are immediately juxtaposed with a series of hop steps under a curved-over torso, the arms swinging back and forth in opposite directions to each other. Rond de jombs en l'air, the body perfectly balanced atop a hip-high leg circling around, are placed adjacent to undulating movements on slightly flexed knees and parallel feet, the hip circling to the smooth rippling of the torso and the arms. Besides the shifts in technique, moments of high spurts of energy are intercut with drawn-out sequences filled with long, sustained lines of energy. A reach of the body into a side bend, pulled by the arm which curves overhead and aspires toward the floor continues into a series of turns, the body whipped around by the other arm which flings itself around the body and leads it around and around itself. If anything, such sections disprove and defy Jowitt's arbitrary judgment about what techniques and movement aesthetics are available to or appropriate for these dancers, and give credence to my perception of the multiple technical skills over which they must acquire parallel command if they are to perform Zollar's choreography. They are also eloquently expressive of the kind of femininity that Zollar is foregrounding: multidimensional, layered, shifting, empowered, and moving through with poetry and power.

Calling on Spirits

Spiritual yearning, understood in particularized ways, is an underlying force in the work of these choreographers. Clearly distinguished from established religion, the spiritual is here focused on issues of self-and-others, self-in-world, and is connected integrally to the formulation of what I have called a politics of defiant hope. The spiritual also enters as a mode of crossing boundaries: the concept of femininity as liberatory mode in Chandralekha's *Raga* and *Sloka* transgresses the boundaries of conventionally gendered bodies, while the story of the artistic aspirations of Minnie Evans allows Zollar to mingle worlds and characters separated by life and death in *Praise House* (1990). Here, the spiritual is a dimension and a perspective; it is understood through the materiality of practice, performed as soul that infuses the work. Moreover, it is always understood as being in relationship with sensual and bodily reclaimings and celebrations, and sexuality is a force intimately connected to the search for self.

First, however, I want to address Chandralekha's use of some concepts and iconography that are Hindu, though in her work they are certainly removed from religious context and implications and reinterpreted in the light of a secular but culturally specific feminism. Among symbols activated in her choreography are abstract concepts such as the inverted triangle as a symbol of the female energy, the concept of the *ardha-narishwar* (half-man, half-woman deity), the harmonious coupling of male and female energies, as well as some more clearly "readable," even though deconstructed, goddess images. Chandralekha's use of these concepts in the juxtapositions and contexts that characterize her work no doubt challenges their "Hindu"-ness, understood as a narrow and conservative doctrine. Yet, this can sometimes be problematic at a time when religious fundamentalisms are aggressively championed, and in terms of an "Indian" women's movement that includes women from various religious groups, dominantly Hindu, Muslim, Christian, and Parsi. This situation is typical of how choices become limited and foreclosed in this dangerous trend of current politics. In a context where firstly, the religious and the cultural are so intimately interwoven with each other, and secondly, where falling back upon "western" sources in the search for neutrality is deeply problematic, the possibility of creating "secular" images is vitiated by the religious affect that has accrued to these images. What are the choices of a choreographer who wants to work with influences that are culturally specific and indigenous to the context in which she lives and works, without denying that in much popular and hegemonic discourse "Indian" is conflated with "Hindu?"

One way of thinking about the usage of such iconography is in terms of a vital but not necessarily efficient separation: Hinduism as religion versus cultural practices that are associated with Hinduism. No doubt the hegemonic position of religion is perpetuated through cultural practices, some ritualized and some quotidian, naturalized. But these latter are often based on Hinduism as lived philosophy rather than actual religious practice, and the distinction between the two, as in other contexts, can often be marked. However, while it is impossible to ignore the genealogies of such practices and images, it is equally unfair to push aside general conceptions of the different bodies of work produced by Chandralekha, all of which have positioned her in unambiguous opposition to such religious bigotries. In this context, her strategy seems to mark heterodoxical practice, signaling the moment of possibility of critique, a form of subversion that still, however, remains framed within or is unable to escape completely the terms of a given discourse.[24] Thus, for instance, Chandralekha's endeavour has been to work with abstract concepts and symbols drawn from her context, but to defamiliarize them both through interventions in form and through reactivating them in a politics of feminist empowerment and resistance. The body of her work, which is overtly antagonistic to fundamentalist Hinduism, also repeatedly undercuts any religious associations that the aesthetic symbols she works through might have. Moreover, the way in which she invokes some images, and then redeploys them to signify differently, is particularly effective, foregrounding powerful alternative interpretations of ideas that could have been co-opted by others for pushing agendas of religio-political dominance.

For instance, distraught at the Hindu-Muslim conflict, Chandralekha created *Bhinna Pravaha* (Different Flows) in 1993, urging tolerance for difference. She used some lines from an old literary text, the *Raghuvamsa* of Kalidasa (Canto XIII), for inspiration. These lines describe a real "confluence of differences" through an aerial view of the meeting of the waters of the rivers Ganga and Yamuna. This very real phenomenon of the entwining of the waters, one light like sandal paste, luminous, one dark like black amber, "flowing together in their separate colors, in their separate currents," which can indeed be seen near the town of Allahabad in Northern India, is evoked to encourage a celebration of individuality and diversity among the Hindu and Muslim peoples.[25] Moving away from her typically seamless choreographic structure, she used two dancers with two distinct training and movement styles, one Chhau (Ileana Citaristi) and one Bharatnatyam (Shangita Namashivayam), to create images of complementarity and collage.[26] Moreover, the exuberant celebration of difference, working with counterpoint and juxtaposition, weaves an aesthetic that disallows the chauvinism of any one style. No doubt the inspiration here too is a Sanskrit Hindu text, but the image itself is from relatively secular descriptions of nature. Moreover, in disembedding Kalidasa's image from its specific context and deploying it in the context of current religious dissensions, the piece, through implication, inserts a Muslim presence into this canonical text of Hindu Indian literature.

Self-Search

The spiritual core of Chandralekha's work is sensed most clearly in that unremitting search for understanding the self, which is both one and greater than one, unique in its individuality yet realized only in relationship to community. The spiritual is also entirely wrapped up in, and interwoven with, the sensual: the choreography constantly reflects a somatic wholeness, where the physical and psychic processes work in concert, exploring new dimensions of self. While this is obvious in almost all of her work, it is most striking in the last work made at the time of this book going to press. *Sharira*, premièred in 2001, is a duet, danced by Padmini Chettur and Shaji John when I saw it being performed in Chicago.[27] Choreographed with an increasingly simple movement idiom, removed from any sustained use of technically superlative moments, with minimal use of rhythmic structure, the starkness of the piece is brilliantly contrasted by the powerful singing of the Gundecha brothers, well-known exponents of the *dhrupad* style of Hindustani classical vocal music. There is no correspondence, thematically, between the lyrics of their song and the choreography, but they work in concert as if they belong together, this man and this woman moving to discover the limits of their bodies, and these musicians and vocalists unraveling the depths and dimensions of a sonic universe, articulating a relationship between self and other that is together yet on its own, on multiple levels. In the dance, limbs interweave, intersecting the space enclosed by other limbs, criss-crossing lines of bodies, creating images of an intimacy that leaves us to ask the question: what is it to know another? What knowl-

Shaji John and Tishani Doshi, Chandralekha's *Sharira*. My descriptions of the piece are from the earlier version when it was danced by Padmini Chettur and Shaji John, while the pictures are from the piece as it is currently performed by Tishani Doshi and Shaji John. Photo © Sadanand Menon.

Tishani Doshi and Shaji John, Chandralekha's *Sharira*. Photo © Sadanand Menon.

Shaji John and Tishani Doshi, Chadralekha's *Sharira*. Photo © Sadanand Menon.

edge of self is gleaned from this inter-relationship with another? What is this relationship of togetherness when self is so distinct? In the absence of "wow" moments of technical virtuosity, we are drawn to notice subtle nuances of technique, expressivity of unfolding hands, the circularity of the journey of the foot that lifts to take a step behind, the breath release of Shaji as he extends his arms overhead just before folding down before Padmini's seated body on the floor. The most vibrant image from the piece remains the beginning and ending one, where the two dancers facing each other, circle around each other slowly, arms lifted overhead, intense series of revolutions dimly-lit, invoking a universe in which we can pay attention to this search for self.

Yet, these moments of quiet revolving and self-absorption have to be arrived at through confrontation and questioning, and through processes of journeying. Early on, Chandralekha had stated her disillusionment with an idealistic philosophy that "gives a 'natural, eternal' justification to art" and "does not explain anything and does away with all dialectics . . . arranges the world nostalgically, harmoniously, so that it appears to be without contradictions."[28] Rejecting the synchronized universe invoked by classical dance forms, her work explores these concepts through patterns and images created by moving bodies, through moments of danger and conflict intercut by reminders of peace and stillness. Her spiritual quest is bodied forth in human terms, something that German critic Jochen Schmidt completely misses as he writes about her in comparison to classical Bharat-natyam dancer, Alarmel Valli. Schmidt lamented the absence in Chan-dralekha what seemed to him to be the essence of Valli's dance: its spiritual fervor. He writes of Valli's dancing that "her spirituality lifts the dance to a level which comes very close to its divine origin."[29] He may not know or may not realize that for Chandralekha these divine origins do not exist, nor does the transcendental location of the dance: indeed, Chandralekha's cho-reography is enriched with a search for the human, not divine, origins of the spirit, and for the immediately physical and spiritual locations of dance.

I am drawn to think of what to me is one of the most powerful choreo-graphic sections of Chandralekha's work: the *netranritya*—the dance of the eyes—section from *Interim. Interim: After the End and Before the Beginning* (1995), was a collaborative project sponsored by the Brooklyn Academy of Music's Visual Arts Initiative program, in which Chandralekha worked with visual artists Kristin Jones and Andrew Ginzel to create a multimedia pro-ject at the Queens Museum of Art in New York, in 1995. Here, juggling the traditional repertoire of *drshtiveda* (the different eye gestures) in different combinations and varying tempi, Chandralekha created this section where, very differently from traditional usage, the ten-minute section with the eyes happens un-conjoined with any *abhinaya* or movement of other limbs. There is also, unlike as in the traditional setting, and typical of Chandra-

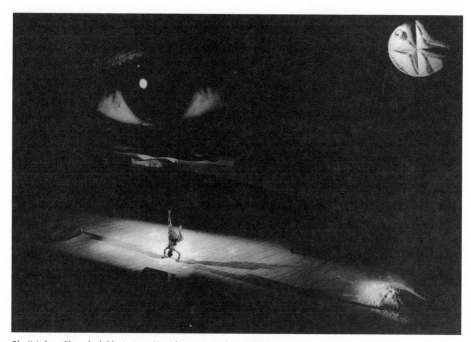

Shaji John, Chandralekha's *Interim*. Photo © Sadanand Menon.

lekha's work, no attempt at narrativization, or at invoking emotion and mood through the eyes, but an abstract sensing of the passage of time, the eyes dancing as if to herald the coming of a time that lies in the beyond.

Three women sit in a tight triangle on the floor, their feet crossed, their knees up and held by the flexed elbows, the forearms running across the shins to clasp the hands in front. They sit in front of a large copper plate, on which the light falls: on a dimmed stage, their faces are lit by the reflected glow from the copper plate, their eyes caught as if in the bronze flush of a setting sun. The six pupils move in perfect harmony, black on white, side, side-to-side, around, up, down, up-and-down, in varying patterns. The measured, slow dance of the eyes is punctuated by a series of quick oscillations, side-to-side, as if watching for the arrival of something imminent. The eyes quiet to arrive at *sama*, front. Then quick flickerings, the eyelids moving for the first time to open and close, like the flame of a candle threatened by the breeze. Their folded legs released from the grasp of their arms, the two women in front turn to face each other, the woman at the apex of the triangle turns to face back. The two women lean toward each other to interweave their arms and cover each other's eyes. Then, as the other woman arches back and we see another pair of eyes in that space held by the three bodies, they twist around to interweave their flexed arms once more to place two layers of hands on her eyes. As the hands move away, the eyes open slowly: it is as if vision is invoked.

Once more the dance of the eyes resumes, all three dancers facing front, around, up-and-down, side, up, side, down, in single and doubled speeds, in different arrangements. Flickerings, like a candlelight, and intimations of something imminent. This time, as the women turn, they effect a different formation, all three of them turning to their right: the woman on the right then faces the upstage left corner, while the other two women face downstage left corner. Of these two, the one in front leans back to cradle her back in the chest of the woman behind her, who now gently places her hands on the eyes resting on her bosom. Then, as the hands open, the eyes open, and still in that intimate position, the women turn their heads to look at the third dancer, who, sitting in a side split on the floor, now meets their eyes. This final meeting of eyes that comes after what I can only describe as an intense search, marks a silently climactic moment in the piece. For it performs brilliantly Chandralekha's ideas about the movement of time, an ephemeral concept, which can be measured only through such momentary phenomena such as the opening and closing of an eye. The blinks, the flickerings, of the eyes are not fixed in the physical time that binds us to routine, but happen in metaphysical time, cosmic and memory time, when in one blink, a whole era, millions of years can be said to have passed by. For Chandralekha, a blink is "the measurement of time across no time."[30] As she once wrote in a letter to me, talking about the past and the future that are always already contained within the present moment,

> I am trying to explore and understand and comprehend the meaning of this *moment*, which receives light from a certain planet which emanated 50,000 years ago, and light from another planet which emanated 20,000 years ago, and light from Sirius which started 2,000 years ago. If all these are received at this end by you in this moment, where is Ananya—in the past, present or future?[31]

This cyclic understanding of time contests logistical notions of time as linear progression, where time can be divided into dated blocks, and corresponds with the way I have theorized the postmodern in this context. Moreover, such relative positioning of self weaves a world-view where a search for the self-in-cosmos replaces both modernist individualism and communities organized on the premises of religion.

Dancing Intimations of Soul

Zollar's works repeatedly testify to how, while referring to and celebrating specific practices associated with the black church as modalities of resistive cultural performance and building community, she continuously distances herself from doctrinaire religiosity. This spiritual seeking reveals itself as emerging from the typical fabric of black life in America, located in all the interstices of daily activity. Ntozake Shange, profiling the company for the *New York Times*, once wrote of Zollar that she takes "Women's bodies, racist myths, sexist stereotypes, post-modern dance conventions and the 'science' of hip-hop and catapults them over the rainbow, so they come tumbling out of the grin of the man in the moon."[32] Shange articulates beautifully Zollar's ability to strip dreams and creative energies of sentimentality and romanticism, embed them in the hard stuff of reality with all its gritty politics of racist and sexist hierarchies, the degradation of poverty and homelessness, and still grope for and locate the power of the spirited body to move on.

I want to refer to an early work, *Praise House*, in talking about the richly layered spiritual universe that Zollar's work invokes, and the unique sense of metaphysical continuity, intersections of conventionally compartmentalized sections of time and space, that particular fluidity of boundaries. *Praise House*, structured in two acts, "Gifting" and "Draw or die," is inspired by the real life story of Minnie Evans (Hannah), a visionary artist, whose predisposition for communing with angels and spirits made her a "problem child" for her mother (Mommy), caught in the throes of reality and the needs of survival. The other central character in this piece is Hannah's grandmother, the elder Hannah, who enjoys similar communion with the spirits and is a soulmate to her granddaughter. The rest of the characters are spirits, angels, denizens of a world in-between, and often the externalizations of Hannah's thoughts and feelings.

By Act II, Granny has passed away, but she continues to be a powerful presence in her granddaughter's spiritual field. A flight of stairs runs up the middle of the stage. The spirit forces or angels stand in groups of two or by themselves around the stage, while Granny stands near the topmost step of the stairs, Hannah stands in the downstage right corner, and Mommy stands in the downstage central zone of the stage. The call-and-response modality takes on rich overtones as the angels, beginning at different times and at different points in the song, begin to sing of the approaching night and darkness. Each group of angels moves in its own time and with its own movement phrase, as some develop the song to its conclusion and others pick up a refrain along the way and layer the breath pauses of the entire song with their echoings.

Mommy begins to speak, her words ringing with frustration: she does not know what to do with her child, who cannot be brought within the regulations of "normality." She sinks to the floor on her knees and leans back on her shins, her arms clasped together at her chest, her elbows joined, as she almost begins to sob, upbraiding god for giving her such a child at one moment, and weeping for forgiveness for such thoughts at the next. She wrings her hands and thrusts them upwards in despair, throwing her head up and back. Her arms and upper body replay the emotional ups and downs her words convey, the utter confusion she feels. Another layer of action is juxtaposed onto this already rich tapestry: from their respective places, Hannah and Granny begin to speak to themselves, yet to each other, one speaking her thoughts as the other finishes, their movements commenting on, emphasizing, the import of their words. Hannah's movements, arranged in waves and circles energized by a constancy of flow, are shadowed or repeated in enlarged form by an angel who stands directly behind her, touching her lightly on one shoulder. The utter difference between the words, tonality, and movement styles of Mommy—more angular, yet reaching, frantic, and broken—and Hannah reinforce the split between their worlds, and while Mommy, surrounded by the angels, recognizes the validity of Hannah's vision-world but resists it, Hannah, situated in the real world, remains oblivious to it, always close to an angel-companion. Finally, Granny, literally located in a zone above them both, signals a world where these contradictory and opposed worlds can meet, where living-dying can be considered in the infinite terms of a continuum.

Connecting with a spirit world that surrounds and often intersects with the realm of logistical realities, this continuity of difference, while very much part of black church practice, is metaphorized and dramatized in much of Zollar's work. It is also this continuity that connects the politics of resistance intimately with articulations of spiritual fervor, while, however, marking two sharp distinctions between established religions and spiritual practices, and between religious observations and cultural forms that have developed around them. So while a personal search for spirituality may be at the center of her work, the typical articulations and energies of black faith, particularly the unique expressive forms of the African American church, often inspire the organizational forms in her work. This, for her, is more about integrating what is a prominent part of African American life, forms expressive of the African American aesthetic, sociocultural interaction, and community formation into her work. "The church as form runs through a lot of our work. The call and response, the peaks that constantly happen throughout a church service, may happen throughout a dance. You may see something come to this point and come back down, come to this point, and come back down . . . it's that drive from the church."[33] Functioning as structural principles organizing Zollar's artistic work, these shared forms encourage both the distinction between religious and cultural modalities that I had talked about with relationship to Chandralekha's work, and also suggest their spiritual potential to invoke renewal and regeneration in the community.

Indeed this commitment to the forces of life and "conjure" is articulated richly in Zollar's work characterized by the interweaving of artistic and spiritual missions.[34] Minnie Evans must articulate her other-worldly visions through her drawings, and in the context of *Praise House*, through her dance. The dancing body here performs a moving spirituality, both in the sense of an embodied spirituality in the tradition of much Africanist practice, and as the experiencing body which "moves" between two worlds and thus shifts boundaries that separate them: "moves," dances, rocks, enacts, is possessed to articulate spiritual fervor; and "moves" or quickens the spirits of those who are present. This dance of spiritual passion works through a rich dialogue between "letting go" and remaining in control. Witness, for instance, this section from *Praise House*, where Hannah appears to give up her body to the control of the angels who hover around her on the stage, and the decentered and shifting centers of energy and control become a perfect metaphor for the unfixed and varying paths for a spiritual search that is outside the predication of religiosity.

Hannah, surrounded by four spirits, runs recklessly in between them. As she hurls her body towards theirs, they close in on her to support her flung limbs. They gather close to continue the momentum of her thrown body to lift her up, her body parallel to the ground, her arms and legs reaching out, her body like a drawn out bow. Immediately she is lowered onto her feet and she runs backward to be stopped in her unseeing motion by the reassuring hand of one angel, placed gently on her back. She continues to rush in between these spirit forces, as if she is swung from one to another relentlessly, but is always protected by them: they share her weight, assume responsibility for lifting and lowering her with speed, turning her around. As she runs forward this time, she hurtles over the back of one angel, who, anticipating the pathway of her run, stands in mid-path, knees bent and parallel, her back flat and flexed over. Running into another angel, who waits, arms extended, to catch her forward-moving body, Hannah is picked up by arms that wrap around her waist and turn her around, as the angel quickly steps around in a circle and then lowers her to the ground.

Mommy's voice is heard in the background, cutting into the song the angels have begun to sing, rising higher and higher, as she frantically calls to her daughter, frustrated at getting no reply. Hannah, who is unable to hear her mother, or is perhaps unwilling to answer, runs to join the dance of the spirits and enters their charmed circle, where one more time, she can apparently relinquish control over logistics of equipoise. Thoughts of balance, precautions, are seemingly sacrificed, as the hip is pulled off-center with the leg that kicks high up, rushing down only to swirl the body around. The turned body drops to the ground on one folded leg, as the other leg stretches out long to the side. She rises up, pulled by the arms, which circle violently overhead and around, whipping the body down and then pulling it back up. A series of back or reverse turns are interspersed with jumps in the air, hip shakes, finger waggings. As the spirits continue to dance around her, Hannah now turns around herself again and again, hopping around on one foot, while the other leg, flexed back from the knee, thrusts out behind her on every step. Stopping, her body is jerked up and down from the hip on low jumps, splashing out in mid-air as her arms and legs spread out on either side. Low jumps also carry her around, as one fisted arm shakes up and down in the air, and the body is convexed up and concaved down from the sacral region.

Obviously spirit possession is one of the black spiritual-cultural forms that is staged repeatedly as a mode of communion with divinity in Zollar's work. In the particular way she casts the experience of possession—finely balanced between choreographed performance and being "in the moment" —Zollar reminds one of bell hooks, who talks about the alternative meaning of possession as a process that makes revelation, renewal, and transformation possible. Hooks refers to the words of Napier who conceives of possession as "truly an avant-garde activity, in that those in trance are empowered to go to the periphery of what is and can be known, to explore the boundaries, and to return unharmed."[35] Zollar's creative process, partic-

Urban Bush Women, Zollar's *Nyabinghi Dreamtime*. Photo by Dona Ann McAdams.

ularly her choreography of possession, seems to reflect this avant-garde potential that Napier talks about. In a particular rehearsal session devoted to this very aspect of performance, where the dancers were training with Steve Kent, a dramaturge who works intermittently with the company, Kent urged the performers to experience the temporary releasing of control within the controlled environment of the rehearsal room: "You've had control over yourselves for at least 20 years. Why do you think that if you let go, you won't be able to come back?"[36] And indeed two of the ways they can "come back" is by the depth of this training and by focusing on others, by watching out for each other with a renewed sense of commitment to the community. Such exercises have also allowed the performers to reach that deep spiritual passion that marks so much of the UBW work.

This kind of work that imbues the dancing with spiritual passion becomes obvious in works such as *Nyabinghi Dreamtime*, which performs a community's movement from loss of control and hope toward revitalization and a resistive spirituality, through ritualistic practices inspired by and reminiscent of Rastafarianism. When the lights come up on the stage at the beginning of the piece, the percussionists are standing behind their drums, and the ensemble of women sit on the floor on folded knees near stage right, facing a woman clearly in a state of affliction. We hear them sob and lament, repeatedly raising their hands up towards the sky, throwing their heads back, as if pleading for deliverance. The priestess, who sits at the

Urban Bush Women, Zollar's *Nyabinghi Dreamtime*. Photo by Dona McAdams.

apex of the cluster of women, rises slowly, palm fronds still in hand, and walks forward with falling steps, her feet crossing one over another to imbue her movement with a curious off-balance swaying motion. Then, as one leg swings forward and high from the hip, it lurches her body to the front: she falls face down, catching herself on her hands. Arching back, she then reaches forward to collect her feet underneath her and rise. As one percussionist steps forward close to her and begins to sing of their suffering in the "Four hundred years in Babylon," the group joins in, singing with him, and moving in the sequence initiated by the priestess. Feet are lifted and dropped lightly to the ground as pronounced gestures in rhythm with the drum beat. Undulating chests and shaking heads are enriched with hips swaying side to side, the arms hanging loosely by the side. Gradually, the group lament gives way to a more assertive movement segment. Once more the priestess initiates a rapid sequence, where quick jumps flicking the body momentarily up into the air, lightly marked step-patterns, high kicks to one side capped by a flexed foot, crowd in upon one another. All the dancers move in a quick circle around themselves with quick, buoyant steps, then still as they raise their voices in compatible but non-unison harmonies as they pick up end segments from the lines of the song the percussionist sings, extending the lyrics while he moves on to the next line. The repetition of this sequence, beginning with the quick, rapid series of movements and ending with the vocalization of multiple tonalities, creates the sense of ritual recurrence that is building up to some climactic moment.

Indeed, as the song ends, the performers pick up one of the last words of the song—"fire!"—and gasp it out regularly, "fire! fire burn!" as they embark on a slower movement pattern. Moving as if the word and what it signifies have taken hold over them, the women, facing the afflicted woman who still sits in the corner of the stage, curve their backs over in a high contraction, hovering over the floor, gathering charge from below, and lifting one leg from the hip. As the leg brushes down to step-step-step-step, the back swings out to a convexity, and head and hands lift forward. The priestess now steps toward the afflicted woman and brushes her up and down with the palm fronds, the latter reacting with shakes and shivers which seem to overtake her body. Her tremblings grow bigger and bigger into agitations that jolt her out of her sitting position and swirl into a dance of kicks, turns, level changes in fast motion, while the drums beat faster and louder in support of her dance. What is interesting about this dramatization of the experience of possession is not just the striking performative embodiment of spirituality, but the way in which the body, which has apparently abandoned any sense of control, balance or verticality, *becomes*, not enacts, the spirit, tossed about in the throes of spiritual anguish. As she stands quietly for a moment, her knees suddenly buckle under her to send her body into a series of dropping tremors, her head rolling back on her neck, then her arms carving through space in a gesture of thankfulness. To the audience it seems that she neither attempts to save herself, nor falls over: her eloquent body gives intimations of an intense revelatory experience that has propelled her into a perception of what lies beyond the everyday, the familiar. Even later, the dancing of the possessed woman in her ecstasy, works similarly, through metaphoric, but intently materizalized, articulations of the body.

Here, the constant presence of spiritual energy is a way of life where the political, the cultural, the artistic, all coalesce into an embodiment of individual resistance. For Zollar this politicized understanding and critique of religion make for an uncompromising search for unregulated articulations of spirit, realized, like often in black practice, through artistic imaginings. As in Chandralekha's work, these emerge as dreams that the spirit weaves from the realities of oppressive situations, dreams that are imbued with the energy and sweat of dancing bodies. The commitment to the processes of conjure and transformation, which are central to spiritual journeys as Zollar imagines them, becomes so clear when we see, for instance, *Transitions*, a piece that is devoted solely to the exploration of spiritual quests, through an interweaving of personal stories and questions, working

Carolina Garcia, Allyson Triplett, Maria Earle; Zollar's *Transitions*. Photo by Cylla von Tiedemann.

through the disillusionments with religious beliefs enshrined in gendered and raced inequities. Even as the name signifies, searches for peace and meaning are precisely that, searches, hence not arrived-at points, but found in the transitions of workings-through, a realization that is constantly reflected in the choreographic structure as well as in the voiced-over score that accompanies the piece. Once again, as the piece carries us through the trials and struggles of different individuals without ever attempting to tell or portray their "stories," to transition into a belief in self and in life forces, we are reminded of that defiant hope that permeates Zollar's work.

Related Structures

As I have pointed out before, this centrality of process, interwoven and interactive lines of development, and openness of structure are typical structural principles in Zollar's work. While Chandralekha's work is also process-oriented and marked by intersecting thematics, the manifestation is totally different here: themes are usually elaborated with a slow but intense continuity and the organization is more or less always circular, like the snake that eats its tail, a repeated metaphor in much Hindu, South Asian visual culture, suggesting the interlocking of beginnings and endings. Zollar's work, on the other hand, works with high contrasts of dynamics and a constant but uneven flow of energy, a constancy of cross-referencing, all of which makes for a rich intertextuality, seen for instance in a wonderfully whimsical, humorous, and touching piece, *Self-Portrait* (1998), whose avant-garde compositional principles contest notions of a "well-made" piece. The name equivocates on the grand focus on self proclaimed by so many masters, particularly white male artists of the classical visual arts. Interrupting thus from the very beginning a monolithic sense of self, the piece not only suggests self as performed, with the dancers evolving character sketches as Zollar imagines them, but also that self is multiple and othered, as Zollar's personal search is played out differently by the individual performers. Of course, typical of Zollar's mode of working, these "selves" are created collaboratively, with a lot of input from the dancers themselves. In thinking about the relationship of the notion of performed selves in *Self-Portrait* to black cultural specificity, I want to refer briefly to Cornel West, who says that a distinctive feature of these black cultural modes is "a certain projection of the self—more a persona—in performance."[37] For West, this spells more than a self-investment, a total involvement with performative modes: "it also acknowledges radical contingency and even solicits challenge and danger."[38] It is this radical contingency, this willingness to go to and over the edge of safety—abundantly clear in the organization of this piece—that echoes both the politics of a defiant hope that I have talked about and the weaving of spirit through the politics of resistance.

Moreover, set as if in a rehearsal space, the piece swings between a clear sense of structured choreography, where Zollar directs the dancers and they follow her instructions explicitly, and failed structure, where dancers occasionally rebel against Zollar's changing her mind repeatedly, between the exposition of formal choreography and its deliberate rupture. These moments, when structure seems to fail, serve, however, as devices of shift, allowing for more dramatic exits and entrances, such as when Zollar finally sends her dancers off to change into their costumes for the next piece to be performed, breaking out of the artifice of the piece itself and referring to the "real" of the performance, while she says she will "work something out."

It is precisely at this moment, when the piece seems to peter out to its end after a flurry of robust dancing, and when the audience is still taken aback by the clear break in performance conventions, that the piece picks up again and moves into one of its most significant sections. Standing in center stage, lit by a spot, taking a line written by Carl Hancock Rux—"You don't know, but this means the world to me"—Zollar works continuously, trying to figure out the best way to perform it, matching text with movement. She plays out the classic trope of alternative postmodern contexts, repetition with a signal difference, as she embodies different characters, in different situations and moods, each imbuing that line with specific tonality and body attitude. The overt question about meaning is resignified with each incarnation, highlighting the negotiated, unfixed process of meaning-making. The lights go out on Zollar, alone, pivoting around herself endlessly, rising and falling with each turn, *you don't know but this means the world to me*, faster and faster, the movements increasing in intensity: the piece is beginning, and the beginning is a continuity.

Talking to me about the piece, Zollar had said: "I wanted to show our process."[39] In *Self-Portrait*, process is become performance. Yet steeped in the cultural specificity of black life, questions about meaning and search, and a deeply spiritual quest, emerge with particular clarity and poignancy, resymbolizing the avant-garde structuring of the piece. By ending with *Self-Portrait*, I return to the notions of defiant hope, of resistive operative structures and forms, of holistic spiritual-sensual journeys that characterize the creative work of artists like Zollar and Chandralekha. In particular, I want to point out how these support, in tandem, an integrated commitment to life with full awareness of and in total resistance to, negativity—a vital marker of the radical edge in their art.

CHAPTER 3   **The Body Mobile, Mobilized, Mobilizing . . .
Or, Regarding Legacies**

I was such an idiosyncratic dancer that I didn't fit anybody else's
choreography . . . Which is probably how I came to look for dancers for
my company. The very first troupe was sort of a motley crew, because we
were all such highly individual dancers. Most of us didn't fit into anything. That's the place I started building from.

> Jawole Willa Jo Zollar, interviewed by Daryl Jung, for *Now, Toronto,*
> Feb. 10–16, 1994, "Tough troupe traces cultural connections."

How are you
I am alright
only
my joints
are
stiffffff
fff
ff
f

Chandraleka, *'68 Poems*

Regarding Slipperiness

It is by now a classic complaint that the body is neglected in academic discourse, particularly Euro-American discourse. But for a little more than a
decade, there has been a good deal of research inspired by, or at least claiming to be based in, the body. It is *how* the body is perceived and presented in
this literature that remains for me a contentious matter. And indeed, literature claiming to write from the body often ends up, conversely enough,
emphasizing the slipperiness of the body, as if dodging the writers' avowed
intention, and escaping through the network of words so that, in the end,
there is indeed no concrete sense of the body in the writing. This perhaps
has to do with internalized convictions about the opposition of words and
bodies, verbal and nonverbal modes of communication that manifest them-

selves in the linguistic structure. But does it also reflect the repeated failure of discursive thought to talk about the body without erasing its particular modalities, to talk about embodied articulations in relation to, not subsumed by, the organizing categories typical to theoretical narration?

As a dancer who works with technique everyday, I am deeply aware of certain ways of working that my bodily processes seem to have, where changes-of-state happen because of a logic internal to the somatic system, one which does not immediately figure as a process in conscious thought. In saying this, I do not want to further perpetuate that vicious mind-body dualism and extend that very reification that I have complained about. But I do think that the rationalities of the body work in ways that are different from intellectual figurings-out. This difference is far from recognized as such, and hence seemingly—but only seemingly—outside the possibilities of articulation through linguistic structures dominated, in their ordering, by the categories of discursive analysis. Thus, within this logocentrically driven epistemological framework, the obvious recognition of bodily processes occurs primarily when it can enter our intellectually ordered consciousnesses, accessible as obvious and external physical manifestations that happen as a result of such processes.

This is how I arrive at my sense of a kind of truancy that my body plays on me when I am inattentive: balance never seems to be a given thing, for instance, and I have to work to find it every day, maybe through different formulations of the physical process. And I often wonder if—as I step into the studio to do my yoga and take that first balance, if I can just focus on registering those little internal adjustments that my body makes to perform the *vrkshasana* position with my body as it is that day, paying attention to the processes of my proprioceptive, kinesthetic figuring out—I would know about my present location differently.[1] Of course there is working knowledge about the mechanisms of the body that enable us to structure, with expectation of uniform applicability, an aerobics class for instance, and to create training programs for particular techniques (like Graham or Horton, for instance) where certain routines are expected to refine technical abilities to a desired level. Yet, in technique class, we are so often told to find "our" extension, for every body is different, work with "our" range of turnout. Especially in dance, then, even the most prescriptive of embodied technical formulations work through translation and negotiation by dancing bodies, defying "uniformity" in understanding movements in accordance with varying body structures. What I want to draw attention to here is the intelligent way in which bodily understanding works, constantly yielding knowledge that is not necessarily accessible to other modes of perception.

And, from having studied Odissi, I am aware of those little shifts of energy inside the ribcage just before stepping into the climactic *tarijham* to position the body in a mobilized *tribhangi* position, to effect that graceful gliding over between the arriving into the position and the marking of the rhythmic climax.[2] From being in "African" dance classes, I know that slight sideways and downward tilt of the chin that goes with the forward swing of the left arm that counterpoints the slight backward swing of the right arm, all of which must be rightly co-ordinated to launch that return to the first combination. From watching students of ballet, I recognize that little separation between the slightly downmoving thumb, the upmoving index finger, and the rest of the fingers, in port de bras, which adds to that sense of lightness and grace. I know there are these and more infinite, subtle, negotiations of the body, seldom articulated in language even in teaching, but imbibed through watching-and-replicating, little *sediments of cultural resonance*, that create the special flavor of a technique. Without those, a specific technique maybe learned correctly, but never quite seems to be "there": these unarticulated details, that make up the stuff of cultural specificity, that slip into some bodies with ease, and evade others.

At any rate, the point of these deliberations is to draw attention to two points. One is the little acknowledged but unique mode of kinesthetic knowing, the intelligence of the body, and the production of culture in and through the body, itself produced through cultural constructions. The second is my conviction that writing that claims to be about the body must at once recognize its multilayered *materiality*, that immediately testifies to the processes of materialization that have produced its current boundaries in interaction with the various sociocultural, political, and economic ideologies in which bodies—we—are implicated. And, of course, these regulations are not just reproduced in the body but are also manipulated and subverted through its acts. Indeed, it seems that even some of the most brilliant scholarship that has emerged from cultural studies, feminist theory, postcolonial theory, and subaltern studies, and even theatre, have often failed to communicate that sense of the body as material entity, embedded in historical, cultural, race-class-gender–based specificities, simultaneously the enactor and the site of layered discursive significance, effected by and affecting discourse. The most troubling import of such theories has been that in analyzing how the body, especially the female body, has been manipulated and rendered "docile," and in insisting on the negative effects of such socialization and internalized policing, they have seemed to erase out possibilities of embodied resistance, or for that matter, of differential understanding of the body as an active site of subversion.

In this light I want to consider briefly the status of bodily articulations in some academic discourse, largely in order to highlight the stakes in a project of "reading" choreography and of locating this project as an important discursive and resistive practice. Indeed, in much sociological and anthropological literature where the body has been commented upon, we come to know it through descriptive, empirical processes, with little active relationship with power dynamics. This is obvious, for instance, even in the landmark project that attempted to think through the ways in which the body is constructed from various perspectives. The essays in the three-volume anthology, *Fragments for a History of the Body*, are written from a variety of approaches, historical, anthropological, and philosophical, and present interesting arguments about the ways in which the human body has been constructed at different historical moments.[3] Editor Michael Feher describes the three distinct approaches that determine the shape of each volume as "vertical," highlighting the human body's relationship to the divine, to the bestial, and to machines that simulate the behavioral patterns of the body; "psychosomatic," studying the relationship between the inner substance ("soul") and outer surface of the body; and as examining how certain body organs or substances have been argued to have a supportive or inverse relation to the social body, and reciprocally, how sociopolitical functions draw on the constructions of the processes of human bodies to justify themselves. Even this last perspective fails to consider adequately the weight of embodiment in active political agency and the body appears as a site that is acted upon. The rich medical, scientific, biological, and thereafter ethical/religious, discourses about the body, reconfirm this effect and render the sensate body an anaesthetic object of the reader's gaze. And, instead of a sense of the historical legacies, specific to race, class, gender, and sexual orientation among other things, which in fact construct the living, moving body, what emerges is a series of ideas about the body. Interesting as they are, these books also illustrate one of the typical trends that problematize such research for me.

Speaking in Women's Tongues

I want to acknowledge the role of much feminist scholarship and some postcolonial scholarship in recognizing and foregrounding the politics of the body, and articulating the political dimensions of the body. Feminist theories have repeatedly reclaimed the body as a significant locus of meaning, protesting against the thought-dominated discourse of Europeanist and other thought systems. However, the body has been fraught with conflicting opinions in feminist theories, which, while revaluing the ignored and othered physicality of discourse, also chafed against essentialist arguments that sought to reduce the concept of "woman" to biological specificities. Reacting sharply to the Freudian dictum that anatomy is destiny and the essentialist argument of the early feminists, and asserting difference, second-wave feminists in the Euro-American world have struggled to liberate women from this anatomical bind, urging more complex understandings of gendered identities. The question Simone de Beauvoir asks in her classic manifesto of early feminist literature, *The Second Sex*, "Are there women really?" and her consequent assertions that there is nothing natural about the "nature" of woman but what is "naturalized" through socialization ("One is not born, but rather becomes, a woman . . . this creature, intermediate between male and eunuch") enunciated one end of the debate, pointing to the complexity of questions regarding women's subjectivities and identities.[4] On the other hand, the insistent exhortations of Helene Cixous that "Woman must write herself: must write about women and bring women to writing . . . Woman must put herself into the text—as into the world and into history—by her own movement" underscored her strategic move to emphasize the evident involvement of the body and movement in women's speaking, capable of exploding the neat arrangement and compartmentalized thinking of phallocentric discourse.[5] As such, much feminist writing in the Euro-American world has strained between such anxieties regarding the female body: oscillating between regarding it as symbolic of "woman," as metaphor for what has gone unrepresented in discourse, or as biological entity with its own brand of "truth," or as the liminal affect of psychoanalytical and deconstructivist discourse, the signification of Cixous's "dark continent" and Irigaray's "two lips."[6] However, probably because of apprehensions of charges of anti-intellectualism, essentialism, or disciplinary "softness," the work of many feminist scholars has tended to reproduce what Vicky Kirby has described as a kind of "somatophobia" that has overturned the earlier biological slant and is different from contemporary reclaimings of notions of embodied discourse.[7] At any rate, while the work of scholars such as Sandra Bartky (*Femininity and Domination*, 1990), Iris Young (*Throwing Like a Girl*, 1990), and Susan Bordo (*Unbearable Weight*, 1993) have been invaluable in demonstrating the manipulated surface of the body in daily power processes in contemporary American social contexts, the female body seems to be layered with interpretive and discursive anxieties in much feminist discourse. For me, however, the difficulties in this area continue to be the tensions between the ways in which female bodies are conceptualized and how represented, and *how* in fact they enter the theoretical domain.

Despite recognitions about bodily articulations' important sites of resistance and despite writing by dance scholars urging the rich possibilities of such interdisciplinary research,[8] the dancing body is seldom addressed within feminist theory, or even acknowledged as an important site for the production of knowledge. A further angle is added to this situation by the fact that a few feminist scholars have actually addressed performance art, where, most often, text is used as a primary element, either as spoken by the performers, as narrated by an invisible voice, as flashed on a screen, or used in various innovative ways. Does the intervention of words aid interpretation and make performance more accessible? Or does this signal a lack of language to talk about and analyze the moving body?

Interestingly, several women scholars of color have written from a feminist framework that is attentive to the ways in which bodily acts and processes can have discursive engagement, though they too have generally avoided talking in any detail about dance. I will mention a couple of thinkers only in order to make this point, scholars whose writing has deeply influenced my thinking. In Rajeswari Sunder Rajan's *Real and Imagined Women*, for instance, she deliberates on the overdetermined subjectivity of the "Third World Woman" with specific reference to the situation in colonial and postcolonial India.[9] Rajan bases her theorizing on the specific practices of rape, wife-beating, dowry deaths, *sati*,[10] where the female body becomes the site of evidence, the burden of proof, so to speak, and the manipulated surface for media constructions of the new modernized-but-not-Westernized woman. She shows how the gap between these specific lived realities and the cultural representations of women in literature, film, advertisements, legal and journalistic texts becomes important considerations in the construction of third world women as subjects of discourse. Rajan also draws attention both to the chasm between the constitutive core of sensory experience of subjects of pain and representations of them, and to how the "real" here seems to mark the outer boundary of linguistic expression. Rajan invokes embodied female subjectivity in order to probe the implications of these silences, but draws on filmic and literary representations for her examples.

Audre Lorde too has constantly pushed for an embodied and material/lived basis for feminist theorizing. In her essay, "The Uses of the Erotic,"[11] she writes eloquently, for instance, about the erotic as empowerment and resource, operating simultaneously on embodied and spiritual planes. Lorde argues that this erotic power mostly lies dormant in women, unacknowledged and distrusted, because patriarchal society mythifies it as a dangerous and nonrational force. She suggests that recognizing their erotic power is central to women's reclaiming of their bodies and to the radical feminist project of restructuring societies. For her, like for Chandralekha, the erotic is an affirmation of the life force in women, the embodiment of their creative force, and the imaginative charge in artistic work. Lorde's concept of the erotic, among other ideas of hers, has invigorated my discussions of the feminist body aesthetics of Zollar and Chandralekha and their projects of reclaiming female sexualities as creative forces.

Of course bell hooks, having critiqued and rejected the specialized language of academic theory, has repeatedly asked for a lived and embodied base for feministantiracistanticlassist theorizing. In so much of her work, black female subjectivity comes to be articulated in intimate relationship with physicality, particularly in the context of a society laden with discriminations and hierarchies. hooks talks about self-reclamation and the creation of positive self-image in the face of commodified representations of black female bodies, and against the grain of excessively sexualized and fetishized images that proliferate the cultural market. Coming to terms with one's blackness must begin, according to hooks, with coming to love one's physicality, which becomes one of the first markers of one's identity in a racist and sexist society.

In several of her essays in *Art on My Mind,* hooks works through different pieces of visual art, discussing her thoughts on issues of representation, with special attention to the representation of the black female body in art. The perspective of discussant, existing outside the artwork, though engaging in a symbiotic relationship with it in order to experience it, changes in "Being the Subject of Art" where hooks talks about being photographed by a visual artist—experiences of embodying the artwork—and is struck by her realization of the transgressive potential of the body and its definitive relation to any understanding of self. Reflecting on the dis-eases in being photographed, she writes,

> we are taught over and over again that the only way to remain safe is to stay within fixed boundaries . . . it is the body that is the first site of limitation. The body is the boundary most of us most of us are unable to move against to recover the dimensions of self lost in the process by which we are made to behold fixed locations, by which we are bound in conformity against our will in many facets of our daily lives. The fact that the word *transgress* appears most often in discussions of the sexual is an indication that the body is the fundamental boundary of self. To transgress we must return to the body.[12]

To transgress we must return to the body. Hooks's comments remind us of the potential power of the body to signify, on many different levels, the ways in which we have conceptualized and layered bodies such that they invoke intense excitement as well as fear, empathy as well as distance. For hooks, being inside of body-centered creative processes turns the focus on the potential of the body to work through acculturated inhibitions, while it reinforces realizations about the ways in which the body is boundaried by constructed conventions. Like a refrain, this line intersects the text with the thought that repeatedly comes to her when she experiences her body as the subject of art: "Writing about art, making art, is not the same as being the subject of art."[13] What hooks is underscoring is precisely that the experience of artistic/performative embodiment asks for consideration on its own terms, differently.

Of course some of the most significant contributions to this field, especially in thinking through the "performativity" of the body, have come through the work of Judith Butler, who in the preface to her book, *Bodies That Matter*, pointed out that "Not only did bodies tend to indicate a world beyond themselves, but this movement beyond their own boundaries, a movement of boundary itself, appeared to be quite central to what bodies 'are.'"[14] Butler deploys these ideas about the material-philosophical dimensions of bodies to argue the discursive and constructive boundaries of their sexed and gendered aspects, to ultimately theorize the political stakes in the normativized performativity of sex and gender. I am grateful for Butler's insistence on the transgressive potential of embodied acts, though clearly her definition of "performance," resting on the citationality of normative, repeatable acts, is different from the ways in which I have dominantly used it here, as particular staged events. While it is precisely the resonances between the different processes of rehearsing and performing as if "for real" that make for the critical power of potential transgressions, it is vital to maintain critical distance between the two. I also want to point to her powerful theorization of the body as located at the crossing-point of power dynamics that are centrally constitutive of sociocultural, political, and economic formations.

Otherwise Speaking

When Frantz Fanon wrote *A Dying Colonialism*, he made obvious the relationship of political phenomena to bodily formulations, especially in a postcolonial situation.[15] Particularly in the section "Algeria Unveiled," he writes with great sensitivity about the changes in behavior that accompany the changed role that Algerian women have had to play in the liberation struggle. Taking on the dangerous task of bearing messages and arms to revolutionary camps, the women must adjust to the scrutiny they were now subjected to. The veil with which they have traditionally covered their faces may be discarded, revealing much more of their bodies, and their breathing, their gait, and their posture—more noticeable now—must reflect a confidence without arousing suspicion. Fanon's writing is permeated with that sense of how the body is a vital site where oppressive and resistive power plays criss-cross and how phenomena such as colonialism evidence themselves in and through the body.

While there is no doubt that Fanon's opposition to the French "penetration" of the Algerian woman's veil is still wrapped up in paternalistic and patriarchal protectionism, he is one of the few postcolonial scholars to work through embodied phenomena as an integral part of his theorizing. In

Black Skin, White Masks, too, Fanon articulates with remarkable power the agonizing physicalpsychic self-alienation experienced under the pressure of the colonial gaze.[16] He writes, for instance, about being the subject of address that identified him only in terms of his race ("a Negro"), and its immediately stereotypical cultural connotations, erasing all other aspects of his identity: "I was battered down by tom-toms, cannibalism, intellectual deficiency, fetishism, racial defects . . . I took myself far off from my own presence . . . What else could it be for me but an amputation, an excision, a hemorrhage that spattered my whole body with black blood?"[17] Bodily processes, however metaphorically understood, bear down with material weight on linguistic structures, rendering the language porous, and marking the importance of body politics in racialized discourse.

However, much postcolonial theory, while acknowledging that colonialism drastically changed all aspects of lived experience, in fact slides over the embodied aspects, moving on to conceptual and discursive analysis of such experiences. Occasionally, even when attention is paid to the female body, it exists only as a passive site of theory, incessantly written upon. Malek Alloula, for instance, attempts what might be described as a postcolonial reclamation of the honor of native women in *The Colonial Harem*.[18] Castigating the French military men for using photographs of Algerian women as postcards, Alloula rightly points out that this obsession with the Algerian women's bodies represents the French proclamation of victory. Algerian women can be photographed and exhibited thus, he argues, because the male heads of society, who would otherwise have surrounded them with prohibitive measures, have been routed, and the women have become "the metaphoric equivalent of trophies, of war booty."[19] However, Alloula is implicated in his own critique, because his own fastidious arrangement of the many photographs, increasing in order of degradation, by his own analysis, reaching a climax with a series of photographs of women naked to the waist, repeats that same gesture. The ultimate concern does not even seem to be the problematic reclamation of the honor of these silenced women, but the reassertion of that male society that can claim its right to represent them. Moreover, the project of "saving" these women's bodies has still not been able to render them real, subjects of historical processes, but has reaffirmed them as objects of representation: the women's bodies exist within the frames of the postcards, flattened and docile, and inevitably there for display.

On the other end of the spectrum, I want to recall Gayatri Chakravorty Spivak's translations of Mahasweta Devi's fiction, particularly the short stories "Draupadi" and "Breast-giver," and her commentaries on the same.[20] In these particular projects of translating these texts from Bengali into English, Spivak's linguistic sensibilities work with Devi's to create a textuality that is permeated with images of female bodies acting, rebelling, and in some ways demanding that they be read in their own terms. Significantly discussed in circles of literary criticism and in terms of deconstructive practice, this aspect of the writing is not so much mentioned. At any rate, at every point, the bodies of the female protagonists are understood through real, physical phenomena, and through the metaphoric affect of these phenomena. When Dopdi Mejhen, the protagonist of "Draupadi," a rebel tribal woman, gang-raped by her captors, refuses to be clothed afterward and insists on facing the male authority figure with her torn and bloody body, she also straddles the position between subject-object, and accesses the power that confronts and silences male power: "Draupadi's black body comes even closer . . . her ravaged lips bleed as she begins laughing . . . Draupadi pushes Senanayak with her two mangled breasts, and for the first time Senanayak is afraid to stand before an unarmed *target*, terribly afraid."[21] She is target, hence object, but also subject, inducing terror, forcing him to recognize the limits of his oppression. The text moves through images of her body, naked, her breasts injured and exposed, bearing immediate witness to her vulnerability (as the object of sexual abuse once victimized) and her strength (as she drops away patriarchal notions of shame and modesty that dictate the covering up of specific body parts), and compels us to recognize how Dopdi Mejhen uses her intelligent body to signify active resistance even at a moment that such possibilities seem to be cancelled out by her sexual exploitation.

In the same way, Devi's story about Jashoda, the "Breast-giver," as Spivak points out, "expands the thematics of the woman's political body. Within liberal feminism, the feminist body politic is defined by the struggle for reproductive rights."[22] Jashoda, the wet-nurse, the mother-on-hire, suckles her own children as well as those of her master's household. This apparent excess of nourishment that her body produces and the terrible demand it supplies read through the physical conditions they ultimately produce in her body and also comment on the capitalization of this female bodily process in an utterly exploitative economic system. The affective and the economic readings of nursing children overlap as we see the production of milk by Jashoda's body both as the "natural" physical effect of her nurturing and mothering actions, but also immediately as the source of economic exchange and as labor. I find these multiple and layered readings of the body, implicated in a plethora of sociocultural and economic processes, and of bodily phenomena, particularly significant for my research in the way in which they read and mobilize the body.

You Should Be Dancing Now

As I have pointed out, though dance studies provides obvious contestations to such theories, while complicating simplistic ideas of resistance, it is seldom, if ever, taken into account in "other" areas of thought. Yet, surprisingly enough, some dance scholarship, influenced by models from disciplines such as anthropology, is often implicated in this very critique of incompleteness. Indeed, though this is an area that concerns the moving, dancing, performing body, much of the earlier writing in the field has paid little attention to balancing movement descriptions and analysis with discussions of the discursive significance of movement. This does not mean that there is not writing that recognizes, and urges the recognition of, the dancing body as cultural-political producer, a site of ideological crossings. But often, the dancing body is regarded as affirming or expressing certain "cultural" values where culture usually seems to be monolithic or immobile, or as reflecting the choreographer's personal experience or idiosyncratic artistry. Questions about what frameworks the body was already implicated in, or where the body is located, beyond the specific experience of the dance—which would highlight the choreographic interventions into sociocultural expectations—are less often raised. Such work often fails to account for the complex positioning of the body, its placement in a mobile network of power dynamics, and its mutually constitutive relationship with broader sociocultural formations. Moreover, such understanding of movements and choreography primarily in terms of an *apparently* "neutral" aesthetic or creative process, or a broadly understood "cultural" framework, often lead to analyses which, however well-intentioned, only reconfirm racist, sexist, classist, or other stereotypes. [23]

Somatic studies, for instance, is a field of Dance Studies that has made vital contributions to scholarship in this field by drawing attention to the particular modalities of the body's workings. Somatic, dance therapy, and other such theories, while not concerned with the potential mobilization of the body in ideological domains, highlight an important fact: that the body has different ways of registering histories and emotions, which may or may not be acknowledged in conscious thought. They also point to the validity of a proprioceptive epistemological mode, the body's knowledge of its own conditions in space and time through proprioceptors, receptors located in subcutaneous tissues that respond to stimuli produced within the body, by initiating nervous impulses. While such scholarship is important in highlighting that body-based processes require understandings on their own terms, there is in fact no attempt to analyze further the affect of such processes, aspiring instead to an universalist mode via broad theories of creativity and such.

I will refer briefly to Louise Steinman's *The Knowing Body*, which explores the role of the body's own wisdom in the process of art-making.[24] Steinman is intent upon showing that the performance piece or the choreographed product that the audience perceives has its roots deep within the native intelligence of the body. She talks to several artists, dancers and performance artists, and finds that remembering is an important part of their process, and memory begins in the body. In particular, Steinman inquires into the choreographic processes of postmodern dance, but for her the wonder lies in the nonverbal sources of information accessed by these choreographers, in their mode of "listening" to the body. Steinman's work is valuable in examining as concrete, felt, sensations, the proprioceptive epistemologies of the body. However, although she speaks to and records the experiences of artists from various cultures, and believes that memories and blocks of sensations stored in the body are entirely personal, she also insists that these memories can be expanded to resonate as human archetypes. These generalizations are mostly problematic for me, especially when the ways memories are produced and invoked are forged through contextual specificities. Steinman's writing greatly enriches thinking about the performance and creative processes, by rendering them complex, ridden with split personalities, questions, doubts, and conflicting feelings. Yet, despite this complexity, the development seems flattened in the absence of registering the unevenness in which the processes of remembering, articulating, and creating are inevitably inscribed in and through cultural specificities and the incidentals of identity.

However, contemporary directions in performance scholarship have inaugurated new dimensions in thinking about such articulation with an emphasis on bringing the materiality of embodiment to intervene in the process of writing. I want to acknowledge the work of performance and dance scholars who are on the edge of such ground-breaking work and to whom I am indebted for methodological inspiration. Informed by concepts and critical thought developed in Cultural Studies and other area studies, I conceive of scholarship in this area of Dance Studies as consistently anchored in the physicality of the moving body. But I should point out that my understanding of the term Dance Studies is not as narrow as this section might indicate. I understand this field of endeavor to encompass not only discursive readings of the dancing body, but also to all the varied self-conscious and reflective practices—training, practicing, creating, performing, thinking, writing—that constitute the field of dance and performance. However, since this emerging field owes this self-conscious gesture of naming to a recognition of the particularity of the research that typifies scholarship here, I believe its cutting-edge and most exciting boundaries are marked by the kind of interdisciplinary reading, where the previous overly anthropological and descriptive focus is replaced by a strongly political and intersecting one, whose genealogy I will trace here.

Tracing the Dancing Body

This new discursive direction in Dance Studies, committed to working through the materiality of the dancing body, seems to take off from Susan Foster's articulation of the notion of corporeality. Though of course there are others, like Brenda Dixon-Gottschild and Jane Desmond, who were also writing in this mode at the same time, Foster is indeed the first dance scholar to articulate this as theory and methodology. This notion of performance first of all draws attention to the widening boundaries of understanding of what dance is and acknowledges that current connotations of dance and performance, often themselves indissociable from each other, are chafing at the limits of their definitional/denotational boundaries. If we then argue that the study of dance is the study of the body-in-movement, of corporeality, of how the body functions in daily activities to signify in different ways, then we change the perspective from which choreography and dance are studied.

Foster's notion was vital in drawing attention to the ways in which embodied knowledges can be central in the act of writing. In her remarkable introduction to the volume of essays *Choreographing History*, Foster, asking for a different consciousness in dance history, writes: "To choreograph history, then, is to first grant that history is made by bodies, and then to acknowledge that all those bodies, in moving and in documenting their movements, in learning about past movement, continually conspire together and are conspired against."[25] The focus is on bodies in motion—interacting with each other, pushing through time and space to make "history"—and on the range of historical information contained in the performing body. Foster's is the most comprehensive and nuanced articulation of this problematic in a series of essays that study embodied enactments at particular historical moments, or in their particular incarnations in specific disciplines such as dance ethnography, advertising, or in relation to endeavors such as music or religious conversion. Taking the same title as the book itself, "Choreographing History," the essay begins by stressing the duality of the body: written upon, but also writing, and emphasizing that the writing body, in its constant process of signification, is loaded with different shades of meaning. This then inaugurates new possibilities for scholarship that takes into account bodily practices:

> The possibility of a body that is written upon but that also writes moves
> critical studies of the body in new directions. It asks scholars to approach
> the body's involvement in any activity with an assumption of potential
> agency to participate in or resist whatever forms of cultural production are
> underway. It also endows body-centered endeavors with an integrity as

practices that establish their own lexicons of meaning, their own syntag-
matic and paradigmatic axes of signification, their own capacity to reflect
critically on themselves and on related practices. Dancemaking, for example, becomes a form of theorizing, one that informs and is informed by
instantiations of bodily significance . . . The theoretical, rather than a con-
templative stance achieved afterwards and at a distance, becomes embedded (embodied) within the practical decisions that build up, through the
active engagement of bodies, any specific endeavor.[26]

Working through poststructuralist thought, Foster also argues that
fixed meaning cannot be attributed to gesture, and that it must be read in
terms of the location and inscription of the distinct historical body that produces it. Referencing the history of Europeanist discourse, she goes on to
enumerate the different ways in which the body has been reified by way of
its re-presentation in such scholarship: as a "natural" object, registering
unknown psychosocial forces; as a mechanics, housing diseases and aberrations, or reflecting the effects of specific training programs, the processes
of chemistry and physics; as a metaphor for the mysterious, the bearer of
the unconscious or the libidinal, the irrational or the perverse; as the bearer
of cultural symbols, often aligned with pleasure, fashion, embellishment.
She recognizes that, even through the work of scholars like Foucault who
amended the general academic neglect of the body, the physical body as
actual meaning-maker, as agent in discourse, not just site of received phenomena, has remained unacknowledged. Importantly, she also charges that
dance studies, in spite of having an acting (choreographing, dancing) and
acted upon (recipient of training among other things) body at center, has
traditionally continued to privilege the logocentric, and has hierarchized
the "thrill of vanished performance over the enduring impact of choreographic intent."[27] Foster acknowledges, however, that scholars in Dance
Studies have recently begun to ask questions that might lead to the development of a complex and comprehensive scholarship of the body and of
movement. She concludes by positing a model of "ambulant" scholarship,
which, having accepted that constant movement must be at its very core,
can write about the body as it is caught in the process of being made and
dissolving, and can, in writing, reflect acknowledgment that in such scholarship the writer as well as the written about are simultaneously moving
and moved entities. What is especially valuable and unique in her theorizing is her upholding of the visceral and reflective sensing of perceived
movement and the multiple layers of the body-in-movement as the center
of scholarship; her balancing of the written-on body with the actively writing body; and also, with specific regard to dance studies, the balancing of

the emphasis on the training and choreographic process alongside the traditional emphasis on the moment of the performance.

In a later volume of essays edited by Foster in 1996, *Corporealities*, she and other contributors reflect again on the notion of corporeality. The introduction foregrounds both the broadening of this field of studies through such discussions and the insistence on the multiple dimensions of the signifying possibilities of the body:

> *Corporealities* seeks to vivify the study of bodies through a consideration of
> bodily reality, not as natural or absolute given but as tangible and substan-
> tial category of cultural experience. The essays in this volume . . . acknowl-
> edge that bodies always gesture towards other fields of meaning, but at the
> same time instantiate both physical mobility and articulability. Bodies . . .
> develop choreographies of signs through which they discourse . . . They
> also illuminate the corporeal play that is vital to cultural production and to
> theoretical formulations of cultural process.[28]

This new direction in dance studies, articulating the thrust behind the practice of scholars such as Brenda Dixon-Gottshild, Jane Desmond, Randy Martin, Ann Daly, Mark Franko, Susan Manning, and others, continues to be developed in works such as Barbara Browning's *Samba*, Ann Cooper Albright's book *Choreographing Difference*, and Amy Koritz's article "Dancing the Orient for England: Maud Allan's The Vision of Salome."[29] I will trace the arguments of some of these earlier texts briefly, only in order to establish the sense of a lineage of writing in which I wish to place my own work, and also to point out what it is, in relationship to such work already written, I want to accomplish.

Foster's own *Reading Dancing: Bodies and Subjects in Contemporary American Dance*, written about a decade before the research just discussed, is an insightful stock-taking of the layered choreographic process, where Foster navigates her discussion to touch upon the correspondences among the development of form, matter, and ensuing training, among ideas about the purpose of art and the dancing body, the definition of a dancer, the sense of selfhood, and conceptions of the expressive act.[30] Even at this point, the body is at the center of Foster's discourse, insofar as it is at the center of the expressive act, centrally connected to conscious meaning-making. As she makes her way through some of the traditions of choreography in American dance history, focusing on the ideas and choreographic patterns of Deborah Hay, George Balanchine, Martha Graham, and Merce Cunningham, and then on the postmodern "reflexive" choreographic processes of artists like Twyla Tharp, Trisha Brown, Meredith Monk, and the Grand Union, she offers a wide range of ideas about the dancing body as meaning-maker and about how differently meaning can be construed. Yet, while Foster effectively destabilizes the concepts of the body that have traditionally accrued to Euro-American ballet by her explorations of the choreographic process of modern and postmodern choreographers, her reflections are hardly moored in discussions of differences of race, class, gender, or sexuality. Moreover, though valuable because of her insistence on conceptualizing the body as a polyvalent signifier, the philosophical framework of this work is definitely at a remove from the much more sophisticated contextualization of the body in a network of signifying systems in her later work. However, it is still one of the first books in Dance Studies to dedicate serious attention to the concept of "reading" movement.

On the other hand, Brenda Dixon-Gottschild is one of the first dance scholars to focus on the complex and mobile racializations embodied in dance. In much of her work, corporeal analysis is deployed to argue the inseparability of white and black influences in the concert dance forms developed in America. In *Digging the Africanist Presence in American Performance*, she renarrativizes the general fabric of American dance history in an "up from under" reading, showing how influences from Africanist aesthetics and movements styles have subliminally or through conscious borrowing been integrated into the very fabric of "American" performance.[31] Similar readings of developments in modern and postmodern dance genres create rich and constantly intersected and intersecting histories. For instance, analyzing the choreography of George Balanchine, and his manipulation of traditional ballet vocabulary and movement style in his work, Dixon-Gottschild argued that indeed what distinguishes American ballet from the European schools is the confluence of African American body attitudes with what was initially a "white" dance form. In this way, she traces the constant cross-flow of cultural influences in American concert dance, even though the assimilation of cultural specificities of the dominated group by the dominating group may be unacknowledged. This is a seminal text for my analysis of postmodern dance in the third chapter and my extension of that argument, and I will juxtapose Dixon-Gottschild's descriptions of the marking aesthetics of black street movement styles with descriptions of the aesthetic of postmodern dance written by other leading dance scholars such as Sally Banes to point out the absences or possibilities for inserting presence.

Jane Desmond has protested against the marginalization of Dance Studies in academia and has argued consistently for opening up Cultural Studies to insights from kinesthetic semiotics, and she has made a strong case for it in her presentation at the International Dance Conference at Hong Kong in 1995. Later, in a seminal essay opening the edited volume,

Meaning in Motion, entitled "Embodying Difference: Issues in Dance and Cultural Studies," Desmond points out even the recent fascination of discourse with "the body" continues to efface the moving, dancing, performing body.[32] In this essay she works her way through several instances to talk about the politics of cultural transmission—the interaction of racial, national, and culturally specific groups and how that affects cultural forms and their valences—in order to point out their impact on social relations, which are as much enacted and produced though the body, as they are inscribed upon it. Later, in an essay introducing the edited volume, *Dancing Desires,* Desmond argues the crucial importance of detailed kinesthetic description and analysis in theorizing the signifying practices of dancing bodies, and particularly in constructing narratives about sexual and social relations in that context. Desmond's essay, titled "Making the Invisible Visible," is particularly significant in this field, urging recognition of the constitutive role of non-normative sexualities and queer aesthetics in dance history, and also that dance "provides a privileged arena for the bodily enactment of sexuality's semiotics and thus should be at the center, not the periphery, of sexuality studies."[33] Particularly in emphasizing the homophobia that permeates the artistic arena as well as areas of production and marketing of dance, and also in pointing to the central role of desire in meaning-making functions in the field of dance and performance studies, Desmond charts out important new territory.

What these scholars have consistently emphasized through their writing is that the dancing body reads as a complex site of cultural and political enactment, imbricated in a complex interaction of social constructions and manipulations of the same. Their practice of reading the dancing body specifically in order to reach through it to access information about the sociocultural relations of a given context and to comment on the relationship between bodies and the political currents of the time is also responsible for inaugurating a new dimension in dance studies. Interestingly, many scholars take on this project of "reading" and "writing" dance self-consciously, that is, with full awareness of the slippages in which it is inevitably inscribed. Randy Martin, for instance, talks about the resistance, inherent in the highly mobilized practice of dance, to inscription, and how that elusiveness to incorporation in words can isolate dance as a mode of scholarship and threaten dance studies with what he calls "conceptual ghettoization."[34] Pulling Foster's notion of corporeality in another direction, Martin draws on the possible link between dance, defined in and through movement, and politics, which is infused with the need to mobilize:

> What I attempt to show here is the way that dance studies could mobilize
> in writing the conceptual challenges that dance offers to conventional

ways of understanding politics and the world, in turn arguing that dance can be specified as that cultural practice which most forcefully displays how the body gets mobilized. The emphasis on dance as bodily mobilization, rather than as any determinant movement form, may ultimately help to efface the distinction between incorporation and inscription that has divided dance as writing.[35]

This of course also helps us to think about the direct political valence of dance, and it reminds me particularly of the kind of street theater and performance that inspires my own choreographic work: that of women's groups in India, who, aware of the constant breakdown of the judicial and legal system, often perform the social ostracizing of a wife batterer or dowry demander. Surrounding the house of such a person (a practice known as *gherao*), the women would sing songs articulating incriminating evidence any time a member of the offending household would emerge from the house. Grass-roots women's organizations like the Stree Shakti Shanghatana would also perform plays in the streets, using a great deal of ritualistic movement, about dowry deaths, women's nutrition, and other issues. Of course, here it is about the power of the images to move, even when words are used in dramatization, which is different from moving through high rhetoric that is primarily used by politicians. At any rate, Martin's formulation of dance studies with an insistent focus on the mobile body that constantly negotiates between processes of inscription and incorporation, while keeping the attention on the materiality of acting, is also an incisive critique of the concept of the dancing body as merely a privileged aesthetic site or object.

One of Martin's ideas that I find important in this trajectory of theorizing the body, though I have some difficulty with it, is his notion of the "composite body," which allows for more complex understandings of how the body might function in a "multicultural" context, across seemingly fixed lines of race. In order to study the processes and practices whereby such composite bodies are produced, Martin analyzes the choreography of Ice Cube's music video *Wicked*, and then, the differential performance of the "same" genre of movement in the context of a largely non-black clientele participating in the hip-hop–based aerobic class in a fitness center in Orange County, California. Through his examination, what emerges is the possibility of understanding a body

> . . . not as a stable presence already available for appropriation but as a composite entity mediated across a conflicted space of the imaginary (literally the representational domain where images appear) and the performative (the practical means through which imaginary forms are enacted).

Dance both appears in the conjuncture of imaginary and performative space and puts the constitutive features of a composite body on display. For dance is both a bodily practice that figures an imagined world and a momentary materialization through performance of social principles that otherwise remain implicit.[36]

Dance then becomes the volatile space where embodiment and the imaginary intersect to create unique perspectives on spaces and lived practices. This notion also allows him to theorize in complex ways about how an immensely popular performance mode such as hip-hop transforms itself as it is embodied, in its migration, across cultures, and how through such reincarnation it refigures the general body of cultural production in given contexts. Martin's notion does not always offer adequate scope to grasp the complex negotiations of racial politics inherent in producing a "composite" body, nor of the subtle political processes at play in negotiating such a body, and Halifu Osumare has recently proposed the concept of the "intercultural" body where the transgression of racial and national borders is foregrounded.[37] She both extends and revises Martin's ideas by examining the politics in the cross-cultural currency and the migration of black popular culture, in particular, the cross-influences between variant yet typical formulation of bodies in hip-hop across diverse communities, in arguing for this notion of an "intercultural" body.

Ann Daly is well known for her incisive analysis of Balanchine's choreography of the pas de deux from his piece *Agon* in her essay, "Of Hummingbirds and Channel Swimmers."[38] Physical images are shown to be loaded signs as she unpacks the layers of association and suggestion around them in order to point out how Balanchine's patriarchal world-view ordered his artistic universe. Differently, Daly's book, *Done into Dance*, is a historical account of Isadora Duncan's career written through multiple ways of reading her body in the sociocultural-political space in which it was located.[39] She discusses Duncan's dance through five prototypical conceptualizations of her body as the natural body, the expressive body, the dancing body, the body politic, and as the female body, the interaction of which Duncan made into a symbol of cultural subversion. In discussing the various ways in which Duncan's body was conceptualized at a particular historical moment, in the context of the paradigmatic ideologies and power dynamics that were at work at the time, Daly suggests the varying fields in which the body is deployed as signifying agent. She also points to how Duncan's body, framed by herself in nationalistic and racial terms, is also weighted in terms of these legacies, so that in spite of her subversion of some cultural expectations, she nevertheless remained supportive of racial (white, distinguished from the African American dance of the era) and nationalistic (American, though drawing on Greek traditions, but opposed to European ballet) hierarchies in the new dance she created.

Susan Manning's study of Mary Wigman's life and work is also interesting for its analytical methodology.[40] Manning self-consciously enlarges the boundaries of dance studies: her critique of Wigman's work is located in an "interdisciplinary space bounded by ongoing dialogues on the history of the body and the sexual and national politics of artistic modernism."[41] As she sees it, Wigman's choreography and the artistic decisions embody different points in a prolonged collision, and occasionally, collusion, of essentialized notions of feminine and national identity. To show how a reinvented male gaze coexisted with its own subversion in early modern dance, Manning draws heavily on historical evidence and analyzes the complex politics of the times, successfully re-creating the charged atmosphere of Nazi and post-Weimar Germany, which is the context of Wigman's work. Manning's analysis of the overt politicization of the dancing body in that context and through the work of specific choreographers, particularly Wigman, is significant in demonstrating the ways in which bodies and moving images in the public sphere of performance can be co-opted by organized nationalistic agendas.

In *Choreographing Difference: The Body and Identity in Contemporary Dance*, Ann Cooper Albright extends current debates about significations-in-corporeality to argue that cultural identities—negotiated complexly through axes of difference such as race, gender, sexuality, and physical ability—gain sharp visibility in dancing bodies. She argues that, while constantly exposed to the manipulations effected by dominant ideologies, dancing bodies repeatedly challenge, and thus destabilize, the rigid compartmentalizations and hierarchies demanded by these ideologies. Ultimately, her argument is directed toward drawing the attention of the wider academic community to the critical contributions made by dance scholarship to contemporary discourse about identities, substantiating, sometimes contradicting, extending, and constantly enriching research in fields of enquiry like feminist and cultural studies. Contending that while dancing bodies are "objects of representation" they are also simultaneously "subjects of their own experience," Albright refuses simplistic and easy tracings of race, gender, and other identificatory norms in performance and choreography, constantly eking out resistive possibilities that cause notions of identity to shift.[42]

Most significantly, Albright reads performing bodies-with-disabilities to suggest that what will intervene effectively in the "visual contract" is not an essentialized notion of a "disabled body," but its particular representation. Albright points out that, almost in reaction to popular associations of the disabled body with grotesqueness, several choreographers have focused their creativity in elucidating the "beautiful" lines the body can still make, which makes for a somewhat apologetic argument, one which seeks to emphasize the embodiment of classical grace, perhaps in the smooth gliding of the wheelchair or in the agility of the torso, despite its moorings in disability. In the dancing of Emery Blackwell and Alito Alessi, on the other hand, Albright sees the continued project of making meaning through physical interaction with no attempt to move away from images of the "grotesque," but rather, a movement through them toward an understanding of this particular physicality.

In the other chapters, Albright weaves her writing through raced and gendered identities, and then revisionings of cultural histories and articulations of selfhood through what she terms the "New Epic Dance" in the works of African American choreographers such as Garth Fagan, Bill T. Jones, and Jawole Willa Jo Zollar. Ultimately what emerges through her probing analysis and sensitive readings of choreographies is the particular complexity of cultural identities when read from the perspective of performing bodies that both inhabit and move them. Albright's scholarship is vital in many ways, particularly in positioning dance scholarship in the realm of "performance studies" where performance itself must be read in a multilayered context, contributing to various fields of discourse. I have discussed Albright's work in such detail because her politics and methodology seem close to my work, though my readings are oriented differently, particularly from the point of view of racialized discourses.

Now What?

How does this emphasized awareness of the multiple dimensions of the body in dance studies mean? And specifically, where does it leave me? I think of one the biggest complaints by my students and myself: why is dance so "dissed" by other "serious" disciplinary discourses and by academia in general? I wonder if, besides a general somatophobia in this highly logocentric culture, it is the messiness of the body, its unpredictability and volatility (which necessitates the daily rigor of practice, but cannot guarantee the constancy of technical perfection), as well as the absence of a language that can talk about it, that are responsible for this erasure? What follows from such avoidance of theorizing the body or theorizing it only partially, as a written-upon surface, is the failure to recognize how the acting, moving, performing body can be instrumental in furthering knowledge and understanding. The consequences of this failure have been serious both for dance studies, which continues to be marginalized and underacknowledged in academia, and for other disciplines whose attempts to include the body without having any kind of apprenticeship in reading both generalized and specialized manipulations of bodily performativity in a given context, a regular repertoire of movement and dance, have often led to evaporations of the material practices of bodies.

Currently, as evidenced by the line I have traced, one of the most exciting areas in dance studies is that located at its intersection with other disciplines such as cultural studies, race studies, gender studies, and queer studies, and some of the most interesting scholarship is emerging from this theoretical engagement. This is simultaneously a body engaged in an aesthetic and immediately political practice that comments back upon, as much as it reflects, these socialized dimensions, a practice which promises to be constantly destabilized, relentlessly negotiating the possibilities of making meaning through performance, as it travels through different embodiments. However, it is troublesome that these insightful analyses and articulations of cultural practice and productions, such as the ones mentioned above, continue to have limited currency: their value seems to be more or less limited to the field of dance studies. I want to draw the attention of other disciplines to dance studies once again, and remind of the exciting possibilities of an interdisciplinarity where material and performative bodily acts are important participants, and suggest that the signifying acts of dancing bodies can be of prime value to their own fields of endeavor. And I also want to align myself with this discursive trend, an exciting and growing practice of conceptualizing the performing body as a material entity with significant ideological and symbolic dimensions, accruing from its sociocultural, racial, gender and class/caste specific, sexually, historically, and otherwise marked contexts, embodied counterparts of what bell hooks has elsewhere described as the "polyphonic vocality."[43]

Now, the notion of corporeality, the conviction about the inscriptive weight of the performing body, and the belief that the study of choreography reveals vital commentary, are obviously fundamental to my work. I have tried to extend this discursive direction to suggest that dancing bodies can, by means of the sign systems they create and "through which they discourse," to quote Foster, comment on, critique, and bend existing discourses, often by re-presenting alternative meaning-systems.[44] Specifically, though, I have tried to ponder over what happens when the performing body whose weight is bearing down upon words and semantic fields, twisting the frames of reference in postmodern and feminist practice in dance, happens to be brown/black and female, markers that are usually overwhelmingly evident in the visual immediacy of performance. And I have tried to insist that these unruly bodies, through their relentless disruptions of apparently continuous streams of meaning and signification systems, are forcing reconsiderations of ways in which we, the general public body (that is admittedly not at all generalizable, but still very much situated in hierarchies and constructs of sociocultural organization), are encouraged by mainstream formulations to think about peoples, cultures, and politics.

I want to mark my work as distinct in this field primarily in terms of an insistent attention to racial and cultural difference understood as much horizontally as vertically, and for articulating a radical politics of solidarity among artists of color, which is sensitive to internal differences and hierarchies even as it reaches toward conversations with each other. I also want to suggest that this insistence on reading dancing bodies through the intersecting axes of racial and nationalized "visual contracts," such that the kind of racial hierarchies that dominate American society generally are not collapsed into the very different hierarchies produced by national citizenship, though they are indeed brought into conversation with each other through a commitment to a specific kind of resistive politics, is my specific intervention in this line of dance studies. The other intervention I have tried to make is in the implication that the ways in which we "read" specific choreographies and the specific political dimensions we invoke in these readings can have greater-than-immediate resonance, such that they compel rethinking of seemingly fixed categories of historiography and aesthetic categories.

Zeroing in on Chandralekha and Zollar

I want to end this chapter by leading the reader briefly through literature specifically about these two choreographers that precede my research. Here, I am interested in looking at substantial writing on their choreography, which identifies itself as scholarship of some sort, different from media accounts of their work or newspaper reviews. In looking at literature specific to these choreographers, there seem to be two major kinds of issues that create problems for the research. Though it is not fair to critique writing for not doing what it did not set out to do in the first place, I mention these texts and what their problems are for me in order to distinguish what I want to accomplish in this book. Writing about choreography primarily through the descriptive methodology, which seems to be a dominant trend, usually serves a more documentary rather than critical function. This is characteristic of Christy Adair's *Women and Dance: Sylphs and Sirens*, where she only briefly talks about Zollar's work though such discussions could have contributed significantly to Adair's arguments about feminist choreographers.[45] Though no extensive discussion is within the scope of her book, her two short entries on Zollar describing primarily the dance idioms and genres used, and the thematic content of one of her pieces, is typical of much of the writing about choreographers of color. I am not placing as much emphasis on published interviews, though they often offer direct reporting of these choreographers's words, because they present few possibilities for interpretation or analysis. Unfortunately this kind of response constitutes much of performance scholarship.[46]

An important predecessor to my book is Rustom Barucha's *Chandralekha: Woman, Dance, Resistance*.[47] Barucha's is an extensive study of Chandralekha's life and work, but it is primarily a biography interspersed with his own critical comments, and his writing about her work is again mostly descriptive. He traces in detail Chandralekha's development from a rebellious child through her short career as young Bharatnatyam dancer, to her evolution, through her feminist and political activist work, into a mature and brilliant choreographer. In the process, he also describes the choreography of most of her pieces in relation to her ideas and beliefs about movement and dance. In this, Barucha does recognize the signifying of the body, but he limits his critical discussion to his own perceptions and does not probe the broader connotations of such signification. Hence, while the depth and power of Chandralekha's work are obvious from Barucha's documentation of the press reviews, strong audience responses, and vehement opposition from traditionalists and from the establishment, his discussion of Chandralekha's own beliefs and comments, and his own impressions of her work, the discursive significance of the moving body, the affect of such artistic production, its effect on the development of theory, remain unarticulated. This is where Barucha's focus and orientation differ greatly from mine. Specifically, my discussion of Chandralekha's work proceeds from a professed location in resistive postmodern/feminist politics. Further, the focus of my writing is a "reading" of Chandralekha's work, which is why I have excluded biographical information about her unless directly relevant to an understanding of her artistic philosophy and practice. On the other hand, the admitted subject of Barucha's book is Chandralekha herself, and while the social and political forces that have shaped the sociocultural history of post-independence India are an inevitable part of his book, they figure specifically in relation to Chandralekha's life and work.

Zollar is one of the subjects of Veta Goler's dissertation, *Dancing Herself: Choreography, Autobiography, and the Expression of the Black Woman Self in the Work of Dianne McIntyre, Blondell Cummings, and Jawole Willa Jo Zollar*.[48] One of the central foci of Goler's research is the ways in which these choreographers use personal and cultural autobiographical material in order to create choreographic structure. This leads Goler to compelling commentary on the choreography of these artists, and on the important elements and processes they use in creating work and in describing the individual aesthetics that distinguish their artistry. Goler focuses on Zollar in the third chapter of her dissertation, titled "Jawole Willa Jo Zollar: The African Past and the Diasporan Present," where she concentrates mainly on the ways in which Zollar interweaves African and African American folk and spiritual practices in the contemporary, multidisciplinary context of her choreography. While Goler's dissertation is laden with valuable critical insights, there is a vital difference in our points of view. Goler sees Zollar, and indeed all three choreographers she writes about, as a modern dance choreographer and writes about her work from that perspective, suggesting that the work reflects the general constitutive characteristics of black female subjectivity. However, for Goler, the feminist awareness in Zollar's work is not a primary area of analysis: it is only in the last chapter, where she relates the artists she has studied to each other, that she explores the ways in which their work debunks negative stereotypes of black women and empowers them through self-affirmation. On the other hand, I have insisted on seeing Zollar as a postmodern feminist choreographer, who refers to African and African American folk and religious traditions and imbues them with irony, double-entendre, and critical sociopolitical commentary. Personal and cultural memories intersect repeatedly here to reflect on the silences and injustices of histories rent with erasures. My perspective privileges a political reading of Zollar's work and has focused on the subversions and revision in Zollar's work more than on the continuities, which is given much more importance in Goler's work. At any rate, Goler's and Barucha's works are important contributions to dance scholarship and are particularly commendable for their focus on particular women artists of color as valuable subjects of research; but mine is different in the way it is oriented toward the "reading" of choreography.

CHAPTER 4   **Danced Disruptions:**
            Postmodern Preoccupations and
            Reconsiderations

Zollar, sitting in a chair on a dimly lit stage, black hat, loose black dress,
a black wooden cross strapped on her torso with a thick white rope that
winds across her body several times. A thick Bible on her lap, a bottle on
hand from which she drinks repeatedly and sprays the stage with liquor
from her mouth with glee. A series of shudderings take her off her chair,
the book falls off, the bottle is placed to the side. The seemingly inebri-
ated body lurches forward, whirls around in looping circles. Yet, suddenly
this energy of excess is pulled inward, where Zollar is right on top of herself, stamping on three beats of a rhythm that is part of the musical
score, and leaving the other two beats of that bar blank. Her heavy boots
emphasize the sound. One leg, the foot flexed up, pulls the body around
as it spins around. Quick subtle shifts of energy. Little shuffles. Coming
front, one arm reaches out diagonally, drawing the body up and out. The
body crumples into a series of staggering walks, Zollar clutching her
stomach. Stop. Knees flexed forward. Waiting. Ease of movement returns
as one arm circles round the chest and across the body, the circular
energy flows through the body as it ripples around itself. Percussive stepping, lunges that fall out, fast direction changes in the hips, leg extensions that pull the body off-center, hip circles inducing body waves, the
cross, the drunkenness, the prophetic screaming, the relentless oscillation from devilish ecstasy to sagging despondency, the crossing of seemingly contradictory symbols on the body. Currents of meanings move
across her body, contesting each other, enriching each other. Is this the
magical rise of empowerment-in-defiance? An aesthetic of hallucination
and transformational power.

LifeDance I . . . The Magician: The Return of She (Jawole Willa Jo Zollar, 1985)

Qualifiers

In this chapter I will chart the theoretical/discursive base for discussing the
work of Chandralekha and Jawole Willa Jo Zollar in terms of "radical" aesthetics and alternative postmoderns, and continue a detailed discussion of
the historical and political context in which the works of these artists are

located in the next. I have framed my argument more generally in this chapter, in terms of pos-colonial societies, or communities that have struggled with long histories of foreign domination, locating general trends under a broad rubric of the politics of artists of color, shifting to particularities in referring to specific contexts. This is in no way meant to ignore the diversity and range within these communities and contexts, and the following chapter will pick up the argument specifically in terms of the particular issues that come to be significant in the still-broad categories of African American and Indian dance.

Personal Longings

Artists dislike being boxed into categories that slot their work into prefigured conceptual frames and thereby imply boundaries and limits. Scholars and historians who work with these organizing genres often end up reinforcing their existence as master narratives of a diverse range of cultural production even as they endeavor to emphasize the very slipperiness of these categorical boundaries. They are, however, helpful occasionally and gather affective significance through their usage as much in academic discourse as in funding procedures, while they play inevitably into the power-ridden politics of naming. Moreover, I admit that I am, like many other contemporary thinkers about cultural politics, fascinated by the concept of the "postmodern," and I think it has to do with a Waiting-for-Godot-esque experience in my growing years. With that apology for inserting autobiography into postmodern reflections, let me segue into a staging of memory. Growing up in urban postcolonial India, some three decades after the moment of political independence, I was intensely aware that my environment was deeply different from that of my parents', for it was during their lifetime that India had as if leapt into "modernity," and we, their children, were born into the lap of "modern" India. Tutored in the methodologies inherited from colonial education, I learned history as straight chronology and linearity. I had not yet been inducted into the world of subaltern studies, and I believed simply: that the "modern" had arrived with the jeans that I was now allowed to wear to college, in the gas ranges where cooking was now being done replacing earthen stoves, with the freedom from the terrible recurring ordeal of vaccination with the eradication of smallpox, through the image of the lovely bikini-clad model in our favorite ad for Liril soap, and in the widespread availability of television sets (black and white no doubt) in private homes in urban upper and middle classes, a total novelty. As someone training in classical dance, however, I was confused by the endless disjunctions between conceptions of "modern" conditions of life and the practice of aesthetic modernism as they manifested themselves in the practice and presentation of dance forms. For I found that the reverence for the traditional "classicism" all but demonized the "modern," constructed it as something to be shunned at any cost, even as some of its terms like the proscenium stage, commercial market, and corporate sponsorship, like class enrollments instead of the *guru-shishya* system, were absorbed into the world of the classical dance. It wasn't until much later that I realized the maneuvered coalescence of the "traditional" and the "modern" in the cultural politics of a postcolonial society, where the neoclassical comes to be an image of the modern. More on this later.

At any rate, the allure of the modern, radiant with and radiating the glamor of the West, and strongly allied to a largely uncritical notion of progress, was incredibly strong: the postmodern, with its implications of going beyond, must only surpass the excitement of the modern, I thought. And just as the modern had seemingly arrived in India, so would the postmodern, going by the implied sequentiality of the terms, probably in my generation? Yet, over the years I realized that the postmodern never did seem to arrive in the artistic realms of third-world cultures. Or that the transformations of different forms of cultural production in these contexts, marking vital questionings of form and content, never seemed to qualify for understanding as radical moments in international recognition that, like Rainer's *Trio A*, inevitably changed our understanding of and relationship to the past and to existing forms. I believe my waiting forever for the arrival of the postmodern moment in the artistic scene in India created this wonder for it: if the modern era had been ushered in even as the British left, through repeated enunciation from the moment of the birthing of the independent nation—in the constitution, in statutes and laws, in official speeches and declarations, in titles conferred upon people—would my fixating on articulating the term postmodern—performing endless *mandalas* in the proscenium stage, footwork-ridden with postcolonial angst—heal the hiatus between the modern and the postmodern here? Would the latter then follow its predecessor as it did inevitably in all of these first-world countries that one caught a glimpse of on the BBC Newsbreaks, and permeate my *mudras* with "postmodern dissonance"?[1]

Even in the naïveté of my expectations, though, I noticed troubling disjunctions in the "progressive-modern-to-postmodern" model. For one of my clearest memories from my growing years is of poring over the atlas with my mother: she would say how the range of colors on the different countries fascinated her because, growing up, the map had seemed so much like blocks of red to her, signifying the expanse of the British empire. Modernity had remapped the world, I thought then, and had signaled the advent of color into the world map? Even in my immediate frame of reference, the Bangladesh war (1971) followed soon after the East Pakistan–West Pakistan war (1965) and it seemed that maps were constantly shifting, and renamings and realignments were quite in order. If the modern broke with the uniformity of color on the world map, then would this fluidity of national boundaries as a demand for freedom from external domination, this rewriting, be a postmodern phenomenon? Correspondingly, might the postmodern then consolidate the play of color in a map of cultural and artistic production? Somehow that didn't seem to be the case. And while I am embarrassed at my juvenile collapsing of modernity into the processes of decolonization, I recognize there was a value to immediately associating the modern, not with the Western mission of bringing progress to less civilized societies, but from the opposite perspective, with the moment that these latter recorded "freedom" from foreign rule. I did not realize then that I was shifting time frames to adjust to another understanding of modernity, one ushered in with the leaving of colonial rule: independence brought modernity to India. Neither did I realize that some of the very conceptual foundations of this freedom, like the organization into a "nation-state," were built on internalized Westernisms and that, in some ways, my "modern" continued the model of Western modernity, that the conceptual break between the two was indeed not that immense.

While these questions could not weigh down the thrilling moments in my forays into the postmodern then, they have returned again and again to haunt me, complex disappointments and dismal doubts. Initially, reading the ideas of postmodern scholars rewriting generic boundaries, commenting on the confounding of the modernist project of empire, and about how postmodern artists were working across genres of spatial organization, I was excited. I wondered over the brilliance of postmodern choreographers and other artists in the West who had ruptured the more static energies of modern forms and presentational techniques and had reinvented understandings of art, its location, and functions. No doubt the coalescence in general dance language, between the descriptors "postmodern," "radical," and "avant-garde," had seduced me completely into a constancy of desiring. But I was intrigued even then by Jameson's concept of cognitive mapping whereby maps themselves have ceased to be possible measures of boundaries, a result of the discontinuous leaps in the expansion of capital and its penetration into areas previously uncommodified.[2] For I doubted the "difference" of the postmodern as I watched religious fundamentalisms escalate at a time when religious frameworks were supposed to have become empty signifiers, and lead to devastating wars over lands, maps, religion and homeland, new versions of age-old crusades; as we learned of the colonization of East Timor, ostensibly by Indonesia, but sanctioned by first-world oil companies and governments. And as I have watched the shifting borders of nations and the spill-over of populations into lands other than where they were born, complemented by increasingly rigid immigration policies, I have realized that these phenomena are as much about the post-modern function of capital as about modernist claims of origins and legacies of empire. Subsequently, I have also come to realize that several western postmodern theorists, in spite of their trenchant critique of American politics and of phenomena as univocally "global," still tend to even out overturnings, ruptures, rumblings marked by third-world peoples that may register only as small tremors on a flattened out world map.

There was the time, for instance, when Thums Up and Limca, the local soft drink industries in India, real treats on summer days, suddenly became less and less available, and all we could find in the markets, the corner-shops, the restaurants, were the international brands, Coke and Pepsi, selling at about double the price of local brands. Was this about the post-modern phenomenon of the exploding of national markets and economies into international systems—that cultural logic of late capitalism? It seemed to have precursors in the imperialistic and colonizing policies of early and late modern European politics, in the trade policies of cotton and indigo for instance. What did postmodernity change then, other than the face of the commodity? For those of us on the other side of the world, it seemed that the manifestations of the postmodern only entrenched some of the markers of the lived conditions of modernity. And, increasingly, my analysis of the ways in which artistic work was being marketed, produced, and com-modified, confirmed this belief.

Meanwhile I have also come to realize, as peoples of color have claimed again and again, that the most progressive and avant-garde edge in mainstream culture has continued to borrow consciously or unconsciously from the inescapable lived realities of peoples who form its underclass: from fashion designer Tommy Hilfiger who drew on the wide-bottomed baggy pants worn by black inner-city youth and felons to create a style he could package under his brand name and make a must-have commodity; to the business enterprise (Guernsey's auction house) who maxed out the cap-italist penchant for the commodification of "expression"—even those forms and voices that are shunned as antisocial and criminal—by running an auc-tion in June 2001 to sell pieces of graffiti in New York City.[3] But, this comes to be marketed as the availability of choice and, as Susan Bordo has argued, postmodernity manifests itself in popular culture in a fetishization of choice, the relentless production of novelty through the proliferation of "new" consumer items.[4] This, of course, obscures differential locationings within this availability of choice and questions of access, and effectively constitutes an effacement of choice. In a different context, Kobena Mercer talks about this as well, reinventing Brenda Dixon-Gottschild's question about cross-cultural influences, in terms of the operating conditions of the field of fashion and body politics:

. . . one cannot ignore how, alongside the commodification of electro and hip hop, break-dancing and sportswear chic, some contemporary hairstyles among white youth maintain an ambiguous relationship with the stylizing practices of their black counterparts. Many use gels to effect sculptural forms, and in some inner-city areas white kids use the relaxer crème technology marketed to black kids in order to simulate the wet-look curly-perm. So who, in this postmodern melee of semiotic appropriation and countervalorization, is imitating whom?[5]

Yet, at other times, I found myself in the midst of some of the typical "postmodern" phenomena that artists and thinkers in the West apparently worked with: disorientation of space, the breaking of boundaries between high and low art. Only, as I recognized them, they seemed to rewrite the discourse of the postmodern from the point of view of those who might never enter or hear of the Westin Bonaventure or ponder the connection between Warhol and Campbell soup cans. This in New York City, for instance, where I met the Indo-Caribbean communities and participated in the Chutney Soca parties.[6] I witnessed the remarkable richness and diversity within these cultures, drawing on several cultural traditions to create new possibilities and cultural specificities, and the irony of the situation became obvious to me: for I realized that it was the very reverse of the classic capitalist modern ploy that becomes a postmodern phenomenon for "others," a nemesis almost to its precursors. This is the popular imploding of national borders: populations from third-world communities initially indentured and shipped off as cheap labor to distant colonies or plantations, later immigrate to first-world countries in search of "better" futures in these more "developed" locations, claiming rights and spaces. Their diasporic reformulations confound attempts made by first-world nations for the containment of "other" racial groups, and challenge the historic self-willed and self-decided mobility and exploration-prerogative of the first-world subject. No doubt they also frustrate attempts of postcolonial nation-states and societies to articulate desires for "cultural purity." In this situation, spatial and temporal concerns necessarily criss-cross and etch out new and volatile world situations. Even as contemporary mainstream politics comes to be dominated, as in recent times, by a frenetic return to conservative politics, communities spill over imposed boundaries and create their own resistive diasporic cultures. They participate in mainstream cultural frameworks and recognize the constitution of identities in terms of these officially sanctioned metanarratives, but still insist on marking their differences, posing larger threats to the existing hierarchies in the first world. I am reminded of Guillermo Gomez-Pena: "For the North American, the border becomes a mythical notion of security. The border is where the third world begins."[7]

And for some, on the other side, the border is there only to be crossed.

It is precisely such practices of mobile intersectionality and of resistance to inscription by and in the terms of the metanarrative of Euro-Western dominance, from a positioning in alterity, that seem to mark for me the recurring characteristics of a postmodern. In her introduction to *Displacements*, a collection of essays on the themes of migration and dislocation, Angelika Bammer argues that it seems that these notions, along with the consequent inscription in "otherness," seem to be the persistent tropes of a "postmodern condition."[8] Yet this seems to have led ultimately to a flattening of distinctive valences of difference, and the positing of a postmodern version of the universal subject, always already displaced. The ways in which location is understood are vital however, and they foreground repeatedly that "differences" weigh differently. Bammer juxtaposes two different readings of modernity to illustrate her point. Fredric Jameson argues, for instance, that the specific shape of modernism between the two world wars in western Europe is predicated upon the structural displacement of significant parts of the Western world onto parts "located elsewhere . . . in colonies over the water whose own life experience and life world . . . remain unknown and unimaginable for the subjects of the imperial power."[9] This doubled and split existence, extended over several here/there ruptures, becomes, for Jameson, the "new and historically original problem" of modernity: "the inability to grasp the way the system functions as a whole."[10] On the other hand, Salman Rushdie, writing from the opposite end, comments on the total arbitrariness with which the "modernist" project was thrust upon colonized and displaced peoples and terrains: "Those of us who have been forced by cultural displacement to accept the provisional nature of all truths, all certainties, have perhaps had modernism forced upon us."[11]

I draw attention to this argument of multiple perspectives particularly to suggest extending it to think through alternative formulations of postmoderns, which is my project here. For, it is the consequent deliberate troubling of Western-style modernity fitted on willy-nilly; the willed not forced destabilizing of nationalist and neo imperialistic regimes of "truth"; the recognition of the questionable logic of Historical narratology, working through considerations of difference, that provide possibilities for the emergence of radical resistive modes. These are modes and forms that constitute alternative forms of postmodern—of a different kind, theorized with different politics. These other local postmoderns, differently from the forms of the modern that Rushdie argues was thrust upon these communities, are realized in reworkings of the power dynamics at play and disruptions of the smooth operation of grand organizing narratives and categories. Through the interventions they effect, these postmodern modes remark the radical edges of cultural politics, a space defined through the imbrication of alterity, agency, and articulation. Therein the radical direction. Here, cultural production contests the typical structures and politics of meaning-making and inaugurates the obvious destabilization of given paradigms, marking perhaps "the shifting ground of signification that makes meanings tremble."[12]

I also want to rethink Bammer's initial idea of displacement in the context of the alternative postmoderns I am invoking, for it seems to me that this juxtaposition, like that of the concepts of modernity articulated by Jameson and Rushdie, reformulates dominant categorizations of the postmodern. Now, displacement as a trope of shifting locations, obviously operates on several levels simultaneously, where "place" is compounded through intersections of geographical locale, with political, sociocultural, economic, and emotional landscapes. Displacements: sometimes in the sense of spatial uprootings, the enormity of ensuing loss, and refigurings, and sometimes, in the sense of total confounding by a disjointed history despite continuity in the same, but totally reconstituted, space. Here, a sense of rupture is built into the notion of displacement, a tremendous interruption in the least. At the same time, in considering the possibilities of an alternative formulation of postmodern, as articulated in the cultural production of specific artists of color and from the third world, there seems to be a way in which displacement functions primarily as premise, and a postmodern manifests itself, beyond a recognition and assessment of this displacement, in a sense of reworking relationships, through terms and possibilities available in contemporary situations, focusing on links or disjunctions that were often passed over in the formulation of modernism, functioning under a different agenda. The typical reading of a postmodern aesthetic through rupture must often be thought through here in simultaneity with projects of suture, working through the political, intellectual, physical, and emotional labor required in interweaving a different set of relationships to familiar yet changing contexts and concepts.

This rupture-suture oscillation is also part of what Bammer describes as the tension that the experience of displacement is charged with: the "historically vital double move between marking and recording absence and loss and inscribing presence."[13] The emphasis on attesting presence, in the face of obvious disjunctions and in one's own terms, is of course a vital part of the project of identity politics that have now come to be re-evaluated as a not so helpful paradigm in theorizing. While identity politics are seldom completely dismissible for artists of color laboring under legacies of appropriative practices, a finely honed politics of location and positionality have come to be central in contemporary practices of presencing, troubling immediate correspondences between place and subjectivity, producing a tense relationship between ideas of cultural ownership and progressive politics. Here, the "double move" that Bammer talks about—the flagging of presences and absences—works through necessarily complex negotiations of location, the process itself inscribed in intersectionalities and shifts. Working through figurings and refigurings of difference, theorizing location disturbs the apparently linear continuity of traditionally aligned communities, notions of organic inherentness of ethno-national relationing, and monolithic and naturalized conceptions of aesthetic "tradition," while opening up possibilities for other coalitions and conversations. In ways and through processes different from how many postmodern scholars in the West have talked about it, then, spaces come to be conceived through these practices as simultaneously resonant and fragmented and, in their saturatedness, potentially disorienting.

It is illuminating, in thinking about shifting locations, to consider the comments of Stuart Hall reflecting on the strange paradox whereby the typical experience of the marginalized populations comes to be constituted, indeed at the very moment that that voice is gathering some force and momentum, as the radical voice in larger left politics:

> Thinking about my own sense of identity, I realize that it has always depended on the fact of being a *migrant*, on the *difference* from the rest of you. So one of the fascinating things about this discussion is to find myself centered at last. Now that, in the postmodern age, you all feel so dispersed, I become centered. What I've thought of as dispersed and fragmented comes, paradoxically, to be the representative modern experience! This is "coming home" with a vengeance! [14]

Hall's ironic assertion of his typical and long-standing experience of migrancy as the home base for the "new" radical politics of postmodernism fills me with hope. It reminds me, in no uncertain terms, that these alternative forms of the postmodern trace a complex and paradoxical phenomenon: Hall's "coming home," like Rushdie's "shifting ground of signification," tells me about the sense of displacement yet continuity, that reworking of Bammer's thesis that characterizes these politics. It also echoes the way in which several peoples of color have responded to the white Western postmodern with irony: as articulations of forms and modalities that, because of directly opposite histories, have always already been their experience. A radical postmodern aesthetic emerging from artists and thinkers such as these is necessarily different from the white Western postmodern paradigms; the search is different, as also the goal, as has historically been the case.

Articulations of this radical edge in the cultural production of people of color excite me. I do not want to reject terms like the postmodern as concepts created by and operative only in the "West"—as if my rejection would have any effect. On the other hand, accepting the inevitability of our implication in the terms of a Eurocentric historiography yet insisting on seizing the resistive possibilities within that, attempting to translate that edge of excitement in that which is post the modern, and avant-garde, I want to examine how they might function in dance and cultural production in specific contexts of color, and tweak their boundaries and definitions in relationship to the context. *How does the postmodern manifest itself in my brown body, Indian passport in hand, when I make dissonant the rhythms of my classically ordered feet, even as I hold on to my tribhangi-bent body? Or does this reincarnation disrupt its possibility completely? Might this disruption be a reworking of a named and self-consciously articulated dominant postmodern in terms of specific located politics and contexts, working through interrogations of particular "traditions" and "moderns"?* I have begun to delineate my theoretical framework even as I have charted longings and disappointments, largely to give these terms a good wash in remembered emotion that also reinvigorates the politics of creativity and artistic intent. I offer the subsequent thoughts not as a grand theory about the works of artists of color, but as readings of stories and discourses of desire and struggle that call urgently for alternative theorizations. I know that neither Zollar nor Chandralekha care to be categorized in any one way. I do not want to force a postmodern categorization on them, but I do offer readings of the postmodern and radical aesthetics, and the near-inevitable coalescence of the two, to set a context for an understanding of their work, and to see how, filtered through such work, these terms get a different hue.

For the sake of achieving a little more clarity than might have been possible through this network of thoughts, questions, and exclamations, let me rehearse the general argument I have been working with, before moving on to consider and develop these reflections specifically as they play out in the field of dance. I want to suggest then, that there are multiple processes at work in these tangled histories. It seems that the modern of the Eurowest, originally meant to define its location as the summit of a progress-driven society, in contrast to the "underdeveloped" nations of the world, spans out to encompass these "others" explicitly, through empire-building, capitalist programs dressed up as "civilizing missions." Implicitly, of course, the "otherness" of the latter serves a vital function: it is what sharpens the definitive edge of the Western modern by inhabiting the space of its lack. But these "others" obviously do not stay passive sites of inscription; the modernity they encounter is transformed and/or translated by them into forms of identity-making that often play into complex politics of individuation and democratic flattening, projects of nation-making, but also highlight long struggles to keep alive or revive "traditional" forms, aesthetics, cultural practices. However, alternative forms emerge thereafter, in these "other" locations, often reactions to Western aggrandizement, earlier projects of empire as well as later modes of industrial colonialism, processes of globalization, but also questioning and reworking the relationships established and accepted by the modern in these communities and reaching toward other forms that illuminate contemporary dilemmas and ideas. I am casting this direction in aesthetic and cultural production as a postmodern precisely because it throws into doubt many of the premises of the modern in these communities and, by extension, its counterpart, the modern of the West. The postmodern I am describing is then primarily a phenomenon of relationality, marked by its negotiations of ways of relating to various periods in the past and to an imaginable future based on a politics that examines and relocates the past variously and differently from other positionalities. Moreover, here, it is not so much that the questions addressed are "new." Rather, it is the forms and modes of formulation that are organized and restructured, marking vital shifts and reflecting a complex relationing to contexts. The Euro-American postmodern is also shown up here as a situated, not universal, category, still laboring under some of the exclusions that had formed the core of the discourse of the modern: avant-garde within a limited framework. Moving on to dancing.

Postmodern Complaints

While the corpus of literature on dance is always meager in comparison to most other fields, there is some greater availability of print source materials for postmodern dance, constituted mostly by descriptive reportage, performance reviews, and aesthetic analyses. However, rarely do discussions in this category include any more than a token representation of artists and choreographers of color, which reaffirms the general conception that postmodernism in dance is a phenomenon limited to Euro-American artists. It is true of course that there were almost no dancers of color in the recognized history of the Judson Dancers, but artists such as Gus Solomons, Jr., though he receives scant attention in accounts of the period, were part of the downtown postmodern movement in dance and working, like the others, in innovative ways.[15] And Susan Foster, in her examination of the "genealogies of improvisation" that supposedly marked the radical in American postmodern dance, discusses the work of African American choreographers like Dianne McIntyre, where the improvisational process played a central role, and other black cultural practices and movements that vitally influenced key players in the happening postmodern dance scene.[16] The question about artists of color in the postmodern movement, however, immediately begs others: is this exclusivity a result of the selectivity of our reading, and of the practices of naming, such that only the very specific artistic processes of a particular group of artists read as the "radical" at that point? And is it this particular lens that did not allow for translations into the different manifestations of similar political concerns articulated in the works of other groups of artists? Or, is it that the contexts and concerns of these "other" artists are so different that their articulation of the radical cannot be recognized as such in terms of what comes to be understood as the conceptual base of the "postmodern revolution" in Euro-American dance? Or did artists of color recognize the postmodern movement in dance as racially and nationally closed and feel unwelcome or uncomfortable? Surely, it could not be that these artists were not interested in participating in a sense of the radical, a questioning of inherited forms and traditions. And why is "postmodern" now, very differently from the sixties and much like the eighties when the phenomenon gained popularity, still the obvious descriptor for artwork that, still remaining situated in an invisible base of mainstream traditions, gives evidence of specific access to "global" influences, with citations of a step from Senegalese dance, some arms from Javanese dance, some hands from Indian dance, thrown in? Who has access? Does the practice of referencing or citing other traditions have equal weight wherever practiced? How is this different from the past of Euro-American dance, laboring under questions of unacknowledged borrowings and influences? Does acknowledgment sanction flattening of the differing political valences of different kinds of borrowings? How do we remember, for instance, the 1984 production of Robert Wilson's *The CIVIL Wars: A Tree is Best Measured When It Is Down* at the Walker Arts Center, Minnneapolis, where the choreography was done by Suzushi Hanayagi, and the principal dancers were Donald Byrd and Maria Cheng? Or, does the naming of the postmodern imply a certain foundational exclusivity where artists of color, few and far between, are present either as proof of the exception that proves the rule, or as singular talented followers in the unending game of catch-up?

Interestingly of course, the "postmodern" is a multimeaning term in dance, operating in multiple contexts, differently. As Sally Banes, one of the first dance scholars to theorize postmodern dance extensively, argues in *Writing Dancing in the Age of Postmodernism*, the "postmodern" means both historically and descriptively in dance. For her, the concept gathers force as a "choreographer's term to draw attention to an emergent group of new dance artists" in the early sixties, specifically the Judson Group and other innovators at this time.[17] Banes distinguishes this from the choreography emerging in the late sixties and early seventies, consciously aligned with the principles of minimalist sculpture, which she categorizes as "analytical" postmodern dance, seen in the works of artists such as Yvonne Rainer,

Trisha Brown, Lucinda Childs, Steve Paxton, David Gordon and others. Also in the seventies are choreographers like Meredith Monk, Kenneth King, and Laura Dean, whose works are more obviously theatrical and fit Banes's descriptor of "metaphoric postmodern dance." Finally, for Banes, postmodern dance in the eighties and nineties seems to be moving away from the earlier repudiation of theatricality, but recovering the earlier Judsonite interdisciplinary eclecticism, to create yet another aesthetic of "abundance and pleasure" and a pastiche of previous postmodern modalities.[18] It is in this last phase that some artists of color figure as important dance makers, and she mentions choreographers like Bill T. Jones, Gus Solomons, Jr., Ralph Lemon, Bebe Miller, Zollar, Ishmael Houston-Jones; and Blondell Cummings, Eiko and Koma and Yoshiko Chuma, in the last phase of the development of postmodern dance. This is also where racialized and gendered understandings of identity are seen as inflecting choreography, though in actuality and seldom-acknowledged, cultures of color are constantly part of the aesthetic base that influences *all* phases of postmodern dance. What also returns in this last phase, according to Banes, is an emphasis on virtuosity, with a special attraction for balletic technique.

What I want to point out through this reference to Banes's analysis is that the concept of the postmodern is an inherently shifting one in the field of dance, meaning differently at different times through the works of different choreographers: "In a sense, postmodern dance began as a postmodernist movement, underwent a modernist interlude, and has now embarked on a second postmodernist project."[19] Even earlier, in her introduction to *Terpsichore in Sneakers*, her classic text of postmodern dance in America, Banes refers to the shifting markers of postmodern choreography and discusses the different concerns that characterized dances through the different decades of postmodern dance, and her conceptualization of the postmodern aesthetic constantly twists to include these differences in its fold. Interestingly, talking about the period 1968 through 1973, Banes writes that three new themes were introduced into postmodern dance at this time: political issues, audience engagement, and non-Western influences. She also points out that what continued to differentiate postmodern dance from modern dance, ballet, and black dance was the "rejection of musicality and rhythmic organization."[20] I have wondered about these statements a good deal. Sometimes it seems, especially if we consider the works of the New Dance Group, certainly of choreographers like Anna Sokolow, those three markers would seem to align the postmodern with the modern, or at least with a certain trend in modern dance. Again, Yvonne Rainer and Sally Banes, at a talk at Walker Arts Center, talked about the great variations among even the Judson group with regard to dramatic elements, ranging from the deadpan face to overt theatricality, with Rainer marking one end perhaps and Carolee Schneeman the other.[21] In fact, by most accounts, the understanding of postmodern dance seems to be more rather than less fluid.

One of its most consistent characteristics, however, seems to have been the focus on experimentation to de-essentialize concepts of artistic validity, to stretch the given limits of dance or, as Marcia Siegel says, "to subvert received ideas about society and art . . . dance that stands given conventions on their head," a description that once again reflects the notion of the immediate "radicalness" of the postmodern.[22] And so, I wonder why despite the bold innovative elements in the works of several black choreographers—their political engagement in thematic material, their interest in breaking down boundaries between high and low art, their interest in working across genres and boundaries—there is no discussion of such "postmodern" practice in their work. For instance, there were artists like Arthur Mitchell, Rod Rodgers, and Eleo Pomare at this time, articulating complex and de-essentialized claims of identity and location through their works— bringing the privileged marker of Anglo-American culture, ballet, to Harlem, recasting Europeanist classics in color, in a strange twisting of the American dream;[23] emphasizing urban decay and the collusion of race and class; bringing the street onto the stage in a reversal of the popular postmodernist move of bringing the performance space to the street in pieces like *Junkie*; insisting on claiming both sides of the hyphenation in the racializing descriptor, "African-American," resisting being bracketed into narrow categories in identity politics, and publishing statements of these ideas in journals like *The Negro Digest*.[24] The politics in their work have important implications for the understanding of postmodernism, often signifying radical departures from the conventions of modern dance traditions, certainly in terms of hybridity, fragmentation, and the breakdown of the myth of cultural purities and essential notions of whiteness and blackness. Again, it is well known that Garth Fagan had started his Bottom of the Bucket, But . . . Dance Theater Company by recruiting inner-city youth from community centers, untrained bodies, as dancers in Rochester, New York, 1970. This has later been subverted in the highly sophisticated training that dancers in his company are now required to have, but little attention falls on this radical beginning. I am also intrigued that many of these choreographers' staging of hybrid identities through the juxtapositions and/or melding of different forms and genres, their moving between different centers of movement, seldom make for comment even now as part of the radical movement in dance at that time. It is in the aftermath of such reflections that I start to disagree with Sally Banes's assertion that "The term 'postmodern' is not an evaluative one, but a descriptive, historical one."[25]

I am also interested that dancers of color, specifically black choreographers and dancers, did not feel encouraged to join the postmodern dance movement, even though several of the white choreographers were ostensibly sympathetic to the "black cause." Rainer for instance talked about the performance in support of the Committee to Defend the Black Panthers in New York University's Loeb Student Center, and of the group's friendship with black leaders such as Amiri Baraka, who introduced them to the black jazz clubs in downtown New York.[26] It does seem that one of the crucial factors in the organization of the Judson and Grand Union eras was the constitution of a group of artists who worked together, but in diverse ways—albeit within a given aesthetic framework—united primarily in their resistance to the established mainstream of modern dance and ballet, and who then came to mark the intellectual and radical edge of dance at that time. How deeply are hegemonic structures entrenched into the sociocultural fabric that, despite critiques of institutionalization that have come from the successive waves of the postmodern movement, the dance scene continues to labor under exclusions and failed understandings? Indeed, while European Tanztheater and French Canadian Danse Actuelle continue to intrigue, in the case of non-Western artists of color working "elsewhere" the considerations hardly arise: other than Butoh artists from Japan, they are seldom mentioned. Yet it is not that they escape categorization in Western terms. In the absence of finer considerations and despite important differences, they often fall into that infamous category of excess and all-that-is-not: ethnic dance.

Such descriptors also show up in considerations of choreographers and artists as part of discussions of "World Dance." Here too, the ways in which they are read parallel the hidden lie in notions of "globalization" that disguises the overtaking, through business and financial operations, of the world by corporations still centrally located in that still center of power. Here, once more, the occasional and uncontexted mention of individuals of color or from the third world serves to highlight them as the exception to the rule of traditional practice. What I mean by uncontexted is not that there is no mention of the sociocultural context at all, but that it seems to have an unchanging face, stuck in petrified and uncomplicated ideas of "Tradition" and "Culture," all of which of course are often promoted by internal governmental policies in these contexts. In the lack of theorizing the context in which they are located, the changing and volatile cultural and political context of their work, they appear as ahistorical figures somehow transcending their otherwise "age-old" legacy. These conceptions continue to affect readings, such that even when perceptions of postmodern and radical have somewhat broadened, disjunctions remain and threaten to vitiate the possibility of formulating postmodern aesthetics based on alternative frameworks and characteristics.

Even now, when critical discourse is highly sophisticated, artists of color continue to ask for a broader yet contexted understanding of what reads as cutting-edge works in specific cultural fields such that, for instance, the cross-genre work of the Bronx-based group *Universes*, where the five actors, Latino and black, movers, poets, rappers, and singers, who both create and perform work that melds artistic, social, and political issues, commenting on urban life and decay, *also* receives attention as highly innovative performance. Or, such that the projects of Carl Hancock Rux, where the artifice of performance is broken down within the structure of the performance itself through the intersecting of music, autobiographical text, poetry, and movement, receives acclaim, not just as a genre of spoken word, but as performance as well. Or that we also analyze the work of *Zuni Icosahedron*, the radical arts collective from Hong Kong, as continuously offering new paradigms of the alternative edge in performance. And that we consider these bodies of work alongside, not way after, the work of artists such as Mark Morris, who are regarded as marking the current front line of the radical postmodern.

Safe Distances

The refusal of the Euro-American mainstream, however subtle, to recognize the postmodernism in the works of artists and choreographers of color is not unrelated to the earlier forgetfulness regarding the influences and inspirations of dance traditions of color in the creation of Euro-American modern dance and assumptions about its self-contained aesthetic. There has always been, at the same time, a marked desire to keep white dance forms at a distance from artists of color. In 1963, dance critic John Martin had commented that blacks were not suited to dance the ballet because its European origins and orientation are alien to them "culturally, temperamentally, and anatomically," while others had repeatedly applauded Katherine Dunham and Pearl Primus for having wisely returned to the traditions of Africa and the Caribbean instead of experimenting with Europeanist forms.[27] Such implicit boundaries and tacit exclusions continue to be operative even though we are well aware of critiques of ethnic essentialisms and racial narratives demarcating categories of possibilities.

On the other hand, the Western world's disillusionment with the forms that its modernity had spewed in the early part of the previous century, associated inevitably with its technological progress, led it one more time to yearn toward the "pure," "unpolluted," traditional forms of African and Asian cultural production. Implicit in this yearning was a discrediting of more contemporary artistic modes in these communities as reflective of contact with the Western world. In this yearning also, and the ensuing rush to "save" performance traditions of these cultures, was the very base for the avant-garde it would now create. Once again, Euro-American dance would re-mark its own forward movement by fixing African and Asian dance forms in tradition, in the past, in a moment that seemed to be unaffected by the vicissitudes of history. As with the modern dance movement, so with the postmodern—history repeated itself. Today, while the influence of African and Asian forms on the pioneers of modern dance in the United States, such as Ruth St. Denis, Ted Shawn, Martha Graham, and others, is generally somewhat acknowledged, the fact that these influences sustain their presence in different ways in the postmodern dance is just beginning to be discussed.

Here, I want to echo Brenda Dixon-Gottschild's call to pay attention to the black street dance forms that very largely influenced the democratizing of movement and the casual energy of much of postmodern dance, and to the flourishing jazz movement at that time led by black musicians that influenced the innovations in open-ended and continuously altering structures that characterized the early postmodern work. I also want to remind that Yvonne Rainer drew upon Indian epics and mythological drama in thinking about interventions in narrative structure, that the circle dances of Laura Dean and Lucinda Childs reflect influences from Sufism, and that several of the postmodern choreographers were greatly inspired by Eastern movement forms such as T'ai Chi Chuan, Aikido, and yoga. However, these are matters of technique, form, and structural innovations, whose acknowledgment suggest once more the inseparable relationship between the Western avant-garde and its "other." But I also want to draw attention to the intertextuality of various modes of protest, the recurrent embodiment of interventionary acts that were a vital part of the context in which these choreographers were working. Clearly, convictions about the political potential of the body, the signifying possibilities of bodily acts, were stronger than ever.

The sixties was a time of political protest and resistance for the black communities in the United States, including individual acts of rebellion like the North Carolina sit-in and Rosa Parks's refusal to give up her seat on the bus, and larger mass movements such as the civil rights movement. While American political conservatism and military aggression reached its peak with the long Vietnam War, different energies were sweeping through the world as "new" nations, decolonized only a little over a decade ago, came into their own. Surely all of these contemporary events functioned, if not as conscious inspirations, as subterranean influences for the artistic community in the United States at that time, seeking to stage their own rebellions against forms they experienced as devoid of meaning. It seems but obvious that the resistant attitude of the Judson group and others fit perfectly into, and was even fed by, an atmosphere of general protest in libertarian struggles and possibilities of subculture, models for which came primarily from local black politics through the civil rights struggle and other movements toward self-determination in the rest of the world, but largely in the third world. Postmodern choreographers presented their work during the Angry Arts Week in 1967, in protest of the Vietnam War, and I have already mentioned the NYU performance, some of whose proceeds were donated to the Black Panther Party. Most importantly, the Black Arts Movement was flourishing at around the same time as the postmodern dance movement in the United States, creating its own impact on cultural production at that time. Some leaders of the movement, like Amiri Baraka, were on friendly terms with the "downtown" arts community of New York. But clearly, the Black Arts Movement galvanized artists from various fields to channel their creative powers to inspire revolution.

However, there is little connection between the artistic or political innovations of the Euro-American postmodern choreographers and those of "other" communities in popular imagination, and often, in scholarly research as well. Implicit in these slippages of remembering, or the unquestioning of access to these influences, is the fact that Euro-American avant-garde arts movements have often defined themselves as such solely in their own terms, unallied in reality to radical politics. As feminist cultural critic Michelle Wallace, pointing to the resistant insurgency of African American artists, intellectuals, and workers in the 1960s, which is usually slurred over in mainstream writing about that period, says, "As ridiculous as it may seem, a white cultural avant-garde, here and abroad, has always believed it possible to make an oppositional art without fundamentally challenging hegemonic notions of race, sexuality, and even class."[28] Wallace's words echo my impatience with much "postmodern" performance in the West. This selective oppositionality, coupled with my observation that some of the most interesting counter-hegemonic performances are being created by artists who cannot but deal with disparities of race, class, political leverage, access to resources: choreographers of color and third world artists, many of them women, artists working in resistive ways.

Of More Arbitrary Irritations
Thinking about appropriations and uneven fields, continuing despite claims of increasing understandings, I find this unequal journey vexing, whereby the selective appropriation or borrowings of "traditional" forms from non-white Western cultures to fuel the innovations of progressive or avant-garde Euro-American artists are brushed over, while claims of radical/postmodern by artists of color and especially from the third world are at least implicitly frowned upon. When established and famous Tanztheater choreographer Suzanna Linke created *Le Coq Est Mort* in 2001 on a group

of eight Senegalese men, apparently about the end of colonialism in Senegal, the project caused great excitement, particularly as a unique intercultural venture. But, the brilliantly danced and produced piece was uncomfortably permeated with images of men, who, beginning with wearing suits, had progressively less to wear; a group of black men performing on a sand-strewn stage, performing violence on each other; black male dancers imitating animals and birds; all images that to me revealed unmistakable shades of primitivism. Interestingly, in a private conversation Linke told me that the movement had come from the dancers themselves, and that she was responsible primarily for the structure, though this was not fully corroborated by conversations with the dancers themselves.[29] A possible reading of this project: "primitive" material brought under the auspices of high civilization; that is, produced in European theaters, through the mediating and shaping hand of European choreography and structuring. The successful European tour of the piece underscored the continued fascination of audiences with a particular kind of avant-garde, despite the problematic imagery.

Moreover, under the scrutiny of internal nationalist and conservative agendas, colluding with the gaze of the West, forms legitimized as "traditional" are glorified and shrouded in some notion of "authenticity," while contemporary forms of artistic production are often charged with being under the influence of the West. I am surprised that I continue to be shocked then, when I read the following review by dance critic Jochen Schmidt, who as late as 1995 writes this way about Chandralekha's choreography, comparing it with a classical dance performance by Bharatnatyam dancer, Alarmel Valli, though one doubts that he could justify such a cross-genre comparison between performances by New York City Ballet and the Judson Dance Theater! Schmidt begins by claiming that "only the writings of Western critics helped (Chandralekha) gain a considerable reputation at home" and then elaborates on how Chandralekha was "discovered" by the West.[30] This implied reduction of India, or other third world cultures, to an oppressive monolith, where nothing interventionary is tolerated, is not new of course. At any rate, neither of these comments are tenable, and one may argue that Schmidt is unable to separate fact from appearance: there are indeed several pieces of lesser-known writings on Chandralekha's work in India over the years, but one has to take into account the differences between contexts where oral transmission has different value and status from the written proliferation of information. Moreover, the capacities of Western media to cast what might often be larger-than-life images cannot compare to the smaller-scale news industries in most third-world countries, something that continues to be true despite the technological "progress" of the latter. Moreover, while Chandralekha's work shocked the sensibilities of conservatives, she obviously received the support of other groups of audience members, one of the reasons why, she herself says, she has continued to remain in Chennai, the citadel of traditionalists, and create work there over the years.

To return to Schmidt's observation, in his dichotomous thinking the two can only be situated confrontationally: he contrasts Chandralekha's move to work with the abstract core of Bharatnatyam, "one of the important Indian dances" (not a classical dance *form* with a full repertoire of its own), with the "charm . . . sublime eroticism . . . divine" dancing of Valli.[31] Of course, Chandralekha's contemporary style is situated at the intersection of several dance and movement forms such as yoga and Kalarippayattu besides the abstract core of Bharatanatyam, while Valli's work is focused on the Bharatanatyam idiom specifically. At any rate, without understanding the historical necessity for the existence of both dance genres in India today, or the politics that underlie their separate yet conjoined positioning, Schmidt writes that "the traditional dance of Valli is so full of art and rich in nuances that Chandralekha's lean modernity seems poor and antiquated in contrast."[32] Not content with this judgment, Schmidt consolidates his self-assumed position as arbiter over the development of Indian dance by concluding with this prescription: "The ideal combination would be Chandralekha's body consciousness and spatial style with Alarmel Valli's choreographic wealth and brilliance in dancing," an arbitration that seems to be arrogant in the least.[33]

Gayatri Chakravorty Spivak theorizes this typical Europeanist gesture of waving away the contemporary cultural attitudes and cultural production in these contexts, evoking instead the "purity" of indigenous traditions, and the subsequent interpellation of third-world artists of color in irrevocable "otherness," abstracting historical processes:

> If one reverses the direction of this binary opposition, the Western intellectual's longing for all that is not West, our turn towards the West—the so-called non-West's turn towards the West is a *command*. That turn was not in order to fulfill some longing to consolidate a pure space for ourselves, that turn was a command . . . today of course, since there is now a longing once again for the pure Other of the West, we post-colonial intellectuals are told we are *too* Western, and what goes completely unnoticed is that our turn to the West is in response to a command, whereas the other is to an extent a desire marking the place of the management of a crisis.[34]

This command, working through manufactured discourses, creates justifications for the West's drawing on what it names as the "traditions" of the non-West in order to revitalize its own sociocultural production and evolution. Think, for instance, of the popularity of the theater anthropology projects of famous director Eugenio Barba who clearly draws on "traditions" of classical performance from India, Bali, Japan, and the Orixa dances of Brazil among others, to reinvigorate European theatrical techniques and create his avant-garde European theater. On the other hand, as I have repeatedly pointed out, Euro-American dance scholars have thus forever chided artists of color for hearkening to "modern" forms (which comes to be equated with "westernized" by the inevitable implications of histories of imperialism), ignoring their own indigenous resources, which are then "saved" by savants from the West who become either master practitioners of this form, or come to be revered for their role in preserving "dying" traditions.

This is why several artists of color experience the niche they find in the Western cultural bazaar to be built primarily on a desire for exoticized "ethnic," admittedly valuable, dance forms, almost to the exclusion of their own contemporary choreographies. This of course feeds back into their communities, reflecting the legitimizing power of white approval, and affects the economic viability of other kinds of work deeply. Very often supported by their "ethnic" communities, themselves rent by internal hierarchies and replicating and sustaining the conservative hegemonic superstructure, these forms of cultural production, valorizing what is constructed as "tradition," are often funded to the exclusion of others, fulfilling the safety valve needs of a multicultural agenda that needs diversity of representation, not difference of politics and aesthetics. Here we get to celebrate qualities that have supposedly dropped away from Euro-American dance forms, through the naturally evolutionary process of civilization and progress, marching from classical to modern to postmodern and post-postmodern, always inventing its "own" avant-garde. What I am also concerned about is the way such terms effectively erase both the continuity of change within the traditional dance forms as well as the vital distinctions of style and genre between, for instance, court and popular dance, or, as Schmidt's review shows, between traditional and contemporary forms within these very cultures. It is important to acknowledge that such a strong tension between West and non-West continues to be operative even at a time when postmodern discourse disclaims the center-periphery theory as too uncomplicated to catch the multiple nuances of power play, and when the world picture is riddled with layered local and global power politics.

A small note here on pop culture will illuminate the looping self-affirmation that keeps the power structure intact. Interestingly enough, the recent spate of films about or from India (*Monsoon Wedding, Lagaan, Mystic Masseur*) running simultaneously in several mainstream movie theaters have sometimes prompted speculations about the growing diversity of the

American movie market. Yet, it is worth remembering that the interest in Bollywood, the Bombay Hindi film industry, was sparked off by a campy citation in *Moulin Rouge*—one of the most potent examples of unquestioning access deployed in a postmodern flattening of differential meanings— and that of course Bollywood is modeled largely after the ubiquitous Hollywood. Here again, the vital distinctions between diversity and difference become impossible to ignore.

Of Norms and Such

It seems that cultural difference has been so grossly commodified, fetishized, and collapsed into superficial notions of diversity that understanding across differences is fraught with increasing problems. What has often stood in the way, of course, is the invisibilization of the cultural specificity of that which is constituted as "norm," and of that "norm"'s power to regulate, name, and boundary. I am moving into these reflections about the immense power of a normativity in order to show how individual intentions often come be shot through with problematic politics through the essentalisms that come to be deeply entrenched in our thinking. Here, it is instructive to refer to the work of scholars and artists who have brought attention to the work of artists of color, particularly of black choreographers, in the area of American postmodern dance, and how their admirable efforts are often undercut by unexamined biases hidden in the textual fabric. In particular, I want to discuss some writing from Sally Banes, who, despite being one of the first dance scholars to write about the radical potential of breaking, and having written about several black and "other" American choreographers, has occasional slippages in her language that cause us to pause and wonder.

For instance, Banes has a very interesting chapter on "Latino postmodern dance" in *Writing Dancing in the Age of Postmodernism*, where she talks about the work of some Latina choreographers working in New York in the eighties and nineties. Throughout the essay, however, one is aware of a sense that postmodernism is a category defined by the white artists she has been discussing in previous essays, into which these Latina artists, working out of New York, have now entered. That is why, in the prefatory statements to the essay, talking about how politicizations of identity have informed their artistic practice, she sees the claiming of postmodernism in their artwork by specific artists of color as a "bicultural" move, claiming to be both sides of a divide, as if postmodernism belonged to a "culture" that is not black or Latino: "But in the 1980s for the first time various groups of young choreographers have identified themselves as bicultural in a specifically avant-garde mode: black and postmodern; gay and postmodern; Latino and postmodern."[35] Is postmodern dance, then, in some essential sense, white and heterosexual? The question, rather, might be how black postmodern dance or Latino postmodern dance differ from a general sense of white postmodern dance, if we are even able to conceive of such categories. Of course, this wouldn't have been the first time that choreographers of color were claiming "bicultural" identities. The earlier insistence by black choreographers such as Rod Rodgers and Eleo Pomare on understanding themselves as African Americans, blacking somewhat the dominant whiteface of American modern dance, had been a similar move.

At any rate, after descriptive analysis of some the pieces created by these choreographers, Banes notes how they use certain formal elements of postmodern dance as compositional choices, establishing a clear relationship of precedence. She talks about the use of language for the purposes of commentary and also to "underscore linguistic and ethnic difference," but for her the "virtuosic display of verbal speed and dexterity" is reminiscent of the "rhythms and tempo of the Spanish language itself."[36] Had Banes carried her analysis further she would have explored how this then affects English, which is the language used. English is broken here, to recall Coco Fusco, and the implicit questions in the performance are how the struc-. tures of English are transformed as they are caught up in the disturbing alterity of Spanish and Nuyorican rhythms.

She also would have seen that though some of these choreographers refer to popular culture as white postmodern choreographers like Jim Self do, the difference between the two contexts, questions of access and representation, the limited places and ways in which people of color find representation in the media, which makes for a deferral of that immediate established meaning, make the two references entirely different. It is this erasure of "difference" in a flat plane of simulated sameness in the reading that I want to object to. Moreover, Banes concludes by saying that "postmodern techniques have been adapted to create a political identity," a statement that obviously sets the cart before the horse.[37] Indeed, as diaspora comes to be theorized increasingly as an important space of meaning-making, and marginalized voices seek out increasingly greater articulation across the world, complex racialized, gendered, and sexualized identities become more obvious, performance being one of the zones of such enunciation. As Banes states it though, it seems that postmodern techniques— which were invested with political power from their inception, and clearly white by the terms of this narrative—are responsible for the formation and articulation of such identities.

The term "postmodern dance," then, has wider currency than the specificity of its conceptual base would warrant, and the symbolic economy of the term, its immediate associations with avant-garde artistic practice, groundbreaking innovations, and brilliant interventions into the history of concert dance, tend to unbalance general understandings of the wider arena of cultural production. This then cycles back to my proposition in the first chapter: that the official discourse on cultural and artistic endeavors in this genre rests on a set of assumptions only tacitly acknowledged, which shuffles to include specific groups and individuals, effecting a class-stratified and racially determined foreclosure of the avant-garde or radical space in art making by peoples of color. While it is obvious that the beginnings of the American postmodern, the Judson era, were populated more or less completely by white artists, I want to, in parallel, (a) investigate some of the subtle ways in which influences from "other" cultural practices form the subtext (sub- also as ostensibly shadowing the primary text, positioned directly below it) for some of the most radical postmodern work in the West, (b) examine the construction of the radical edge of the postmodern through a politics of specific kinds of unexamination, and (c) suggest some alternative formulations of the postmodern in keeping with different contexts, histories, and concerns.

How might it be to conceptualize the philosophical and political bases of the postmodern such that the radical innovations of choreographers of color can be part of that creative range? Can we see how these artists transform these categories and offer radical insights on these formulations? For instance, can we begin to probe what happens when ballet, reared in the lap of the European upper class, is taken up subsequently, via socialist Russia, in Mao Tse Tung's China in the wake of the Cultural Revolution? When militarized ballerinas come to symbolize the dropping of feudal trappings from cultural production in "modern" China in the Revolutionary ballet, *The Red Detachment of Women*, a production claiming to be a progressive antithesis to the "degraded" traditional opera? How does this resignify Euro-American ballet and the innovations in this field in contemporary times? Does it comment on the aesthetic of modern ballet, or does it pass as a shadow from the frame of cultural production in the West? Can we begin by pondering in general the seldom acknowledged, but inevitable reflexivity, circularity, and implicatedness of "others" in the construction of the Western "radical," the always already doubleness of the narrative of innovation and revolution in Western dance history? I want to posit a model of always asking questions from the other end, without simultaneously proposing a binarized meaning structure, but asking for alternative and localized perspectives in the responses, as a constitutive force in the alternative postmodern that I am attempting to theorize.

Marking Moments: The Crisis in Meaning
One of the bigger searches, especially for the early postmodern choreographers, seems to have been the location of "meaning" and its role in deter-

mining choreographic structure. In fact questions around meaning in movement seem to be pivotal in the distinction between modern and postmodern, and meaning is an important factor enabling the shift from the modernist position that "movement does not lie" to the postmodernist "mind is a muscle," or to the sense of the body as a composite location of different kinds and genres of movement. Particularly, it seems to be the question of *how* movement means and functions that fuels several other questions in the postmodern search, something that becomes apparent in some of the discourse about this period. I am also focusing on the function of meaning and the related "expressive" and communicative functions of dance because I think it is key to understanding how the radicalness of postmodern dance in the West is constructed.

Michael Kirby, in a special issue of *The Drama Review* focusing on the postmodern dance, said in his introduction to the volume that what was being called "the New Dance," while one of the most radical innovations in the performing arts, was no longer so new. He then renamed it "postmodern dance": "This at least has the advantage of making a historical point: 'postmodern dance' is that which has followed modern dance."[38] Kirby then goes on to discuss what he considers to be the markers of this postmodern dance: here, choreographers do not apply visual standards to their work, but work through an "interior" view: "movement is not preselected for its characteristics but results from certain decisions, goals, plans, schemes, rules, concepts, or problems."[39] For Kirby, this exemplifies postmodern dance's rejection of the musicalization of movement that typifies modern dance. He goes on to discuss the postmodern choreographers' rejection of overt concerns with meaning, characterization, mood, or atmosphere, so that dance exists for itself, not in order to convey messages or make statements. Neither do the dancers here represent characters, forces, or archetypes. Kirby thus introduces essays that describe and document performances by artists such as Batya Zamir, the Multigravitational Group, and Nikolai Foregger, and reflections on their own work by artists such as Laura Dean, Trisha Brown, Lucinda Childs, Simone Forti, Steve Paxton, and David Gordon.

On the other hand, for Susan Foster, writing a decade later, the central difference between the modern and postmodern genres seems to be the recognition and conscious marking of the political agency of the dancing body.[40] She highlights the shift from the idea of the body as an expressive agent in modern dance, to the postmodern affirmation of the body as a signifying, hence avowedly political, agent. So the "fact" of the body, even as shorn of other affective functions, is its own "meaning." This is an important idea and I find it vital in thinking through different conceptualizations of the postmodern. Yet, in most of her early work, Foster falls short of making the connections between the aesthetic politics of these artists and the cultural, social, and racialized power politics of their context, so the politics of the body that she is referring to here operate within a circumscribed area. Importantly though, her later research, picking up on the mandate sounded by Brenda Dixon-Gottschild, seeks to examine the black cultural influences in the interstices of the postmodern aesthetic.

In examining Sally Banes's classic about the early postmodern period, *Terpsichore in Sneakers*, as well as other writings on postmodern dance, one finds a preponderance of the descriptions of movement and choreographic structure as neutral and ordinary.[41] This assumption of neutrality/ordinariness, along with Rainer's more explicit desire for "uninterrupted surface" and "nonreferential forms," signals an evacuation of overt content, of movement as metaphor, and ultimately of meaning, which in turn functions to evacuate cultural specificity and disguises norm as abstraction.[42] Clearly, meaning is not inherent in any movement, but is always produced by context and interpretation. Thus, even when the argument is that the movement and the choreography have no narrative function, and no valence beyond the immediacy of embodiment, clearly the inevitable signifying power of the dancing body, performed and witnessed repeatedly in the domain of public culture, hence recalling history and reflecting context, creates circuits of "meaning." The ability of the white postmodern choreographers to work with structures based on tasks and random juxtapositions, to play with whimsicality and flux, to resist the dominant paradigms of concert dance, indicates artistic *choices*, and choices of course illuminate what is at stake, that is, the politics of cultural production. It is the locating of these choices in the zone of "neutrality" or "ordinariness," which, while connoting nonnarrative, non-concert dance, also connotes meaninglessness, that obscures their racial and cultural specificity, and effectively positions all choices as equal in the realm of postmodern flattening. It also effects the phenomenological position where it is possible to talk about "the body" without immediately complicating its recognition in terms of cultural, racial, engendered specificities: clearly, however, bodies of color inevitably signify difference in this context, and racial and cultural differences cannot be wished away.

One of the recurring features of another, more recent genre of postmodernism is the heterogeneity of cultural references that seemingly proliferate the global cultural field, invoked through the practice of citation, so that notions of unity of style and genre are disrupted through these references from "other" cultures. Yet, such aesthetic practice, while creating interesting comments on hybridity of cultures, deserves further thought, for often they merely underscore the conditions of access in a postindustrial society marked by the commodification of ethnicities. Moreover, these overt references exist alongside a host of covert influences, which, inevitable part of the diverse worlds we inhabit, are still vital to acknowledge. In reverse, forms and signs of the modern and postmodern as defined by the West, and which have become part of third world cultures, are not matters of such choice, but rather, the effects of processes of economic, political, and cultural domination. Such citation then, along with an apparent celebration of diversity, only masks an unchanged centralization of power. Here, the flattening of meaning under the rubric that movement simply is, movement for its own sake, is often hard to swallow.

A quick example: To a Tamil film song, Mark Morris choreographs *Tamil Film Songs in Stereo* (1983), caricaturing a dancing master (Morris himself) ruthlessly training a young ballerina (Nora Reynolds), who eventually breaks down, using hand gestures to symbolize tears streaming down her face. The score reflects a similar pattern of male master-female disciple relationship. Then, again, in 1984, he choreographed *O Rangasayee* to a recording of the same name by Sri Tyagaraja. Morris danced this piece himself, bare-chested, the soles of his feet and his palms reddened as Indian dancers or women often do using the dye *alta*. In some performances he wore white shorts, while in some others he wore a *dhoti*. It would be silly and paranoid to drop into reactionary and essentialist theories of cultural ownership at this. We all call it postmodern hybridity. We could also, with reference to the second piece, think about the kind of possibilities offered by spaces that are carved out through such partial, and often decorative, invocations of otherness, a consistent theme throughout modern and also postmodern dance history in the West.[43] But I would at least juxtapose it with Deborah Jowitt's comments on Chandralekha's work that I have referred to earlier, celebrating the latter's innovations on traditions: "If artists of her caliber borrow from the West, they borrow primarily the credo of freedom and personal expression," a comment that implies an oppressive and silencing indigenous cultural context into which Western influence breathes liberation.[44] I want to highlight the unevenness in this terrain of global cultures, so that "borrowings" never have equal effect. Morris's references cannot be spoken of in the same vein as the Kerela Kalamandalam's production of *King Lear* in the Kathakali movement idiom: because of colonial histories, we in middle-class India grew up studying and acting Shakespeare, while for Morris the reverse isn't true. It is even vitally different from black ballet choreographer Alonzo King's creating a piece (*Who Dressed You Like a Foreigner?* 1998), inspired by the poetry of Bengali poet Rabindranath Tagore, to a score created and performed by Indian percussion maestro Zakir Hussain, who, like King, is a San Francisco–based artist. Despite postmodern breakdowns, cultural practices and histories form a rugged field, rent with hierarchies and missing links. The question of how things mean is vital here, even though it is seldom acknowledged as such.

"So Yvonne, I was Just Wondering If . . ."

Continuing to think about meaning in dance. The direct relationship of the performed expression and narrative and emotional meaning, or the lack thereof, remind me of *Trio A*, and the deliberate positioning of the dancer away from direct eye contact with the audience. I want to ponder the subtext in the discourse briefly to reflect on the many ideas and influences that were present in the context in which postmodern innovations were spawned. This in order to examine the tacit assumption of self-containment about the creative universe of these early postmodern artists, and to point to some ways in which "other" artistic practices and traditions have been part of the subterranean consciousness of artistic work that seems overtly white. Traveling through India, seeing a lot of dance and apparently thinking constantly about ways of conceptualizing of the performing body and its function as expressive agent in performance, Rainer eventually arrives at an impasse as she encounters again and again in Indian dance and performance modes the investment in the emotive expressivity of movement. From reading her "Indian Journal" it seems that she is constantly thinking through her ideas about meaning and structure, and that these are shifting boundaries, open to redefinition. In fact, some of her questions seem to echo much of my perception of what seems to be problematic in the formulation of the postmodern. Quite taken aback as she reflects on a Kathakali performance she had seen, Rainer, who can hardly be accused of romanticizations of any sort, writes: "But this guy actually projects *emotion* . . . all through extremely small changes in particular parts of his face . . . A chart of human feeling . . . I simply responded kinetically. I haven't experienced kinetic empathy for years."[45] A series of reflections in this tone lead up to the following comments after experiencing a Bharatanatyam performance: "I refuse to believe that my enjoyment of it must be dependent on understanding the meaning. But maybe we in the Western avant-garde are really fooling ourselves in our contempt for that question, 'What does it mean?' "[46]

There is another of Rainer's reflections that calls for attention: her surprise at how meaning and emotion are embodied. I mean to emphasize the slippery connotations of how, in how many different, constantly shifting ways things mean. It seems to me that this devaluing of "meaning" in Western performance avant-garde also often disregards the complex ways in which meaning-making might function in "other" cultural practices where there might often be several variable threads connecting movement to what it signifies. For instance, it is precisely the layers of metaphor in a *mudra* that make it different from American Sign Language—the logic of abstract imagery versus the logic of linear narrative—and that make comparisons of the two, not an uncommon project in the currently popular drive for multiculti, cross-cultural work, deeply problematic. The basic semiotic multiplicity of the *mudra*—the varied *biniyoga* or applications of the hand gestures in different contexts to signify differently—or other elements of *abhinaya*, the dramatic/narrative performance mode, suggests the constant shifts between how each gesture or movement means (elaborating the narrative in an *abhinaya* piece) or does not "mean" in the above sense (marking the abstract aesthetic framework of a *nritta* piece) in the context of each particular piece.[47] There is no direct functionality of meaning here and the possibility of significance and signification are constantly renewed. Again, as an in-depth and contexted reading of gesture in African American street performance, or of Ebonics, will show, meaning often proceeds in parallel or opposing lines, making evident a clash of semantic fields, the encoding of history in linguistic structure, and the politics of claiming the underside and reinvesting it with "different" meaning.

I am trying to point out that meaning-making happens on multiple levels, and if *Trio A* meant nothing specific at one level, it meant many different things at several others. Indeed, Rainer talks about showing the piece at a studio in Delhi to a group of friends, where her host, one Sonar Chand, comments that the piece seems to be about human frustration. What becomes obvious through the pages of her "Indian Journal" is that the question of meaning—how meaning is embodied, performed, and interpreted by the audience—is one of great weight for Rainer. In an extraordinarily poignant section, at the end of an entry about the Kathakali performance, Rainer writes: "The energy in the audience is unbelievable . . . An old toothless man sat next to us both nights, head bundled against the chill, blanket around his shoulders, gaze riveted on the stage, mumbling and chanting to himself. He was really in there. It means more to him than a moment's entertainment and escape from his life. And something other than what opera is to westerners."[48] At another point, she is moved to tears as she visits a temple and writes "how much more interlocking, overlapping are history, everyday life, fact, myth, superstition, daily worship in this country than anything I have known about. In India the earthly and divine are all mixed up together."[49] Elements of the late postmodern pastiche for some, just how things function in a postcolonial society for others . . . In other words, some of the deconstruction of meaning, the radical juxtapositions, the rearrangement and fragmentation of the organizational logic of "meaning" that were part of the postmodern revolution, were already part of the experience of many other peoples positioned on the other side of the spectrum.

I want to recall Rainer's comments on the Kathakali performer one more time. To her, what is amazing is that the performer is actually able to perform an emotional state and arouse emotion in the audience through a set of codified and learned physical movements. Here is a critical moment: Rainer and other postmodern innovators had rejected codified and stylized movement as empty: movement was complete in itself and material for dance. Yet, this highly elaborate and stylized gestural expressivity arouses "kinetic empathy" in her. She obviously does not "understand" the meaning of the gestures on the narrative level, and hence the emotion is not related to the narrative; rather, it is an immediate response to the movement. Here, technique, that had seemed to be the roadblock to achieving process-oriented work, comes to be seen in a different light. Yet, not even Rainer takes this question further to inquire into whether technique and the formalized presentation of the dancing body might, in other contexts, still be connected to other processes of meaning-making, or to examine whether even the early postmodernists were really deploying a different set of skills and techniques in achieving the look of low virtuosity. The adherence to notions of pure motion, which was also posited as transparent, ordinary, and hence accessible to "everybody," was of course broken by later generations of postmodernists, but I think its remnants stand in the way of recognition of choreographers working with specific non-Western movement idioms, even when they are pushing the limits of these idioms, working innovatively with them. The question of meaning comes up again in thinking through the apparent neutrality, and technique-less-ness of the postmoderns, signaling a kind of universality. As if motion can be pure and culturally unspecific.

For me, these conversations around Rainer's *Indian Journal* are significant: they are but one example of the many subtle, unnoticed, ways in which the "other" fed into the creative fire of the postmodern movement and prompted its directional changes. There are other more obvious examples: for example, Ramsay Burt talked about how Rainer had once planned on performing *Trio A* in tap shoes.[50] Again, "Yvonne (Rainer) . . . does a quasi-Kathakali number standing on one leg, gesticulating with rubber-capped fingers."[51] Instead of listing every one of them, however, I want to quote Brenda Dixon-Gottschild who elaborates how the Africanist aesthetic is a "pervasive subtext in postmodern performance," indicating the implications of similar readings with references to Asian and other cultural practices:

> . . . it is naïve to assume it is coincidence that postmodernism and
> Africanist traditional performance share parallel processes. The fact that
> postmodern culture exists inside of, around, and on top of Africanist cul-

tures is a fact of intertextuality, not merely parallel development. The problem is that the chroniclers of postmodern performance have credited only
sources from the European historical avant-garde."[52]

Dixon-Gottschild continues to argue that historians of postmodern dance
have acknowledged Asian inspirations while they have not recognized
Africanist sources at all. While I agree that different communities have
been racialized very differently particularly in the United States, and that
some influences from Asian sources have been acknowledged, many of
them have not been. More importantly, the way in which these have been
thought and written about have only reinforced the modern/West-Tradi-
tion/East binary, implied the static state of these other cultures from Asia,
while their traditions have been recycled to create "new" and radical juxtapositions in a postmodern aesthetic.

Unmarked Spaces

I want to mark the articulation of postmodernism in the fields of Indian
and African American dance through crisscrossing journeys, to read them
as moments of rupture engaged paradoxically in articulating practices
marking continuity: disruption yet suture. Typically, postmodern aesthetics
in these contexts seem to be constituted through continuities, not rejec-
tions, of specific dance/performance traditions that have been reimagined
and reframed, even as such revisioning immediately foregrounds interruptions and dislodgings of continued practices, where the seams show. Such
postmodern practices, marked by a critical distance from unproblematized
notions of "tradition," are also characterized by intensive self-reflexivity and
analysis of the historical constructions of cultural and political practices,
ultimately reaching towards rearticulations of existing relationships from
the perspective of contemporary political, economic, and social realities.
The complex intersection and conflicted interaction of local and global cultural fields comes full circle in the work of artists like Zollar and Chandralekha, exposing the numerous levels of power relationships at work in
the field of cultural production in communities of color and in the third
world.

In his reflections on how postmodernism might be conceptualized,
Fredric Jameson begins by saying that the postmodern consciousness
might not amount to much more than "theorizing its own conditions of
possibility."[53] Indeed, for him, it might best be characterized as a self-
reflexivity turning in on itself to locate, not new worlds in the modernist
fashion, but ruptures, events which, with ripple-effect, make for an undeni-
able break, "shifts and changes in the *representation* of things and of the
way they change."[54] This echoes my earlier reflections on other postmodern

aesthetics, and it also supports my notion that it is indeed such kinds of awareness and investigation that motivate and permeate the formation of alternative aesthetics that, in certain contexts, are best described as post-modern, and radical. On an immediate level, I think of the doubled gaze choreographed in Chandralekha's *Angika,* two sets of audiences, objectify-ing and re-objectifying the female dancer: a section that critiques official narratives of Indian cultural history, as well as national and international spectatorship, from a feminist perspective. Or, the refracted choreography of Zollar's *Self-Portrait,* performing choreographic process, the structure fluctuating between group improvisation and fixed movement, finishing with Zollar endlessly trying out versions of a movement and text sequence, performing rewriting even as she reconceives the notion of a "well-made work." On a broader level, I think about the ways in which these choreogra-phies repeatedly undercut essentialized ideologies, draw attention to passed-over moments in narratives of the past, and position themselves in a politics of defiant hope even as they destabilize past histories. Chan-dralekha's dancers, clearly Indian in body attitude, idiomatic specificities, but busting the typical image, formal and stylistic tenor, and thematic specificities that dominate notions of Indian concert dancers; Zollar's dancers, never relying on monolithic rituals of tradition or essentialized ideas of Africanness, weaving, through an eclectic movement repertoire, contemporary images of black women; both artists choreographing richly political commentary: such practices, intent on their questioning of form and structure, history and convention, and on working out their relation-ships to these paradigms, stage and embody that tracing of breaks and changes in representation that Jameson talks about.

Moreover, this self-reflexivity, the awareness of the conditions of its own possibility, also makes for a re-examination of history and the past in ways that lead to restaging notions of cultural specificities and differences. First of all, the experience of foreign domination and the devaluation of indigenous cultural traditions have spurred strong resistance movements that have in turn fuelled projects, in these communities, of reviving and celebrating older cultural practices that had been marginalized. But there is no simple process of reversing the changes wrought by historical events or of performing an even continuity when, in fact, memory is interrupted by struggles for survival and fraught with erasures. However, because the need of the moment is often understood to be cohesion, verifiability, legitimacy, all of which had been besieged so long, the process of "adequate" narra-tivization often overrides lived knowledges. Typically then, in many soci-eties of color and third world societies with histories of colonization and slavery, the move toward a revival of the content and forms of what might be cast as "originary" aesthetic traditions in that community, without neces-

sarily examining or acknowledging the inevitability of certain centrally constitutive changes in them, characterizes modernist politics. This is no
doubt a recurring phenomenon in communities engrossed in the political
necessities of revival, invested in (re)building national or racial pride, seeking to impart some measure of consistency and continuity to cultural traditions that have been under attack. Yet, these given relationships with the
past do not simply stand uncontested, and different histories of displacement and silencing within "traditions" claiming continuous practice and
validity come to be questioned. Complex and difficult solidarities that have
been engendered by revivalist beliefs, and have, in turn, remarginalized
other groups and politics and led to other "internal" hierarchies, both in
terms of artistic and cultural work, and other sociocultural phenomena,
come to be critiqued. Nationalism, for instance, that was a viable and powerful modality for galvanizing movements for independence and liberation
and moving into modernity, so to speak, now clearly exposes itself as a jingoist and dangerous philosophy. Here, artists often find themselves
inevitably implicated in an examination of whether performances of such
"tradition," charged with the mission of preservation of "culture," often
legitimize power hierarchies and uniformities in the name of cultural
legacy, and of the disjunctions, silencings, and problems that recur when
these "traditions" are re-embodied in vitally different contexts.

The radical cultural politics of the postmodern are here woven from
the recognition of the problems and failures inherent in the forms of the
modern, as well as in what has come to be recognized as traditional.
Awareness of historical necessities, processes and contemporary power
plays emanating from them, and critiques of the same then invigorate the
formal, thematic, and structural concerns of the postmodern aesthetic: the
failure to take up women's questions, the needs of alternative sexualities,
the multiple positioning of identities in the visioning of new democracies;
the unresolved confrontations between what is posited as "tradition" and
what as "modern"; the postcolonial emphasis on the narrativization of a
more or less uniform "national culture," or of racially and ethnically determined cultural directions; these, among others, are vital forces fuelling the
direction of the postmodern. In the attempts to conjure up visions and
images of reimagined pasts and invoke different futures, passing through
the uneven terrain of a present, forms and structures, motion and stillness,
from different locations, find unique resonances, alliances, and reworkings,
and what is refigured as postmodern is more often than not experienced
simultaneously as déjà vu and entirely new and contemporary. It is in such
uncanny juxtapositions, the reworkings of "tradition" through culturally
specific modalities, the reinterpretations of cultural conventions in ways

that compel rethinking of static and essentialized aesthetic categories, that I locate the radical postmodern aesthetic.

Think of Zollar's *Batty Moves*: six black women who back up on us relentlessly, their butts pushing toward us, performing what I have called the "scoot back." Remembrances of objectified and tortured black bodies and the ignominy of the Venus Hottentot meld with ballet vocabularies that are repeatedly dislodged and yet held onto. Feminist reclaimings of black female bodies and sexualities calling on long histories fed by racist mythologies as well as contemporary commodifications of music videos sustained by misogynies, working through reinscribing movements from "traditional" West African dance with an insistence on women's pleasure and play. Chandralekha, advancing deliberately, riding on the back of a man who crawls forward on his hands and knees, mobilizing a pre-Vedic image, and energizing it with a vibrant sense of contemporary politics, in *Angika*. A stone relic from a time prior to written history deployed in contemporary choreography in complex symbology, bypassing goddess images from later times, to indicate the radical need of contemporary women's movements to harness patriarchal power before it destroys life-energies, and possibilities of growth and movement. Importantly also, a woman in a sari, apparently a loaded signifier of "tradition," embodying a call for a radical sexual politics, refusing to be locked into an economy of reproduction and glorified motherhood.

The returned gaze of moments like these, upsetting audience expectations nurtured by mediatized endorsement of hegemonies, and hierarchical narratives of history, read on multiple levels as performances of resistance. They necessarily disturb the possibility of the dancing bodies of women of color being considered the docile bodies of "traditional" knowledge, or anthropological research, or sociocultural testimony, who can be applauded for the richness of the dance they embody, their courage, their talent, and maybe still for the rhythmic complexities and colorful costumes characterizing the dance. They perturb the possibilities of simple interpretations of "tradition" and particularly of patriarchy and heterosexism posing as "tradition." They rework feminist agendas in culturally specific terms, challenging the domination of the conception of a global women's movement by white western agendas. They challenge the audience to articulate layered, nuanced, and different concepts of the radical, the avant-garde, the postmodern edge, where histories of the past and desires and resistances of the present are summoned up to intersect with each other in the same bodies, in complex plays of boundaried segments of time and space. Here, the postmodern is not a focusing on looking for the "new" that overturns a set of cultural practices, a gesture of rebellion in the tradition of Anglo-

American adventurism, but is a constantly renegotiated search, in terms of a politics arrived at through contemporary life situations, through divergent existent or remembered practices that can be reimagined to create meaningful images and commentary. In such work we witness a politics of disruption, intervention, and refiguring, not dismissal. A question asked repeatedly of Chandralekha's work by western critics: yoga dressed up or Bharatanatyam dressed down? Familiar but unfamiliar, difficult to reduce to known categories of movement. Here too, the insistence is on a postmodern that dismantles Americo-centric "universality," and, insisting on its own variability, refigures notions of radical, avant-garde, and postmodern in local terms, with references to the specific incarnations of the modern, the classical, tradition, that form the context.

Not for These Choreographies the Effervescent Body

Talking about the avant-garde artists of the sixties, Sally Banes argues that the concept of the Bakhtinian grotesque body was central to the work of these artists and inspired their tendency to blur the ways in which different genres and defining categories were embodied. In a profoundly insightful discussion, Banes suggests that the body of this avant-garde is dialectical: "always in the state of becoming, [it] includes within it dual states—animal and vegetable, death and birth, childhood and old age."[55] It is also "an anticlassical body": "It is the medium for a cluster of artistic genres that challenge elitist classical representation with their unbridled bodily images . . . a body of carnivalesque performance."[56] Moreover, the boundaries of this body are fluid where artistic forms "harness it to a utopian conception where disparate strata of cosmos, society, and body are unified."[57] Because of all these reasons, the effervescent body is, for Banes, a layered political symbol. Banes goes on to talk about artistic explorations of the "gustatory body" of open orifices, challenging the closed, private notions of the modern body. Moreover, she claims the effervescent body mixes races and genders and thus "ignores the boundaries of sociobiological classifications."[58] But she is quick to point out that though the intention of the work of these artists was quite the opposite of racist, there was a strong element of what she describes as "essentialist positive primitivism" in their attitudes.[59]

I am fascinated by these concepts and wonder how they might be read in the context of postmodern choreographies in alternative contexts. Of course, I do not know that essentialism of any sort can be positive because it shortchanges some part of the equation and inevitably leads to some kind of disempowerment. However, this discussion once again brings up the importance of localized arguments. For most peoples of color, whose bodies were often regarded as ultimately grotesque because of their differing ideas about sexual practices, hygiene, certainly dancing and the like, the sanctity of whose bodily privacy had been ruptured through the violence of lynchings and other atrocities common in colonization and slavery, the abandonment into carnivalesque performance is not necessarily a marker of the postmodern. Moreover, forms of modern in these communities had regulated bodies, particularly dancing bodies, and had strictly defined the limits of the classical dancing body. The postmodern here cannot work though an anti-classical body, but can instead be interpreted as reframing the idea of the dialectical body to intersect the classical with the carnivalesque at moments (as in Zollar's *Batty Moves*), or the classical with the pedestrian (as in Chandralekha's *Sri*), or the ritual with the playful (as in Chandralekha's *Sloka*), the high modern with postmodern looseness (as in Zollar's *Shelter*) the sexual with the spiritual (as in Chandralekha's *Raga*), the rehearsal mode with devised performance (as in Zollar's *Self-Portrait*), in the same bodies, simultaneously. These multivocal bodies, equivocating in their categorical affiliations, trespass the borders that have governed audience expectations in different ways to conjure up dancing bodies of what I have described earlier as overwhelming presence. Such presence, manifested in the returned gaze in the choreographies of these artists, in the intersecting but sharply defined contours of these dancing bodies, in the movement between disruption yet suture, in the multiple layers and sites of presencing, calls for theorization in terms of a clearly defined politics of transgression. The trope of effervescence, of the dissolution of boundaries to create a new chemical substance is not so effective here. The resistance to Euro-Western dominance, aesthetically, conceptually, and politically, disallows such dissolution, and makes instead for a location in cultural specificities even as what these specificities are and look like are constantly refigured. Yet, in the ways in which these resonances of cultural preferences and practices are located, in complex relationships with committed progressive politics (thus different from the modern insistence on essentialized cultural identity), constantly emphasizes mobility, border-crossings, and artistic awareness and deliberate challenging of the sociobiological differences that the white avant-gardists could "ignore."

The work of artists such as Chandralekha and Zollar then beckons to realms beyond the known: their work is post both the "modern" dance of Anglo-America, which drew on the "other" in various ways but most often failed to acknowledge that source of inspiration, and post what was created by choreographers and artists in their own communities during this "modern" period. Moreover, in locating a radical avant-garde that politically, conceptually, and aesthetically, works with indigenous cultural practices, as well as forms of the high concert tradition—ballet, modern, Bharatnatyam, Kathak—and juxtaposes elements of cultural practices with the radical politics generated in a contemporary context, these artists show up the limits of the Euro-American postmodern that has failed to recognize a radical framed in "other" terms. I find that the most apt descriptor for forms and aesthetics created in these modalities a radical postmodern. No doubt there is a sense of periodizing inherent in my conception, but this linearity in the sense of occurring as a response to, or critique of, the modern—understood in that double sense, the Western project, and the response from those peoples implicated in that project as necessary "others"—is only one of the senses of time in such work. I have pointed out that there are multiple relationships to the past and future at work. This is not, however, postmodern eclecticism, but rather necessary intersections of synchronous and diachronous modes to create cultural contexts of depth, without modernist nostalgia. Also, as I have said before, I also want to underline my characterization of these postmoderns through attitude and relationality, because of how they negotiate their positions in relation to any number of factors such as essentialized notions of black dance or Indian dance, dominant notions of purity of form and genre, concepts of tradition, relationship to narrative, in resistance to Euro-American hegemonies, and certainly, in the articulation and embodiment of a radical female subjectivity. So they are not boxed into a temporal frame: the neoclassical modern, local folk traditions, as well as other genres continue to be practiced along with postmodern explorations.

Finally, the politics of location that emerge from such work rework the structure, form, and content of this aesthetic framework, and these revolutionary politics are different from those of the sixties in the United States, but continue the age-old struggles of women, peoples of color, same-sex partners, labor unions, and other marginalized populations, for some notions of hope and excellence. These resistances, reminiscent of these continuities, take different forms because the ways issues are formulated are contemporary and contexted, and they are permeated with a reworking of essentialisms that might have been necessary strategy at some point for liberation struggles, but which can no longer hold a community together. In artistic work, we see this in the search for and consequent reworkings of indigenous cultural practices that can be deployed to articulate contemporary sensibilities, an examination of structures and practices that have come to be problematic in this context. These are aesthetics that emerge under the pressure of politics overlying age-old racial hierarchies with contemporary epidemics like AIDS, forged through difficult conversations about sexuality that have characterized coalition politics in the women's movements, through anxieties about survival and commitment to activist artistic work that does not always make for economic viability, let alone economic success. This radical claiming of the possibilities of reframing worlds in the face of relentless negotiations, open-ended questions, and shifting realities, denying the feel-good solutions of easy nostalgia, failed acknowledgments, or facile dreamings and celebrations, foregrounds the defiant hope that I find energizing this avant-garde of artists of color. The danced images, vital and lived, however, do not promise permanence, alive only in the moment of their embodiment, but the danced hope, while necessarily renegotiated and processual, is defiant in that it assures its endurance and its commitment to a difficult yet brilliant politics. In the end, I want to remember bell hooks talking about photography as a vital engagement for black folk, a project of decolonization: "Using images, we connect ourselves to a recuperative, redemptive memory that enables us to construct radical identities, images of ourselves that transcend the limits of the colonizing eye."[60] Danced images like those that inhabit the works of choreographers like Chandralekha and Zollar, despite their impermanence, have energy and the power of liveness, spirit, and the fiery passion of their creators' politics. They shore up in other but vital ways the project of decolonization, creating aesthetic frameworks that are permeated with an interventionary politics, working not solely in reaction to hegemonic structures, but generating beauty and power that, while creating specific kinds of pleasure and value, resists reinscription into reigning dominant constitutions.

Usha, Chandralekha's *Mahakal*. Photo © Dashrath Patel.

Chandralekha Group, *Mahakal*. Photo © Dashrath Patel.

CHAPTER 5 **The Historic Problem:**
Historicity As Legal Alien

Two women sit cross-legged in stage center facing each other. One bends forward, cups the other's foot in her hands, slowly raises it to place it on her chest and caresses it. The other leans back, allowing that touch to resonate through her chest, as it reaches in a full curving line behind her. Around them dancers perform martial arts sequences: energies sharp and cutting whirl around them evoking memories of war, violence, and destruction. The two women remain enraptured with each other. In a time of war, elsewhere lies a time of love. In the audience, I witness time as moving in multiple layers, as progressing in circular pathways as much as in linear ones, but importantly weighted through our experiencings and personal encounters that imbue it with heights and depths.

Mahakal (Chandralekha, 1995); Program Notes:
"The dance of Time danced by Timelessness"

I am reminded of another moment like this. Three women lying on the floor, their knees flexed out and then in to meet the soles of their feet together, a series of floored mandalas. A male dancer enters the space and begins to climb the long black pole that is placed upstage left, stepping slowly and deliberately on the small rods that emerge from the pole at regular intervals around it, like a winding staircase of thorns wrapped around a huge desert cactus. As he spirals his way up, he occasionally stops, reaches one arm out to the side and swings the outer leg out to strike the open down-facing palm. Now at the height of his ascent, he underlines the curving motif of his winding pathway with a deep arc of his spine backwards to catch the light in his eyes, destabilizing the linearity of his rise upwards, even as he extends the verticality of his climb with the spatial architecture of the women's bodies on the floor. I evidence the spiraling intersecting movement of time-in-space.

"Interim: After the End and Before the Beginning" (Chandralekha, 1995).

Reflections on "Historiography"

Everywhere, projects of constructing historical narratives are often subsumed under Western, Europeanist models of historicizing, dominated by organizing modes such as modernity, development, and other post-Enlightenment structurings of linearity and coherence that have come to be legitimizing factors in any understanding of history. Indeed, as is evident in categorizations and sitings of "primitive" and "tribal" art that continue to plague current understandings of the evolution of dance as a concert art, one might argue that "history" as a category of organizing knowledge has been the Eurowest's attempt to legitimize its putative civilizational superiority. This has made such projects suspect for scholars working from locations that are logistically, discursively, and politically "different." Scholars of the subaltern studies group, in particular, have urged the recognition of dominant models of historicizing as the affect of a "hyperreal" Europe that inevitably obscures alternative voices and modes in historiography.[1] At the same time, scholars such as Dipesh Chakrabarty acknowledge that historical undertakings are unavoidable, but they urge reconceptualizations of history as a contested narrative, where supposed "facts," documented in texts privileged as sources of "truth," grapple with memories and unheard testimonies, where hegemonic logocentricity is dislodged from its position of power and has to engage with oral histories, incomplete memories, myth and other modes and sites of recounting remembered and also reimagined pasts, where the naturalization of choices about what constitutes "historical" material is challenged. This effectively challenges and forces a rethinking of the "universals" that masquerade as history and also govern the supposed historical value of ideas and incidents that constitute our understanding of our pasts. In contesting the thematization of "history" in accordance with grand Europeanist paradigms, such scholarship points to the inevitably incomplete historical narratives that currently exist.

I want to keep in mind the vital rethinkings of notions of structure, validity, and historicity, necessitated by subaltern studies and other recent scholarship as I begin this specific context-setting discussion for the work of Zollar and Chandralekha in an effort to align my project with the concept of "hybrid histories," "contrapuntal narratives" that deliberately coalesce and layer, "necessarily inconstantly and incompletely" the evidence from dancing bodies and historical texts.[2] I am invoking alternative modes of narrating the past in the realm of dance history specifically in order to urge rethinking conventional academic understandings of non-white, non-Western cultural contexts, such that they are not restricted to being studied in terms of Western linear chronological models. In fact, specifically because of the vital oral traditions and modes of direct transmission in several of these cultures, the greater emphasis placed on the practice itself and less on documentation, and other differences in sociocultural values and ethos, the history of dance in "other" cultural contexts is seldom texted in detail according to a chronologically developmental history. In fact, understandings of dance produce interesting critiques of linear time-bound and evolutionary models of historiography. This does not mean, however, that they escape being subsumed in categories generated by Western epistemology and aesthetics; rather, in the absence of validating "texts," and despite the presence of other kinds of evidence, they come to be scripted in an ahistorical "lack." This in turn confirms their location in the notion of unmoving tradition that I talked about earlier.

In invoking some of the terminologies generated by the very histories that I find problematic, specifically in staking a claim for the "postmodern," I have several intentions. First of all, ignoring these categories does not make them less ubiquitous than they are, especially because of the already pervasive organizing metanarratives of modernity and the collusion of history with linear chronology. Moreover, as I have pointed out earlier, as in the history of the modern, there are specific hegemonic investments in keeping the postmodern a limited category, especially in its coalescence with the avant-garde and the radical. This in turn creates the huge black hole of the "ethnic," into which all "other" artistic production is conveniently shoved in the absence of thought-through relationships to categories and marking criteria. Ironically, the logistics of a global market make it almost impossible to avoid these categorizations. The presence of an audience centrally constitutes a "performance," and the gathering of audience members, unless one is willing to work only in nontraditional spaces such as street corners, requires publicity and marketing efforts. It is frequently in passing through these circuits that we all get caught up in standardized (read Eurocentric) categories. I have earlier suggested the possibilities in claiming, as subjects, not covert objects, such categories as the postmodern that continue to signal a radical presence. In fact, given our inevitable implication in these dominant historiographic modes, albeit in negative ways, signifying the "others" of such history, shying away from them only reinforces our location in ahistoricity and timelessness.

To insist on timed and complex understandings for non-Western dance forms, cast as unchanging "traditions" marked by a transhistorical continuity, while recognizing both the multiple ways in which time works and the necessity of reworking the different terms of such narrativizing, offers scope for reading the continuity of shifts and changes in those forms, or in the way relationships to "tradition" are questioned and examined over time. I do not call upon that category of the postmodern in some form of what Anthony Appiah has called "the Naipaul fallacy," but rather to urge a situated yet shifting narrative for cultural production so that we can begin to understand what informs the choices made by contemporary radical choreographers such as Chandralekha and Jawole Willa Jo Zollar, and to place them in a continuum that is marked by disruptions, disturbances, and resistances.[3] Indeed, rather than ignore the power and affective significance of these categories, I would rather take up Dipesh Chakrabarty's charge to "provincialize Europe," insist on localizing the terms and conditions of Eurocentric historiography by reinterpreting them as they are deployed in other contexts.[4]

As I have discussed in the previous chapter, the postmodern is not deployed here in the contexts of Indian and African-American dance, only in the sense of a chronological term. Further, it is largely a classification determined by political foci that are reflected in choices about artistic form and content, and so it is not just an aesthetic category. I use it importantly to indicate locations that distance themselves, despite an obvious relationship, from opaque narratives of history in order to examine the ways in which notions of "stream of tradition" and narratological conventions have operated and determined a time frame characterized as "modern"; to investigate the possibilities of negotiating different relationships both to "tradition" and the forms of the modern in that context; and ultimately to examine the formulation of contemporary artistic practices in these contexts.

In this brief "historical" venture, I will work primarily through late twentieth-century political ferment and the evolution of performance forms of the modern in these contexts. It is interesting to analyze the coalescence of the emergence of "modern" forms in cultural production, particularly in performance, with the development of nationalism and see how in fact they ultimately come to be managed by notions of ethnocultural determinism, which of course is related to agendas of producing unified cultural identities. In their introduction to *The Politics of Culture in the Shadow of Capital*, Lisa Lowe and David Lloyd point out the rich possibilities and contradictions inherent in these historical junctures:

> . . . nationalism invokes tradition in order to assert the antagonism between irreconcilable social and cultural values. For this reason, in fact the moment of anticolonial struggle is generally very productive of "emancipatory" possibilities far in excess of nationalism's own projects . . . But the ultimate fixation of anticolonial nationalism on the state form tends to reproduce the articulation of tradition and modernity by which traditional society requires to be modernized—even if the forms of postcolonial modernity are modified to accommodate a fetishized version of tradition through which a distinct people is to be interpellated by the nation-state. State nationalism then seeks to mask the contradictions that re-emerge between formal political independence and economic dependence (the contradictions of neocolonialism) and to contain the excess of alternatives released by the decolonizing forces of which it was a part.[5]

This relationality is significant: it emphasizes precisely why the forms of "tradition" inscribed on moving female bodies come to be vital signifiers in the articulation of nationalist agendas. And those very moments that, cloaked in high nationalism, generate notions of tradition and culture that are hegemonic, essentialized, yet vital in the anticolonial struggle, also generate the possibilities of their own disruption through gradually emergent practices that I am describing as alternative postmoderns. Such relationality also re-emphasizes the disruption yet suture of these latter modalities, the way in which this meshing of continuity and difference, of the contesting forces of liberation and control, only signals in sharper terms their transgression. In this kind of work the "post" of the postmodern, insisting on a location in cultural specificity, even if understood in shifting terms, still signals a critique of the modes of modernity that have characterized the politics of specific liberation movements that have preceded them, as well as the recurring menace of Western cultural, economic, and political domination. Such projects obviously call for articulations in the manner of history; how that history will be imagined, revisited, or intersected, and how the terms and categories of a hegemonized discipline will be manipulated and realigned is what determines the direction of the radical in the work of these choreographers. Tracing these realigned, refracted directions is the focus of my current project.

Without attempting a dense and fully figured-out narrative, I will work through a series of invocations and some general comments, attempting to dig up what subaltern studies scholar Ranajit Guha has called "the small voices of history."[6] These voices disrupt an official or "statist" history, which, thematizing and evaluating the past according to the specific schema and criteria systematized by ruling authorities, also tends to "forbid any interlocution between us and our past."[7] This version of history—whether it is the story of "Other" cultures forwarded by a Eurocentric center, or the narrative nominated by the postcolonial government of India, or by the leaders of a narrowly conceived Afrocentric nationalism—denies us the plurality and variability of choices about our relationship to the past. To rewrite history then is both "to choose means, in this context, to try and relate to the past by listening to and conversing with the myriad voices in civil society" and specifically to "put the question of agency and instrumentality back in to the picture."[8] These are some of the ideas I want to keep in mind in writing this chapter. Indeed, while the conditions of cultural production in the black American and Indian contexts are totally different, the need to think through the kinds of choices that are and are not available, and the politics in choosing, become increasingly obvious when we consider, for instance, stagings of women's agencies and desires, non-normative sexualities, and performed quests for safe yet public spaces to articulate alternative positionings.

In fact, as will become evident subsequently, an important difference emerges between my argument and the work of scholars such as Chakravorty, who, searching for other sites for historicizing, arrives at spirituality as an alternative modality, but reads spiritual movement primarily in terms of the emotional and psychical workings of faith. Perhaps largely because the enactments on and of the body are at the center of my project, it becomes clear that critiques of Eurocentric historiography must be as much and immediately critical of the ways in which sexuality is conventionally constructed and deployed. For, clearly, Eurocentric categories as well as internalized nationalisms and essentialized identities are sustained importantly by constrictive heteronormative and gendered structurings, and postmodern difference in these alternative contexts is inevitably wrapped up in critiques of these categories. And while search for spirit is at the vital center of the work of these choreographers, obviously the search is articulated as sensual, embodied, desired, and cherished, a dimension that necessarily impacts the narrativizing of history.

Historicizing the Moment

How did artists like Zollar and Chandralekha arrive at the spaces they inhabit? In raising this question my aim is to invoke a specific sense of context through brief if fractured reflections that trace the issues and indicate the kinds of questions that might have helped to direct these choreographers' creative trajectories. First, I want to invoke the figures of women whose shadows hover around the figures of Zollar and Chandralekha and to draw attention to some patterning of history on the bodies of women who dedicated their lives to creating a legitimate space for, and "tradition" of, concert dance, and on whose dancing bodies was forged the history of modern concert dance in India and in black America. On one of the ends of the spectrum stands Balasaraswati, artist from the devadasi lineage, whose Bharatanatyam, suffused with the erotics of performed passion, came to be problematic for the new image of "ancient" tradition enshrined in religious devotion and projected as classical glory;[9] on the other, Rukmini Devi Arundale, daughter of respected Brahmin parents, well-educated, married to Theosophical Society member Lord Arundale, inspired by Annie Besant and others to re-form the "debased" *sadir nac* according to the tenets of the *Natyashastra* and institute it as the classical Bharatnatyam dance style through her Kalakshetra school.[10] Rukmini Devi in effect "classicalized" and de-eroticized the dance practiced by the devadasis, renamed it Bharatnatyam, and effectively cast it as the primary classical dance of an India recovering from the shame and debilitation of years of colonization. On the other side stand two women, whose dancing bodies forged a recognition of the depth and variety of a distinct African American concert dance tradition and highlighted, in tandem, its aesthetic and scholarly contributions: Katherine Dunham, whose choreography was enriched by her research in Haitian and Caribbean dance forms, who ran one of the most successful touring dance companies by any standards, and who now lives in East St. Louis, Illinois, working with underprivileged African American youths; Pearl Primus, anthropologist, choreographer, and dancer, whose research in Africa tapped into the creative fount that continues to inspire so much choreography in America today. Both these women, in their different ways, insisted on connectivity: the links between dance and other sociocultural phenomena, between the practice and scholarship of dance, and between dance in the black diasporas of America and dance in other Africanist cultures.

Of these four women, Ms. Dunham is the only one alive and still continuing to work with dance and education. Their legacies inform and vitalize not only the work of established and mature choreographers like Zollar and Chandralekha, but also young developing artists today. However, I am drawn to Veve Clark's exhortation of her audiences in her introduction to a collection of essays, interviews, correspondence, and writings by and on Katherine Dunham. Talking about the activism that continues to characterize Dunham's work, and her primary reputation as a dancer/choreographer pioneer, Clark urges, "Dance people, the reverence you show her must continue, but in the present tense, for Dunham *is*. She energizes and plans strategy; she smiles and makes others laugh in East St. Louis, Port-au-Prince, wherever she travels or sends emissaries on her behalf."[11] And I wonder if—even as the technical innovations and choreographic legacies of Dunham, Primus, and Rukmini Devi have been somewhat institutionalized and continue to be studied, even as Bala's plastic dance was documented on celluloid by famous filmmaker Satyajit Ray as national treasure—these women, whose bodies literally bridged the gaps between an era they put behind them and the new one they ushered in, seem to have been incorporated into the annals of history in ways that have petrified them in the past and that constrict current understandings of them from various perspectives?

Clark's comments also draw me to think about the little-acknowledged connection between dance and politics, the minimizing of the deep political impact of the work of these women in the field of cultural production. I remember the large stone image of Rukmini Devi at the entrance to her school, Kalakshetra, in a meditative pose, garlanded, perfectly embodying notions of the Great Mother that patriarchal circuits later inducted her into. At least, it seems important to underline that all of these women, cultural leaders, were caught up in the specific complexities of their context and were responding or reacting to the typical politics of "modernizing" communities, especially in the connections they were seeking to locatable origins, though of course they were positioned differently, even oppositionally within that framework. Bala, for instance, was marginalized in the modernist struggle for a respectable national culture while Rukmini Devi was enshrined in the legitimacy conferred by the "classicism" she designed, but for both, the burning questions were about authenticity and legitimacy in terms set up by nationalist politics.

Yet, if we pay attention to Clark's remarks, there seems to be the sense that despite lack of adequate histories about these women and their work there is a general satisfaction with their images as consolidators of "tradition," albeit from different takes, as modernist pioneers, such that investigations into the complex politics that foregrounded them in particular ways, and interpretations of how their work meant and means through changing contexts, get much less than the attention they deserve.[12] I am reminded of Chakrabarty's warnings about the functions of a modernist and Western model of historical narrativization, which replays and consolidates all of the hegemonies in place in the regulated functioning of that society. Given modernist beliefs about "tradition" and "revival," for instance, and the typical nationalist thinking about these issues—the tradition-holder as matriarch—do we not need to ask how these women managed their sexualities and desires in resistance to, or in compliance with, the demands placed upon them? Of course, these issues came into sharp and specific focus in the Indian situation, where state management of female sexuality and the yoking of necessary chastity with the staging of "tradition" were central in the intense conflict between Rukmini Devi and Bala. But these anxieties were continuous in both historical contexts: we know for instance, that many audiences were puzzled by what they perceived as the opposition between the rich sexuality of Dunham's pieces and her vocation as "serious" anthropologist, and that censors bothered her constantly about the explicit sexuality of several of her pieces. At the same time, especially in her work in Hollywood and in the entertainment art genre, she had to constantly guard against attempts to portray her and her dancers as sexual objects of a dominant gaze, embodying and performing seduction. While these questions are being brought up within the small and eclectic field of dance research primarily, many others remain about the ways in which they impact historical narratology generally.

I also want to insert an apologia for mentioning only four of the several figures who have worked on the modernist project of recuperation, of constructing some notion of tradition and of a deliverable past on the concert stage. At any rate, my invocation has two prime purposes. One is to indicate the constancy of cultural activism that has characterized the dance field in these communities, how dance has continuously been a key signifier in the politics of the time, and how this work has been carried out largely, though not exclusively, on the bodies of women. This, in turn, suggests the legacy attendant upon the bodies of contemporary dancers and choreographers in these contexts. Another purpose is to emphasize the necessary project of translation that is implicit in the work of these women, embodying the transitions necessary in the shift from a vernacular mode to a concert stage mode. What they embody is a crucial conversation, admittedly interrupted at points and moving through subterranean routes of retention and memory, staging a past, if an imagined one, to validate a present. They stand as prime links in histories where the modern recasts the traditional, and the postmodern travels through the modern and the vernacular and engages them in a bricolage with the contemporary. Both Chandralekha and Jawole, in their own ways, continue the pattern we see practiced by these women: they weave elaborate tapestries, drawing on the cultural practices that form their ground of "tradition" even as they envision different embodiments of them. This invocation then puts in clearer perspective the very different kind of negotiations choreographers like Chandralekha and Zollar are engaged in, how their work continues, with signal differences, the project launched by these pioneers, and how it disrupts some of the ideological premises of their predecessors while recognizing that these legacies inflect, in particular ways, how and what choices are available in the present—all of which complicates a vertical notion of lineage.

Arrested Histories and the Stakes of Postcolonial Criticism

It is problematic then to institute the pathways etched out by these pioneers as generalized and necessary models, as having charted pathways that validate and authenticate. And this is often how processes of mainstreaming work, effectively limiting the interpretive possibilities of creative projects and critical examinations of artists of later generations who, while respectful of the work of these women, are working in different ways. However, they often find their work being understood *primarily* in terms of the paradigms of artistic work established by these forerunners.[13] Specifically, Zollar's work is inspired by the anthropological approaches and artistic styles of Primus and Dunham, the technique formalized by Dunham, the choreographic practice of melding African American experience with Africanist dance material familiarized by Primus. At the same time, despite apparent similarities, differing politics and contexts create different choreographic methodologies: *Shango* (Dunham, 1945), for instance, is vitally different from *Nyabinghi Dreamtime* (Zollar, 1994). Both take off from anthropological research and set the choreography in a context of ritual. But while in *Shango*, there is a gesture towards some kind of "truth," accuracy of representation, clearly a necessary methodology at that historical point when black dance seemed to be underwritten by an educational mission, in *Nyabinghi Dreamtime*, inspired by the Rastafarian tradition, which itself is a culture of protest, Zollar does not dramatize a certain Rastafarian ceremony. In other words, though it is based on substantial research about the Rastafarian traditions, it is not an "ethnographic" piece, recording the alternative religious practices of a particular sect: it does not draw on the expected sequence of any ritual from this tradition. Instead, based on that idea of protest and of creating an alternative channel of communion and community-based spiritual experiences and some of the symbology of that practice, Zollar creates an abstraction of the themes celebrated in that tradition combined with her personal beliefs. The various cultural-artistic forms that have developed around religious ceremony are integrated, not just to inspire content, but to contribute elements of form and organizational principle, and to bring to the work a sense of renewal and joy valued by the community.

In this, it really completely belies Deborah Jowitt's comments about it, which seem particularly imperceptive when read in conjunction with the program notes that describe the piece. Jowitt complains about Zollar and her composer-collaborator Junior "Gabu" Wedderburn's "noncommittal approach to a Jamaican Rastafarian rite."[14] For her, "the treatment is reminiscent of Katherine Dunham's theatricalized rituals (for example, *Shango*)."[15] It is not that anything would be amiss if the previous statement were true, but as I have pointed out, in fact, it is not. Jowitt fixates on some of the points of the piece and stereotypes them as markers of a certain kind of theatricalization: "Here is the silver cloth with candles and ceremonial objects, the kneeling 'lost sister' . . . the powerful priestess lashing branches around, the celebrants singing and dancing and crying out," all of which can only be elements in a scenario familiar to her.[16] What Jowitt does not see is the avant-garde structuring of the piece, how these elements are used to set up its ritualistic mode. The piece is choreographed from abstracting the key ideas in the ideology of protest and alternative spirituality that mark the Rastafarian tradition, and it is based on notions of access to and alignment with "other" cultures that are substantially different from those that underlie *Shango*. The program notes, succinct but direct, make the point:

> *Nyabinghi* is a ceremony of dancing, drumming, and singing from the Rastafarian traditions that lasts from three to twenty-one days.
>
> *Rastafar* is a way of life, a political movement based in protests

and resistance. The Rastafari movement incorporates teachings from the old testament into their traditions.

Dreamtime is our place of visioning where the world is sung into existence and the different spiritual traditions of the African diaspora meet and merge.

Babylon is the force that has colonized and enslaved people for 400 years and still counting.

Zion is that place of remembrance of freedom and liberation that exists in our hearts and minds. The dream of its existence will never die.[17]

These notes emphasize the connection between the struggles of black peoples in different parts of the world and between the different African diasporas through a shared politics of resistance, not through a finding of roots, or origins. In both Dunham and Zollar, then, the point is about connection but the modality is different, reflecting the specific different historical necessities of the moment.

There is also a deliberate attempt to move the piece away from a sense of spectacle, or the sense of a "tradition-on-display" that was a natural corollary of Dunham's mission to uncover the diverse premises of black dance. *Nyabinghi Dreamtime*, on the other hand, works to dismantle the sense of a performance event: it begins even as the audience is filtering in and the auditorium lights are still on. The priestess walks in from stage right and places a long strip of cloth on the floor close to the scrim on stage left corner. She moves on and off stage bringing lighted lamps and placing them in a line on the cloth. She then brings out another woman, clearly afflicted and in need of some kind of blessing. The priestess's arms are wrapped protectively around the shoulders of the suffering woman and she supports her unsteady movement as they walk diagonally across the stage to the downstage left corner. The priestess helps the other woman, whose head still droops forward, to sit on the floor on folded knees, and then she walks back off the stage. Finally, she returns to stand before the lighted arrangement, holding palm leaves in both hands and waving them, her back still toward the audience.

It is only now that the lights go out: when they come back on, the ensemble is on the fully lit stage and the piece continues its beginning. It is important that the prefatory moments of the piece happen relatively inconspicuously, outside of the conventions that govern the performance of a dance piece. While the artifice of performance cannot be denied, it is diffused: the priestess inaugurates the piece without drawing attention to it with the aid of lights and a silent house. The audience members are gradually wooed into the piece as they begin to notice her. The choice is interesting and effective: the "high" ritualistic mode that marks the beginning is mediated by the low-key presentation, the audience is hushed into silence and attention, drawn into what it is witnessing, not switched into watchfulness by the parting of curtains and the coming up of stage lights. In contrasting these two works my intention is not to upstage one in favor of another, but to establish the different needs of the two different choreographers situated at different points in a historical continuum and to highlight the movement in the choreographic practices of black artists in recent times.

Chandralekha, on the other hand, went to Rukmini Devi's school, Kalakshetra, in search of her dancers—rigorously trained and technically strong—yet, through these dancers she brought back into the dance eroticism, something that Balasaraswati had lamented the passing of, though of course in Chandralekha's imagination it is conceptualized and embodied totally differently from Balasarawati's. While the devadasi repertoire is dominated by the exposition of heterosexual love where female sexuality is elaborated and performed strictly in relationship to male sexual love, the inevitable reciprocity of male-female and of love and sexuality is absent in Chandralekha's work. Here, while male-female sexual complementarity is often staged in striking terms, the focus is always on sexuality, and particularly female sexuality, as a vital aspect of self-realization and spiritual awakening. In Chandralekha's case, differently from Zollar's, it is the inability of critics to see how she has distilled and brought into interaction the legacies created by these two women, and then forged a different direction for her own work, that makes them often respond to her work as the product of "Westernization."

I have prefaced my exploration of the historical context with reminders of these remarkable women and their work in order to suggest, among other things, that these histories, while caught up in patriarchal agendas and often dominated by male nationalist leadership, are nevertheless largely women-centered: populated by female figures who are crucial as dancers, choreographers, characters in pieces, in effecting the historical transitions that indeed constitute history. However, it is the transformation of such women-centered work into work fired with a politics of radical local feminisms in relation to the same nexus of aesthetic and political issues that marks for me one of the ways of passage from modern to postmodern aesthetics in this context. While the former enables the latter, it does not make it inevitable; so while the context is vital in understanding and appreciating the works of these artists, the pathways they have traced must go to their credit.

I have not attempted to structure evenly the following sections discussing the Indian and African American situations. Rather, I have responded to the different needs and issues inherent in each; for instance, while there are some texts that trace the historical development of black concert dance in America over the last hundred and fifty years, there is little such work in the classical dance forms in India. In both cases, however, I have attempted to refer to erasures, and to sound a deliberate reminder of historical aspects that are less documented and less known generally, in order to highlight the ways in which Chandralekha and Zollar have engaged with these legacies or intervened into them. It is also my intention, in this chapter, to render uneven the surface of existing, seemingly seamless histories, in order to highlight events and moments in this narrative.

Painful Transitions, Devadasi to Concert Stage Diva
The history of the Indian classical dance forms in the colonial era is troubled by erasures, largely because of the stigma that came to be attached to the dancers, whose embodied knowledge of the traditions had kept alive the dance from generation to generation. The devadasis, literally translated as servants of god, were women dedicated to the service of the deities in the temples, a long-standing practice. They were trained in the arts from an early age and married generally to a male deity whom they served through various means, among which was singing and dancing before his image. On the one hand, because they were his brides, their performances were expositions of their love and desire, spiritual and physical; on the other, as women dancing before god, their performances were devotional offerings, and there was no conflict between the two. Attached to the temple, the devadasis received the patronage of the Hindu, and sometimes the Muslim/Mughal rulers of India, and were often granted land endowments to support them in their old age. They were also described as "nityasumangali," forever brides, for their husbands could never die, and their presence was regarded as auspicious at many important social ceremonies. The devadasis, however, were clearly perceived as living on the fringes of society, in particular because of the sexual freedom granted them: one of the ways of communicating with their lord was through his representatives, the king, the royalty, the temple priests, with whom they could, and were often forced to, have unlimited sexual encounters. Even later, when they came to be regarded more as courtesans, dancing for the king and royalty at court, the devadasis remained paradoxically located both at the center of society, as brides of god, and no temple or social ceremony was complete without their presence, and at the margins, mistresses of the royalty. Here, I am referring to a valuable nexus of research that has been documented in detail by scholars such as Amrit Srinivasan, Saskia Kersenboom-Story,

Avanthi Meduri, and others, both in order to provide a context for my readings, and to situate my take on what constitutes the "modern" in Indian dance. In order not to detract from the issues at hand, I will work with broad strokes, admittedly generalizing some aspects of a finely diversified scenario. Moreover, while this history is more or less specific to Bharatnatyam, one of the first forms to be revived, renamed, and claimed as a "classical dance," this pattern is generally true of several of the major dance forms of Indian concert dance today.[18]

With the establishment of the British Raj in India, the so-called secular colonial government discontinued any support to the temples and the devadasis were suddenly left without any income. These women, who could hardly find their way back into a more-or-less strictly regulated social system, were often forced to earn their living through prostitution. The British administrators had already complained bitterly about the indecent and lascivious dancing of the native "nautch girls" and they were seriously disturbed by the increasing sexual encounters between such native women and British officers.[19] The Bengal District Gazetteer of 1878 reported the words of an indignant British civil servant, William Ward Hunter (1872), regarding the dancers of the Jagannath temple at Puri, Orissa: "Indecent ceremonies disgraced the ritual, and dancing-girls with rolling eyes put the modest worshipper to the blush . . . The baser features of a worship which aims at a sensuous realization of God appears in a band of prostitutes who sing before the image . . . In the pillared halls, a choir of dancing-girls enliven the idols' repast by their airy gyrations."[20] Reportedly, red light areas sprang up around British encampments in great numbers. In 1864, the colonial government devised a way of establishing some measure of control over this situation: they passed the Contagious Diseases Act whereby prostitutes were required to be registered and examined medically. Many women committed suicide in frustration at police harassment at this time.[21] By this one stroke of pen, the devadasis in whose bodies the dance had lived, the nautch girls, and courtesans, who had different levels of training in the arts, were all reductively categorized as prostitutes only, supposedly lacking both decency and morals. From that point on, history usually referred to these dancing women primarily in this negative light, delegitimizing their artistry, without simultaneously theorizing that without any form of support from the state, hounded by daily worries of survival, it was hardly possible for these women to continue to practice their art with the kind of attention and dedication that earlier characterized their practice.

The dance gained prominence only years later, during the cultural revivalist movement of the 1940s, when the sculptors of modern India realized that here indeed was great wealth of cultural practices which should be "revived" and celebrated in the project of reconstructing India's grand culture, a project influenced by the Western Orientalist scholars of the nineteenth century. The influence of theosophical thought, which can be traced in the philosophical base of the Kalakshetra College of Dance and Music established in Madras in 1936, no doubt entered this arena through the advice and guidance given by Annie Besant and Lord Arundale to Rukmini Devi, the architect of modern Bharatnatyam. Dislodged from the practices of the devadasis, the dance was reborn as classical art form located on the proscenium stage, when, in 1947, after a long drawn-out anti-nautch struggle, it became illegal to dance in the temple. Concomitantly, the secular government of independent India announced its support of this "classical" dance as age-old "tradition" reincarnated as concert stage forms.

Modernity was caught up, in the Indian situation, with the struggle of discovering "Indianness"—the notion of essential characteristics of a nation brought into being on the bodies of continuous but separate kingdoms united under the banner of the British domain and modeled on the European concept of nationhood. Modernity was also about recovering from a public failure, the revival of national self-esteem that had been stunted and disfigured during the struggles of the colonial era and the ensuing fight for freedom. This was a moment of national self-consciousness, birthed in the grand proclamation that India was indeed an independent nation and needed to reassert its own cultural legacies. It was also a moment of political amnesia and utopianism where the crafters of modern India did not come to terms with the fact that the "Indianness" they were seeking to project as part of the "national" identity was inevitably entangled in an ambivalent relationship with the once-colonizer, and would inevitably come to be contested, as the unfinished negotiations and enforced silences upon which this uniformity was built fought their way to voice.

Modernism thus evidenced itself in the "revival" of the classical dance, infused it with a large degree of the Europeanist Puritan thought that had become part of the mindset of the English-educated Indian intelligentsia. The dance was transferred from the precincts of the temple to the proscenium stage without acknowledging that it was predicated in sociocultural and religious beliefs that were at odds with the structure of this modern performance space, the site of commercially packaged stagings of "culture." Primarily Bharatnatyam, then the other dance forms following that model, were now restructured in keeping with a modernist uniformity: they were organized according to the tenets of "classical" performance delineated in the *Natyashastra* and other age-old scriptures of performance, and in terms of a developmental hierarchy leading up to a fully evolved repertoire, and could now be held to be truly representative of the rich "classical" performance traditions of India. Most importantly though, the slurs of sexual impropriety cast on the devadasis, which seemed to pollute the dance they performed, could now be wiped away in these new Brahminized forms.[22] The reincarnated form of *sadir nac*, Bharatnatyam, removed itself from the traditional belief in an embodied spirituality, where human love for the divine was expressed through the metaphor of sexual union, and from other erotic themes that were the staple of the courtesan repertoire. Instead of being based in *sringara rasa*, the erotic mood, then, where the focus was on various expositions of love and lovemaking, the dance form came to be based almost exclusively in *bhakti rasa*, the devotional mood, which distanced it from its previous associations with sexual desire and embodied spiritual longing.

This resituation, projected as continuity, is thus in fact based on a rupture in the premises and functionality of the dance forms. It marks the site of a disjunction between temple and court dance forms, predicated on an articulation of the sensual-spiritual and part of a lifestyle that received royal patronage, and concert dance forms based on a performance of religiosity and its packaging as a consumer item, a commercially viable mode of entertainment as well as high culture. This is evident in the following well-known anecdote from the 1960s: when Balasaraswati (a descendant of the devadasi lineage) wanted to dedicate her art to Lord Muruga before a performance, she was confronted with a government injunction that had foreclosed the possibility of her practice and faith and that of many such women who truly believed they were the brides of the deity and danced for and to him. By default, the government, acting as culture broker here, indicated that her spiritual fervor could only be reserved for the concert stage. Since dancing in the temple was now forbidden by law, Balasaraswati had to engage in all kinds of subterfuge in order to send the priest out of the temple grounds on some pretext so that she could dance a short prayer before the deity.[23] The question of "faith" has lost its importance in today's secular market where the dancer is part of a fiercely competitive professional circuit, and its performance is more or less ritualized, but the formal shifts in the dance from a form predicated upon the articulation of faith and passion to one concerned more with abstractions of line, classicism, and state-sanctioned religiosity are virtually unaddressed. An important pillar in the modernizing project of India, the dance forms are projected as continuous forms of tradition, cleansed from the degradation that accrued to them through the sexual excesses of the devadasis, and supposedly reflecting the glory that once characterized them, resuscitated through the efforts of the cultural leaders of modern India.

Following the model of Bharatanatyam, other styles such as Kuchipudi and Odissi were subsequently reorganized in the format that was followed in organizing the Bharatanatyam repertoire in terms of an evening-length performance, in order to legitimize their claims for "classicism" and prestige. This rush to adhere to some given notions of classicism based on the *Natyashastra*, which was cast as having pan-Indian relevance, subsequently resulted in the minimizing of the regional and culturally specific aesthetics that had characterized these forms. The different levels of formality, varying organization and goals of the plethora of cultural practices in India, reflected in loose groupings of these forms as *desi* or *margi*, were reified and hardened with the mistranslation of the above descriptors as "classical" and "folk," with their inevitable implications of high and low art. Inevitably also, these categories remained messy, unable to cover up overlaps, with several forms demanding categorization as at least "semi-classical." These, of course, are part of the slippery negotiations of a postcolonial culture seeking to develop its own, often problematically uniform, identity, and while I must bring these politics to the fore in this discussion, I do so without lament or nostalgia for an "unadulterated" past, if there were indeed any such discernible moment. Indeed, it is well known that at the time of the cultural revivalism, in the 1930s and 1940s, the repertoire of much of these dance forms was greatly diminished and the technique rent with gaps. It is well known, for instance, that in the 1950s the surviving Odissi repertoire—today a rich "legacy," however contemporary, and lasting at least an hour and a half even for the basic concert format—was no more than fifteen minutes long. What I do want to insist on, though, is a consideration of these forms as living practices, *neoclassical* forms reconstructed in keeping with a modern aesthetic, and draw attention to the aesthetic and philosophical shifts and slippages that accompany their reformulation as concert stage forms. I also want to keep in mind that the colonial apparatus, as it regulated gender and sexuality, also instituted new forms of temporality that often clash with current projects of "retrieval" and render them problematic, if not utopian. Finally, I want to draw attention to the high stakes in upholding ideas of classicism and tradition, and the to manipulations of power inevitable in the intertwining of cultural and national agendas.

What might be seen as the modern dance of India, or the dance of modern India, then, is really primarily the neoclassical dance, though in keeping with the projected continuous legacy of these dances they are understood to be "classical." And in the official narratives of culture, the "classical" made for much more respect than what came to be designated as the folk and semi-classical forms, and more contemporary forms imagined from these genres by pioneers such as Rabindranath Tagore and Uday Shankar. This neoclassical dance, embodied for the most part by female dancers, beautifully adorned with flowers and shining jewels, and embraced warmly by many upper- and middle-class women of post-independence India as a socially sanctioned artistic mode, worked effectively in

the Indian government's tacitly implemented cultural policy of moderniza-
tion-without-westernization, where the female body came to be tacitly
scripted as the reservoir of "tradition." Indeed, in order to create a national
cultural identity that could inspire and encourage, a link had to be created
to the "glorious" past, a link that the terrible experience of British rule had
apparently not been able to sever. The ringing bells on the ankles of the
classical dancer creating marvelous rhythms, the splendor of her costumes
and jewels, the poses she created resembling the temple sculptures,
seemed to imply that the divine *apsara* was still incarnate in the modern
classical dancer.[24] The history of disjunction could be forgotten, at least
momentarily, as she recreated the temple art on the proscenium stage, no
longer reserved for the viewing pleasure of a select few, but open to all who
could purchase tickets for the show. In fact, her presence, which resonated
with "age-old" artistic excellence, sculpted in idealized embodiments of
femininity, was necessary to hold on to "Indianness" while the nation itself
marched toward the modernization spelled out by the Euro-American West.

I have laid out this argument largely in terms of a female subjectivity
deliberately, though there were several male exponents of these classical
forms who were then at the forefront of both the revival and continuing celebration of dance in India, largely because dance came to be perceived as a
female space, one also populated primarily by female dancers at this time.
This despite philosopher Ananda Coomaraswamy's famous treatise, *The
Dance of Shiva,* a text that elaborated the idealized premises of Indian dance
for Western audiences for the first time, albeit in terms heavily influenced
by an Orientalist rhetoric, a text which also reinforced the mythologization
of origins through the foundational philosophy of Shiva as Nataraja, Lord of
the dance. Interestingly, when one of the strongest supporters of the dance,
a leader of the resistance against the anti-nautch movement, E. Krishna
Iyer, Brahmin by accident of birth and lawyer by profession, decided to
prove his point about the richness of the Bharatanatyam form by demonstrating it in a public performance, he appeared in drag. Cross-dressing is
by no means uncommon in Indian performance traditions, but this event
had unique significance in that his announced female persona served to
legitimize the taking on of dance as a not-so-disreputable career by women
of upper and middle classes.

In this context, postmodern performance comes to be characterized by
a coming to terms with the difficult legacy of colonial experience and the
managed double-talk of postcolonial politics, and by repeated questionings
of projected "originary" moments, of the investment in the legitimating
power of classicism and tradition, and of the slippery boundaries of that
very "national" culture that the builders of modern India had sought to consolidate. There is also the acknowledgment of disjunction between the rhet-

oric about the avowed philosophical base and aesthetic context of the neo-classical dance forms, and the logistics of its current staging and propagation, contexts that seemed unable to converse with each other. Certainly, in my generation, there were many of us who were caught in this difficult dichotomy: beautiful and deeply spiritual as we found these dance forms, in which we could submerge ourselves, they were being increasingly co-opted by capitalist commodification, and we were disturbed by our inability to situate these experiences in the middle- and working-class worlds in which we lived. We found it difficult to dance invariably about the ideal heterosexual love of divine partners like Radha and Krishna, however metaphorical, after we had just participated in a street play about domestic violence, especially when we knew that the beauty of these forms also covered many violences, certainly those rent upon the historical body of the devadasi. Caught up in the immense disparity between the two extremes, groping for some unknown notion of a resistant and differential aesthetic, our dance was fraught with contestation.

As I think about the popular and governmental endorsement, at both national and global levels, of specific forms as national cultural signifiers, I am repeatedly reminded of Frantz Fanon's thoughts about the problems that might be inherent in a postcolonial society's attempt to create "national" art forms. In *The Wretched of the Earth*, Fanon writes that artists aiming to create such national works of art imprison themselves "in a stereotyped reproduction of details . . . these people forget that the forms of thought and what it feeds on, together with the modern techniques of information, language and dress, have dialectically reorganized the people's intelligences and that the constant principles which acted as safeguards during the colonial period are now undergoing extremely radical changes."[25] For Fanon, the insistence on denying the processes of change and on cocooning cultural traditions in a fabricated net of uninterrupted continuity is a "demonstration of nationality . . . which is a throw-back to the laws of inertia. There is no taking of the offensive and no re-defining of relationships. There is simply a concentration on the hard core of culture which is becoming more and more shriveled up, inert and empty."[26] Fanon's words provide insightful commentary on the fraught debates between classical purist and experimental artist camps in India, especially in the field of dance, where contemporary work seems to threaten "tradition" and signal the onset of full-fledged "westernization." On the other hand, it is that dialectical reorganization of intelligences and sensibilities that Fanon talks about, as well as lived logistics, that I believe the postmodern in these situations recognizes and responds to.

Interestingly, this classic text of decolonization was recalled recently in the first International Conference on Bharatnatyam in the United States

Shaji John and Tishani Doshi, Chadralekha's *Sharira*. Photo © Sadanand Menon.

held in Chicago from September 6–9, 2001. Collaboratively organized by Natya Dance Theatre and the Dance Center of Columbia College, the star-studded conference brought together many celebrities in the field of Indian dance from different parts of the world, dancers, choreographers, and scholars. At a panel discussion focused on the performance of *Sharira*, choreographed by Chandralekha, an audience member asked the former a question that triggered a series of exchanges ridden with anxieties: Where is the Bharatnatyam in your choreography? In the ensuing discussion, the question was picked up by famous exponent of Bharatnatyam, Malavika Sarukkai, while others, including myself, tried to argue that while the ostensible characteristics of Bharatnatyam were not obvious in the work, the core of the idiom—its groundedness, energy, notions of bodily architecture—was certainly the abstracted formal qualities of that dance style. The discussion reached a frenetic pitch soon with questions about what indeed could be given the name Bharatnatyam. Finally, Sadanand Menon, cultural critic, invoked Jean Paul Sartre's introduction to *Wretched of the Earth*, where the latter says that while France was once the name of a nation, it had now become the name of a nervous disease. Menon recalled the nerve-wracking procedures most delegates from India had had to go through in obtaining visas in order to attend this conference: long lines at the United States Consulate in Indian cities, arbitrary decisions, less-than-polite reception. Paralleling Sartre's remarks to this experience, he said "Bharatnatyam too was once the name of a dance form, let it not become the name of a paranoia, where we have to show our visas and passports in order to enter its realms."[27] His incisive commentary points once again to the conflicts at the heart of cultural forms governed in their staging through the tumultuous debates in a postcolonial society, especially one that has chosen to capitalize on hierarchies of Nation and Tradition in negotiating its identity in the global cultural market.

Here, it is instructive to recall Richard Shechner's comments on restored traditions, where he cites the case of Indian Bharatnatyam as a typical instance. For Schechner, restorations need not be "exploitations. Sometimes they are arranged with such care that after a while the restored behavior heals into its presumptive past and its present cultural context like well-grafted skin. In such cases a 'tradition' is rapidly established and judgments about authenticity are hard to make."[28] I can only agree partially with Schechner: indeed, Bharatnatyam, and some of the other classical dance traditions that were "restored" or "revived" in modern India have seemingly fallen back into their historical place in the continuum of long traditions. Questions about their continuity or "authenticity" are not so much contested because clearly these are not totally manufactured or "invented" traditions, but do have substantial past histories and legacies. However, what Schechner does not realize and what I have tried to emphasize is what is keenly obvious in the dancing body—the graft shows, and the tears and wounds of erasure and restoration, the pain and suppressed violence in the troubled history of the devadasi's dance, the adjustments of the postcolonial condition, do not really heal perfectly. Today's dancer of these neoclassical forms inherits a legacy where beauty and magnificence are inextricably entangled with fractures, painful memories, and unacknowledged disjunctions. The postmodernism of Chandralekha's work lies, in the most rudimentary analysis, in her acknowledgment of this unhealing, her willingness to deconstruct the power that has come to accrue to the idealized classical dancing body as cultural-political signifier, and to re-examine its construction through time. In this, she also recognizes the necessarily muddied relationship to the past, first by distancing herself from this restored tradition where it did not work for her, and then by reaching to various overlapping indigenous cultural practices through diverse movement systems, that both create a context of depth and allow for the chiseling of a different version of this dance idiom.

Painful Transitions, Repeatedly Recreating the Magic Circle of the Dance

There is now a more substantial body of historical documentation of African American dance than there is of Indian dance, so there is really no need to repeat that scholarship. Instead, in this section, I want to work through some of the issues in that scholarship, analyzing and interpreting some of the trajectories and patterns traced, and draw out some of the silences even in these histories. The narrative of African American concert dance coming into its own charts a trajectory of repeated disruptions and unremitting reachings towards cultural continuity, of the dancing body as a record of repeated interruptions and retentions. This pattern of attempting to build connections across disturbed and broken continuities through dance is inaugurated early in African American cultural history. This rejection of a linear movement both in history and in the life of the community and the insistence on reconnection and circularity could be argued to reflect what Sterling Stuckey has described as the "circle of culture," whose use was "so consistent and profound in slavery that one could argue that it was what gave form and meaning to black religion and art."[29] Stuckey also points out that enslaved Africans from different countries adopted this formal and ritual convention common in several Central and West African cultures despite their ethnic differences, as a dominant configuration in spiritual and cultural expression, which functioned as one of the means for them to achieve oneness in America.

The practice of Africanist dance traditions among the enslaved Africans was repeatedly forbidden by the managers and owners of the plantations, who refused to allow any practices or entertainment that they ostensibly regarded as potentially inflammatory, licentious, or threatening. Yet they could hardly contain the creative spirit of their African captives who repeatedly invented new modes of dancing that still kept within the increasingly stringent injunctions issued. Dancing and creating dances was a way for these enslaved men and women to remain in touch with the cultural fabric that had been an integral part of their lives, and they continuously reinvented these forms in order to overcome the prohibitions that were placed upon their dancing by the slave masters. At the same time, as Dixon-Gottschild has suggested, subliminally and perhaps unknown to them, the whites were absorbing the very iconic forms of the African cultures that they declared they abhorred. These manifest themselves in the midst of and intertwined with white mainstream cultural forms, creating the uniquely diasporic fabric of American culture.

This urge toward recovery and retention of cultural specificities, marking itself in terms of a sharp "difference" to hegemonic aesthetic norms, becomes a specific direction shaping the development of the "modernist" phase of black dance in the United States It seems, in fact, that much of the early modern of black American dance insists upon its difference through its invocations of "roots" located elsewhere, as seen for instance, in the work of Asadata Dafora, Katherine Dunham, Pearl Primus, and others who also work on the premise of a continuous genealogy. This outward directed gaze reflects back on the self located here (in American concert dance), illuminating its difference and suggesting the complex cultural practices in which African American dance was enmeshed, thereby legitimizing its tradition and historicity. Describing Dunham's "modernist vision of renewal," for instance, Veve Clark writes,

> Dunham taught her various companies that the performance of "forgotten dances" was not merely a question of learning steps . . . Dunham performers contextualized the dances and re-presented them in a climate replicating the original settings as they simultaneously "signified" on their legacy following a continual process of transformation and revision true to African American cultural production . . . In a sense, her dancers became repositories of memories.[30]

Implicit in the work of these early moderns are the two prime modes that Houston Baker describes as the directive tropes of African American modernism, *mastery of form* and *deformation of mastery*. Baker is speaking primarily in terms of literary and musical production, though he invokes minstrelsy and the use of masks to elucidate his concepts; but I believe that these ideas also illuminate some of the forces at work in the dance world. The mastery of form works through irony, it "conceals, disguises, floats like a trickster butterfly in order to sting like a bee."[31] Deformation of mastery, on the other hand, is predicated on an unhesitating proclamation of difference; it is "go(uer)rilla action in the face of acknowledged adversaries . . . it distinguishes rather than conceals. It secures territorial advantage and heightens a group's survival possibilities."[32]

There is a plethora of stories of how these early moderns, having finally entered this world, were quick to pick up on the formal conventions of dance studios and concert stage, how they seemingly adopted the white liberal position of emphasizing their "difference" but ultimately ensured their place in a predominantly white-dominated circuit of "high" performance and touring, that is in artistic production, and not just as entertainers.[33] The fact that there was a great degree of comfort in the "difference" of black forms for white audiences, a difference that then allowed for trivializing and dismissal is unarguable. Consider, for instance, the comparison of *New York Post* critic John Mason Brown, writing as late as 1940, likening Asadata Dafora's efforts to choreograph African material as serious art to children playing in the attic. Consider also the much more affectionate and apparently benign appellations that teachers Martha Graham and Charles Weidman had for their student Pearl Primus, respectively, a "panther" and "his little primitive."[34] Because "difference" is incomprehensible in terms of the dominant culture, those "aliens" who articulate the different cultural forms come to be constructed as deformed. As Baker reminds us, there are two dominant ideas about the dynamics of deformation: "first, the indigenous comprehend the territory within their own vale/veil more fully than any intruder . . . second, the indigenous sound appears monstrous and deformed *only* to the intruder."[35] Again, Baker is speaking primarily of linguistic forms, but this conflation of "different" with monstrous or, sometimes, childish, is an institutionalized strategy of hegemonization that works across genres of cultural articulation. It is always a reaction to the acquired mastery of form by people who were debarred from and so far deemed unfit for these highly sophisticated cultural forms, a reaction that relocates them back in primitivity.

Moreover, there were continuous attempts to contain African American dancers in the field of social and popular dance, and the entertainment circuit, that foreclosed serious considerations of artistic endeavor. Such a phenomenon of double displacement runs through the history of American modern dance: while black influences were both unconsciously absorbed and consciously integrated into these forms mostly without acknowledgment, black dancers who wanted to be part of this field, either as performers, choreographers, or teachers, seldom found their way in. Aspiring black artists, vying for a place on the modern or ballet stage, were strongly discouraged—even a talented artist like Talley Beatty was reprimanded by important dance critics for his "dallying ballet technique."[36] African American dancers were also directed away from modern dance forms and advised to create their dances out of their Africanist heritage, which would distance them from the mainstream. Pearl Primus and Katherine Dunham, in particular, were applauded for having "wisely gone back" to their cultural traditions in order to search for movement inspirations.[37] Joe Nash reports that the appearance of the category "Negro Dance" in 1931 was met with not-too-delighted surprise; a set of stereotypical conceptions about the natural rhythm and talent of Negro dancers, such that they did not need the discipline and training essential for white dancers; and the recommendation that the Negro dancer avoid the dance forms of the white race in America: "There was never a reference to Negro artists as modern dancers or as participants in American modern dance."[38]

The reason the trope of "mastery of form" is so effective here is because, of course, this reaching outward to highlight the difference of Africanist roots on the concert stage, despite appearances, is no acquiescence in white directives. For while white cultural leaders and audiences wanted to mark difference and therefore distance, and urged black artists to study their "roots" instead of Western forms, there was little premonition that notions of the inferiority of black cultures would be upset by this, or that concert dance would become contested ground. But through their painstakingly acquired mastery of the forms and conventions of mainstream concert dance, black artists of the time made this a mode of validating "other" artistic modes and cultural influences, for staging their desires for locatable origins. Yet, in situating this different aesthetic on the modern concert stage, in claiming its status as black concert dance operating through the established channels of staging, touring, and institutionalization, this difference served to radicalize notions of black dance and ultimately transformed the content and forms of American concert dance.[39] And therein lies another way to interpret the phenomenon of the deformation of mastery—this time as a successful move on the part of those "others" who have worked to acquire mastery of form, such that it ends up "deforming"/revolutionizing the master forms. Such deformation is obvious in the ultimate transformation of the American concert dance scene—such that, even at that early stage, one of the largest and most successful touring companies was that of a black woman's, Dunham's—and of related effects on the field of cultural production, funding, and programming despite institutionalized racism and intolerance. That strategies like these were necessary at this time when exclusions and appropriations abounded is, of course, obvious. For instance, Brenda Dixon-Gottschild's analysis of Balanchine's choreography shows how the master introduced into the linear forms of ballet, Africanist subtexts and body attitudes, working through rhythmic structures instead of through defined steps, using off-center weight shifts, sudden mood changes, and movement styles from the Charleston, the Cakewalk, and other popular African American dance forms. And while the research of Dixon-Gottschild, followed by the work of scholars like Constance Valis Hill, has unearthed the influences that artists like Katherine Dunham and Arthur Mitchell had on Balanchine's choreography, there has been little acknowledgment of this generally.

These complex and antagonistic forces also helped create a historical field apparently ridden with different and opposed temporalities: because "difference" cannot be read as such, but only as a version of the "primitive," the "progress" made by black artists in mastering the forms of modernity only still reads as a demonstration of their primitiveness or otherness, hence reflecting an always already arrested temporality, highlighting the relentless forward moving-ness of white cultural forms. It seems surprising that even the most "radical" minds in this area labored under prejudices that are difficult to reconcile with the other philosophies and beliefs they championed. Let us look momentarily at Isadora Duncan's manifesto, *I See America Dancing*: this pioneer of the modern dance in America, who advocated the freedom of the spirit of the body and the mind, who broke with social convention in many ways, and whose dancing seemed, for the first time in white mainstream dance, to be in harmony with her femaleness and her sexuality, still created this constricted vision of national identity based on essentialized and hierarchized notions of race and gender. In this document, Duncan opposed her vision of "the dance of the future" not only to European ballet, but also, in terms of great disgust, to the contemporary popular jazz and Charleston. In this, she casts European ballet and "Negro" dancing as essentialized entities on the two ends of a despised spectrum, for neither of which she allows room in her modern dance, which expresses the national spirit of America:

> It seems monstrous for anyone to believe that the jazz rhythm expresses America. Jazz rhythm expresses the South African savage. America's music will be different . . . Long-legged boys and girls will dance to this music . . . not the tottering, ape-like convulsions of the Charleston, but a striking upward tremendous mounting . . . And this dance will have nothing in it either of the servile coquetry of the ballet or the sensual convulsion of the South African Negro.[40]

Ironically enough, later postmodernist choreographers would find in the very jazz rhythms she despises inspirations for the improvisational mode and ways to play with structure. Ironically, too, jazz would come to be upheld as a cultural form uniquely "American" in origin! Despite Duncan's vision of a society moving toward "freedom" and clearly because reigning notions of "progress" were so skewed, these attitudes did not disappear with time; as I mentioned before, modern and postmodern dance in America continued to be filled with unacknowledged influences from African American culture. It was these conditions that pushed for strategies that deployed modernist liberalism and constructed Afrocentric lineage in order to bolster the claim for a serious artistic concert dance tradition.

These maneuvers are indeed successful in opening up the field of concert dance and make for some changes in the direction of work that is produced. It is only in this later period that black choreographers like Ailey and McKayle created work with a distinctly different focus: work that is continuously saturated with the explicit flavor of African American life, that is self-conscious of its "difference" in its immediate context, the difference that is a necessary corollary of blackness in American culture.[41] In this context, a postmodern consciousness often picks up the trend set in motion by the early moderns of articulating a relationship with other Africanist cultures, but like the later moderns is deeply conscious of its geopolitical location, and thus particularly attentive to the politics of its own production as well as of diasporic cultural production. Think, for instance, of the collaborative projects of Reggie Wilson, Alonzo King, Ralph Lemon, and of course Zollar, whose work with black artists from other cultural, national, and artistic contexts reflects an acknowledgment of the different locations they inhabit and a desire to work across those differences in order to share creative spaces.

Consequently, such work also reads as critical of an essentialist Afro-centricity and the modernist validation of linear temporality as legitimate history.

Postmodern dance in America, like ballet, modern, and social dance genres, drew in different degrees on images, movement styles, and rhythmic structures, attitudes, and stylistic nuances that mark Africanist aesthetics. Specifically, Dixon-Gottschild argues, much of the avant-garde principles of the postmodern movement, such as the aesthetic of the "cool," the relaxed, loose, laid-back energy, the radical juxtaposition of ostensibly contrary elements, the embodied and verbalized play of irony and double-entendre, the dialogic relationship of performer and audience, are actually informed by recycled Africanist principles. Thus, writes Dixon-Gottschild,

> When Douglas Dunn quotes ballet without straight legs or heroic energy, or Yvonne Rainer creates a solo, titles it a trio (Trio A), and bases it on movement clusters and an indirect approach to the audience, they redefine their idiom. They may not be aware that the Africanist aesthetic is nonlinear and values dance steps that are dense, self-referential, and choreographed in clumps or clusters. (This approach to dance making, from a Eurocentric perspective, has been regarded as "cluttered" or "bad.") . . . Irony, paradox, and double-entendre, rather than the classical European, linear logic of cause, effect, and resolution, are basic to the Africanist aesthetic and offer a model for postmodernism, subconsciously as well as cognitively.[42]

Dixon-Gottschild's reading of the postmodern aesthetic, which fills in an erasure and insists on a double narrative in writing the history of dance, particularly in America, challenges the factual verifiability of history narrated by prominent dance historians such as Sally Banes, who in her *Terpsichore in Sneakers* does not make this connection between the American postmodernists and their African American influences. Banes, for instance, writes, in a language that parallels Dixon-Gottschild's, but instead of making a connection with African American dance can only contrast postmodern dance with its predecessors in "white" dance: "The bodies of the postmodern dancers were relaxed but ready, without the pulled up, stretched muscle tone of the ballet or the classical modern dancer . . . the down-to-earth style, the casual or cool attitude, the sense that 'it is what it is' . . . constituted a crucial aspect of the dance's import."[43] Banes merely mentions that the overturning, by the later postmodernists, of the early postmodern rejection of musicality and rhythmic organization has seen the emergence of a group of black postmodern choreographers, who have joined Gus Solomons, who was alone in the previous generation of avant-gardists. Interestingly, though her classic book goes on to focus on the early avant-gardists, she does not write about Solomons anymore, or explain why she did not include his work in her focus. In fact, discussions of Solomons's experience of the Dunn workshops and of his early highly innovative pieces such as *Neon* and *Bone Jam* are extremely difficult to find,[44] while Joan Miller, a black dancer-choreographer who was also part of the early avant-garde, is barely even mentioned in the increasing body of literature that exists on postmodern dance.

Journeying through volatile and vicious racial relations, the diverse community populating the concept of "black dance" in America, however, comes to be ridden with troubled negotiations over identity, anxieties over how in fact this blackness means, what the "traditions" of black dance in America are, and the "authenticity" of these traditions. It is in the course of these struggles that the political binary –black versus white—and essentialist notions of blackness that seem to have percolated out of the polarized and narrow politics of modernist nationalism, emerge as troubling and constrictive paradigms. For some choreographers, like Bill T. Jones and Joanna Haigood, it becomes befuddled or stifling, urging a need to work with more complex articulations of sexuality and spatiality, for instance, in the lack of which, notions of identity become increasingly reified. For others, like Chuck Davis, African American dance must derive its strength only from its roots in Africa, or in some cases in the Caribbean. Identity is embedded in an essentialized notion of "Mother" Africa, and unwittingly a hierarchy is set up whereby the artistic traditions of the originative country are celebrated over the diasporic choreographies of the African American peoples, instead of articulating continuities and resonances. In Anthony Kwame Appiah's critique of the formulation of a "reverse discourse," he reminds us that

> the terms of resistance are already given us, and our conversation is trapped within the western cultural conjecture we attempt to dispute. The pose of repudiation already presupposes the cultural institutions of the West and the ideological matrix in which they, in turn, are imbricated. Railing against the cultural hegemony of the West, the nativists are of its party without knowing it.[45]

This seems to me the constitutive problem when Euro-American nationalism and its corollary, ethno-national identitarianism, are transplanted onto "other" communities especially with little negotiations of the terms and conditions of such organization. Particularly with reference to this context of "black dance," aesthetics formulated in reaction to frozen hegemonies instead of working through resistances, remain caught up in the Americanization of race relations determined by the ghettoization and polarization of difference (often passing as "community-based work") underlying melting-pot cultural policies.

Let me offer a reading, at this point, of the performative oratory of Chuck Davis as master of ceremonies at the DanceAfrica festival, held at the Brooklyn Academy of Music on June 5, 1988, as an illustrative instance of the essentializations marking the latter end of the spectrum. In his welcome address, Davis introduced the theme of the program as "Africa's dance and America's answer" and spoke of the agendas of the different artists on the program as "using traditions in a more contemporary sense," represented by the Urban Bush Women, and "preserving the traditions,"[46] represented by the Sabar ak Ru Afriq Dance Theater Company based in New York City, and the dance company of Rosemarie Guirard from Abidjan.[47] It is interesting that the African American companies are referred to as such whereas the company from Africa is referred to metonymically through its artistic director, "Sister Rose." This is not only because she is an extraordinarily talented person, for so are the others; nor is it because her ensemble is not institutionalized: the name of her company, which is not mentioned by Davis, is *Les Guirirvoires*. Rather, in this context, this seems to be related to the fact that she symbolizes the pure ground of "the motherland" that Davis invokes repeatedly with nationalistic fervor, speaking of the beauty of the dances of "Mother Africa" and of the continuity of heritage from the motherland to African peoples in America. In the opening ceremony that follows, Davis repeats this gesture: "Africa, my Africa, *my* Africa . . . There is none like thee in all this universe . . . Africa, my Africa, *my* Africa," the emphatic tone further underlined by hands placed on the chest.[48]

On the one hand, this is the claiming of the cultural lineage of peoples forcibly displaced, but who have struggled and persevered in maintaining their cultural difference from the mainstream into which they were forced to assimilate. On the other hand, it is impossible to ignore the "mothering" of Africa, coinciding here with the body of Sister Rose who is celebrated for her "preservation" of tradition, and the fervent nationalism of the dispossessed son. Later too, in a statement about the 2001 DanceAfrica festival, Davis proclaimed that this program of what he termed "edu-tainment" was necessary "to pay homage to the motherland."[49] The implicit polarization of the Urban Bush Women, who "use" the traditions in a contemporary setting, versus the work of Sister Rose, is also somewhat problematic because, while the approach and modality of the choreographers to what is regarded as "tradition" is different, there are some overlaps in the ways in which they work with movement. Sister Rose preserves "traditions" by, at least, rearranging them for a stage setting—her web page in fact lists all of her repertoire as "choreographies"[50]—as does the Dance Sabar company, which according to Davis, presents "the truth of the traditional dance," while Zollar refers to them in a varied innovative framework.[51] Interestingly, in conjunction with this reference to an originary "truth" and his sanctification of the notion of a singular and hegemonic "Tradition," what Davis went on to say seemed to reflect his own anxieties about "purity" of origins. For he also proclaimed that though they were originally performed surrounded by the community, in the village square, putting these dances on the concert stage had not blemished their "authenticity." As elsewhere, the masculinist claiming of a feminized motherland insists on an unchanging point of origin, the source of an essentialized national identity. For Davis, identity, fired by nationalistic and racial pride and the demands of modernist recuperation, is a matter to be reclaimed through accessible means. He talks about how he was nurtured by friends in Africa, where he ate "all kinds of traditional foods," and about how his friends sent him the traditional costume he was wearing, which, however, was not available except on the continent. The consumerizing of Africanness, the reach of the access in "developing" countries that comes with the holding of an American passport, the complex negotiations in the creation of contemporary art forms from long-standing cultural practices, the multiple jeopardy in which African American womanspace is inscribed, are completely glossed over in this arena, where Africanness is an unproblematic "truth" reclaimable through the materiality of specific practices.

This hierarchizing of a "pure" and "original" African dance is also seen in the tense reception visitors or immigrants from Africa sometimes extend to some African American dance companies who refer to their dance style as "African." The former often react with surprise to what they see as the African American insistence on "sameness" with African, because, for them the dance they see is not really African, but different: African American.[52] While I am referring to specific conversations I have personally had with colleagues, Senegalese, Nigerian, Ghanaian, Somali, and African American, these are not uncommon perceptions: different contexts, different logistics clearly have their impact on cultural preferences, training systems, aesthetics. The politics of naming are complex, however, and reveal different power plays at work, among which are as much notions of purity of origins, as the differing effect of location in a first-world versus a third-world situation. One side insists on claiming "roots" in no doubt a somewhat monolithically conceptualized "African" dance, resisting the pervasive influence of Anglo-American forms, and often also on projecting continuity without adequate acknowledgment of the changes inevitably wrought by ruptures and by the violences of displacement and disjunction, and to differences attendant upon diverse geopolitical locations; the other insists on bringing up the slippages in such continuity, marking differences between cultural production in African communities and their diasporic counterparts through notions of authenticity, ultimately privileging and sometimes implying a superiority of the dance in Africa, as source. Both of these positions can be problematic, based in hierarchical notion of origins, neither adequately attentive to the shifting meanings of signifiers, ideas that have been brilliantly theorized by scholars such as Stuart Hall. Neither position allows for the recognition of the complex ways in which the "black atlantic" is constructed, or of the politics of delineating cultural specificities in black diasporic cultural production.

One of the forums where the tensions running through contemporary notions of "black dance" in America came into sharp focus is the Black Choreographers Moving Conference held in Los Angeles in 1989. Throughout this conference, several young choreographers seemed to be chafing against being labeled according to narrow notions of "race." Marilyn Tucker's comments are particularly illustrative of the doubts and fears that were voiced:

> My feeling about watching programs that can be viewed as Black dance, specifically after having watched the Black choreographers' program BCM, is that themes which Black choreographers seem to be addressing are far more universal than could be directed solely to Black culture . . . What I'm trying to say is that I think that if this is the way Black choreography is going, perhaps Black themes are not being specifically addressed by Black choreographers anymore. I don't know, I may be wrong.[53]

Again, at a panel deliberating "Will the Black choreographer always be Black?" artists such as Bill T. Jones wondered whether the contemporary need to claim a black heritage would be so strongly felt by posterity, while the comments of some others hinted at a desire to work with more "global" themes. These ambivalences have, of course, to be understood in several ways, political, economic, and artistic. To some extent, the dominant definitional location of blackness (and of non-whiteness, for that matter) in lack within American society projects a deep negativity: it drives the wish that Langston Hughes lamented in 1925 as a desire "to be as little Negro and as much American as possible."[54] Moreover, as the history of arts funding in America shows, survival often depends on some kind of alignment with the establishment and its ideas: a claiming of a resistant "blackness," diversely formulated, reads as problematic, while the assumption of sanctioned blackness, themes and forms that "diversify" the artistic scene but do not immediately disturb the status quo with the staging of unmistakable "difference," is often preferred. Yet, what I believe Bill T. Jones was trying to signal was the desire and urge shared by him and several other artists, for claiming the complexities of their African Americanness, revealing the many contradictions, complications, and submerged hyphens within that denominator, the many differences that characterize the "black" communities of America, and the possibilities of diverse alignments along lines of sex, gender, and class differences within these. The assertion of such a potentially volatile diasporic location is particularly threatening when juxtaposed with the celebration of "traditional African" dance forms, where, one more time, "black dance" can be kept at a safe distance from "white dance."

Moreover, clearly the category "Black Dance" comes to be experienced as constrictive when it becomes commodified and reified, stereotyping expectations and limiting the possibilities of choreographing alterity and confrontation. As Lula Washington said at the same conference,

> When you think of Black Dance, you automatically think 1) you have to do gospel, 2) you have to do jazz and blues, or 3) you have to do African dance. I don't necessarily think that those are the full extent of what I am as a Black choreographer or as a Black person. I think I can utilize those elements, but I don't necessarily have to be put into a category that says what I have to do . . . I utilize the elements of my heritage in an abstracted version.[55]

In fact, Zita Allen has pointed out that the term "Black Dance" was initially deployed by white mainstream critics to separate artistic endeavors by African American choreographers and dancers from the rest of concert dance in America as a kind of cultural apartheid, and it implied some decisions taken on behalf of black artists, about what belonged and did not belong in this field. Allen asserts that dangerously enough, "in spite of the fact that this label has no clear-cut definition, it has acquired a power almost as great as its meaning is obscure."[56] Indeed, even while the term has been diversified and reclaimed by some black artists, imbuing it with different kinds of power, it functions in a context pervaded by an oppressive racial hierarchy and hence has larger implications than might be denoted very simplistically by concepts of "aesthetic preferences."

The postmodern here is often characterized by the inevitable recognition of the continuity-yet-rupture, the marking of difference between the diasporic cultural formations and aesthetics, images of "tradition," and of the negotiations that mark the reconstitution of blackness as a vital if shifting signifier. As Stuart Hall has argued, disaporic cultural identities can hardly be understood through models of unitary or uniform experience, and are better theorized through tracing the shifting positions inhabited in relating to the formations of culture, history, tradition. Cultural identity, in this sense,

> is a matter of "becoming" as well as of "being" . . . It is not something which already exists, transcending place, time, history, and culture. Cultural identities come from somewhere, have histories. But, like everything which is historical, they undergo constant transformation. Far from being fixed in some essentialized past, they are subject to the continuous "play" of history, culture, and power. Far from being grounded in mere "recovery" of the past, which is waiting to be found, and which when found, will secure our sense of ourselves into eternity, identities are the names we give to the different ways we are positioned by, and position ourselves within, the narratives of the past.[57]

It is interesting to reflect on Zollar's own ideas on identity in the context of these remarks by Hall. At the Black Choreographers Moving Conference that I referred to earlier, Zollar expressed explicit concern at the need that some African American choreographers had voiced, to resist categorization of their art in racialized terms, arguing that this did not necessarily predetermine artistic choices or yoke them to a narrow label, but rather suggested a *context* for their work, influences, and politics.

> When I hear choreographers say, "I'm a choreographer who happens to be a Black person," I understand what they are saying, but it's an unfortunate choice of words. Something about that statement is very painful because what I hear them buying into is, "Yes, I see Black as limited, too, so I don't want to be defined by that," rather than saying, "I am an African or Black American choreographer, and I choose to work with this aesthetic, or I choose to work in a culturally specific aesthetic based on growing up as an African or Black American person and everything that means." It doesn't mean any limitations. It hurts me to hear people say, "I'm colorless." . . . We are artists; we are working with an art form that we are passionate about; and we are bringing all of who we are into that art. I don't think Americans can recognize that fact.[58]

For Zollar then, like Hall, identities are also created at the intersection of being and becoming, which is why Zollar can overlap her critique of the anti-abortion policies of the American Congress with prayers to the African goddess Oshun to inspire the journey toward self-healing and potential empowerment, can juxtapose laments about the practice of female infanticide in different countries, and telephone conversations about the headlines of the *New York Times* in her critique of state-sponsored patriarchy.[59] The possibilities inherent in the diasporic fabric of American cultural forms, and the rich, intertextual black presence in the aesthetic forms of this context, thus suggest different relationships to existing cultural practices, specific aesthetic and cultural preferences, and political convictions. Here, "blackness" becomes a location to be claimed, not for ethnic marking, but for indicating the crucible of historical and cultural specificities that aesthetic choices have been filtered through. Artists like Zollar then, overturn both the conflation of blackness with "tradition" and the reading of blackness as the trope of "restriction," and instead mobilize blackness as an intervention and a critique of the projected "universality" of Euro-American modes.

Hall also suggests theorizing diasporic identities as formed by the dialogic relationship between two simultaneously operative and intercutting vectors or axes, which yields rich insights into the various relational formations that are articulated here:

> . . . the vector of similarity and continuity; and the vector of difference and rupture . . . The one gives us some grounding in, some continuity with, the past. The second reminds us that what we share is precisely the experience of a profound discontinuity: the peoples dragged through slavery, transportation, colonization, migration, came predominantly from Africa.[60]

For Hall, then, a recalling of Africa, a return to the source of this continuity in spite of dislocation, is inevitable, but it cannot happen through a linear, simplistic route. Remembering or embodiment of that connection, then, must work through acknowledged intersecting pathways to refer to "what Africa has *become* in the New World, what we have made of 'Africa': 'Africa' as we re-tell it through politics, memory and desire."[61] This, for me, is a singularly important marker of the postmodern here: this notion of reclaiming the past through politics, memory, and desire, rejecting a simple notion of recuperation, subverting some of the obvious attitudes and assumptions of the modern, mediating a contemporary relationship with "tradition" and "culture" through constructed and reconstructed narratives.

There are ways in which, then, these historical fragments of Indian and black American dance share grounds: as the little acknowledged presence in several genres of Western, Euro-American dance, and specifically in modern and postmodern dance, and then in terms of the politics and strategies of nationalism, recuperation, and naming. However, the trajectories develop very differently in colonized India and among enslaved and struggling African Americans: the long black presence in America coupled with the insistent activism of cultural leaders has made it imperative that the work of black choreographers and dancers situated here be taken into account, though this has often happened in terms that are frustrating for these artists and unmatched with the availability of opportunities. On the other hand, cultural production in the third world is seldom and erratically noticed, and then is often deployed to demonstrate the lip service to "multiculturalism." Moreover, because of the different and hierarchized ways of racializing of different ethnic groups by a white hegemony here, artists of color located in the West, and nonwestern artists from third-world countries, often find themselves positioned oppositionally and seldom have opportunities to converse with each other. There are also the conditions of the current cultural marketplace, where America emerges as one of the wealthiest producers and hence legitimators, of artistic work, and where the call of a multiculturalism, conceived primarily as a safety-valve operation, pits people of color against each other as they are called upon to play out necessary representations. What makes it possible to discuss choreographers such as Zollar and Chandralekha, choreographers in the contemporary world, in the same book, without attempting a "cross-cultural" study in the mode of liberal relativism, are emerging notions of global resistances to white and Western dominance, and the urgent energies gathering around possibilities of alliances along lines of progressive politics and color and across national borders. What is also significant about these two choreographers is that their works resist interpellation in the conditions of hegemonic notions of success and salability, both as determined by the Euro-American mainstream and by the dominant rhetoric of nationalism emerging from their communities, and necessitate constantly different terms and frameworks of understanding and articulation.

The Women Refuse to Acquiesce

In this section, I want to draw sharper attention to that particularly critical site for historiographic reconsideration that I invoked earlier: questions about women's subjectivities and sexualities. Focusing specifically on how the construction of nationalisms is bound up with repressive notions of gendered and sexualized agency, I want to point out how many of these issues spin out in terms of performative representation, and how this history complicates an understanding of the location of the choreographers I am looking at. I have described the work of both Chandralekha and Zollar as feminist, as have other critics. Though this is common knowledge by now, it remains imperative to point out that women's movements across the world, based on specific contextual issues, have taken different forms and shapes. These differences are not so much acknowledged in the discourses that emerge from Europe and America, and feminists from non-white and non-Western contexts have come to resent this hijacking of a wide series of global movements and their representation in terms that are inevitably Eurocentric. Though this is changing in response to incisive critiques, these politics have bred a fear of and resistance to the term "feminist," which sometimes ends up reifying the situation further.

One of the important ways in which activists of color understand their feminism continues to be the coalescing of concerns of gender and racial and cultural difference in the first instance, such that issues are understood through a complex intersectionality. Moreover, there are considerations of how these factors coincide or clash with locations in class, sexuality, citizenship and other factors. There are further considerations of the specific histories of control of female sexuality and the subjugation of female desire in the service of larger political projects: in contexts dominated by conditions of colonization and enslavement, women particularly have struggled against multiple layers of objectification and silencing, used as pawns in the efforts to establish colonial rule and slavery and thereafter in nationalist movements. Because of the way in which hegemonic systems are institutionalized, women of color and especially from the third world have found it imperative to critique the narrow vision of an agenda dominated by Anglo-American feminism and to push instead for a more finely negotiated discourse. This is also to point to the many insidious forms of racism that have dogged the possibilities of a solid footing for a global women's movement.

Some more historiographic fragments then, to highlight the specific debates involving female subjectivities that have complicated questions of performance and representation in these contexts, and how the particular paths of these struggles permeated history to charge the work of choreographers such as Chandralekha and Zollar with the specific politics and awareness of a situated feminism. Clearly, the ways in which female sexualities are performed in the works of these choreographers, specifically in the light of that history, invites a "feminist" interpretation, albeit understood through difference. It is useful to think of Alice Walker's concept of womanism in this context, especially when we keep in mind the specific context of African American women's struggles which gives to the concept its particular potency and power. The idea of womanism has been particularly useful in thinking through a differential politics of women-centered liberation struggles in a transnational framework. At any rate, I have stuck with using the descriptor "feminist" in an attempt to underscore its reclamation: though Anglo-American women's movements have attracted the lion's share of global attention, a wide range of resistance movements led by women and centering on women's issues have been and continue to be vital part of communities in the third world and communities of color here, and have constituted a crucial, if unacknowledged, part of the legacy of a global "feminism."

I have previously alluded to the practice of devadasi dedication in India and the conflicted space it came to occupy, particularly in the latter half of the colonial regime. A brief reference to the politics of the struggle that ensued in the wake of the anti-nautch movement, which began as early as 1892 urging the abolition of the devadasi system, will show how the sexualized body of the native dancing woman came to be deployed as a trope embroiled in the politics of the colonial rule and the nationalist movement, while the image of her physically absented body was spread out as metaphoric war ground, on which several issues could be debated.[62] In 1930, a social worker, Muthulakshmi Reddy, introduced a bill in the Madras legislative council, under the aegis of the Women's India Association, to ban the dedication of women to Hindu temples. This Devadasi Abolition Bill was accompanied by a demand for the amendment of the Madras Hindu Religious Endowment Act to dispense completely with the services of devadasis in all temples. The bill sparked off a heated controversy, dividing those at the helm of cultural and political policy making into opposed camps, each upholding cardboard images of the devadasi to bolster arguments that in reality erased her voice.

For the supposedly "progressive" nationalist camp, what was really at stake in this bill was the essentialized image of Indian womanhood, linked to the "pure" body of Mother India. Like the motherland, which had to be rescued from rape and plunder by the British, the devadasi had to be rescued, forcibly, if necessary, from the lust of men (and, seemingly, from her own rampant sexuality), for they also embodied the cultural practices that gave evidence of the nation's claims to artistic greatness. The opposers of the anti-nautch campaign, as it came to be known, were closely allied in thought to Indian nationalists for whom *"Power, in order to be used, must be controlled . . .* Woman as the terrain of nationalism was the object as well as the teleological end of the process of control."[63] It is worthwhile recalling, in this context, the emphasis placed by Gandhi on the role of the woman in mothering and nurturing, and by extension transforming the society through nonviolence. Gandhi, who had proclaimed that Hindu temples, shamefully enough, were more brothels than houses of religious worship, calls upon the women of India thus: "Let her forget that she ever was or can be the object of man's lust. And she will occupy her proud position by the side of the man as his mother, maker, and silent warrior."[64] The implication is that the women of modern India must sublimate their desires and reduce sexuality to a function of reproduction only. Fitting into their larger roles as mothers and makers of men will ensure their place of respect by his side, not behind him; the couching of their warriorhood in silence is only befitting of these ideal roles.

Muthulakshmi Reddy, who led the campaign, was herself descended from a devadasi lineage and cited personal knowledge of the horrors of the lives of devadasis "who would otherwise turn out to be legal and chaste wives and loving mothers and useful citizens . . . being forced by their dependents to sell their flesh to make a living."[65] The campaigners also gained substantial support from Christian missionaries whose vociferous denouncing of the system pressured the government into taking their side on this issue. Of course, the colonial government hardly needed much per-suading when it came to a matter of denouncing the heinous practices of the natives. Besides, this legislation castigating devadasis as prostitutes had a very influential predecessor in the Contagious Diseases Act of 1864, which introduced among other provisions the compulsory registration of brothels and prostitutes and the periodic medical examinations and com-pulsory treatments of prostitutes found to be infected with venereal dis-eases. Like its precursor, this issue could also be used as adequate proof of the moral degeneracy of Indian society.

Support for Reddy's bill also came from associations representing non-Brahmin castes in the South such as the Sengundars and Isai Vellalars, from which a large number of devadasis were dedicated. But even here it was not necessarily concern for the devadasis themselves that prompted action: the members of these associations denounced devadasis as a dis-honor to their castes as they supported the bill. Of course the support of the men from these groups has to be viewed in the light of the fact that the anti-nautch campaigners advocated that men who were willing to marry (and thus domesticate) devadasis should be encouraged by offers of employment and other benefits. Further, as Amrit Srinivasan has shown, the support of the men from within the devadasi community for the bill was largely motivated by the determination to stamp out the woman-cen-tered, matrilineal traditions inside the devadasi institution. Obviously, they did not hesitate to collaborate with the emergent Indian patriarchy and campaign aggressively for legislation that would yield them dominance both within the household and in wider political society.

On the other hand, for the Brahmin-dominated conservative camp the bill read as an attack on traditional Hindu practices. S. Sathyamurthy of the Madras Congress urged the "protection" of the devadasi system as part of the project of rescuing indigenous national culture from extinction. He warned that this would only lead to a demand by non-Brahmins for the abo-lition of temple priests, who were incidentally Brahmins, and to further such onslaughts against the ancient Hindu religion. Another group that opposed the bill were the leaders of the cultural revival movement, lead by eminent personalities who, also often Brahmins, formed a large part of the cultural elite of the community, such as lawyer and cultural activist, E. Krishna Iyer, and Rukmini Devi Arundale, closely associated with Annie Besant, the founder of the Theosophical Society. For them however, what was to be resisted was the phenomenon of throwing out the baby with the bathwater: the system of devadasi dedication was perhaps harmful, but it was to be remembered that the devadasis themselves were the bearers of performance traditions. If devadasis were no longer to dance in the temples, the ancient artistic and cultural heritage supposedly embodied by them must be "rescued." This move, based on the vital distinction between a devadasi and a prostitute and on prescriptive notions of women's sexualities, was no less patriarchal or conservative than the positions of other groups. As I pointed out earlier, influenced greatly by Brahminical puritan values and the Christian religious biases of the Theosophists, the leaders of this movement succeeded in appropriating her dance from the devadasi and recasting it as high "classical" art. The upper-class, high-caste, educated, privileged, and apparently sexually chaste dancer of this classical art was a far cry from the devadasi who had come to be marked as prostitute and whom no legal rhetoric could represent within the systems of the newly crafted nation state. As Srinivasan has shown,

> it was the model of the ancient temple-dancer as a pure and holy, sexually chaste woman which was stressed . . . By thus marking her off from the living "devadasi," they hoped to attract the right clientele for the dance. The argument that without the attendant immorality the dance was a form of yoga—an individual spiritual exercise—abstracted it from its specific community context, permitting its rebirth amongst the urban, educated elite.[66]

As research has shown time and again, the devadasi's own voice was nowhere represented in the debate, though her sexualized body was snatched up repeatedly, often as an effective cover, to argue for several issues. Essentialized images of her, either as immoral prostitute or as the guardian of art, were tossed about in the debate, and serious stock was never taken of the situation in which she now found herself, economic and sociocultural, and of how that would be affected with the legislation. This is not to deny total agency to the devadasis themselves: they registered several complaints in writing, to the government, to the Congress, and to individuals at the forefront of the debate, bringing up, among other issues, the glossed-over matter of economics. Even as early as 1927, they had written in protest to the colonial government, invoking their status as the brides of god and asking for the religious neutrality promised by Queen Victoria.

However, heed was never paid to their words, and the bill was finally passed in 1947, regardless of anything the devadasis had to say about how this legislation would hereafter change their lives drastically.

These specific debates show how the arrival of the "woman question" at the scene of nation-making or community consolidation is never easily accommodated within the politics of the time: most often it is relegated to the margins. For it inevitably disrupts the aspirations toward a stable space, intervenes in justifications of modernity, progress, homogeneity, the nation-space, cultural organicism, and threatens the small measure of security arrived at, even if through various silencings and a projection of consensus. Therefore, it must be silenced, resisted with doubled force, and the issues must be co-opted at the earliest possible opportunity. The disturbing presence of spaces marked by alterity within the margins of this nation/community, can no longer be attributed to problems created entirely by external hegemonies, but points to erasures within the constitution of community, citizenship, and national subjecthood that form its very base: "It becomes a question of the otherness of the people-as-one. The national subject splits in the ethnographic perspective of culture's contemporaneity and provides both a theoretical position and a narrative authority for marginal voices of minority discourse."[67] The vexed questions of native female subject-formation and of othered sexualities thus become the point of silence in much nationalist discourse: the metaphoric woman-space of the nation, embodied by individual real women at home, comes, via a remarkable circuit of ventriloquist shiftings, to mark a space of nationalist reclaiming when so much has been lost to the dominance of the West.

Problematic gender relations also afflict the histories of African American liberation movements, where racialized hierarchies intervened in the possibilities of conceptualizing a finely nuanced agenda for "freedom." This of course does not mean that women in these communities have not continued to eke out means of resistance even within the small spaces in which they found themselves. The histories of these communities are bolstered with legacies of women who, individuals or groups constantly negotiating between the different centers of power, continued to push forward women's issues. Case in point: Josephine Baker. Baker's struggle to move from impoverishment, helping support her family through her job as chorus girl, to stardom in Paris is well documented, and there is no need to repeat that scholarship. What I want to draw attention to instead are the ways in which she worked her agency in an extremely difficult situation. There was little room for talented African American artists like her to work in the heavily racist climate of America in the 1940s. And while many of these artists consented to living and working in Paris, giving life to the famous Jazz Era that flourished there, these artists were painfully aware that they continued to be framed in racial terms that were still derogatory. Even when she was revered as brilliant performer and one of the most beautiful women seen, Baker was celebrated for her "wild" sexuality and her "primitivism." Indeed, there is no doubt that the erotic fascination with her body and her "uninhibited" movement was completed wrapped up in notions of the wild "other," with intimations of the teeming sensual riches of Africa that had been brought under control through the civilizing processes of Europe.

Indeed, even in her film career, beginning with roles like that of Fatou, Baker might have seemed doomed to fulfilling colonial fantasies about the savage and primitive sexual excess of the "other," and to some extent, perceptions and representations of her would always remain sexualized. However, seizing that small window of opportunity, she positioned herself in ways that captured the imagination and attention of the audience and presenters to an unprecedented degree. But, and this is her subtle yet sharp intervention, she also changed the textures of the roles she played. In later roles such as Zou Zou and Alwina in *Princesse Tam Tam*, her self-consciousness about the power of her sexuality permeates her performance, such that it becomes difficult to fix her in object-position or to deny her agency. By foregrounding always her own pleasure in the kind of sexual play that was the very source of her unique success, she constantly gestured to an autoeroticism which deferred considerations of others' pleasures.

For instance, even in the one scene in *Zou Zou* where we see her dancing, which leads to her discovery by the manager of the theatre as "star" potential, she begins by playing with her own shadow created by the stage lights behind the curtain. Unaware that at some point the curtains have been pulled back and that she is being watched, she "performs" for herself, fascinated by her own movement and shadow: dancing for her own pleasure, taunting her shadow through a wagging finger, challenging her shadow to perform the same high battements and floor splits. While this may be argued to have been part of the script, I believe that it is Baker's ebullient performance style, the way in which she plays with herself and submits herself to her own gaze—dancing with her shadow—that imbues the section with its surprisingly subversive and ironic qualities. It is the gaze of the white men that is secondary here, presenting them somewhat as intruders in a "self-contained" scene. What also comes across in sections like this is a remarkable sense of self-sufficiency, an intervention that seems to me to be Baker's very own because unsupported by the rest of the movie, one that acts in fact as a fine and clever reversal of the rest of the script.

Nonetheless, despite her validation as brilliant performer by diverse audiences, the irony that underlay her style, the subtle maneuvering of the roles she was supposed to play to create larger-than-life figures hovering on the borders of real and fantastic desire, the subversiveness of the ways in which she created but remained in charge of her eroticism, got less attention than the other aspects of her work and personality. Much conservative African American writing at that time found her work deeply troubling and subversive of the integrity, self-respect, and principles they had been fighting for, for a long time. Caught between the "respectful" agenda of a new black middle class and the colonial fantasies of the dominant gaze, Baker no doubt struggled to find ways to articulate her own position.[68] Recent scholarship about Baker has in fact examined, in great detail, questions about her agency in a difficult and overdetermined situation where racial stereotypes abounded, yet it often seems that more than her dancing itself, it is her body image and sexuality that are the objects of terribly public discussion. And no doubt, if we examined Baker's work from the point of view of a homogeneous and idealized feminist agenda, we might misread the narrow pathways she carved to arrive at resistive representative possibilities, tweaking the ways in which she fulfilled the desiring and primitivizing gaze of the audience in order to arrive at her status of a glamorous star. We might miss how she reversed her performance persona by creating her off-stage but still extremely public persona as its obverse—subtle, dignified, human rights activist, lover of animals, characterized by political and cultural savvy—refusing to be boxed into the images that were created for her and desired of her. We might miss how her self-presentation typified what Houston Baker has described as the fluid power of conjure: "conjure is a power of transformation that causes definitions of "form" as fixed and comprehensible "thing" to dissolve . . . African conjure meant to move the spirit through a fluid repertoire of 'forms,'" so much so that she became a genre unto herself.[69]

I have referred to Josephine Baker in order to point out once again, how considerations of women-centered choreography by women artists of color are always implicated, because of the hyper-patriarchal politics during slavery and colonization, in the skewed representations of gendered and sexualized bodies that have been the legacies of those politics. It is when we consider the complicated rhetoric debating the status of the devadasi in India at the verge of independence from colonial rule, and Baker's meteoric rise to fame and the consequent negotiations she effected in her representations that we recognize once again both the frustrating conditions of representational success in spaces created by a hegemonic order, and the narrow position given to women's questions and sexualities in the projects of nation-building/community-consolidation that are formulated in the face of colonial domination. It is in terms of the vicissitudes of these histories and the particular needs that arise in these contexts that we can best understand the depth and the complexities of the feminist consciousness that runs through the work of choreographers like Zollar and Chandralekha and energizes their particular brand of radical politics, and also recognize the significance of their work in re-producing the contours of female sexualities and in staging women's desires.

CHAPTER 6 **Text Dances:**

Pieces and Thoughts

SUBVERSIVE DANCING

The Playful Interventions in Jawole Willa Jo Zollar's *Batty Moves*

(1995)

Introducing the piece before a performance, Jawole Willa Jo Zollar said: "I wanted to create *Batty Moves* because I had started to get confused. I started out dancing as a young child, having fun, and then I went to college (step right) and started studying modern dance and ballet and I started kinda holdin' and pushin' and tuckin'. Then I'd go over to the African dance class (step left) and party and be all loose an' movin', and I'd go to my classes over here (step left) and I'd be holdin', pushin', tuckin' and apologizing and everything, and I'd go back over here (step right) and be movin' it, and and I . . . I just decided I needed to find a way to bring both traditions together."[1] Out of these unruly intersections and the decision to claim the multiple facets of her aesthetic palette, emerged a beautifully crafted, ironic tour de force. In examining the choreography, I want to argue that *Batty Moves* is peculiarly subversive, particularly because of some of the "interventions" that Zollar integrates into it. By the term intervention here, I refer to the practice of interrupting or bending expectations in technical or choreographic structures, particularly so that other possibilities for meaning-making are opened up.

I want to quote from some mainstream reviews of *Batty Moves* before I offer my own readings of it as typical examples of incomplete or misreadings, because it is often such public commentary that introduces artistic production to audiences and influences their viewings of them. These reviews are particularly troubling because of the ways in which some of the stereotypical popular notions about black female bodies are uncritically adopted and reaffirmed in them. Deborah Jowitt, for instance, writing in *The Village Voice*, captions the picture of Maia Claire Garrison from the piece "Rear unguarded . . . ," and titles the review "Interior Itch." For her, the dance is "full of interesting rhythms and moves that present the dancers as a strong sensuous woman dancing for the joy of it as well as for the seductive effect she knows it's having."[2] Jennifer Dunning, writing for the *New York Times*, mentions the solo section and describes it as a "care-free lexicon of moves with a lilting bottom as the choreographic motif."[3] None of these comments capture the specific cultural nuance of the piece: it is significant that the woman celebrating her sexuality is a black woman, after all. And this is particularly significant in the context of a history where black women have been stereotyped as either hypersexual in the image of Jezebel, or completely desexualized as the Mammy figure, and the celebration of sexuality has to be carefully thought through and performed so as not to unwittingly reaffirm any existing stereotypes.

However, *Batty Moves* is much more than a comment on sensuality and sexuality: it is also a strong statement about the politics of aesthetic preference. Indeed, given the complex and challenging movement vocabulary, the comment about the "carefree" lexicon is more than surprising. Again, Janice Berman, writing for *New York Newsday*, is deeply appreciative, but quite misguided: "Just think of Prentice-Ryan as the opposite of a so-thin-as-to-be nearly-transparent ballerina and her dance as the opposite of classical ballet, and you'll be on the right track."[4] But *Batty Moves* is also not the polarized opposite of ballet, as I will later show. In fact, what the piece does is show the balletic potential of these superb dancers but then make a decision to follow a different aesthetic, and if we were to construct the

Urban Bush Women, Zollar's *Batty Moves*. Photo © 2003 Bette Marshall.

dancers in the piece as the exact "other" of the ballerina in order to appreciate them and the choreography, then we would in fact be missing much of the point. Further, as I have said before, "interesting rhythms" and "carefree lexicon" and all of the other references to the piece's strong celebration of female sensuality say nothing about the technical challenges of the piece and its incredibly difficult maneuverings between different aesthetic preferences. Nor do any of them cut it as assessments of the complexity of the choreography. In reading the choreography of *Batty Moves* with reference to the deep historical, cultural, and political commentaries that are embedded in it, I want to highlight the resistive potential of the work, which gets little attention, as the above reviews show.

Zollar choreographed *Batty Moves* in 1995 because she felt strongly that in Euro-American modes of training, specifically in ballet and most modern idioms, dancers' butts were usually drained of movement, poetry, and passion. "There is 'expressivity' in the African-Caribbean way of releasing the hip or hyperextending the back . . . in African dance hip movement is accepted as an integral part of both sacred and secular dance," she has said.[5] In this piece, most of the movements are initiated by or end in the butt, while several others take traditional movements from modern dance vocabulary and subtly transform them by substituting the erect spine and aligned pelvis for more curved lines of the back. However, despite the seemingly descriptive title—the word *batty* is Jamaican slang for *butt*—the piece reaches beyond making the technical point about the beauty of hip/butt movement to invoke and comment on history and cultural politics through choreography that is at once celebratory and resistive.

I will start with some movement descriptions from the beginning up to a point in the piece when what I call the "scoot forward" happens, a movement phrase that functions as a trope of the kind of resistive practice that characterizes Zollar's choreography generally and this piece in particular. Lights up. Three women on stage, standing in a triangle, their backs to the audience. Each has positioned her body so that the hip and the butt jut out and the line of the spine is deliberately dislodged into an ending curve. The women begin to sway their hips so as to reflect and continue this movement impulse in the rest of the body. As the drums come on, the soft movement of their swaying hips becomes even more smooth as, balanced on one leg, hip pushed out to that side, the other hip pulls out and in to dip the toes to the floor and off, and then becomes more pronounced to execute a step pattern. Four women now enter from upstage right, their swaggering hips and shoulders moving in twice the tempo of the feet, which easily rub on the floor to move forward. A hip circle is emphasized with a large flourish whereby the palms come to embrace the hips on either side, and is complemented by a series of torso circles and roundings of each shoulder.

The four women move diagonally forward to end up in a line facing the drummer, who sits on the downstage left hand corner. This introduction has then prognosticated that every movement here will have a special flavor because of the involvement, whether immediate or ultimate, of the hips and butt. A rond de jomb en l'air, an attitude, a kick, a bending forward—all will involve some movement of the hips or the butt, sometimes exaggerated, sometimes just to not suppress the movement that might happen naturally as a result of the movement in the rest of the body.

As the rest of the women file out with a percussive, side-to-side swinging of the hips (only to re-enter in a little while from the other side), they leave one woman on stage, directly facing the percussionist. She suddenly lowers herself to the floor, balancing herself on toes, feet placed apart, and on her forearms, which prop the rest of her body up in the air. This signals almost a signature movement in this piece, repeated several times in varying tempi, from varying angles and positions. We see her in profile as she begins a fast shaking and circling of her butt in the air. This lowers the butt to the floor, and the impulse spreads, so that the entire lower back shakes and circles vigorously. The butt peaks again, marking a slow round in the air. As it marks the far contours of this circle, the butt—the highest point of the body in the air—pulls on the knees to dip them to the floor and up. Gradually, the butt lowers to pull the arms off the floor and return the body to standing, the hips continuing to sway from side to side.

Meanwhile, the three women who have re-entered the stage from the opposite corner begin moving to a rapid sequence, an elaborate choreography of leaps, rolls on the floor, kicks, and balances, which gradate to weave into one another. As this goes on, the percussion begins to slow down, and the rest of the women re-enter the space and join in this zestful dancing. One dancer signals a break as she steps forward, sharply displacing her butt to one side, and circling her wrist with a large flourish to place her hands on her hips. As the others gather around her, she introduces herself to the audience, the friendly tone of her voice still holding a veiled warning to the audience to note those special dancing hips. One by one, each dancer steps forward and raps out a sharp introduction, punctuated by her circling hips and snapping fingers, each woman moving and speaking with distinctly defined and different attitudes and tones, always doubling the import of her words with gestures that mark her personality. The lyrics and full-bodied gestures work in concert to create the highly sensuous yet playful images of these women, as they identify as different versions of "Big Mama," in charge of their bodies and sexualities. As they all join their voices in a final clamor, moving around in tightly knit chaos, we see them arriving upstage in a horizontal line, their backs to the audience.

From one end of the line, somebody calls out "Hey! Hey!" and, in immediate response, the seven women embark on a side-to-side toe-step-flat step pattern. Their upper bodies are flexed slightly forward, their fore-arms held straight in front of their bodies, and every weight shift is underlined by the side-to-side pushing of the hips, the head turning on every step to note the movement of the hips. The command comes, "Take it down!" and their knees flex and their torsos slant all the more forward as they continue the step pattern. Now the voice charges—"Take it back!" Sud-denly, the women, backs bent forward, butts jutting out, easily flexed knees, scoot forward rapidly toward the audience with a series of hop-shuffle steps. This marks a climactic moment in the piece: the audience who has until now seen mostly the backs of the dancers are now faced with a line of pushed-out butts advancing briskly toward them. This is Jawole Willa Jo Zollar's rejoinder to a sociocultural system that has fetishized one part of the African American female body, and her reclaiming of her body and its inherent beauty and sexuality. The movement of the hips and butt is also emphasized by the white UBW t-shirts that the dancers have tied around their waists in typical dancer-like style. The white fabric hangs loosely over their butts over their short black unitards, catching the light sharply and emphasizing the movement with the rippling of the loose ends of the t-shirt around the butt. The dancers now mark an energetic step pattern that carries them somewhat away from the audience. Stopping abruptly, they begin a rapid shaking of the butt, clasping their arms behind them as if to frame and ornament their shimmying hips, slowly stepping back toward the audience. The entire sequence in the line starts over again.

Obviously, choreographic intention in *Batty Moves* is multilayered. Movements that emphasize the hips and the butt become more than about invoking "other" cultures, cultural preferences, and aesthetics, though of course given the context in which this piece was created and performed—that of concert dance in America—this invocation of an "other" aesthetic and culture, which is also not-white, not-Europeanist, already marks it as "different." Importantly, however, the piece emerges out of Zollar's celebra-tion of black female sensuality and her revaluation of black female bodies, and much of her interventionary practice has to do with upturning histori-cal perceptions or misconstructions that have accrued to them. Specifically, the movement phrase described above—the scoot forward—invokes that fascination of nineteenth-century Europe with the genitalia and buttocks of Saartjie Bartman and others, women brought over from Africa and paraded from country to country as novelty items, freaks of nature, reportedly because of the enormous size and protruding shape of their butts.

Sander Gilman has shown through an analysis of visual art and litera-ture that since the seventeenth century, the occasional presence of black servants amid the otherwise uniformly white European figures in the foreground seems to mark the presence of illicit sexual activity.[6] This notion was taken up in the early part of the nineteenth century by scientists such as J. J. Virey, Henri de Blainville, and Georges Cuvier, who specialized in the study of racial differences, which then seemed to be contiguous with divergent behavior traits that seemed to typify "other" racial groups. The interest in Hottentots (or Khoikhoi) and Bushmen, culturally distinct peoples who lived in Southern Africa, is part of this apparently scientific research of comparative anatomists who studied both the body and the earth. However, as has been shown again and again,

> From the start of the scientific revolution, scientists viewed the earth or nature as female, a territory to be explored, exploited, and controlled. Newly discovered lands were personified as female, and it seems unsurprising that the women of these nations became the locus of scientific inquiry. Identifying foreign lands as female helped to naturalize their rape and exploitation, but the appearance on the scene of "wild women" raised troubling questions about the status of European women. Hence, it also became important to differentiate the "savage" land/woman from the civilized female of Europe.[7]

Indeed, when Saartjie Baartman was put on public display in 1810, it was as part of this program of violent but scientifically dressed-up racism whereby she was reduced to her sexual parts, and what was repeatedly pointed out was her steatopygia or protruding buttocks. What was also talked about but could not really be examined while she was alive, for she repeatedly refused to permit it, was the "Hottentot apron," the hypertrophy of the labia and nymphae, reportedly caused by manipulation of the genitalia. When she died at age twenty-five, after five years of public exhibition, the police prefect gave Cuvier permission to study her corpse. Baartman had been, in life, successful in preventing this ultimate probing into her body, but in death she lay docile, and Cuvier was able to examine and report to the world the "abnormalities" of her genitalia. All of this in order to finally complete "the comparison of a female of the 'lowest' human species with the highest ape (the orangutan)" and explain the pathological sexual nature of such women, and the obvious bestiality of her people. [8] This also to put to rest anxieties about hidden secrets about European women, and to brush over the obvious fascination and attraction that the European male felt for this "bestial" woman by pseudoscientific (but equally pathological and dangerous) discourses.

The "scoot forward" then picks up deliberately on this typical racist move of labeling anomalous, prurient, and bestial something of the "other" that is attractive, exciting, and interesting for various reasons, particularly in the realm of sexual attraction. Convenient metonymies are created—woman = (necessary misconceptions about) her sexual organs/body = racial typologies or characteristics of animalistic, lesser developed behaviours = enabling categories for a hierarchical ordering of the world and its peoples—and through these, dehumanizing reductions are effected, thus justifying the destruction of a people who have been "scientifically" and logically proven to be lesser beings.

This history of misperception of the black female body and sexuality as anomalous is deeply linked to the abuse, particularly the sexual exploitation, heaped on African American women throughout the slavery years. Yet, in *Batty Moves*, Zollar does not respond with sadness or anger to the memory of such abuse. Instead, she confronts that history and treats these constructions with supreme irreverence and witty sarcasm. She changes the pace and energy of a traveling phrase found in the movement vocabulary of several African dance styles, for instance, turns its facing around, places it at a climactic moment in the introductory section of the piece where it is emphasized through multiplication—a line of seven black women stridently performing it—thus overlaying the aforementioned associations with those of fun, power, and beauty.

In this way, her response goes beyond earlier reactions of the black diaspora to European stereotyping and misrepresentation, resistance modes that have been described by Cornel West as "moralistic in content and communal in character."[9] Here, the struggle was to present positive images of black life in order to combat the dangerous negative images in mainstream culture, but these attempts remained trapped within the same logic of binaries that they sought to combat and were further problematic because they were propelled by a homogenizing impulse, flattening the differences within the black communities. Zollar's response—not a response at all in the sense of a reaction, but witty, sarcastic, creative, and empowering, aesthetic and political at once, presents these women as complex human beings. They are subjects in control of the politics of representation, not objects upon whom it is thrust—changing in vital ways what Stuart Hall has described as "the relations of representation."[10] The piece thus simultaneously addresses histories of abuse of black peoples and the sexual exploitation of black women in particular, challenges the reduction of women to their sexual parts, actively creates a different aesthetic, and performs claims for the redefinition of beauty. This does not make light of the stereotype nor deny the havoc it has wreaked, but rather, disallows the further internalization of that history and thus refuses it power to cause further damage.

Talking about the work of artist Felix Gonzalez-Torres, bell hooks describes counter-hegemonic art as that which requires that we identify neither with the artist as iconic figure nor with the beautiful art object, but rather with ourselves as subjects of history through our interaction with the work.[11] Though concepts articulated in the realm of visual arts often do not work when applied in the realm of performing arts, or in embodiment in general, this notion of counter-hegemonic art encourages us to look at the broader commentary that *Batty Moves* evokes. Though the history of the Hottentot Venus is not directly brought up, it is recalled repeatedly through movement phrases such as the "scoot forward," and the piece disallows the viewer's sliding over that uncomfortable remembering. This is a moment of testimony as well of interrogation: the dancers' embodiment of this focus on the hips and butt does not provide an escape into a world created by the artistic imaginary, but testifies to the history of fetishization and abuse that has layered the black female body in much Eurocentric imagination. At the same time, it compels us to interact with the in-your-face way in which that history is evoked, and with the way it actively bends that history to refigure the politics of such representation. The gaze is returned as the piece leads us to examine our locations, our experience of these events in history, our relationship to the aesthetics of difference, our stand on how we represent ourselves, and, more specifically, how we react as we sit in our chairs watching these seven black women backing up on us relentlessly, their butts in our faces. Such representation is not just a rebuttal of negatives, it emerges from a different framework: from a learning to love and value one's physicality and a calm assertion of one's need to have control over how one is represented.

At another level, the epic memory of Africanist movement styles, marked by the get-down quality, the high contrasts, hip movements, curvi-linearity, are celebrated and woven into the very texture of Euro-American, specifically "white," movement styles to create a comment of unusual depth and perspective. In such choreography, subversion and critique are braided with celebration and creativity. I want to highlight this multidimensional-ity—this weaving and layered texture—as marking the embodiment of Zollar's complex and unique movement aesthetic.

With their backs still to the audience, in a horizontal line, the dancers now begin to sway their hips from side to side, the arms swinging, lassoing around the body. The measured regularity of the motion is cut off by one leg that swings sharply to position the body at an angle to the front. Stand-ing in relevé, arms flexed forward from the elbows, on a heavily empha-sized breath pattern, the dancers wriggle their butts percussively, thrusting the hips back and forth at the same time as one foot steps back and forth. This develops into a freeze, from which the dancers are propelled into movement again by a ringing directive: "Party time, yo'all!" From one point of the line the movement spreads, as one dancer claps her hands and jumps lightly on both feet, and then swings her hips in a marked rhythm, arms by the sides of the hips slashing up and down to underline their movement. As the rhythm travels down the line, mutating here and there, becoming more and more complex in the process, it grows louder, more insistent. Suddenly it is interrupted as the dancers break into a quick one-two cha-cha-cha footwork, the hips swinging sensually from side to side as the feet mark the pattern with ease. This takes the dancers to delineate different rhythmic patterns with their hips, twisting and turning the body above in counterpoint. The next injunction "Snake yo'all!" makes one hip jut out to slither the leg on that side out and curl it up and back in. As the leg slides back to the floor, the hips pull to one side and then the other to draw a smooth figure-of-eight in the air. The last directive is an ironic tour de force. The voice calls out "Attitude walk"—and instead of that hallmark of balletic and modern dance technique, a walk or "promenade" with one leg in attitude, the dancers give us a walk with an "attitude" indeed. They strut backward diagonally, legs crossing at knees on each step, hands on their shaking hips, chin tilted to observe their own proud bodies.

Like this section, *Batty Moves* abounds with surprises. Moments of high contrast, while in keeping with an Africanist aesthetic that celebrates the richness of oppositions, are still surprising in the general context of American concert dance, where notions of unity of style dominate.[12] As the piece draws to a close, we see the seven women in two horizontal lines, backs to the audience. As if in a "regular" technique class, the dancers flex into a grand plié to the floor. But in the rising, the unilinearity of the spine is jostled away as the hip swings from side to side, curvilinearity marking the body's ascent to verticality. This is followed by a typically balletic port de bras, pulling the body in a long line in a side bend and then forward as the arms sweep to the floor. Immediately though, the feet jump into a wide parallel position and the floored palms are flung up into the air, one after another, to mark the alternate beats of the rhythmic cycle while the swinging hips mark every beat. Only such a multiply delineated rhythm can coax the dancers back to their upright positions.

This, then, is part of the brilliance of Zollar's choreography, particularly evident in *Batty Moves*, this easy juxtaposition of the high and the low, the high and the high, and the low and the low, Africanist aesthetics commenting on and intersecting with the lines of modern dance. A sharp, rhythmic step sequence may be softened with a phrase where the movements are slow, full, and circular, integrating the hip with the body which moves as a whole, but will almost immediately be undercut with another sequence, sharp and percussive, marking rhythms with isolated body parts, always emphasizing hip and butt isolations.

The subversive practice in *Batty Moves*, a recurrent enough technical marker of Zollar's idiom, is also a unique embodiment of the intentionally equivocating signification we see so often in black literary and cultural practice. In such practice, dominant codes from mainstream rhetorical usage collide with typical reinterpretations in black usage, and traditional meanings are invoked only in order to be resignified with critical difference and ultimately upstaged. In this collision of black and white semantic fields, what is deferred is the primacy of the dictionary or syntactic meaning, while the recoded signifier sits in parallel capacity with it.

Zollar doubles the irony of this tradition through her double-bodied choreography. Let us look, for instance, at a traveling movement phrase from *Batty Moves*. The dancers enter from the upstage left-hand corner, one by one, and rush across the stage in a diagonal line, performing what seems to be a series of rapid chainée turns. But the chainée turn is invoked here only to be dislodged, for its strictly vertical alignment is recast into twiced-curvilinearity in the bodies of the Urban Bush Women. The dancers here, firstly, open their shoulders and arms slightly beyond the line of the chest at the initiation of each turn, so that the back is pulled into a convexity with every turn. Secondly, the line of the spine is curved as, on each turn, the pelvis pushes out with the outward movement of the arms, defying the favored linear positioning of the spine in the typical chaineè. Further, the dancers ground the up-reaching energy that is supposed to mark the chaineè, going through their turns with more of a gliding motion of the feet working with the ground, instead of pressing against the ground to remain in relevé. Because of the rapid pace at which this phrase is performed, these subtle changes in the initiation and execution of the movement, its energy, and spirit, are not very pronounced. So, at first glance, one might think one is seeing, in fact, a series of chainée turns, but the difference becomes obvious as the series of dancers perform it repetitively across the floor, and the recalling of the classical move only to be revised becomes all the more subversive.

In sections such as this, where Zollar takes a movement from the classical vocabularies of ballet and modern dance forms and soils it, so to speak, with body attitudes deemed antithetical to its very definition, she embodies redoubled, tongue-in-cheek, and critical resignifications of dominant cultural tropes. Here, many of the features that Geneva Smitherman lists as typical of a "black mode of discourse" are present: in the invocation yet not of formulations from mainstream (white) American dance, there is the indirect way of making a point, there is irony, punning, and play, and, specifically in the wider context of the piece, there is the use of the metaphorical or the imagistic mode, where the images still remain rooted in the everyday or real world.[13] Further, in this double-bodied play, where a series of hip shakes might follow on the heels of a rond de jomb en l'air, performed according to the specifications of a ballet dictionary, so that questions about capability are constantly deferred by the assertion of preference, the politics of the larger sociocultural world, its misconceptions and stereotypes, are constantly called up and exposed.

In doing this, Zollar is both reaffirming black traditional cultural practices and extending them, for the practice of signification has been articulated and theorized primarily with regard to black literary and musical practice. Of course, this revising with a deviation, this celebration of playing with the exact delineations of "technique" so as to imbue them with a totally different aesthetic, and with the caveat that the dancers are capable of executing the first with aplomb, is not typical in Euro-American performance practice, the mainstream tradition of concert dance in America. However, it reminds one of music scholar Samuel A. Floyd Jr.'s rearticulation of Henry Louis Gates's theory of critical signification. Floyd talks of signification in music as troping:

> . . . the transformation of pre-existing musical material by trifling with it, teasing it, or censuring it. Musical Signifyin(g) is the rhetorical use of pre-existing material as a means of demonstrating respect for or poking fun at a musical style, process, or practice through parody, pastiche, implication, indirection, humor, tone play or word play, the illusion of speech or narration, or other troping mechanisms.[14]

Floyd also emphasizes Gates's point about the *materiality* of the signifier in his discussion of the physical presence of the body in the ring shout, and the embodied troping mechanisms of clapping, shuffling, and jerking of the shoulders. "Such dance movements are material signifiers in the music/dance experience, joining the Signifyin(g) musical tropes . . . as material tropes that should be the focus of our perceptual and analytical attention."[15]

Again, musical troping can be, as in the literary practice, synchronic or diachronic. Extending this to dance, we might describe synchronic signifying as a response in the performative moment: like the rise from the "perfectly" executed plié with swaying hips and curving butt, rewriting rules of linear alignment. Diachronic signifying might be described as an ironical dialogue with, not just a recalling of, moments in history or historical predecessors. I see the "scoot forward" move as a typical example of this, where Zollar invokes the construction and history of the Hottentot Venus and, as if in conversation with her, flaunts that fetishized body part in our faces. These tropes layer each other and point to the many levels at which *Batty Moves* functions. Throughout the piece, in fact, the (*mis*)placement of the butt and hips at key points effects a *dis*placement of critical focus and exposes fissures in concepts of the purity of origins, whether at the level of racial histories, or at the level of body aesthetic and dance technique.

Obviously, the materiality or embodiment of the signifying devices, which function through diverse modes such as synchronic and diachronic, call for a specific, contexted reading of such cultural production that is missing from general reviews of such work. For it is in the mode of embodiment, the way gestures or movements are taken on, that illuminate both the structure of "difference" and the text-less critique that is danced. Here, I quote again from Floyd to comment on my own methodology of constantly and immediately interweaving analyses of technique and movement with invocations of historical and cultural context, in order to accomplish a dense reading of choreography and emphasize the importance of dancing bodies as vital registers of cultural politics.

> It is this materiality and its solid cultural grounding that prove the impropriety and futility of applying to black music, an aesthetic determinant, the European notion of transcendent, abstract beauty (which leads to formalist analysis and criticism in which "good intonation," "ensemble blend and balance," "proper harmonic progressions," "precise attacks," and other such concerns take precedence over the content of what is expressed and communicated), and that therefore suggest, or demand, a cultural-studies approach to black music—that is, the ring shout itself contains within it the very basis for inquiry from within the tradition.[16]

Indeed, as Floyd suggests, the critiques can be seen to lie within the choreographic structure and movement content once we are attentive to context, and while, in this case for instance, references to Saartjie Bartman are not explicit in the choreography, the ways in which the butt is used and the piece is choreographed pry open questions about these histories.

The power of *Batty Moves* lies in its choreographic and idiomatic structures whereby imprisoning stereotypes about the black female body, often internalized to the extent that natural movement and sensuality were consciously curbed in an attempt to live down that stereotype, are confronted and demolished through choreography filled with surprises. Zollar disallows the dictum of mainstream dance training in the West about the linearity of spinal alignment that permeates the performance of ballet and modern vocabulary, and unravels an alternative aesthetic characterized by extensive isolated hip and back movements. But rejecting complicity in white, and later black, eroticizations of the black female body, Zollar refuses to be locked into isolated hip and butt movements alone, but intercuts them with movements from a strict modern vocabulary where the butt is kept in line with the rest of the spine, implying capability for adhering to any one given body image but rejecting it in preference for one more complex and shifting. The activity is richly creative—the butt and the hips swing, not just to dislodge the lines of ballet, but because their movement is perceived as beautiful, if according to another register of beauty. Another aesthetic is in place here—as a matter of choice, with full knowledge of the other possibilities. This layered choreography where idioms comment upon each other also challenges the one-dimensional re-sexualizing of the hip and butt that marks the representation of black female sexuality in much contemporary popular culture, and which, bell hooks has suggested, reinforces these body parts as sexual signs even as it challenges negative racist assumptions about them.[17]

Further, in laughing/dancing off an imprisoning stereotype about the black female body with total irreverence with specific reference to dominant American culture, Zollar repeatedly refuses to image black women in terms of the racist hierarchies of this culture, and points to the complex imbrication of domination/objectification and resistance/creativity in the formation of identities. She creates series of images of six black women contesting definitions as they play fiercely with movement, challenging us to see these black bodies as anything but beautiful and sensuous, swinging with hidden subversives and taking pleasure in their bodies and sexualities. Finally, then, in constantly taking movements from mainstream dance styles and "soiling" them, so to speak, from under, she plays with established cultural and aesthetic concepts and repeatedly inserts her presence into them in a way that demands their redefinition.

ANGIKA (1985)
Rehistoricizing Cultural Legacies

One of her earlier works, which immediately earned her national attention, singling her out as an important artist to be watched, *Angika* can almost be regarded as marking the beginning of Chandralekha's career as contemporary choreographer. Having left dance to work with the women's movement and other artistic disciplines for a while, Chandralekha returned to dance when she was invited along with other well-known dancers and choreographers to show her work at the East West Dance Encounter organized by the Max Mueller Bhavan and the National Center for Performing Arts in Bombay in 1984. She had not performed in public for twelve years, and people did not quite know what to expect. For this showing, she revived parts of older works, *Devadasi* and *Navagraha*, and collaboratively created a duet with well-known male dancer, Kamadeva, *Primal Energy*. The unique minimalistic use of the Bharatanatyam idiom in these pieces created great excitement in dance circles and she was invited to show her work again the next year. It was at the following East West Dance Encounter in 1985, that Chandralekha premiered *Angika*, subtitled "Traditions of Dance and Body Language in India." This was a piece that altered perceptions of Indian dance inexorably. As one critic, Sumitra Srinivasan, euphorically pointed out; "*Angika* sets the body free . . . after this, Bharatanatyam need never be the same again."[1]

Even as I distance my reading of this piece from the romanticized rhetoric of "a free body," it is vital to begin with an investigation into the widespread impression of its liberating potential, which marked its premiere in different places across the world. I will want to take this discussion in two directions. First of all, it seems that this setting free of the body lends itself to a feminist reading. I think that the classical dancing body in India comes to perform, be imaged in terms of, and constructs, clearly differentiated gendered behaviors. Hence the possibility of *ekaharya abhinaya*, where the solo dancer tells the story enacting the roles of all the characters of the story—possible only because the performance of male versus female behav-

iors, in the first instance, and thereafter, the defined classification of archetypal characters, is so distinct. Moreover, since realism is almost never the
goal, behavior is highly stylized and heightened, such that dailiness never
intrudes into the realm of classical performance. There is no attempt here
to locate a "natural" dancing body, or to perform movements as functional
only, or as naturalized through repeated citation. This heightening also
serves to sustain and systematize several sociopolitical hierarchies: it renders opaque the constructed binarization of genders and sexes, and it also
supports the mythology of divine sanction for the dance. *Angika*, by making
transparent the manipulation of movement to reflect gendered hierarchies,
also allows for the staging of female and male bodies that have access to an
undifferentiated repertoire of movements, particularly in the first few
scenes, built on yoga and martial arts movements.

The second direction has to do with the metanarrative of divine origins
that looms over Indian classical dance. This avowed divine beginning for
the dance has tended to lock it into an ahistorical category, unchanging
through time, a notion no doubt popularized particularly in service of the
Orientalism of the Modern Euro-West. In contrast, in *Angika* Chandralekha
explores the historical development of the performing body through various cultural and artistic traditions. What is at work here, however, is a
unique kind of mytho-poetical imagination, which, while still intent on
drawing out the metaphysical and remarkable potential of the body, still
refuses to journey through magical stories of gods, goddesses, and larger-
than-life figures. Instead it moves through aesthetic explorations of yoga,
Kalarippayattu, and Bharatnatyam to weave connections between different
physical traditions and create an intertexted framework of cultural practices
from which the classical dance forms emerge. Clearly, in this project Chandralekha was choreographing her explorations of the ancient tenet from the
classical scripture of performance, the *Abhinaya Darpana* of Nandikesvara,
which avowedly lies at the root of much of her work: "Angikam bhuvanam
yasya," the body is your world. Hence, a history of the dance necessarily
engages in a world-making project—its aesthetic framework, its philosophical base, its principles of pleasure and excellence—through explorations of
bodily practices. Related to this idea is one of the avowedly central intentions of this work: Chandralekha's effort to recast dance history divorced
from the usual sentimentality and religiosity that have come to be regarded
as inseparable from it. Thus, while the *Natyashastra*'s delineations of the
body and movement could be valued and explored in contemporary performance, Chandralekha insisted on discarding the theory of the divine origins of classical dance, which shrouded the dancing body in mythology and
mystery. It is indeed through this simultaneous rejection of divinity,
mythology, and mysticism in understanding the roots of the dance, and the

embracing of a wider context of physical forms, connected through their philosophical moorings, that the dancing body is resituated in relationship to a diverse set of physical practices that form part of its historic and cultural framework.

Moreover, the contemporary specialization of dance, its commercial packaging as saleable commodity, prevents us from seeing the breadth of the context in which it is set. In historicizing the development of the dance, especially Bharatnatyam, *Angika* draws our attention to these obscured links and urges the viewing of dance in terms of somatic processes such as breath, energy, embodied principles of geometry, that invigorate all of these disciplines. In this, *Angika* accomplishes a denaturalization of what masquerades as tradition, as divine authority, as heritage, and ruptures the claims of "purity" that frame classical dance. It refuses the policing of boundaries that seems to become a necessary marker of "tradition" and "classicism," and it seeks relationship with other forms, even a cross-fertilization of influences among these practices. It also thereby historicizes Bharatnatyam, even as it rewrites the traditional anthropological perspective that might suggest that cultural practices are discrete, evolved in isolation, proposing instead their "contamination" through exposure to other forms and their evolution through cross-influences from various movement genres. It is also in this project of historicizing, then, working through material practices and thereafter through political manipulations, that the "freeing" potential of *Angika* might be located. What might also be clear by now is that while Chandralekha's commentary is embedded in the history and context of Bharatnatyam, there is a clear sense that the other classical dance forms, in fact, the notion of classicism itself, that are implicated in this political curve.

Angika is choreographed in six sequences and was danced initially by three women and seven men but, with the composition of the company and the choreography having changed several times, it has been danced later by different casts. I will delineate the ideas basic to Chandralekha's historicizing of bodily practices as artistic development in this section with general observations on the movement ideas in *Angika*, relying less on detailed descriptions of the sequences because the specific choreographic structure for this piece has changed with changing casts and contexts. This is, however, a seminal piece in her repertoire that most of her dancers are familiar with, even if they have joined her group recently and have not had a chance to learn the choreography, since *Angika* has not been performed lately.

I also want to offer some thoughts about the sequentiality of the piece before I go into the descriptions of the sections themselves. Undoubtedly there is a sense of the linear development of physical genres in this piece, a sense that the piece travels through temporal frames designated as "pre-history" and "historical time," marking the development of various physical traditions that culminate in the development of the dance, which then is co-opted by a patriarchal culture for its own uses. Indeed, the program notes, which I will quote from as I go through the different sections, foster that impression. However, the choreography itself undermines the fixity of such a teleological direction. No doubt the piece is fueled by research about indigenous cultural practices that either predate the development of the performance traditions that are scripted in the *Natyashastra*, or are at least simultaneous with it. Moreover, there is a marked emphasis on the way the development of patriarchy distorts cultural production and "tradition." However, the way in which the choreography progresses—the earlier scenes exploring the different physical traditions by themselves, the later sections working increasingly thereafter to coalesce these traditions, positioning them in simultaneity and conversation with each other—makes two important statements. First, the dance developed as a physical discipline in a context where practices such as yoga and Kalarippayattu existed or were developing and influenced the movement aesthetic, hence primarily a statement about concurrence, simultaneity, and relationship, rather than one of chronology. Second, the exploration of the disciplines by themselves clarify the shared philosophical, spiritual, and material bases of these forms, suggesting that they be viewed as connected practices that constitute a broad movement base. While this emphasizes the spiritual dimensions of the dance, it also humanizes it: dance is posited as one among several embodied cultural practices, developed in human terms, not perceived as a "gift from the gods." Moreover, the apparent temporal linearity of the piece, while self-consciously rendering these "timeless" classical forms historical—that is, registering changes and shifts in moving through time—also in fact disrupts Eurocentric history's progress-bound model by foregrounding a more oscillating and discontinuous historical model, a claim I seek to support through my following descriptions of the piece.

Interestingly, there is also another way in which this sequentiality can be read, which both comments on and challenges a time-bound historical interpretation of the piece. In the way it is organized, moving from explorations of elements and characteristics of movement and energy deployment to increasingly complex dance sequences culminating in a vibrant sequence, it recalls and signifies on the structure of a contemporary Bharatnatyam performance. Such a performance, arranged as a presentation of concert dance, progresses through "items" such as *Alarippu, Jatiswaram, Shabdam, Varnam, Padam,* and *Tillana,* each section symbolic of stages of a journey, physical and/or metaphysical. While *Angika* directly refers to or names only two of these items, also the most significant categories, the

Varnam and the *Tillana*, the others are implied in the movement of the piece.[2] Such an arrangement of repertoire might reflect on the fact that this structuring is contemporary, part of the needs of a concert stage presentation, which in turn is very much a result of the very historical changes mirrored in this alternative interpretation of "item" categories Chandralekha offers. If then *Angika* is also an exposition of Bharatnatyam like other classical concerts claim to be, then, it clearly shifts the structure and understanding of the form in this incarnation.

The piece begins by recalling the unique positioning of the human body, its vertical location between earth and sky. As if he would stretch the body to its utmost as a medium between the two spaces, a man (Nandakumar) stands balanced on one leg, the other flexed twice to place the sole against the thigh of the standing leg. This, the first asana of the yogic repertoire, *vrksasana*, in which the body, atop such a balance, reaches tall, and the arms extend past the ears to join the palms in a salutation above the head, is only held momentarily. He opens out his palms and pulls them outward, etching two diagonal lines from his shoulders. His neck stretches to tilt his head up and he fixes his gaze skyward, his foot remaining steadily rooted to the ground. It is as if, in that moment of ultimate stretch, he realizes the spatial relevance of the body, as if for that instant sky and earth, upward and downward energies, meet in his extended body. Now the nine dancers, who are organized in a grid of three rows in this opening sequence, embark on a similar exploration of yogic asanas, as if in order to

Chandralekha Group, *Angika*. Photo © Dashrath Patel.

realize the concept of yoga as a meditation on the extensive possibilities of the body. Because they are performed continuously, melding into one another, the asanas do not seem to be practiced as virtuosic body positions, as demonstrations of remarkable flexibility and balance, but rather as archetypal and shifting forms that set the performers out on an exploration of their bodily capabilities. Dancers positioned at different points on the stage begin to elongate the line of the spine continuously in backbends which bridge the body as curve between hands and feet, the yogic *urdhva dhanurasana*, or which fountain the body over toward the heel of the back leg where the only contact point of the body with the floor are the feet positioned parallel and away from each other, the yogic *parsvottanasana*. The curving of the body forward to reach the forehead to the feet is similarly explored in different levels juxtaposed against each other: one dancer stands in a wide second position and flexes from waist down to reach her head to the floor (the yogic *prasarita padottanasana*), while another sits on the floor right in front of her, her legs flexed out from the hip and in from the knee so that the soles touch each other in front of the pelvic floor, and curls her head down to meet the ground near the feet (the yogic *baddha konasana*). Another dancer on the other side of the stage works his way from a prone position on the floor, the legs reaching slowly overhead to touch the tips of the toes to the floor in an extended *halasana*. These transmute into other asanas that seem to flow organically from them, without large energy shifts to reposition or without having to move away from the initial point of movement. It is as if these points in space in which the dancers begin to move are themselves elasticized, stretched in multiple directions, but never themselves resituated. This seems to signal the beginning of the conscious formalization of movement, the tuning and centering of the body to realize its capacities for line, flow, and balance, marking the material origins of the dance.

The next sequence moves on to explore another formulation of the body through a different use of energy and a focus on momentum. On either side of the space, dancers position themselves at the entrances of the two wings in two parallel lines, squatting. One by one, pairs of dancers from either wings run in. With a typical jump from Kalarippayattu, where one leg kicks up in the jump to slap the palm of an arm raised in front the body at shoulder level, they arrive at a more central point on stage and sit on the floor, knees reaching out to the sides. The principles of the martial arts are explored here, through movements that integrate the modes of attack and defense and show the body's progression to develop movements around the concepts of control, balance, coordination, endurance, alertness, lightness, tension, and relaxation. Men and women, women and women, men and men partner each other in this exploration where the prime focus is mastering principles of energy and fine manipulation of the body-in-space, not the relative strength of bodies. In this mixed partnering attention is drawn to the characteristics of the movement itself: the energy with which elbows reach out forward while the body lunges out and down, and how those lines are maintained as the arms suddenly pull back. What Chandralekha capitalizes on in this section, which is based more or less completely on marital art sequences but never becomes a straightforward demonstration of them, is the principle whereby attack and defense can coalesce in a single movement: a moment of cautious self-protection whereby parallel and closely joined legs are flexed forward, arms folded forward and joined from the elbows up, palms folded in front of the face, the body flexed forward from the hip, leaning over the thighs, can be a preparatory moment for, and lead into, an aggressive lunge, one leg sliding back to extend to its full length, the torso rising to continue the diagonal line of the leg, the arms slashing across the air to extend in front of the body, still joined from the elbows. This is one instance of Chandralekha's choreographic realization of some of the basic laws in Kalarippayattu, which Chandralekha's martial arts consultant Pandian V., for this piece, describes as knowing "how to defend, how to attack, how to defend and attack at the same time, how to defend without attacking, how to attack without seeming to defend, how to attack the *marmas* (vital nerve centers), how to lunge and attack, how to block with the hands crossed in *swastika banda.*"[3] Attacks, for instance, with fisted hands cutting straight across the air, bodies in strong wide lunges, are explored with six dancers facing different directions. They are intersected with swirling kicks that move the dancers and cause the lines of the surging out legs and arms to cut through each other's spatial orbits, creating a network of attack and defense, cycles of mobile and mobilizing energy.

One particular move that recurs in this scene, dissolving shorter sequences of high martial energy only to rebuild them again, is significant in the way it emphasizes the sense of quickly shifting energies. The dancers on stage begin to move swiftly, in a sideways run. Other dancers from the wings enter and run similarly across the stage and back again. Again and again dancers enter and leave, some facing, others with their back to the audience, as if mobilizing all linear directions in that space. The lines become increasingly dense as more and more dancers converge on stage, moving through the space at the same time, vibrating it with their quick-moving energies, and then they thin out, leaving only the dancers for the next section on stage. This also creates a sharp contrast with the other sections where the dancers move with intense energy, sometimes with slashing-out lines of the limbs, sometimes with slow focused concentration, but generally holding the ground on which they start to move.

These above sections clarify the specific physiological theories that both yoga and Kalarippayattu are based on. Unlike in many Western physical disciplines, the body is conceptualized, not through an emphasis on the musculature, but rather on the nervous and skeletal frames. Understanding the functioning of the nerve centers is vital in order to control the use of one's energy flow, while the skeletal frame, with the help of the muscles and ligaments, houses the organs that keep the body functioning. The body is then constantly viewed as imbued with intelligence whose workings, as seen in the highly evolved organizations of life-continuing and life-supporting circuits, are distinct from, if working in consonance with, conscious intellectual activity. It is significant that Chandralekha relates Bharatanatyam to disciplines and body theories such as these, for they immediately mark a very important difference between the dominant ways technique is approached in the West, for instance, and in several parts of Asia, certainly in India. None of these physical disciplines—dance, martial arts, or yoga—work primarily through muscular manipulation and control, but rather through the principle of openness, attained through an increasing focus on breath.

In the next section, the focus shifts to tracing connections between life activity and work activity and the consequent evolution of physical practices with an obvious interest in understanding movement, from the perspectives both of its functionality and aesthetic dimensions. Drawing one more time on movements from kalarippayattu and martial arts, the dancers develop locomotive styles from their observations of animal movements. These walks are not realistic imitations, nor are they close to the more stylized walks later described in the classical scriptures of performance. As they are deployed here in *Angika*, they are ways of discovering the body and the rudiments of how it operates, of understanding the concept of propelling the body vertically in space through a jump, of coming to realize the possibility of changing the direction of one's journey through a turn, and of discerning the basic principles in pace, level change, and body attitude and how they effect movement. Stealthy weight shifts are learned from the tiger, while continuously grounded motions across space are understood by watching the snake. A gallop-like movement where both forelegs (hands), then both hind legs (feet), are thrust forward, effecting a very different kind weight shift from the cross-lateral movement of the tiger, comes from following the horse. This is differentiated from the spring-like motion inspired by the hops of the rabbit, where the entire body is lifted up and down in short spasm-like elevations. The cockatoo is evoked through a sitting-in-air posture and small, stalking motions of the dancers, their chests flexed forward over joined thighs, elbows joined before knees, forearms rising to point joined palms, beak-like, before their faces. The leap returns

Chandralekha Group, *Angika*, Animal walks from Kalarippayattu. Photo © Dashrath Patel.

once more in the frog-like walk, particularly daunting in this humanized form as the dancers, locking their heels into their buttocks, jump up into the air to land in a low crouch on all fours. In an exploration of the crocodile walk from kalarippayattu, the dancers hold their bodies parallel but close to the floor, propped up by palms and toes pressed against the ground, and continuously jump forward on all fours, like a crocodile stalking its prey. Alternating with this is the camel-like walk where the dancers, bent over double, the pelvis raised and the palms flattened on the floor close by the feet, shift their bodies unevenly in space, resembling the dipping, humped gait of the camel.

Elements from familiar everyday movements are expanded and extended, and the different nuances characterizing them are highlighted through unique juxtapositions. The joining of the palms, for instance, makes the *anjali hasta* in the repertoire of hand gestures in Indian classical dance, as well as in everyday social gestural codes, to signify a basic greeting. Moreover, while the *anjali hasta*, like all other mudras/hand gestures, can signify several different meanings depending on the impulse of the narrative context (*biniyoga*), the particular doubled connotation here, recalling the beak of the bird (cockatoo) that inspired the movement, and functioning as part of a defense-attack mode, is interesting. No doubt this usage is common for a specific audience knowledgeable about kalarippayattu, but for a contemporary dance audience, most of whom are not familiar with that style, the usage of the *anjali hasta*, flexed forward from the wrists to jut out from the face, working on the imagistic and functional representational levels at once, and combined with small, strutting, bird-like steps, resignifies it. This technique of defamiliarizing the familiar, of recontextualizing the known in an unknown setting, lies at the root of both Chandralekha's revolutionizing the traditional movement base available to her and of her redefinition and expansion of the idiom of dance. The entire concept of humans learning about locomotion by studying the animal world is also interesting: it destabilizes the evolutionary model where human beings are placed at the pinnacle, superior to other animals.

This leads into the more formalized series of eight animal walks from the kalarippayattu repertoire, decontexted from their location in specific, determined fight sequences, and intercut by martial and yogic leaps, turns, and splits. Technically difficult, the *ashtavadivu* (eight animal walks) include gaits that are inspired by the different movement principles and the body sizes and shapes of the elephant, the lion, the horse, the boar, the peacock, the cock, the fish, and the serpent. Once again, though these sequences are choreographed into the general movement flow with the dancers adhering exactly to the technical specifications that mark their execution in kalaripayattu, they are interwoven with such variations and choreographed as such a continuum of energies peaking and ebbing instead of being isolated movement units, that they open up a vast range of movement possibilities and energy lines. The floor becomes more than usual surface, as feet as well as hands tread on it, and torsos brush up against it in a curving movement, in several "grounded" walks. Interestingly, this section also invokes the former, emphasizing the point about connections between forms: especially for those familiar with yoga, the crocodile walk of kalarippayattu recalls the yogic *nakrasana*, where the floor position of the latter is mobilized across the floor, and the camel walk seems to evolve from activating and manipulating the *uttanasana* where the body is still flexed over from the hip and the head tucked in between the knees.

All of this creates adequate preamble for exploring the bases of the abstract aesthetic of the dance. The conceptualization of the body in the *Natyashastra*, the world's first text on the body and movement written by the sage Bharata, now provides a specific base for this exploration. Chandralekha focuses on the basic elements of style, exploring Bharata's categorization of gestures, his detailed repertoires of movements for primary limbs (*anga*), subsidiary limbs (*pratyanga*), and tertiary limbs (*upanga*), all of which can be used variously in different contexts, and his refinement of the concepts of body positions, jumps, turns, and gaits into a highly evolved repertoire of dance movements to define the grammatical base for an expressive movement form. Obviously these are not merely strung together in a catalogue of movements, but even while they are performed with minimal elaboration and adornment, the choreography creates juxtapositions, contrasts through manipulations of pace and direction, to create a rich movement fabric with many dimensions. *Mandalas*, for instance, are performed by all the dancers simultaneously, sometimes one lined up behind the other contributing to the depth of the image, sometimes positioned at angles to each other to create a kaleidoscopic picture. We notice the difference from the previous sections: instead of the arms reaching in extended yogic lines, or slashing out the sides in attack-defense mode, they are positioned in asymmetrical lines, one overhead flexed at elbow and wrist, the hand in inverted *katakamukha hasta*, the other in curving around the torso, the hand forming the *katakamukha* at the center of the chest. The jumps begin to emphasize the take-off and landing points of perfect *mandalas*. Yet, occasionally, in the way space is covered through lunging movements, in between specifically recognizable stepping patterns of dance, we seem to catch glimpses of the previous scenes. These scenes are also recalled in the some preparatory moves that occasionally enter the choreography: for instance, in the last of a series of jumps where the legs kick high to reach the toes to the extended palms, the body stilled momentarily in mid-air to move through this position.

The dancers then move on to longer dance units, the *adavus* (basic movement phrases) of Bharatnatyam, which they perform with variations of speed, order, and direction. Movements, whose rudiments could be discerned in the earlier sequences, are now seen elaborated and developed: this pure dance (*nritta*) section marks the transition from martial arts and yoga to artistic engagement where the centrality of the body in elaborating this abstract symbolic framework is celebrated. At first, we see stilled moments from the *adavus*, slowed-down footwork patterns, the intended reaching points of the fingers at the end of a particular step sequence marked with deliberation. Then short step units—a jump, a side bend—are danced, the dancers juxtaposed in various ways, and plays on direction, pace, and the crossing of lines that also reveal the intermediary points between two steps. Then, entire *adavus*, in several tempi, some marked by rapid stepping patterns, some by the curving and turning lines of the torso, some by jumps. We also see here the danced versions of animal walks, more stylized than in kalarippayattu, more weighted toward metaphoric representations, using the *hasta*s or hand gestures that signify those animals. As the repertoire of eye, head, neck gestures (*drshtiveda, sirveda, grbaveda*) choreographed on a group of dancers who perform them, not as exercises, but as movement that enliven the body and the performance space, meld into longer *adavu* sequences, we witness the unfolding of idiomatic elements—grammar and syntax—into poetic articulations.

It is only fitting that this reference to the development of pure dance should be followed by Chandralekha's re-examination of *nritya* or expressional dance, where dramatic elements and expressive intent (*abhinaya*) are woven into dance movement. The choreographic focus now shifts from the body-in-movement and the exploration of characteristics of movement as abstract aesthetic mode to a highly poetic and evocative use of movement in *abhinaya*, elaborating, reinterpreting, and layering the emotional context invoked by the lyrics of the accompanying song, even as an implicit narrative about the co-opting of the dance by political-economic hierarchies and gender inequalities is played out through implication. Here is a point again when the teleological historiography is significant for what it achieves: by casting the development of patriarchy and the way in which it imprints the dance as posterior to the development of the dance itself, *Angika* suggests that the gender biases that now seem inherent in the dance, the typical ways in which women are conceptualized, particularly in the *abhinaya* sections, are in fact part of a historical development, very much a function of the shift of dance becoming a women-dominated practice in a social context riddled with gendered hierarchies, geared somewhat at entertainment and increasingly spectacular display. In this scene, Chandralekha choreographs a scathing comment on the development of the classical dance in a patriarchal society, and the process of commercialization of women's bodies, where the vibrant moving bodies of the previous scenes appear weak and controlled by outside forces, the strong promise of their potential clearly attenuated. The program notes ask difficult questions: "Bharata gave us the concept of *sharira-mandala*—our body as the center of the universe. What happened to that inspired body language?" As the sequence shows, without taking recourse to a simplistic narrative, the forces that energized these dancing bodies were subverted, fragmented, and negated through the socialization of the dance in time.

> First, the transformation of the body as a vehicle to serve gods, religion, priests. Then, the transformation of the body as a vehicle to serve kings, courtiers, men. The shift of the dance from the temple to the court, of its content from "bhakti" to "shringara," of the focus from the abstract divinity of gods to the concrete divinity of kings. Then the transformation of the body as a vehicle and victim of moralistic society. Devadasi becomes . . . "thevadiyar" or a plain prostitute . . . a common "janadasi."[4]

The cosmic, martial, and material origins of dance are thus obscured in the religio-mythical shrouds that are cast over it. Moreover, dance becomes increasingly cosmetic, divorced from real-life concerns, and inscribed in a system geared for the subjugation of women's bodies through the later

Vedic ages, the eras of repeated foreign invasions, of colonization, through the postcolonial era up to contemporary times. Again, the program notes are somewhat problematic in that the female body seems to be a passive site of inscription, overwritten by political institutions such that the possibility of a dialectical relationship between the body as acted-upon site and actor is pre-empted. Once again, too, the choreography, particularly the following sequences, presents somewhat different ideas, especially when considered in the context of the totality of the piece.

However, in a striking choreographic venture, Chandralekha sets up a stage within the stage and duplicates the structure of an audience on stage. The two women dance for a double audience: groups of men are seated on either side of the stage, observing the dancers. The dancers face the men on stage as much as they do the audience, and occasionally seem to dance to them, as if offering the dance to them. At one point, some of the men turn their focus outward toward the audience, as if to return to them the same scrutinizing and objectifying gaze with which they behold the performing body of the woman dancer. Chandralekha also improvises on the structure of a *varnam*, where the dancer interprets in multiple ways, and elaborates on, the lyrics of the song that accompanies her. She disrupts the tradition of solo performance of the *varnam* by putting two women dancers on stage, each interpreting the song in her own way. This also interrupts the traditional technique of *ekaharya abhinaya*, a solo expressive technique, and becomes a particularly ironic intervention in this *varnam* where one woman complains about the "other" woman, her rival in love. Both women, though they do not explicitly register each other's presence, are part of the same scenario of being-watched. Irony continues to mark the choreography of this section: the lyrics of the song Chandralekha selected to accompany the *varnam* are openly erotic, the singer complaining to the king Datta Rajendra about his attentions to another woman. It is important to recall here, that Kalakshetra, the institution of classical dance and music which had been largely instrumental in the revival of *sadir* and its recasting as Bharatnatyam, had insisted on "purifying" the content and style of the devadasi's dance by spiritualizing all of the erotica that characterized the former. In this tradition, the sexual metaphors of such lyrics are almost always subsumed under a veil of spirituality and interpreted in terms of human love for the divine. Also, the doubling of the solo abhinaya tradition apparently pits the two women against each other, a graphic realization of the "other woman" syndrome, where male desire operates in the conferring of value. However, paradoxically enough, by the end of the section, they find themselves thrust in the same situation by a ruse manufactured by the very patriarchal system by whose rules they seemed to have been playing just moments before. More importantly, through an ironic tour de force,

Chandralekha invokes the familiar elements of a classical dance perform-ance such as *pushpanjali* (offering of flowers) and *varnam* to question the increasing marginalization of the devadasi, while the concert stage marks the space where, and the contemporary form of classical Bharatnatyam marks the form through which the devadasi and her legacy had been effec-tively erased in contemporary times.

The last few moments of this section recall the tragic consequences of this history for communities of dancers. The lights focus on the two women who back away from the audiences toward each other, their feet dragging them along in faltering steps: their bodies are weighted down, held diffidently, with shoulders drooping and eyes downcast, casting into doubt the confidence with which they seemed to have danced a few moments before. In a vignette that lasts for a few seconds only, we see one woman lowering her head while the other, eyes low, turns away from the gaze of the audience. No applause from the audience here, no exhilaration for the dancer. Chandralekha's succinct comment points to the violence of a system where, by an unacknowledged slippage, those who are victimized have been persuaded of their own criminality, so that they go out silenced, with loss of self-respect, unable to argue for their rights. The comment is made in silence, and without sentimentality: the power of the image puts the issues in high relief, marking a strong emotional climax in the piece. The lights black out on this vignette with the dancers still moving. One is inevitably reminded of the movement around the banning of devadasi dedi-cation, where the dancer-prostitute conflation was viewed simplistically as moral degradation, of the appropriation of the devadasi's dance, and of the entire problematic rhetoric of purity-sin marking the revival of Bharatnay-tam as classical dance form. I am reminded of postcolonial feminist scholar Lata Mani talking about the debate about *sati*, which reflects similar issues of control and manipulation: "Tradition was thus not the ground upon which the status of women was being contested. Rather the reverse was true: women in fact became the site on which tradition was debated and reformulated. What was at stake was not women but tradition" (1990, in Sangari and Vaid, *Recasting Women*, p. 118). "Tradition" is, of course, a polit-ical construct, more often than not deployed for the purpose of justifications and exclusions, and imbued with the power to legitimize.

As if acknowledging the need for resuscitation after this devastating comment, Chandralekha now looks back into indigenous images of female power, reaching far back into the depths of time, creating a cyclical notion of history. Indeed, this strategic maneuver is also telling of her own way out of this situation, her own devising of a dance beyond the modern forms of the classical dance, which has become ridden with this history of degrada-tion. This is also the most celebrated sequence from *Angika*, perhaps the

Chandralekha and Nandakumar, the naravahana image, Chandralekha's *Angika*.
Photo © Dashrath Patel.

most threatening for conservative audiences, choreographed as a collage of images drawn from the ancient pre-Vedic Harappan culture, enabling us to reimagine a social organization that is women-centered. Indeed, though these patterns have long disappeared, their presence in the contemporary Indian cultural matrix persists only minimally through such images in stone and terracotta as of women riding ferocious animals and men. For Chandralekha, these are important sources of inspiration in "reappraising ourselves of the power and potency of the human body—a memory of the past vibrant and alive with images, symbols, cults, rituals."[5] As the lights come up one more time, a man crawls onstage on all fours. Astride his back, one leg folded in to rest on his back, the other hanging over his shoulder, sits a woman, Chandralekha herself, tall and powerful. This is the *naravahana* (man as carrier) image, where the woman, goddess-like, rides the man. Though it can be linked to a series of goddess images in the later Hindu tradition where she is portrayed riding on ferocious animals such as tigers and lions, it remains difficult to read this sequence in religious terms or as a deification of women, particularly because of its positioning between the two sequences that flank it, which connect it to the broader theme of re-cognition of movement sources.

Moreover, even if it is interpreted in terms of the dominant Hindu ideology that structures the prevailing interpretive possibilities for audiences of Indian dance whether in India or elsewhere, where Shiva and Shakti, the primal male and female powers, are balanced powers, it is difficult to see

this as a naive reversal of hegemony. In fact, this image has a certain resonance in terms of this Hindu mythology: the goddess Kali, a manifestation
of Shakti, is visualized at a moment of arrest in her path. This is a moment
in which she has unwittingly stepped onto the chest of her husband, Shiva,
who lies prostrate in her pathway in order to prevent her tumultuous journey destroying all that came in her way. Though Shakti is always imaged
thus, stepping onto her husband's chest, there is no implication of any
imbalance of power here. Shiva and Shakti are in fact worshipped together,
as this unity of complementary powers. Moreover, this meeting of powers
is celebrated in the common belief that Shakti inserts the "I" in the concept
of Shiva, who would remain *shava*, a corpse, lifeless, without this union
with her. In this striking section, Chandralekha recalls the directionality of
the energies of Kali-Shiva image, without repeating it literally: Shakti is the
vertical energy, perpendicular to the ground, while Shiva is the horizontal
energy, parallel to the ground. The remembrance of these images reawak-
ens the Shakti inherent in women, and we see the coupling of the archetypal male-female Shiva-Shakti energies to combat forces that imperil
survival. It is important to mention that these images are performed without the traditional *abhinaya* that would accompany the portrayal of any goddess, or without invoking the valorous mood, the *veera rasa*, that might be
expected of a classical rendering of a military sequence.

However, the recalling of this image of female power without any
direct reference to the goddess figures is significant: the strong traditions of
goddess worship in contemporary India coexist with patriarchal systems
that attempt to restrict, in particular, their sensual and sexual powers, besides other aspects. In the *naravahana* image onstage, on the other hand,
conceptions of the goddess resonate but are not directly represented. In
Chandralekha's choreography, this goddess-like woman, as she sits atop her
human carrier, uses hand gestures to symbolize the weapons she wields—
tigernails that rip apart, a spear, a bow and arrow, a sword. She also wields
objects more related to cultivation than sophisticated warfare, a scythe and
a chopper. All of this links her to agricultural traditions and fertility cults as
well as to martial traditions, in which she reclaims her active participation
and her central role. This contributes to secularizing the images: the man
and woman on stage are just that, and while she is divine-like in the
confidence of her power and her grace, and reminds us of the goddess-
strength in her, her translation from awesome womanhood to goddesshood
is hardly possible. Again, because the images are delineated with intense
energy but in silence, with remarkable economy of movement, and without
overlayings of heroic emotion, they refuse idealization into *devi*-images.

As if the wilted energies from the third sequence are revived by the
next one, *Angika* finally moves on to a celebratory ending, where the ener-

gies from the different physical traditions of martial arts, yoga, and Bharatnatyam come together and are juxtaposed to create vibrant and unusual col-
lages. This is Chandralekha's version of the *Tillana*, which is a pure dance
(*nritta*) composition marking the finale of a traditional Bharatnatyam
recital. At one moment in the piece (I am referring here to a later version of
the piece when it was danced by six women and three men), three of the
women dancers, in a horizontal line, facing backstage, advance rapidly
upstage with a quick stepping pattern, their arms extended in one diagonal
line slanting from stage left down to stage right. Facing the women on
either end of the line are two other women, their arms extended similarly
so that the four arms, held by closely placed and simultaneously moving
bodies, appear like intersecting lines radiating outward from their meeting
point between two bodies. The quick step pattern, the curling of their
hands into the *alapadma* hand gesture signifying among other things, a
fully blossomed flower, the perfectly balanced lines of their bodies, evoke
the beauty of the classical dance, though in its most austere form. The
receding line of the dancers is intercut by the kalari artists who now move
in rapidly, but with an entirely different energy across the stage, from left to
right. They perform a series of martial walks and kicks in profile to cover
the space. The *nerkal*, where one leg is swung straight up from the hip to

Chandralekha Group, *Angika*. Photo © Dashrath Patel.

touch the knee to one shoulder, the arms parting sideways across the chest to make way, is alternated with the *iruttikal*, where the leg swings up again from the hip, but brushes down to cycle down underneath the hip and pull the body to the floor while the other leg extends straight in front on the floor. The variations of momentum through the flick of the upswinging leg and the slow descent of the body to the floor cuts into the measured, symmetrical choreography of the Bharatnatyam sequence, creating new spaces and possibilities within the existing vocabulary of Indian performance.

Again, two couples of dancers, three women and a man, facing backstage, move towards the scrim, marking a fast rhythm step pattern that moves them side, side, and then forward. The two couples stand close together, their elbows out and overlapping, their hands on their waists. Not only is the simple step from the Bharatnatyam repertoire transformed through the density of steps performed by pairs of bodies moving together and the repetition and intercutting of the angles of the flexed elbows. The dancers are placed as if in high relief by the two men who stand downstage facing, and at some distance from, each other. In contrast to the rhythmic and quick stepping of the dancers, these two men move on breath-rhythm to extend the definition of the yogic padangusthasana position. Extending their arms above their heads, they flex down from the hips to pitch forward, their heads touching the floor, their legs and chests creating inverted "V" shapes. Their arms extend out on the floor beyond their heads, and they nearly touch each other with their fingertips. It is through this valley of their downsloping backs and arms that we see the dancers moving backward in a quick stepping pattern. Other combinations of kicks, steps, walks, turns, and stretches, choreographed into a seamless flow, bring the piece to the final moment, where all the dancers perform one last salutation to the dancing body in unison. Facing different directions, and creating a complex juxtaposition of bodies, the dancers step forward in a lunge, stretching the other leg far behind the flexed leg to ground the body deeply. Raising the arms slowly around and up, they join their palms above their heads and extend their torsos in a back curve, moving the arms with the torsos.

Melding the energies of a yogic asana with the lines of a dance movement, *Angika* ends with this homage to the rich collage of bodily practices that are available to us, and to the intersections—the explorations of the dynamics of body and space, the tension generated through the lines created by bodies-in-space, the crossing of movement genres and styles to reveal startling juxtapositions and dialectical relationships—that might spark rearticulations of dance. Indeed, the scriptures conceptualize *angika* as one of the four aspects of abhinaya or expressive performance. The modality of *vacika* is language, that of *aharya* is costumes, make-up, scenography, of *sattvika*, the physical expression of psychic states, and that of *angika*, bodily movements. In highlighting *angika* and exploring its expressive potential in isolation from the other three aspects of traditional abhinaya, and in historicizing the development of dance through it, Chandralekha puts at the disposal of future generations of dancers a contemporary and secular idiom, still rooted in the cultural specificity of its context. Moreover, by disconnecting this movement repertoire from an obvious narrative function contained by mythology or traditional love and/or devotional poetry, and yet deploying it to dramatize a personal search for historicity and connections, *Angika* invokes different functionalities and modalities for both the disciplines of dance and historiography. In this, too, resides the challenging and liberatory potential of the piece. Indeed, while Angika might not have "set the body free," it did offer a poetic lineage of bodies gendered and controlled by dominant ideologies, particularly through the medium of dance, and opened up possibilities for imagining dance and movement as forces that can mobilize resistance against such control.

WOMB WARS (1992)
Embodying Her Critical Response to Abortion Politics

On a table placed in the center of the stage squats a woman dressed in a rust-colored dress. The focus of the lighting on her, which keeps the rest of the performance space darkened, underscores her presence in isolation. Her arms are stretched out in front, parallel to each other, reaching to no one. The palms are rigid, the separated fingers are taut with tension. Her voice reaches out in a deep undertone, the mouth opens wide to enunciate each word by itself, reinforcing the strange disconnectedness between the relaxation of her lower back and pelvis, and tension of her upper body, the emphasized separatedness of her fingers. Her eyebrows are raised, furrowing multiple lines of puzzled anguish across her forehead. Almost motionless, her eyes wide open and unflickering in the trembling light of the candle that is placed in front of her on the table, she speaks in near-choked baritones:

> I go down to the river to cleanse myself. I see the stranger dumping
> sewage in the river. The stranger, he see me. He beat me and rape me.
> I go to tell my father. He beat me too. I go to tell my mother. She stay
> silent. I go to tell the doctor. The doctor, he cut my insides out. Who
> gonna care 'bout the river? Who gonna care 'bout me?
> I'm
>   lookin'
>   for
>   God. . . .[1]

The voice reaches a pitch of agony with those words. In the ensuing silence, the lights dim, her eyes, her face, lower, her outstretched arms fold in, and her body shrinks into a low crouch.

The above is a description of the beginning moments of *The Empress . . . Womb Wars*(1992), a piece choreographed and performed by Jawole Willa Jo Zollar. Using movement, theater, narrative, as well as vocal and instrumental music, this performance piece centers on the conflicted debate about abortion rights. However, it insists that the issue be understood in the context of global patriarchal practices that attempt to curb female sexuality, of experiences such as rape, unplanned childbirth, adoption policies, poverty, and of the long history of race, sex, and class-based hierarchies and oppressions.

I want to read the piece in the light of the specific cultural context in which it is located as well as the broader context it evokes, and comment on the complex politics it embodies. In particular, working through close analysis of sections from the piece, I will explore how, negotiating through complex histories and legacies, the black female body weaves a choreographic structure that travels from time past to the present and future, and back. I will also suggest that the black female body becomes, in Zollar's choreography, the ground as well as the mode of memory and commentary, of a community's renarrativizing of history as well as of personal resistance, and the ground of attack and healing. Through this reading of the piece I intend to draw attention to the ways in which performance and cultural production can comment on political or legal debates in ways that refigure their very terms. I also underline the unique ways in which Zollar's choreography complicates theorizings about the representation of female bodies, particularly in the context of sexual assault.

Jawole Willa Jo Zollar, Zollar's *Womb Wars*. Photo by Dona Ann McAdams.

In this piece, Zollar makes it clear that the issue is located on embittered battleground. So much is at stake—body, soul, values, desires—and as Zollar moves to the rhythm of the drums, swinging out right arm, right leg, left arm, left leg in wide gestures, her back convulsed with every step, she declares war: "Throw your blood into the river woman . . . we have no choice but to fight!"[2] Yet the piece insists that the war is not *only* about abortion rights and that it will lead to no simple victories, but that it is imperative to fight for unconditional choice over our bodies as a basic condition of life. The rhetoric that is used must be complex and nuanced, for as Angela Davis has shown, self-imposed abortions and reluctant acts of infanticide were common during slavery but they were motivated by the inhuman life conditions African American women were trapped in, and "most of these women, no doubt, would have expressed their deepest resentment had someone hailed their abortions as a stepping stone toward freedom."[3]

Peggy Phelan has shown through her brilliant analysis of the Operation Right campaign how the manipulation of images of the fetus as an entity in its own right, separate and separable from the mother's body, covers deep anxieties about paternity and dislodged hierarchies, invokes deep and complex emotions, and shifts the debate significantly. Images generated by this campaign represent the fetus as always already gendered male. Abortion handbooks and activists refer to the fetus in (hu)-man-izing terms, such as "the little guy." Through the simulation of this identification, man comes to speak *for* and *as* the fetus, forcing an obliteration of the fetus's immediate condition of possibility inside the woman's body.[4] In *Womb Wars*, it seems that Zollar addresses this very erasure of the female body and insists on weaving the choreographic fabric through numerous images of the same, and simultaneously through layering conception and maternity with situations predicated in violence, pain, and ambiguity.

As Celeste Michelle Condit has argued, the pro-life lobbyists advance their legislative claims by projecting them as "protective" legislation for the fetus and for women's reproductive and mothering roles. Yet, of course, "the articulation of social conditions through rhetoric is a substantively different artifact than those supposedly primary social conditions themselves."[5] It is on this apparently opaque public discourse, based on an elaborately constructed rhetoric of pain on behalf of the fetus, that Zollar's images inflict their disturbing presence. Indeed, these images of black female bodies, relentlessly enacting their pain, betrayal, humiliation, desperation, anger, and hurt, constantly moving through the complex intersections that mark their experience of these issues, gnaw away at the secure right-wing rhetoric in which they cannot be represented, for their presence would immediately destabilize it.

The dark, brooding, intense mood that opens the piece is re-empha-
sized in the following segments. When the lights come up again, we see
Zollar sitting at the table, recalling the moment of her entry into the womb
wars. She speaks in pairs of contradictories, the second statement overturning the first. The coupling of a nondescript face and tone of understate-
ment with the weight of the actual statements that are being made
underline the irony of her words. The doctors had told her mother that she
could never get pregnant; she had five children. The doctors had insisted
that if she did manage to conceive, she would never carry the baby to full
term; she carried all five children right through. When the first child was
born, everyone regarded it as a miracle and a blessing, and was ecstatic.
But, by the time the speaker herself had been born, nobody thought it a
miracle or a blessing, and her mother drank quinine to quell the growing
life inside her. The baby was born nonetheless. Questions rise repeatedly in
the minds of audience members and undercut the scene with deep irony:
How much does the medical institution really know about women's bodies,
or doesn't it matter much? How then does it arbitrate with such smug
assurance, and issue unhesitating pronouncements on matters that are of
great significance in people's lives, when there are obvious gaps in knowledge? These are also questions that compel the recognition that the survival
that is endangered here is that of many people in many difficult, complex
situations, and cannot be understood as a unilinear issue of fetal life.

Suddenly, as if the remembrance of her own birth overtakes her, Zollar
rises and rushes to the side of the table. Standing feet apart, her body tense
with terror and panic, she flings out her arms to one side, flexing her hands
to shove an imaginary object of terror into some space beyond. This is her
imagining of the moment of her birth: another womb/girl-child in a long
line of daughters, unwelcome. Over her heaving motions trying to push the
imaginary head of the emerging baby back into the mother's womb, her
utterance—reflecting the words heard by the baby at the time of its birth—
rises to a frantic, high-pitched, incoherent, babble, still communicating the
mother's anxiety at being unable to prevent the birth of this womb-child.
No explanation is offered for the situation, no apology, and no blame is
affixed to the mother. But what is unexpressed does not escape implication,
and the tacit comment emerges as strong as the spoken word. While her
rocking, heaving body connects with the pangs of the mother's body
fraught with labor pains, the words we hear seem to be uttered by others,
by society, who clamor around the birthing mother, drowning out her
words. How do we understand the agency of a working-class African American woman who, forced to raise her children on meager resources, drinks
quinine to abort a fetus? The situation makes its own devastating comment
on the socioeconomic system in the land of opportunities, whose demo-

cratic provisions and notions of "welfare" cannot include specific groups of individuals in its fold.

The irony of the narrative makes for gaps through which questions emerge, questions that intervene in the narrative itself and make the belief system in which it is based dysfunctional. There is a sequence, for instance, where Zollar picks up the receiver to talk to her friend Marcia. Quite outraged, she asks whether Marcia has seen the front page of the *New York Post*, which proclaims that "God is a man, I am not kidding, it's on the front page of the *New York Post!*" She goes on to tell Marcia about the story carried by the paper: it's the story of Cardinal O'Connor, who is protesting vehemently against these "feminists" and their revisionist ideas, talking about goddess this and goddess that. The clinching statement comes at the end of this conversation, when Zollar repeats again the headline about the maleness of divinity, as if trying to bring herself to believe it, and then adds: "And you know what, I really really think he meant to add white!"[6]

Meanwhile, the chorus of women, cloaked in black fabric, have entered the space and stand in a clump in the upstage left corner. This invocation of God prompts the chorus to a chant: "O-O-O-O ye sinner! O-O-O-O ye sinner!" However, the way has been opened up for disrupting the uniformity of religious practice and piety alluded to by the hymn. And Zollar pitches into a high evangelical mode at this point but her text refers to preacher Jimmy Swaggart who claimed to speak from the visions he received from God. If so, he must have been working under divine commandment when he was "picking up sex workers from every city he visited and taking money from people in the name of something that he should have believed in himself." If the divine source of his authority indeed encouraged him in such hypocrisy, and forgave him for his aberrations, then, of course, "God is a white man." The choral voice enters one more time into the fabric of the performance but reworks the invocation sung earlier: indeed, it rings out only to fall in an irritated and bathetic "O-O-O-O shit!"[7] The rewriting implicit in the doubling of the invocatory singing intensifies as Zollar immediately switches back into her character and returns to narrating the story of her birth. She tells of the disappointment of her parents when they learned that their child was a girl—a womb-child, and not a boy—a penis-child.

And the narrative flares out to reflect on a world in which womb-children are held to be much less precious than penis-children, and touches on practices such as female infanticide and genital mutilation in many parts of the world where this dislike has been taken to an extreme. The current struggle of women for rights to control their bodies is thus framed in a global situation of patriarchy and even misogyny. The chorus begins to sing one more time and the irony falls with redoubled emphasis on the paralleling of the lustful preacher who is forgiven with the newborn baby who is barely tolerated for being born a womb/girl child, and, in the context of the piece generally, of the brushing over the unbridled licentiousness of the religious leader, with the claims to clamp down on women's rights to decisions about their bodies and sexualities.

This is the way in which Zollar typically broadens and layers her stand on the abortion issue. First, by bringing in Cardinal O'Connor's critique of feminist views of religion, and by referring to the preference of boy over girl children and practices such as female infanticide, she makes clear the widespread dominance of patriarchal law. Then, by invoking the religion and the hypocrisy of those who speak in the name of religion and God, a very influential voice in the anti-abortion campaign, she exposes the manipulation of religion for personal gain. The commentary also resonates with the previous story of her birth, fraught with pain, rejection, and the desperation of her mother at a moment where the concept of options has become a matter of increasing privilege. The closure of choice is also emphasized later in the piece when Zollar, as the central character, talks about the anxieties surrounding giving up her child for adoption: The authorities had told her that they would only have a home for the child if she were a girl. So the first question the mother asks after the child was born is about the sex of the child. And though it is in a different context, her frantic questions recall the similar situation of women who know that their girl children might not live long—the practice of female infanticide is rampant—and who fear for the safety of the children they have just given birth to. This is the midnight hour, when meaningful choices seem to cancel themselves out endlessly, though other choices, which are not choices in any significant sense at all, seem to abound. Symbolically enough, the child is born at midnight, and the authorities at the hospital repeatedly ask the mother what day they should put down on the birth certificate. They need to "put down one day or another, midnight's not one or another" they repeat, while she, trying desperately to come to terms with the situation, wonders why that is so important.[8] In the face of lack of real options, there is urgent need to forge the grounds for choice. What manifold needs arising from multiple complex situations are being silenced in the simplified arguments that frame the abortion debate in the legislature?

Further, the bankrupty of religious pronouncements that are used to suppress the rights of selected groups of people and the failure of the impartiality of law are emphasized repeatedly as they are juxtaposed with material practices of women trying to survive through the centuries and as the piece moves through personal recountings and commentaries to show how these issues are inflected by the differences of race and class. As Zollar picks up the phone again to talk to Marcia, who needs an abortion and is

Jawole Willa Jo Zollar, *Womb Wars*. Photo by Dona Ann McAdams.

desperately searching for a place where the procedure is still available, she warns against using coat hangers that will destroy her insides. There are histories of practices, deeply spiritual and embedded in the resources that surround us, that have helped women to survive through such crises before. As Zollar talks about the herbal tinctures, about calling out to her goddess with sincerity, her voice rich in intense invocation, she brings different meaning to the repeated statement, "I'm looking for God."[9] Godliness here becomes about making decisions on the side of life. Further, by foregrounding images of black female bodies struggling, pushing, falling, running, making a desperate bid for life in the midst of so many crises, she underlines both the preciousness of women's bodies generally that are so readily sacrificed in the right's pro-life arguments, and the continuous resistance of black women, whose voices are seldom heard in the debate, and who are so often the "expendable" commodity in this situation via the heinous coalescence of economic and political hegemonies.

Also, as she tells Marcia about the respectful process of honoring the right of the spirit who wants to be here, and then honoring her own "absolute right to help it leave," Zollar is invoking other spiritual traditions, specifically here, the Yoruba concept of the Abiku, spirits who come to go.[10] As she speaks, it becomes clear that the emotions are complex, there will be pain and the need to mourn, but it is important that the decision to abort does not become about opening oneself up to unresolved energies, but that it is laden with the spiritual responsibility to oneself and to the spirit, to honoring the separate paths of each. And as she advises Marcia to reconnect with her own body and Africanist indigenous traditions, slowly massages the oil made of several herbal tinctures into the pressure points of her palms, as she gently places crystals around herself and lights candles in intense prayer to Oshun, she performs her final homage to Marcia, who has become a prisoner of this war over women's bodies and who has no rights in this democracy, for "Big Daddy bought the rights to her soul."[11]

Another way in which Zollar refuses to accommodate a simplistic reading of the issues in the abortion debate is by locating her piece about this issue of great current political valence in a layered time frame. Through this mechanism she enables audiences to realize that the debate on abortion extends beyond the present and rings differently for different groups of people, largely because of different, often opposed, experiences through history. The piece then comes to insist that the debate and any understanding of it be inflected with the politics of race and class along with gender, and the specificities of histories.

The complex choreographic structure where past, present, and future, the history of a community and individual experience, and the political, the social, the economic, and the intensely personal intersect with one another, makes for a rich fabric of meaning where movement and text, gesture and song comment on each other. As she talks over the phone, Zollar's posture and her rising voice spell increasing desperation, and she tells Marcia that she will probably need to go underground in order to emerge from this situation. This is a particularly poignant moment in the piece: the thought of going underground brings back to her body ancestral memories of secret flight, and her experiential knowledge of institutionalized state-sponsored assault on women's bodies coincides with the historical legacy of African American peoples. Rushing to the other side of the table at which she was sitting, she begins to run in place. She runs faster and faster, picking up her feet higher and higher, her arms flexed forward, her hands fisted. But unlike those who run the marathon, she is caught in an endless running that takes her nowhere, certainly nowhere safe. Her next words, panted out, echo the sense of being trapped in an eternal cycle of running: "Sometimes I have to run, like my ancestors. Running from Louisiana, running from Mississippi, running north to freedom. Sometimes I have to run, like my ancestors."[12] Locked, like her, into a repetitive reflection on a destiny of running, her words repeat themselves. Personal and racial memory intersect here to reflect on the uncanny intersection of issues in African American life, on persecutions and oppressions that return in different forms and contexts, like ghosts that arise from the past and haunt the present relentlessly. Pounding feet: the rhythm of her running feet is picked up by the percussionist (Junior "Gabu" Wedderburn) and rumbles on from offstage.

This invocation of past time opens up the ground for surfacing of personal memories, which merge with the memories of other women, to become about collective remembering. As Zollar returns to the role of the central character, sitting on her haunches, she speaks of "that place inside of her where memories scald like pieces of searing flesh." These memories of wounds that remain fresh, of what is unspeakable, building up to a place of rage, are memories of sexual assault and rape and the shame and humiliation that comes with them. Zollar then begins to articulate her painful memories of rape, still a child, by a trusted family "friend": this was the dawning of her realization of the close relationship between the threat of violence and sexual submission. The range of emotions, the shifting moods, are placed in high relief when the enactment of pain is split into two zones, in the performances of two women, in both of which the body-in-pain is laden with suggestions that it is penetrable and penetrated, degradable, and in this, always already feminized. As the central character recedes to her spot at the table, humming low and pained, "I said I wasn't telling nobody, but I couldn't keep it to myself," another body, naked, female, spills onto the stage (Valerie Winborne). Her head is stretched back, every pore of her face contracted and flushed with pain, her fists clenched, legs flexed up at every joint in screaming agony. Her body is flayed about with violent convulsions punctuated by helpless sobs as she pleads for somebody to take her to the water. She scrambles around on the floor, lifting her pelvis high and then dropping it, dragging her body from side to side and around, like a caged animal in the throes of death. The central character sinks into a low crouch under the table, pressing her limbs together and close to the body, yet unable to close off the memories of rape that, inside of her, "scald like pieces of searing flesh." Her protective posture and its seeming impenetrability are mocked by her inability to prevent the recurring memories of the pressing shame and humiliation, of rotting, dismembered, and tortured corpses, of the terror and rage that again and again overtake her body. In this place where her body is reduced to an object to be used, as if lifeless flesh, she has had to wait "with no language . . . with no answers."[13] The experience parallels those of women with unheard voices, who must await the outcome of the legal battle, which will be executed upon their bodies.

The echoing images of the body-in-pain mark an emotional peak in the piece. Following a particular line of argument from Elaine Scarry's theory on the ultimate inscrutability of physical suffering: pain, a uniquely object-less experience, a wholly internal and passive state of agony, "becomes an intentional state once it is brought into relation with the objectifying power of the imagination."[14] Here indeed, the imagination and performance of intense states of pain, intent on marking and re-marking themselves, invoking a collective remembering or empathy with such anguish map the psychological and emotional terrain in which the political argument must also be located. But Zollar confronts Scarry's notion of the inscrutability of pain with images of subjects who perform their pain, who articulate their pain through metaphors of immense power in verbal and nonverbal mediums, who locate their pain in a larger political complex. In this, she also complicates the ways in which bodies-in-pain are usually constructed as the objects of our sympathetic or horrified gazes.

Zollar repeatedly faces African American women's legacy of rape and assault, of multiple levels of oppression, of battered yet struggling bodies in her work. Images of the black female body, violated and forced open, are often found in her works, but they are always followed by images of healing, of replenished energy, of women who, admittedly through struggle and through a difficult journey toward self-determination, return strong and in control of their destinies. The female body, constantly the site of pain and violation, is at once the site of restoration and source of strength. Most importantly, Zollar, while refusing to aestheticize this violence, infuses her representation/re-embodiment with deep respect for subjects who have such histories. So, there is no shrinking away from the painful representation of violation, no metaphorizing the struggle against the harshness and aggression of the threats to female bodies. But there is no sense of the excess that typically attends the fetishized gaze through which such events are reported upon in journalistic coverage, eroticizing suffering, especially that of women and people of color, as visions offered up for voyeuristic consumption.[15] In fact, these images are so integrally woven into the structuring of the piece, so layered with political commentary, that there is never a sense that the choreography of violence is gratuitous. But we cannot but gasp at the intensity and complete arbitrariness of the violence that is enacted on women's bodies. The complexity of the representation, in which commentary and embodiment intersect and layer each other, and where the invoked histories throw up multiple ghostly images to juxtapose the moving ones onstage, implicates us immediately in the situation and leaves little distance for an objectifying gaze.

The piece does not end, however, in this welling up of shame and pain. The "womb wars" are unlike the wars commanded by military diplomats where hundreds of people must be sacrificed for some yards of enemy territory, where the suffering human body is publicized as erotic spectacle, indissociable from the restoration of the nation, its wounds washed by the figurative tears of the motherland, its private and individual identity ultimately broken down. The wars Zollar urges us to join are about restoring to female bodies their rights to dignity and privacy, and about women reclaiming their power, about creating spaces of safety where these invasions cannot destroy. So, while *Womb Wars* does not brush away the fragility of the female body, nor diminish the threats that relentlessly accrue to her, it does end with a celebration of a woman's ability to resist controls imposed upon her through her ability to regain peace and benediction. Here I am reminded of Rajeswari Rajan's problematizing and revisioning of Elaine Scarry theorizing of the body-in-pain as an essentially unrepresentable entity and as the inalienable other of language, a thesis fraught with strategic and political difficulties for Rajan.[16] Instead, she urges the importance of seeing pain as a stage rather than a state, a non-perennial state of being, and to regard the subject in pain as an acting, moving, being, rather than a passive space.

> The subjectivity of pain, it is important to stress, needs to be conceptualized as a dynamic rather than passive condition, on the premise that the subject in pain will be definitionally in transit towards a state of no-pain (even if this state is no more than a reflexivity) . . . It is therefore as one who acts /reacts, rather than as one who invites assistance, that one must regard the subject in pain.[17]

Indeed, the way in which Zollar weaves together the bodies of black women in pain reflects this notion and also recalls my earlier statement about the difficulty of deploying the objectifying gaze in such work. Her choreography of pain does not offer static visions to be wept over. Instead, they are part of the mosaic of future activism, of what Zollar wants to move us to

Urban Bush Women, Zollar's *Womb Wars*. Photo by Dona Ann McAdams.

make a choice to act for limiting the widespread recurrence of this pain. Zollar's earlier exhortation, "We have no choice but to fight!" resonates even in the pained cry of the woman who wants to be taken to the river as she thrashes around in the throes of pain.[18]

Ultimately, in the last segment of the piece, the chorus of women gathers around the central character, holding flowers and singing. Zollar, slipping into an autobiographical mode, now recounts her recent meeting with her daughter whom she had given up for adoption at the time of her birth. As gesture and voice warmly soften and quicken to retell of the reconciliation between mother and daughter, of the restoration of a love-filled relationship unnaturally severed at its inception by the unholy conditions of its occurrence, the reconstitution of their lost umbilical connection is performed. The women in the chorus, who have gathered behind her, now pick up the candles she has lit in the course of the piece from the floor, and gently hand her the flowers they have been holding, all the while singing "No! No more! No! no! no! no more!" to this pain, to oppression, to such violence.[19]

As it goes through Zollar's testimony about her personal experience of sexual assault, the performance implicitly evokes the history of sexual exploitation of black enslaved women in this country and the courage of black women who decided to abort the fetuses of their unborn babies so that they would never know the terrible suffering that was the inevitable fate of black peoples in America at that time. The audience has earlier been reminded of patriarchal hegemonies that continue to reign in countries across the world where male children are valued over female children, of practices of genital mutilation. Other histories are also invoked here: that of the enforced sterilization of non-white and poor women in the early part of this century in America. There are also histories of African and Native American children being forcibly taken away from their parents by missionaries so that they could be raised as Christians; of assumptions that crept early into the movement for birth control that poor women, black, Native American, and Puerto Rican women, had "a moral obligation to restrict the size of their families."[20] For these communities then, the debate on abortion reads very differently because the possibility of pregnancy and childbirth had been violently torn from them.

If anything, this piece, which insists that the female body, constantly the site of pain and violation, is at once the site of restoration and source of strength, makes a vital statement while it draws out the complexity of the current debate on abortion. Zollar makes it clear that here the female body bears the entire brunt of the situation, of the assault of rape as well as the ensuing legislations—where decisions will be taken by those who most probably have no real knowledge of the experience. Here, simplistic, reified, moralizing judgments are dangerous. Her dramatization of her politics in performance where her own body as well as the bodies of other women in her company literally and metaphorically bear the weight of the testimony, reveals the epistemic fracture that marks the politics of legislation, the unbridged divide between those who know practically, and those who decide from a distance. In performing the female body in the throes of complex situations that are understood more in the abstract in the legislature, invoking a layered imaginary, and mobilizing the images created on stage in multiple zones, *Womb Wars* foregrounds the issues in unique and immediate ways and comments on current politics in a way that complicates them immediately. Finally, the piece makes clear that simplistic categorizations of attitudes as "pro-life" or "pro-choice" erase the fine complexities that shape the discourse for women, and the different experiences and contexts that visit the bodies of the women upon whom politicians legislate and wage their power battles.

YANTRA (1994)
Infinite Erotica

In her introduction to *Dancing Desires*, which highlights an exciting new research direction interweaving dance studies and sexuality studies, Jane Desmond outlines the two main arguments the project seeks to make: "It suggests that to understand dance history and dance practices, we must analyze them in relation to histories of sexualities. Conversely, it suggests that the analysis of dance, as a form of material symbolic bodily practice, should be of critical importance to gay and lesbian studies and to 'queer theory.'"[1] While the arguments are specifically set in the context of exploring the articulation of alternative sexualities in and through dance, it seems to me that their relevance and significance in fact spans the broader field of sexuality studies in general. In fact, as I suggested in Chapter 5, it seems that sexuality is both one of the most potent sites of alternative historiography, and one intimately woven into dance history. Further, while I believe it is vital to guard and protect the distinctions between heterosexual and homosexual desire and sexuality and the resultant affect, it is also important to question the apparent "straightness" of all heterosexuality, and to wonder to what extent women's desires and sexualities, even when heterosexual, are "queered" in resistance to the heteropatriarchal domination that structures most contexts. This is precisely the kind of question that is raised by a critical reading of *Yantra* (1994).

Moreover, the importance of Chandralekha's *Yantra*, in fact, is best realized with reference to the regulations and economies that currently construct the field of sexuality in India, in which context the piece is created. Introducing *A Question of Silence?* which looks at representations of diverse forms of sexual relationships and institutionalizations of sexuality in contemporary India, editors Mary E. John and Janaki Nair mark the dominant stereotypes that mark the field: "Is there a way of charting sexuality in India that does not begin with the *Kamasutra* (the text) and end with 'Kama Sutra' (the condom), separated by an intervening period of darkness illuminated fleetingly by the laborious pieties of erotic temple sculptures and miniatures?"[2] Locating what they call a "conspiracy of silence" regarding sexuality in India, their project proceeds to thematize this field primarily in order to illuminate how issues of sexuality are embedded in the major debates, issues, and investigations that are currently under siege or contestation. In this, they insist on conceptualizing sexuality as "a way of addressing sexual relations, their spheres of legitimacy and illegitimacy, through the institutions and practices, as well as the discourses and forms of representation, that have long been producing, framing, distributing and controlling the subject of 'sex.'"[3] Particularly in a postcolonial context, one that is further ravaged by continuing conflicts over national boundaries, religion, and other issues, women are subjected to the representational boundaries demarcating acceptable and illicit sexualities and desires, and norms about "appropriate" sexual behavior in their expected embodiment of national chastity. While *Yantra* apparently works within the boundaries of heterosexual representation, the context from which its assertion and celebration of female sexuality emerges, the particular kinds of juxtapositions through which, and the slow deliberateness with which this is articulated, underscore the boldness and anti-normativity of the choreography and situate it on the edge of a radical politics of sexuality.

The apparent coolness of its title, *Yantra: Dance Diagrams*, and indeed of its structure, belies the rich passion that suffuses this piece. Indeed, to me, the piece reads as an exposition of Chandralekha's conceptualization of sexuality as a richly creative and generative force that mobilizes other energy fields. The piece is inspired by the ninth-century Sanskrit poem, *Soundarya Lahari*, in which "the perception of beauty is related to awareness of the body expressed through the geometrical diagrams, *yantra* and *chakra*, signifying male and female energies."[4] Throughout the piece, the choreography interweaves these themes: the celebration of the erotic as the prime creative force and the elaboration of yogic and dance movements, and movements drawn from Kalarippayattu, creating constantly moving and merging images of triangles, squares, and circles, geometric poetry that is inspired by the movement of the erotic. At the same time, the technique, characterized by extensions of known forms and the blending of genres, charts an embodied journey towards self-knowledge, as if to discover and awaken erogenous zones and pores buried deep in the body, internal energies lying dormant.

In fact, *Yantra* begins with Chandralekha reciting from the *Soundarya Lahari*, stanzas that are central to this piece and that she interprets in terms of the human body and sexuality. She stands in a pool of light on a stage set simply: a backdrop of red and black intercut by occasional lines of white—a large square piece of cloth hung from the back wall, on which sits an inverted triangle, folded around its edges to reveal surprising intersections of the red and the black, revealing more squares and triangles within the larger structures, offset by a red circle which sits in the center. She speaks: "Centered in the immortal seas, encircled by timeless trees, this island jewel. Within this, groves of *kadamba*,[5] and within this, the chamber of wish-fulfillment gem. Here man is the platform on which she turns. Blessed indeed are those, the very few who see her here, the goddess mounted and melted in tides of pure awareness and of perfect joy."[6] As she speaks of the island jewel, Chandralekha joins the tips of her index fingers and her thumbs to perform the *yoni mudra*, or hand gesture, that abstract symbol of female sexuality. The square enclosed within her hands echoes the square on the wall, striking the two major themes of the pieces: the celebration of the infinite powers of sexuality, particularly of female sexuality, and the multiple energies that are brought to life and charged through the arousal of the female spirit and the conjoining of the opposite male and female forces.

While it is impossible to avoid recognition of the dancers' bodies as gendered and sexed, however, there is a way in which these material bodies invoke and activate archetypal energies and principles from conceptual and philosophical realms. Thus, to read the images in this piece in terms of a straightforward male-female binary would only be reductive of its conceptual scale. What might yield a richer interpretation would be to read these dancing bodies as working through their physical and visceral immediacy, through their movement, breath, and energies, to mobilize their symbolic, often epic, and discursive dimensions, and to invoke larger fields of energy. Here the intimate connection of the dominant thematic concerns of the piece, such that the erotic force charges this exploration of energy circuits, creates a structure where marked metaphors of sexual union, such as the *lingam-yoni mudra*, intersect with abstract symbols of male and female energy fields, the triangular (*yantra*), square (the shape of the *yoni mudra*), and circular (*chakra*) circuits. In the *lingam-yoni mudra*, the right hand is in *shikhara* gesture with the upraised thumb symbolizing the male phallus, and the left hand is in *pataka mudra*, symbolizing the vagina, which encircles the phallus at its base. On the other hand, the abstract symbolism of triangular, square, and circular pathways are explored in diverse ways by the dancers, both individually and in choreographic arrangements of the ensemble, as is the pattern of coupling, where dancers move in pairs, male and female, female and female, as if held together by a central coil of energy between them. Yet, the choreographic structure works to emphasize understandings of these forces and images in terms of complementary energies that come together to invigorate a journey toward realization of potential.

Even within the framework of exploring male and female energies, there is an emphasis on the primacy of female forces, their potency to renew life in multiple ways. Particularly in this piece, Chandralekha's idea of the "ancientness" of the female body, which symbolizes that richly creative force continuously replenishing itself through the cycle of life, is explored at great length. Once again, this concept of ancient-ness is not so much a mystical notion, but relates, rather, to the idea of the body as layered with philosophical discourse and rich traditions of thought that construct its ideality, and the processes of history. Chandralekha often talks about her concept of the "primeval accumulation" that is the inspiration for much of her choreography, a notion that is related to this idea of the ancient-ness, and which allows her to reach into the past and weave it into a vision of the present and future. For instance, she describes seeing a woman by the roadside once, squatting, looking at her as she passed by, an image from daily life in current time. Chandralekha felt she saw in that woman—the way she sat by the roadside, the way her body was positioned, butt hanging, back leaning forward, arms loose, the way her eyes turned to look, her unflickering glance—resonances of many sculptures, paintings, poems from a long time ago, both specific similarities and abstract echoes. As if that image had traveled through history assuming different forms through time, but had retained some recognizable core physicality. This is particularly poignant when women have so often been the "silent" bearers of history; when their bodies have been the site upon which so many historical and political battles have been fought; but also when these bodies are witness to repeated resistances and revolutions; are the mode of enabling continuities despite interruptions; and when all these processes of change and retention have formed and boundaried female bodies. In such richly troped images, when past and present seem to be encapsuled together, Chandralekha finds confirmation for her claim that bodies are historically charged, bathed in ideas and events from the past, existing simultaneously on many zones. Importantly, these ideas are not deployed to support some grand narrative of decline or dislocation and subsequent recovery; rather, they are revisited, interpreted, and embodied to envision a possible liberatory sexual politics, particularly for women, in contemporary sociocultural economy, drawn entirely from indigenous sources.

Related to this is also Chandralekha's idea that "men come from women, from women's bodies."[7] Once again, it would be a misreading to understand this statement literally, in terms of the procreative power of women, reproductive processes where women are the source of life for all human beings. Rather, it is testament to the creative potential of female energies, their inherent power to bring the world into being and keep alive the process of renewal and regeneration. In fact, Chandralekha draws on the ways the body is activated within the discourse of early Hindu mythology and philosophy to arrive at this notion of the female body as endowed with magnificent powers. This is also no doubt a vision that is clouded over with the development of patriarchy in later times. Indeed, early and pre-Vedic texts give evidence of conceptions of the female force as the Great Mother, endowed with supreme creative powers, but also de-link it immediately from direct and necessary relationships with biological motherhood. Pupul Jayakar, writing about the early images of Earth Mothers found in rural India, dating back to the second century A.D., describes the following striking image, where the image of the Mother recalls no Madonna figure, but instead holds in her hands a cup, not of milk to feed her child, but of blood, a symbol of fertility.

> In her manifestation as the great Mother holding within her the secrets of life and death, she is conceived in the northern river valleys as a woman with virgin breasts and massive thighs, holding a baby in one hand, while in the other she holds a cup of blood to fecundate the earth . . . The body is moulded by hand and the texture of clay is uneven. The massive arms have withes of clay coiled around them. The body and ornaments are pitted with holes. The face of the Mother is a grim mask, the eyes are indicating links with rituals of death, magic, and fertility.[8]

The idea of *apitakochamba*, undrunk-from breasts, is particularly fascinating to Chandralekha. She recognizes clearly that while motherhood is socially respected, it has also come to function as a way to institutionalize and control women's sexualities. So it has been an important mission for her to create images that articulate the power of women's immense creative potential and of female force as a source of life, without immediately tying it to actual mothering processes. In untethering women's sexualities from motherhood while celebrating them as the central regenerative force in the grand scale of creation, *Yantra*, compels a reconceptualization of women's bodies.

Chandralekha visualizes these ideas in this striking segment from the second section of *Yantra*. After a section where the ensemble, five women and one man, execute complex footwork patterns, four of them leave the stage, leaving two women standing in *alidha pada* in downstage center,[9] their bodies facing and close to each other. They lean their torsos sideways away from each other, their gazes still intensely focused on each other, creating a fan-like opening out of bodies remaining together at base. As they move back to center, keeping one arm fixed behind, they circle the other out from the shoulder to the chest so that the palms of the two women meet at center, between their bodies. One woman spreads her palm flat in the *pataka mudra*, the other places her hand folded in the *shikhara mudra* in the center of that palm, jointly creating the symbol of the *lingam-yoni*, the male and female in coitus. Like a lamp circled that is around in ritual worship,[10] the women raise and lower their hands with slow concentration and the drums reach a crescendo roll in fast tempo. This raising and lowering happens in mobility as the women edge their feet around to turn half a revolution. It is vital that this adoration of the shiva-shakti or male-female energy coupling is performed by two women, which disrupts heterosexual expectations associated with that image and opens up the interpretive possibilities of this erotic-spiritual symbol. Then, lowering their arms, the women now embark on a series of rapid steps to move together to the center, and away from each other to stand on the two opposite corners of a diagonal stretch of light across the stage. Now, one woman stands in the downstage right hand corner facing the opposite corner, arms on the sides of the body, back extended, legs apart in a wide parallel, eyes directed forward, unhesitating in her glance. Another woman steps on stage to join the second dancer and they stand in the same posture, one behind the other, in the upstage right hand corner of the stage, diagonally across from and facing the other woman.

From the downstage left hand corner enters a male dancer: we see him as he drops himself catching himself on his hands. As the nattuvanar begins to utter, for the first time in this piece, a series of rhythmic syllables, he glides through the legs of the woman standing there, emerging from between her legs still on the front of his body, and arrives in a smooth shift at the feet of the woman in the opposite corner. As he rises and begins a sequence inspired by Kalarippayattu and yoga, he seems to be dancing out his adoration of the feminine. He loosely swings one leg back, then forward and high to slap the palm of one hand extended at shoulder level in front. Using this added momentum, he propels himself into a turn in mid-air to land facing the opposite corner in a low lunge, leaning slightly forward, his palms flat on the floor by his front foot, while the other leg extends long behind him. His palms joined in *anjali hasta*, the traditional gesture of salutation, at his chest, he raises his torso from that low position to stretch his entire chest, bow-like, into a back bend to regard the two women toward whom his back is turned. Returning to verticality, he circles his folded hands lowering himself onto his back foot, the other leg extending long in front of him, then moves through a weight shift in that lowered position to arrive at a low lunge on his forward foot, extending his hands long in front of him.

In such sequences repeated several times with variations, he moves between the women, marking the space between them repeatedly with his gestures that evoke the sense of ritual worship. Finally, he arrives at the upstage right corner in a low lunge, his hands in *anjali hasta*, extended forward diagonally, to face the women standing close together there. This time, as he rises to stand with bent knees in a wide parallel, he points, with the tips of his jointly held palms, to the women toward whom he has advanced and moves his hands slowly to the floor, as if paying homage to the cardinal points in their bodies. Now, the woman in front lowers to stand in a wide *mandala*, as if to receive his homage as he circles his body around from the chest to lower his head in front of her as he arrives center. Both rise together, slowly. Apart from this, throughout his intense movement, the women neither move nor look at him. After having danced within the space contained by the women, his body still emitting a tensile energy, he lowers his entire body to the ground and waits, his body stretched and poised on his flattened palms and his toes which are his only points of contact with the ground, recalling the crocodile walk of Kalarippayattu. The women at either end of the diagonal space-hold, now shuffle forward in deep *mandalas*, compressing the long corridor between their bodies and stand facing each other, their bodies close, rising above the male dancer's prostrate body beneath them. The directional architecture of their bodies resignifies the *lingam-yoni* icon where the male rises from, and is surrounded by the female. As the women remain focused in their mutual beholding with their intense gazes, waxing their torsos toward each other, then in a small circle, he exits the stage, emerging from underneath their bodies and traveling back out in a series of short jumps in that pushup position returning to the outside he had come from. It is now that the women begin to move fully, embarking on a footwork pattern and creating a triangular spatial pattern.

The above is a key scene in *Yantra* and in much of Chandralekha's work: the man dances his adoration of the female creative potential without deifying the women. In fact this ritualized homage recalls the practice of *varana* that is performed by priests in invoking the spirit of the goddess in her image. It is also performed by mothers in ritually welcoming their offspring and their spouses-to-be to the marriage ceremony through which they will enter the next stage of their lives. In either case, this is a signal practice marking the awakening and mobilizing of spirit and is performed by appealing to centers of concentrated energy located in the regions of the forehead, the shoulders, the heart, the knees, and the soles of the feet. But even in this recalling, Chandralekha dislodges the practice from its traditional contexts, where the only invocation performed by male figures, priests, is that of the goddess spirit, never of women, unless the women are, in rare cases, specifically conjured as representative of the goddess. Typically, in fact, the patriarchal system is sustained through the physical verisimilitude yet ontological distinction between women and goddesses, so that the popularity of devi-puja or goddess-worship practices have little connection to women's oppression, and in fact is often used to further regulate women's sexualities. Here, in a reversal of general norms and hierarchies marking such practices, the lone male figure dancing in the space defined by the three women, welcomes the rising of their sensual-spiritual power, and then exits, without contesting their domination of the space.

In *Yantra* then, Chandralekha continues her commentary on the body and her celebration of its material dimensions that she had begun in *Angika* by illuminating, in striking embodiment, its seemingly intangible dimensions. Further, while she had always spoken about the body as organized in terms of circuits of energy, it is her moving invocation of these forces, which set up an arousing chain of vibrations palpable in the movement, which reaches a peak in *Yantra*. Specifically, it is the awakening of the female sexual principle that sets in motion a complex circuitry of energy that seems to sustain larger creative processes, articulating, in that movement, a "resonant" body. Bodies, in other words, receptive to these mobilized and mobilizing energies alive on many levels, resonating with possibilities for further growth and articulations through an interwoven spiritual-sensual arousal. Here, dancers play with the specific motifs of triangularity and circularity, not as static linearities, but as mobile forces, which, imbued with certain potencies, intersect and invigorate each other. Never are these presented as shapes with rigid dimensions: instead, triangular lines melt into rounded body stretches, paired-off dancers move the sharp edges of inverted triangular formations toward the *bindu*, the central energy point which seems to be holding their two bodies together. Rapid footwork patterns create and merge distinct frames into one another in the choreographic arrangement of the ensembles.

The piece, in fact, opens with one such sequence, setting up a pattern that will be repeated again and again, where yogic positions are manipulated and expanded beyond their yogic dimensions, combined with improvised formations to create the excitement of discovering the multiple layers and dimensions with which the body is potentially endowed. The force of such movement, however, is not in the robust athleticism, amazing elevation, and strength that is typical of much concert dance movement in the West. Rather, Chandralekha's focus is on a grounded, tensile, and constantly mobile power, which enables a process of constant "becoming" rather than one of "performing." It is the openness of the body, not the possibilities of its muscularity, that is stressed as being at the root of energy. All of these sections also emphasize slowness, bodies moving in extensions against the ground with unhurried concentration. Moreover, as several dancers position themselves closely, one behind another but slightly off to one side, and movements unfold in somewhat of a canon, there is also the sense of echo and resonance, awakening ripples of movement. It is through

Chandralekha Group, *Yantra*. Photo © Dashrath Patel.

these techniques that the movement acquires its mythic proportions, and what could have been the most simple, and in terms of Indian classical dance repertoire, ordinary, gesture, becomes endowed with ritual significance.

Witness these segments from *Yantra*, most of which are danced to the live singing of classical vocalist Aruna Sayeeram. As lights come up to inaugurate *Yantra* in a diffused spot center stage, we see a complex mobile formation of four bodies, sitting close behind each other in a vertical line. The first woman sits with her legs bent at the knees to join the soles of her feet on the ground in front of her. Her arms interwoven through the crook of her knees, her palms on the floor, she reaches her torso forward from the hips to lay it on her legs. This recalls, momentarily, the yogic *Kurmasansa*, where the legs are extended in front of the body. The echoing of this *asana* at the inception of *Yantra*, a piece that celebrates the richness of female sexuality, has its own double-entendre: kurmasana is said to be sacred to a yogi, for it prepares the practitioner for the pratyahara stage of yogic practices, which marks the withdrawal of the senses from the outside world. On one level, *Yantra* repeats the withdrawal from an engagement with the outside world to focus on what lies within. On another level, *Yantra*'s insistence on realizing the sexual dimension of the self and the location of soul within the sensual insists that the journey toward self-realization be charted through the body and the full richness of sensual life. It is also this unremitting principle of invoking a familiar traditional practice only to dissolve it or carry it to another unpredictable place, sometimes to dismantle the original text, sometimes to resignify it from the point of view of another movement philosophy, and sometimes to create images resounding with multiple, and often contesting suggestions, that makes the choreographic layering of *Yantra* so rich.

Here, the simple lines of the *asana* are conjured up, only to be built up into pyramidic complexity. The two women who sit directly behind the first, their legs turned out and flexed in a wide mandala position, their knees raised and feet touching the floor on their sides, echo the raising and lowering of her torso. Now the second woman raises her legs from her hips and places them on the shoulders of the woman in front, while the third woman repeats this gesture to place her feet on the knees of the second. As the first woman, who repeats the raising and lowering of her torso, reaches the upright position, the two other women lower their legs and all three, in canon, stretch their legs to either side in a near-split position. The formation reaches its final opening out as, simultaneously, the male dancer, who has so long been lying prone at the back end of the line, his presence unobvious to the audience, raises his legs in a long vertical line from the floor, his soles facing the audience. The articulation of the thematic concerns of the piece proceeds through the processual intercutting of verticality and horizontality, of flexion and extension, opposite but complementary lines that resonate throughout *Yantra*, as does the counterpointing of rhythms, which happens immediately following this sequence as the dancers rise with one sharp movement to create complex footwork patterns and floor designs.

In another sequence, three of the women arrive center stage to stand in a formation that marks the three corners of a triangle whose apex lies upstage. In a series of openings out initiated by the feet, where first the toes and then the heel fan outward, the initial close parallel stance of the dancers is broadened substantially. Each woman turns out that foot that lies toward the center, to point to it, and turns her body in that direction. Flexing the forward leg in a deep lunge, the other leg extended behind, and placing one palm on the floor by the forward foot for support, the women reach their upper bodies to touch their waists sideways to their thighs. The long diagonal line of their upper bodies is elongated by the other hand that stretches overhead, fully opening up the line of the waist through the shoulder and neck. At this point, the torsos of the two women at the base of the triangular formation are facing the front, the fingertips of their extended arms touching to create the sense of another triangle which stands perpendicular to the floor intersecting the other which lies on the floor, its apex marked by the women's hands. The dancer marking the apex of the grounded triangle, who so long had her torso facing stage right, now allows her extended arm to initiate a rotation of her torso forward, and raises the supporting arm to extend overhead, parallel to the other arm. This intensifies the choreographic intervention whereby the dancer's previous performing of the traditional *utthita parsvakonasana* of yoga is not only manipulated to reveal movement contained within it, but the adherence to the exact dimensions of the *asana* melts away as its lines are mobilized and, phoenix-like, dance movements originate from its dissolving structure.

The three pairs of forward stretched arms, pointing to the central energy point of the space contained by the three bodies, now pull the torsos of the three women slightly upward and then stretch them in the reverse direction as they extend into the back space. The long stretch of the back and the sides in the *utthita parsvakonasana*, extended by the line of the arm, resonates in this long curving out of the front surface of the body in a back bend, while the linearity of the former is enriched by the circularity and constantly moving line of the latter. As the women come back upright and revolve around to repeat the same sequence at the outer rim of the circular pool of light in which they have formed their triangle, their shadows cross and re-cross at center, imaging the concept of the multiple energies that move and interact with each other, bringing alive the apparently static diagrammatic representation of the *muladhara chakra*.[11]

I have drawn attention in the movement descriptions to the ways in which yoga *asanas* enter and dissolve into dance in the choreography. There is also another way in which yogic conceptualization of the body enters the work: that is the way space is conceived both inside and outside the body. Space is live medium here, outlined and charged by dancers' bodies, articulating the richly interwoven circuits of energy. This is of course a recurring theme in much of Chandralekha's work: dancers bring their bodies close to each other, almost but not really touching, and guard that distance between them as they move through the sequence, occasionally expanding and shrinking that space. For Chandralekha, this is the difficult task she imposes on her dancers—that of "moving the inter-subjective space"—so that the attention falls, not only on the two faces that breathe so close to each other, but on the shifting shapes of the space enclosed by the two bodies in profile, both bodies generating forces to charge the space they hold between them. This charge connects the dancers with larger energy circuits, rendering porous the apparently fixed and boundaried limits of their bodies, suggesting also that the exploration of self happens in context, inevitably as self-in-world. Indeed, in Chandralekha's choreography dancers come together in close proximity, not as individuals existing enclosed in marked-off zones, but as dancers who emit awareness of their location, with others, in spaces electric with energy and connective possibilities. And when dancers come into close proximity with each other in the course of the choreography, their focus on breath, space, and line seems to suggest that their meeting with each other happens not just on personal here-and-now terms, but as individuals with larger-than-life dimensions, archetypal figures resonating through time and space.

Talking about the circuits of energy creating this sense of the resonant body Chandralekha emphasizes their complementarity: "it could be up and down energies; it could be the male and female in us; it could be inner and outer space."[12] One particularly striking exploration of this theme occurs about mid-way through *Yantra*. Three of the women dancers arrive, through a footwork pattern, downstage off-center, slightly toward stage left. They stand in profile to the audience, facing stage left, one behind the other, their bodies close. The woman closest to stage left moves away from the other two through a series of distinctly enunciated footsteps, and crosses her legs to sit on the floor. As the drums stop, the female vocalist sketches a melody which, having elaborated the base notes, rises to explore the higher variations on that scale. As the two standing women broaden their stance into a wide parallel, the dancer on the floor stretches her legs long in front of her and, supporting herself by palms placed firmly on the floor by her hips, lengthens her spine to curve into a back bend which finally lowers her to the floor. Of the two women standing, the one facing

Sujata, Meera, Usha, Chandralekha's *Yantra*. Photo © Dashrath Patel.

Chandralekha Group, *Yantra*. Photo © Dashrath Patel.

the third dancer on the floor stretches forward from the hips to reach all the way down, placing her palms on the ground by the ears of the prone dancer, her face coming to an encounter with the other dancer's face. The latter now circles her arms out and overhead, her palms brushing the bending dancer's face and her feet and ultimately placing them by her own shoulders. As the second dancer raises her lowered torso upright, the other now picks up her body in a magnificent arch bridging over the space between the arms and the feet that remain on the floor, supporting her weight. The yogic simplicity of her *urdha dhanurasana* is eroticized and reinvigorated by the movements of the second dancer that emphasize the beautiful length of her stretched body. One more time, this second dancer reaches forward from the hips, lowering her torso all the way down, her breath brushing the contours of the stretched body of the other woman. This time the faces meet in mid-air, suspended in opposite directions from reaching torsos, and then move on in their circuits again. Every moment of this not-long sequence seems to be stretched beyond its dimension in clock time, as is every point in the space surrounding and in between the bodies of the three dancers. This prolongation and layering of discrete time and space monads happens in rhythm with what seems to be happening in terms of the dancers' bodies: internal energy circuits, erogenous zones, creative forces are aroused, and the harmonious interrhythms of breath, blood flow, and release vibrate the dancers' bodies as they emerge from this sequence to be joined by the ensemble. This insistent attention to these larger-than-immediate physicalities of bodies underlines the notion of their "resonance" that I have introduced, their signifying potential on many simultaneous levels.

As *Yantra* progresses, its imagery becomes more and more dense through the layering of thematic material. The rich metaphors of the initial textual inspiration come alive in the following sequence where yogic and tantric perceptions collaborate with bodily and movement poetry. Recalling the floor design at the beginning of the piece, three women and one man position themselves in a vertical line center stage. This time, however, the relative simplicity of the former design is replaced by more complex formations from the very beginning of the sequence: the two women in front stand in a wide parallel facing each other, while behind them lies the male dancer on the floor, his legs facing the fourth dancer in the line, who stands in a wide parallel, arms by her side with her back to the audience. As the last two dancers remain unmoving, the two women in front circle their arms around at shoulder level to clasp their hands between their breasts and then unclasp them to place them by their sides. Then, each in a different direction, turning one foot out and rotating the chest to face that direction, these two dancers reach their hands behind themselves to form *anjali hasta* on their backs, and gathering momentum from a slow back curve, they reach forward to rest their torsos on their thighs. This performance of the yogic parsvottanasana is further vitalized not just by the movement explorations that surround it, but more by the complex formations of bodies that are revealed interstitially through the constantly moving asana. As the two bodies bend back and forward in opposite sides, repeating the sequence in different directions and looping through the central axis in between their bodies, we catch glimpses of the male dancer etching a circle on the floor with his arms, of the last female dancer turning her legs out and flexing into a deep, wide *mandala* and coming up again. The dancers at either end of the line, both facing back, now circle their hands, one in the *pataka mudra*, the other in *shikhara*, to the center of their chests in the *lingam-yoni* gesture as prologue to the next movement. The two women in front now take a wide step out to offset the verticality of the line, standing on either side of the two figures who remain at center, still facing back.

Their stepping aside reveals the third female dancer in a wide mandala position, seated on the shins of the male dancer, whose raised legs are folded from knees to hold the shins parallel to the floor. The female dancer dismantles the *lingam-yoni mudra* that she has been holding straight in front of her so long and extends her arms overhead and around, rising from her seat. As the male dancer lowers his legs, turns them out, and flexes them to place his feet close to his pelvis on the floor, she stretches her entire body into a back bend. Supported by his knees, she reaches her back low, her upturned face between her forearms, her palms now planted on the floor beside his waist. The flexed architecture of their legs join as her legs fold over his, and she rests her back softly on his front. One more time, the rich energies of the female creative power "mounted and melted in the tide of pure awareness" is refigured through startling images. The symbol of the coupling of forces, the *lingam-yoni mudra*, is revisioned through the contexts in which it is invoked, which stretch it beyond its traditionally exclusively heterosexual domain to invoke a yoking of energies that sustain life-flow. One more time, too, the celebration of the coital reveals itself as a celebration of movement, of process, of energies that move through and in the body. The dancers are never stilled in any position, nor do such moments mark the climactic moment of a sequence. Rather, reinvigorated through the imagery they create, the dancers constantly move on to new combinations. Given the intimate connection of dance history and sexual politics, it is only fitting that dance should be the space for such dismantling of hierarchies and the articulation of an alternative vision. Moreover, because Chandralekha is working with movement forms that have valence as "tradition," and disrupting this affect from within to suggest radical departures in the philosophy upon which they are based, she reminds one of theater critic Rustom Barucha, who talking about the possibilities of making secular art, describes how form might become "a site of confrontation for the content itself."[13] It is this confrontation within the formal and structural framework that both disturbs and marks the dancing body as a fertile site of meaning-making.

Of Chandralekha's works, *Yantra* particularly brings to mind again and again the ideas of Audre Lorde, for whom the erotic—"those physical, emotional, and psychic expressions of what is deepest and strongest and richest within us, being shared . . . the first and most powerful guiding light toward any understanding"—bridges the dichotomy between the political and the spiritual and is the power of connectivity within the self.[14] For Lorde, as for Chandralekha, the erotic is understood in terms of rhythm, sensuality, desire, power, knowledge, and the capacity for joy. Conjuring up the image of margarine at its melting moment as a rich, soft yellowness, she writes: "I find the erotic such a kernel within myself. When released from its intense and constrained pellet, it flows through and colors my life with a kind of energy that heightens and sensitizes and strengthens all my experience."[15] This is how for Lorde, as for Chandralekha, the erotic flows continuously into the spiritual and becomes an empowering and profoundly creative source. For Chandralekha, as for Lorde, the erotic comes into its own once unshackled from patriarchal conditioning and becomes a liberating force, actively engaged in world-making on its own terms, reinventing the self and surrounding context repeatedly.

For me, what is radical about the notion of sexuality articulated in *Yantra* lies precisely in the sense of the infinite erotica that permeates the piece. In the way it weaves together the power of sexuality with that of creativity, in the way it locates female sexuality as the prime force sustaining the continuity of life, linking it immediately to the flow of multiple energy circuits, *Yantra* imbues sexuality with dimensions that extend far beyond an understanding of the sex act only. The flow of erotic powers thus foregrounds bodies that are resonant, and this resonance is infinite precisely because it draws on forces that circulate beyond the finiteness of sexual activity. It is also to make pleasure synonymous with awareness and realization of potential. To make such claims about female sexuality at a time and in a global context where women's sexualities are constantly under threat, repeatedly subject to legal, societal, economic, and political injunctions, is radical. While *Yantra* may not directly address the question posed by John and Nair that I quoted in the introductory paragraphs, and while it does not offer a linear history of sexuality that spans the distance between *Kamasutra*, the text of erotic performance, and Kama Sutra the condom, it does offer the possibility that the sustaining forces of life through time have been feminine creative energies. And even while Chandralekha plays with the synergy of masculine and feminine energies in celebrating creative flow, she displaces the unmarked yet hegemonic male subject and desire that dominate social formations of sexual behavior and cultural understandings of appropriateness in male-female relationships.

METONYMY MINING HISTORY
Hands Singing Song (1998)

This piece, for me, marks a paradigmatic moment in Zollar's choreographic practice: one where the way in which she focuses in on some part
of the body and unravels, in full-bodied dance, its metaphoric and symbolic
reworkings in a particular cultural context, is wonderfully successful in
rewriting historical perceptions through a complex interweaving of multiple progressive politics. "I was mining history," Zollar says of the inspirations for *Hands Singing Songs*.[1] And indeed what impresses immediately
about this piece is its tracing of the multiple practices and histories from
the recent past to ask questions about possibilities of personal positioning
and political organization in African American communities today. This
piece currently survives as several short pieces, but I want to talk about it in
the form I saw being performed several times. At that point, it was
arranged as a suite of five sections, each revealing different aspects of black
historical and cultural practice, connected to each other but not linked in
narrative necessity. While I think each of the individual sections stands well
as shorter pieces, I believe that their juxtaposition to constitute a larger
piece accomplished a vital overall commentary, and that the sections also
energized and complicated each other. Because they are so distinct in flavor,
I will comment on each of the sections, paying more detailed attention to
sections that are significant for my analysis, in the order that they were
performed.

Give Your Hands to Struggle
Voices inaugurate the piece in darkness: one by one they name well-known
activists of color, heroes and leaders of the struggle for a life with more dignity, justice, and respect. As the lights fade in, we see a woman (Maria Earle
or Michelle Dorant) standing in a crisscrossed pool of light at center stage.
Her arms reach to corners, pulling her torso along and undulating it. They
whip around in a wide circle, turning her. One hand brushes over her head,
the side of her body, to fall gently down. A group of performers is clustered

together on upstage right, dimly lit: voices ring out weaving a lineage of struggle, primarily but not exclusively black leaders in this country, who have changed the lives of others: "Sojourner Truth, Harriet Tubman, Frederick Douglas, Nat Turner, W. E. B. Dubois, Chief Seattle, Sitting Bull . . . Ella Baker, Medgar Evers, Malcolm X, Martin Luther King, Lorraine Hansbury, Cesar Chavez . . ." The soloist dances to the sound of voices articulating names, movements that that connect deep into the floor with grounded palms to propel the body in different directions easily. This rolling list of ancestors is followed by a continuous naming of current leaders, those who are continuing that previous history of struggle: "Rosa Parks, Angela Davis, Nelson Mandela, Winnie Mandela . . . Bernice Johnson Reagan, Katherine Dunham." Individuals working in their own ways to further the common goal of enriching and strengthening "community." The focus on the act of naming, of filling in silences in history, and constructing a lineage of black struggle, thus becomes as much about engaging with that history in the present. The dance reads as a metaphor of that mobilization and that active connecting with a past to inspire movement in the present.

The dance grows in momentum. The lights grow in intensity to cover the entire stage so that the soloist and the group are seen continuously, as part of the same lit zone. Her arms reach out and then back toward her body, rippling across the air. She repeats a motif: one arm returns from a turn to swing across her chest and push it into a back curve. This immediately reflexes the body down, doubling it over the knees. Elbows out, the arms curve the chest back up. One after another, the arms push forward, hands flexed up, while the effort registers itself in the softly rippling torso. As the arms come to the chest to reach out to the audience in an outgoing gesture of reaching, the group begins to sing: "If you see me struggle, don't stand back and look on . . . give your hands to struggle!" The soloist's arms move outward as if in offering, they draw luscious circles around her body pulling her along in diagonal lines across the space. Hers are hands that reach out into space as if to catch something, that extend the body in undulating lines across space. They are paralleled by the hands of the group, which come together to clap out a rhythm to the song, syncopating the meter of the tune so that the words fall in between the claps, creating a dense soundscape. This collaborates with her movement where the smoothness and directed flight of reaching hands—one fisted hand reaching above the head, coaxing the body to lean into its extended line, the palm then opening out toward the audience, reaching even more—are intersected with more percussively timed series of movements: the shoulders shimmy twice on the beat rocking the body forward, one hand caps itself onto another to shoot up in the air, flexed palms pulling out in half-circles to jump the body in short, springy releases from the floor.

Maria Earle and Urban Bush Women, Zollar's *Hands Singing Song*. Photo by Cylla Von Tiedemann.

While the soloist dances across the area of the stage, the group contains itself where we first saw it, and we come to understand the relationship between them through the vocal and clapped support the group offers to the soloist's dance, as their song emphasizes her danced exhortation to join her in her fight, "give your hands to struggle." Her palms reach to the floor as she moves with a slight leap to her side, and then curls her spine up and ripples her arms forward. One gestural motif reappears several times: one hand extending diagonally outward, the other reaches to it, curving over the torso, and clasps it as one leg rises in back attitude. As if energized by each other and that clasp, the hands open outward, while she remains in attitude, a picture of perfectly centered balancing and outward reaching simultaneously. Hands—that part of the body that reaches out to make contact with others through gestures like handshakes—here come to embody a constant reaching toward an as yet unseen vision of a moment that is the aspired-for beyond of the present struggle.

The individual's persistence in struggle is supported by the community's history and commitment to that collective vision: it is this partnership that makes the struggle meaningful. Yet in a general context of a community in struggle, the resistance of each individual is significant and difficult. As we see the soloist slowly revolving around herself, her outreaching arms looping out to fold in on her chest, the lights fading out on her, we sense her sensitivity at being touched by this history, by the remembrance of the struggle. One is reminded of Audre Lorde's words, "the transformation of silence into language and action is an act of self-revelation, and that always seems fraught with danger."[2] While we do not have so active a sense of the danger here, the lyrics, fraught with the possibility of failure and sounding a call for support—"if you see me falling, don't stand back and look on . . . give your hands to struggle"—and the occasional tenderness in the movement, the choreography of falls and turnings away, hands that seek contact with others, give us a clear sense of the vulnerability and fallibility in the struggle.

Hands Singing Song

Five women stand close to each other in a horizontal line in a central pool of light. The long garbs of the previous scene are replaced by short dresses. Girlfriends play with hand gestures creating game structures. Silence, except for the sound of hands cutting through the air. If hands are about struggling and reaching here, they are also about aggression, especially the aggression children internalize growing up in a violent world. The play suddenly gets more tense, the hand gestures more abrupt: they are interrupted by a group phrase that returns several times in the piece. The women, in a horizontal line, their bodies in profile to the audience. One hand reaches out in front of the body toward the audience. They walk forward, deliberate steps, marking the ground with the heels. The other hand circles over the head to clap onto the extended hand and grip it firmly. The arms flare out at shoulder level as they walk back, the palms flexed up and watchful, the fingers taut and separated from each other. One more time, standing still, one hand reaches out, the other claps itself on, the clasped hands rush to the shoulders as the elbows axe them out to the sides. Clarity and aggression: especially as the women move toward, then away from, the frontline together, menacing in their posture, leaning forward, facing the audience with a dead-on look.

They return to their individualized choreography but seem to chance upon moments where everybody, having arrived at the starting point by a different route, still performs the same movement simultaneously with the others. In one such moment, all five women find themselves with their arms held up high, their hands clasped together. One woman (Christine King) from stage right, starts to sing; "We've got the whole world in our hands, we've got the whole wide world in our hands." The other four move as she sings, often reworking the motif of the clasped hands with varying energies and emphases. Five black women, performing to a song of make-believe abundance as they play with hand gestures. This could read as children's play, sung with the wide reach of innocent belief. But it also reminds us of black women's long history of self-reliance, of carving meaningful

Christine King, Francine Sheffield, Joy Voeth, Allyson Triplett, and Carolina Garcia in Zollar's *Hands Singing Song*. Photo by Cylla Von Tiedemann.

moments from difficult circumstances, their strongest resources being their laboring bodies and their emotional and creative fortitude.

Throughout this section, the dancers pick up on children's songs, infusing them with irony as they resituate them on the shifting borderline between girls and women. The emotional climax comes in the next game song they sing together: "You put your right hand in, your put your right hand out . . . that's what it's all about." As they move to this rhyme in chorus, the woman at the far left end of the line (Christine King), looks up sharply, exclaiming, "What?" She cowers, slowly crumbling to cover her face, as the others follow suit, trying to protect themselves as if from a blow in stunned silence. Suddenly the game structure falls away and we see in-turned violence as the women begin to attack each other, jerking each other into movement, threatening each other in a line of transference. As each woman hurls out the rhyme, she manipulates the body of the woman next in line roughly into accompanying movements, punching the last line with a final attack. Even as she reels from the attack, this next woman continues the chain of violence, repeating the same words and actions, no longer sung as a melody, but spit out as prose with hard and angry emphases. As we reach the last woman in line (Carolina Garcia), we see the last stages of internalization of this violence: there is no one left to lash out at, so she turns on to herself. She brings her hand sharply to her face, as if slapping herself, which sends her whirling around from the force of that slap, even as she almost sobs out, "THAT's what it's all about." She turns in suddenly, clapping her hands together right in the face of the woman next to her. Claps read like slaps as the woman keels over, and sends that violent gesture echoing down the line, and back. And girls who learn that violence is the way to go about the world turn into women who extend their arms out in front of them and gesture with their hands the sign of the gun.

But here moods shift quickly and the sharp, attacking anger of the previous moment dissolves suddenly into laughter and another series of games, where the girls, sitting on the floor and doing each others hair and nails, complain that they got "the hand-me-down blues" from wearing all the shoes and clothes handed down to them. The locating of the moment of violence within a context of play has a deep impact: it serves to emphasize the impression that those who play these games, innocents, internalize the violence that is meted out to them, either directly or indirectly what they absorb from their surroundings. It urges us to recognize the violence and potential damage that young girls of color are exposed to in this society. The reaching, struggling hands of the previous section can also be these slapping, pushing, trigger-pulling hands.

On the Black Hand Side

Give me five, on the black hand side. The five women still standing in center stage, arms crossed across their chests, heads cocked to one side, their body attitudes and facial expressions signaling challenges thrown out to each other and to us, the audience. From the edge of the second wing on downstage right, Zollar begins to read from a text of her interview with Abiodun Oyewole of The Last Poets. It refers to the histories of black artists in Harlem in the 1960s, and their conscious articulation of a typically black performative style, sometimes resignifying existing codes in the dominant system of social interaction, sometimes culling from the specificities of black cultural practices to create new codes of social interaction. Here specifically, the reference is to the handshake that was developed by black artists and activists at this time both to emphasize the personalizing of a common gesture and to communicate a certain political stance—"a handshake was just a record of how you were supposed to be while winning this revolution—so you had to be precise, you had to be clear . . ."[3] One dancer twists and circles her wrist in elaborate patters, another moves her hand percussively back and forth, finally coming to round in, on her chest. Playing with one's hand before it reaches another in a handshake, creating a personalized "code."

The lights create a pattern of two lines crossing on stage. Two women (Christine King and Allyson Triplett) walk in from either end and meet at center. In their first encounter, they raise a hand out toward each other but miss contact and walk off. They turn back and walk toward each other again with intent. Close to each other, they stop: hands move towards each other, palms come to face each other packing a narrow layer of air between them. Sandwiching hands move together in circular pathways and then again with angular turns. The fingers ripple, and pull away toward the chest. They fist and come close as if to touch, one on top of the other: but they still refrain from actual contact. The next time they come together the touching of hands leads to more elaborate moves, like a handshake giving the support to slide to the ground and into a somersault. Wrists circle around each other as fingers make contact on the beats of a defined rhythm. Hands reach to the ground and fling the legs up. Each meeting of these individuals creates occasion for further creative activity, spontaneous improvisation and invention, playing off each other; each meeting makes for a handshake that is different, so that the originality of each encounter is emphasized. Grasped hands lead to floored jumps where both dancers, their palms moored to the floor, dip their hips to the floor down and up. One dancer leaps up nimbly and walks over to where the other is balancing her lengthened frame on one arm, the other arm flexed up, palm facing upward. Hands come to together again in midair, and again, only to pull apart and snap out the emphases of the music.

They are riffing on the text that Zollar is now reading, from another section of that same interview: "Cool Like that," where Aboidun talks about the musicians' Dap, the hand-to-fist greeting that was developed during the Black Power Movement as an expression of black solidarity. The musicians' rendering of the Dap is different from the revolutionaries' according to Aboidun, because for them this greeting is also an artistic form, and it's "always interesting to see what the artist does with what the people have created."[4] The accompanying music is created and played by composer and musician Michael Wimberly on the piano, jazz grooves syncopating rhythms here to draw out that same melody another place, which gives the two dancers room to play with their movement as the others dance back in. Clustered together in center stage, some sitting, some standing; exclaiming all at the same time, creating an extraordinary clamour of voices, they throw their hands into the center of the circle as if for a group handshake, some focusing on this choreography of thrown hands, others looking away deliberately, too cool to not rely on their creative flair and the unseeing accuracy of their moves.

Hands also elaborate other gestures; they underline the attitude of a walk, for instance. Here, they further a play on the Harlem walk, so that we are reminded again that the walk is never simply about the functionality of locomotion. Rather, it too creates spaces for an outburst of creativity: Give me five, on the black hand side. They re-embody this typical "Harlem

Joy Voeth in "On the Black Hand Side," Zollar's *Hands Singing Song,*
Photo by Cylla Von Tiedemann.

walk," emphasizing the dipping knee with an incurved shoulder. Walking
back, to a downbeat-emphasized percussion score, they arrive upstage
center. One leg extends out long even as it remains capped with a flexed
foot, it rond de jombs around only to dip the body down as the knee bends
and pulls the entire body weight groundward, and the opposite shoulder

gives in to that pull. As the body curves up again, the move is repeated, but this time the rounding leg kicks out with the flexed foot as the torso exults in waves on movement atop this series of close-reaching kicks. Occasionally, the dancers and musician pause to remind us of the result of their explorations: "cool like that!" or "chill like that!"

As the dancers are launched into hectic, complex movement phrases, the choreography rides the improvisational mode of jazz as the dancers work within the grooves of select signifying gestures, each stamping the movement with her individual style. When the dancers suddenly come together in unison movement in the middle of that highly individualized choreography, we are reminded of a notion of community organization where a group of people share some codes and sensibilities, but where there is still room for the originality of each individual within the expression of group solidarity. Give me five, on the black hand side. The dancers burst into one such moment of group choreography, as the six women form a horizontal line upstage. The drums explode into a fast-paced, blood-racing, percussive score, and the women charge forward, their bodies in profile but faces turned towards the audience, their fisted hands circling around and around as they scoot forward rapidly. This inaugurates an elaborate and highly charged choreography of swings, drops, jumps, and turns, dancers weaving individualized movement scores with sections of unison movement. Propelled more often that not by arms, bodies swing backwards into curves, emphasizing every note of a rhythmic cycle; hands slice through the air to pull the torso down reaching head to knee, and shake up in the air as hips to the drums. Here cool blends into hot, and our attention is focused on the riveting power of this group energy. The revolution may not have been televised when it happened, but its spirit is remembered and staged here with power, through movement metaphors that remind us that the cultural is immediately political.

My Female Hand
The next section, separated from this one by a musical interlude played on percussion, flowing in waves, takes us to an entirely different place. Short sharp exclaims from a female voice. Four women in individually lit circles marking the tips of a triangular formation on stage, one (Carolina Garcia or Joy Voeth) in center upstage at the tip of the triangle, one in the right base corner, and two in the left base corner. The light falls only at an angle on their bodies creating, in the intersection of long shadows and half-lit body-lines, a sense of a scene that can be seen only partially. More clearly though, the light shifts constantly so that there is never a point when all three points are lit. The movement of the light suggests the idea of roaming flashlight, catching bits and pieces of scenes as it scans the range. It illumi-

nates that which is unseen and only hinted at. The woman at the center touches herself lightly, her fingers brushing against her thigh as her hand circles around and then moves lightly up her body and gently pulls her into a loosely held arabesque balance, arms reaching out in front. The light moves to the two women in the downstage left corner who carry over the impulse of that curving reach of the arm to reach an arm in a circle around the body. Their palms walk up their bodies, from their thighs over their stomachs, their chests. Suddenly, as if to remind us of the secrecy that this exploration is enmeshed in, they look up at the audience, fingers on lips, and breathe "Shhhhhhh!" A series of more fast-paced movement, rolls on the floor that end in kneels, punctuated by hands folded as if in prayer, and then opening questioningly. One more time: "Shhhhhhh!"

The light moves to the woman in the central circle. She is on the floor, lying on her chest. Her butt peaks up and twists her body slowly to one side. The light flashes over to the woman in the downstage right circle, who too is lying chest to floor, butt peaked, balanced on toes. But the self-absorption of the dancer in the center is replaced in this woman by a sharp nervous energy: she constantly jerks her head from side to center to side, as if watching for something. The lights come back on the woman in the center. She is sitting back to the audience. The right elbow, raised above her head, flexes the forearm down to reach across the middle of her back. The other elbow reaches down and flexes the palm up to the middle back, reaching toward the other palm. The reach takes her back down to the floor, her legs fan out in a wide V and sweep her over to her stomach. The legs flex at the knees to bring the heels together in an elaborate dance of heels and ankles. She swirls around to rise, coming to stand on her knees. Her arms ripple out to the side as her pelvis undulates in luscious circles and her torso swells with pleasure. The drum grows and ebbs in unceasing waves of rolls. She dances alone in the central pool of light, her hands traveling from her legs up her body and rising finally to cross over her head, creating her own pleasure, as her body ripples in the throes of delight.

This woman reminds me of the central character in Toni Morrison's *Sula*: "She is new world black and new world woman extracting choice from choicelessness, responding inventively to found things. Improvisational. Daring, disruptive, imaginative, modern, out-of-the-house, outlawed, unpolicing, uncontained, and uncontainable. And dangerously female."[5] It is interesting but not too surprising that this is a section that producers are uneasy about marketing.[6] Women's auto-eroticism is deeply threatening to the stable hegemony of a patriarchal system that relies largely upon the internalization of a sense of need for the symbolic law of the father for its smooth operation. The images in this scene perform desire and pleasure, but what is singular is the staging of self-generated pleasure.

This is a precious moment in the history of concert dance in America, where the performance of black female subjectivity—often routed through the reconstruction or celebration of historical legacies and cultural practices, or the typical fabric of black women's fortitude in the face of adversity and pain—comes to insist on an articulation of sexual pleasure and erotic fulfillment in her own terms. The hand that touches the vulva and creates pleasure and fulfillment also enters the realm of the symbolic to overturn the old discourse in the Anglo-European thought about the definition of woman in lack. Hers is not the practice of self-policing whereby women render their bodies docile. At the same time, the embodiment of this "dangerously female" sensibility is not unrealistic: clearly it must be protected by some kind of secrecy, "shhhhhh!" and happens in the shadowy zone of half-light. But the privacy surrounding acts of such pleasure do not take away from the power of their pursuit.

Hazel Carby and Angela Davis, among others, have written about the remarkable ways in which female blues singers like Ma Rainey and Bessie Smith, both in the ways in which they presented themselves physically and in the lyrics and modes of their music, "reclaimed female sexuality from being an object of male desire to a representation of female desire."[7] Zollar picks up on this tradition but extends and twists it, so that the representation of female desire is immediately accompanied by the dangerous assertion that the desiring body contains possibilities for its own ecstasy. She also extends the epoch-making declarations of the French feminists, Helene Cixous and Luce Irigaray, in the 1970s about the particular nature of female sexuality and subjectivity. One is reminded of Cixous's call to recognize the power of female desire from a location in the "female" imaginary, rather than in a phallic discourse of lack. The mobile pleasure of the soloist, exulting in the sensory delights of her own touch, reminds us also of Irigaray's assertion about the multiplicity of female desire and her emphasis on touch as sexual and symbolic catalyst: "the intimacy of that silent, multiple, diffuse touch."[8] Yet the embodiment of female desire on a black body, the focus on pleasure, and the unmistakable self-sufficiency in the performance of the arousal of desire, its exploration, and orgasmic fulfillment within the boundaries of self, make this scene a radical statement of black female subjectivity.

Hands Singing Hallelujah

Notes from a piano. A woman (Christine King) enters the stage from the right upstage wing, stepping through a strip of light. She walks slowly, rubbing her hands together. She begins to speak her memories of her grandmother's hands: nurturing, caring, gentle hands that rubbed her chest to ease congestion, comforting hands that held her so close, hands that prayed and guided her on her own way. Her hands come together and then widen out again in gestures of offering, and reach to her chest and touch her body gently. Behind her, upstage right and dimly lit, three women move gently, suggesting mutual support and caring. The soloist's stories about her grandmother, and the care embodied in the loving touch of her hands, layer this generally less-conspicuous movement with references to cradling, nursing, healing, and caring. The soloist's voice reaches a crescendo as she celebrates the marvelous life-affirming power of those hands: Hands that sang *Hallelujah*. Her movements become smaller as she walks out slowly, the lights dimming on her, the piano extending her resonance of her trailing-off voice with the refrained melody of the last line. This too is the legacy of black women: loving and caring for their own, even as they labored to take care of others' families. It is important that this section is positioned in between one where there is an active desire for sexual fulfillment and desire, and the following, where the women are in revolution. While these women have led different movements that have articulated their own emotional and political aspirations and needs, they have made time to care for others. It also signals the multilayered and multidimensional legacy of black women in this context, all of which Zollar lays claim to as she dances this complex picture of black female subjectivity.

Hand to Fist

This last section picks up on some of the energy of the third section, *On the Black Hand Side*. As the last notes from the piano from the last scene trail off, Zollar comes on at the side of the stage and begins to read. The text for this section too comes from Zollar's interview of Abiodun Oyewole of The Last Poets. Michael Wimberly, the percussionist, takes us into the spirit of the scene as he walks into the light casually, pulls on his black cap and, leaving his drums, comes to sit facing the stage, still to the side but more visible, and begins playing on an unturned bucket with his drumsticks. For Wimberly, this is a reminder of his own youth: young black men, aspiring artists, growing up in the sixties in New York, beating out rhythms as they improvised them, creating rhythms on the hood of someone's car in the streets, creating something out of minimal resources.[9] The text refers specifically to the fervor of the artists in the sixties Black Arts Movement who were struggling to individuate themselves and assert their presence in a socioeconomic situation that sought to control them and destroy their will. "We took our revolutionary posture and put our African natural style with it to reaffirm and to try to define our particular place and our accents on what we wanted to make important this time and we would say this is our thing."[10]

And it is individual accents that become significant in this section,

even as they are highlighted by the coming together in the unison performances of "codes" of empowerment. One by one, three women in short
dresses and doffing black caps, walk in from three directions to meet in the
center of the stage. The walk is assured if cocky, clearly directed if suffused
with attitude. Hands on hips swing off to sign in "codes" for a basic moment of reckoning. Caps are adjusted, two hands clap together in a handshake. With recognition of "belonging," the shoulders begin to pulsate to
the rhythm of the drums, turning the body from side to side. This gradu-
ates suddenly into a fisted hand shot out, so that two women end up facing
each other, one arm extended toward each other, one's fist placed directly
above the other's. The third woman's fist is raised high above her head and
placed right above the other two fists. Signifying on the Black Power sign.

This is not a simple recalling of the revolutionary movement, though,
and the women immediately move on from that moment to different movements. Using their bodies percussively, they pick up the rhythm of the
bucket, which goes off momentarily, and move into a circle as two more
women join them. As the drums pick up again on the choreography, one
woman marches in from the downstage right wing. The rest of the women
are in a loose diagonal line. She weaves in between the women, performing
an elaborate handshake with each one of them, one of them dipping down
to the floor or jumping off, pulling on the shaking hand to complete the
gesture. This immediately launches them into an exciting, high-energy section, where jumps move into swirling kicks and fast-shrugging shoulders,
and arms beating the air propel the body into a series of lunges.

From a more simply syncopated score, Wimberly now goes into a
faster, highly complex, densely structured rhythmic sequence based on a
Zimbabwean warrior rhythm.[11] Quick somersaults mingle with fisted
hands beating the rhythm on the floor, kicks with flexed feet swivel the
body into side-to-side hinges. Voices rise becoming increasingly urgent. We
catch glimpses of locked fists and hands shaking in complex gestural combinations. The rhythm changes again, the deliberate articulation of each
beat hitting the air with its own force. One by one the women join into a
movement phrase where they march forward, hurl the arms out to the side
from their chests, marking the movement with heeled emphasis. They
march back to meet with the others who now join in. Suddenly they all
pivot around to face the audience, standing close together, and shoot their
fisted hands up into the air. The sign is held but for a second. Angular
edges and insistently syncopated rhythms fill the choreography. Again, we
see a coded moment: the women still fleetingly, close together, feet wide
apart, fisted arms held out low to the sides, their gazes fixed forward. The
next moment liquid torsos flexing down and curving up are charged by
butt-kicking jumps and arms that slash through the air. Stepping forward

with jump-kick motions they move in a circle, arms flexing up to the sides, occasionally thrown up and shaken down, always empowering the basic rhythm cycle of the percussive instrument.

Zollar now moves on to another text: her own reflections about the Black Power Movement and why it fell apart. She talks about the exhaustion that comes from being constantly on the frontline, about the disruption caused by internal contradictions of sexism, homophobia, and authoritarianism in the movement, individual selfishness and short-sightedness. The dancers are still in a circle, but their energy is clearly flagging, the movements get less clearly delineated and less complex. Hands are thrown in gestures of obvious frustration. A couple of them leave, walk off. She talks about the dangerous dissensions caused by the FBI's notorious Cointelpro policy, which ruptured the organized energy of many progressive movements in the sixties and seventies. There are only two dancers left on stage now. Suddenly one of them turns on the other, her hands flaring out into the other's face in a demanding gesture. The other ignores her for a bit then suddenly repeats the in-your-face question performed at her. They are in each other's spaces, their profiles in close but threatening proximity. One of them suddenly whips off her cap and thrusts it into the other's hands, who stomps off. The lone woman on stage continues to move again. But the texture of her movement is now totally different. Instead of the hard-hitting articulation of beats with gestures, she weaves a choreography of pliability, her body hinging back to take the floor, her arms waving in over her chest and billowing out, and then elongating the body horizontal in a held balance.

The text has changed in tone too. Zollar speaks now of her conviction that despite the apparent failure of the movement, most people did not in fact give up on their commitment to fight for justice for disenfranchised peoples. Rather, they realized that they needed to work in ways different from the more confrontational and violent tactics used by the Movement, and have continued to forward those same ideals, fighting in their own small ways, building toward a vision of a better life in their communities. Obviously the struggle continues: the lone dancer on stage moves fiercely, her jumps melding into her upreaching turns and fast footwork. As Zollar's voice rises, exhorting those who are working to continue their valuable labor and understand that they are part of an inspired group of individuals, the dancers file back onstage one by one. Their movements are individualized but they all emphasize the theme of "building" that Zollar calls out again and again, they dance with fierce intention and robust energy, accenting the drummed rhythm that now grows more insistent and fast. As they move, they are once again in a circle, but this time the lights narrow into a central pool so that the dancers mark the outside rim of the light circle.

Zollar insists at a breathless pace: "we gotta work it out, gotta work it out, gotta work it out, work, work, gotta work it out."[12] The percussion is lured into her pace and is furiously marking each second. But the dancers still. The revisiting and immediate re-scripting of that moment in history is now faced with quiet and unshakable determination. One by one they raise their fists in the Black Power salute and then draw that arm back to cross their chests. In the fading lights we see them pulling that fisted hand close, placing it softly on their bodies.

Urban Bush Women, Zollar's *Hands Singing Song*. Photo by Cylla Von Tiedemann.

The piece reaches to the larger context of this time through the text and through the resonances of the primarily abstract choreography, where the only direct reminders of the Black Power Movement are the doffed cap and the raised fist, both resignified in their gendered "difference" and through the way in which they are mobilized in the choreography. These images also fall into the network of the entire piece that highlights the project of remembering, re-experiencing, and therefore rehistoricizing through specifically marked lens, politically charged and personally powerful. At an informal talk given at the Race, Ethnicity, and Migration Center at the University of Minnesota, Paul Gilroy talked about the migration of movements, for instance, the way in which hip-hop has travelled from the United States to the United Kingdom and within other contexts.[13] In relation to this phenomenon, he urged attentiveness to the potential danger of the reductions of democratic aspirations when disempowered people take on images that signify conventional notions of power, and of the possibilities of militaristic fraternalism inherent in such embodiment. While acknowledging the subtlety and power of his argument, I want to rethink it in reading the way the Black Power sign is taken on in this piece by the women. Contrary to Gilroy's apprehensions, their embodiment and performance of the "sign" seem to signal a powerful moment in the rewriting of history: it reminds us of the continuity of political participation and leadership that is part of black women's history, a claiming of the legacy of Sojourner Truth and Rosa Parks. Moreover, it claims the movement and its drive for self-determination even as it remembers the sexism inherent in it. Many black women at that time found themselves lodged between a difficult set of choices: a feminist movement dominated by white middle-class agenda, and a movement for black liberation, exciting in its vision but based on "compulsory male leadership."[14] Elaine Brown's reminiscences of her participation in the Black Panther Party show how disruptive and simultaneously celebratory this remembering is.

> A woman in the Black Power Movement was considered, at best, irrelevant. A woman asserting herself was a pariah. A woman attempting the role of leadership was, to my proud Black Brothers, making an alliance with the "counter-revolutionary, man-hating, lesbian, feminist white bitches." It was a violation of some Black Power principle that was left undefined. If a black woman assumed a role of leadership, she was said to be eroding black manhood, to be hindering the progress of the black race.[15]

Abhorring this heteropatriarchal control of the movement, many of the women struggled to support it as part of their own political agendas. Yet their participation in that movement, which obviously offered some vital affirmation in terms of racial and cultural identifications, and concomitant commitment to transforming that movement by struggling for greater agency within it, is a valuable history which, seldom acknowledged within larger historical narratives, is set into relief in this choreography. Here, the work of revolutionary women like Katherine Eldridge and Angela Davis are juxtaposed with the problematic politics of the Black Power Movement to create a complex, contested narrative. History, in fact, is mined here, because official narratives are not taken for face value; rather, in reaching deep below the surface, Zollar throws light on the underside of historical phenomena, signifies upon them, and brings valuable perspectives to light.

This highlighting is always a powerful moment in the piece, all the more dangerous because the embodiment of the sign is on bodies female and black, those apparently low on the rungs of the hegemonic power ladder, but who are obviously committed to fighting for their dreams. Moreover, the ways in which it is staged, and the way the rest of the narrative frames it, the performance of this last section becomes anything but unreal, confined in an isolated space—the useless mimicking of forms of power by those who have none of it—but a foreshadowing of the future resonating with a rewriting of the past, a strategic move in the call to organize in a broad-based fight against institutionalized hegemonies. The way in which the Black Power sign is mobilized in the piece is significant in that respect: performed against a text that is urging the forging of a politics of resistance on multiple levels, the fisted hand appears but is not held. It dissolves, as it is revisited, celebrated, and then let go, its energies absorbed into other movement. This choreography recalls, for me, Toni Morrison's concept of "rememory," which, because it is both so personal and yet also interpersonal, involves a character's renegotiations with and of the past. In *Beloved*, Sethe talks about walking down the road and encountering a "thought-picture," a clear sensory image that seems to have taken shape in her imagination, but in fact that is a moment when "you bump into a rememory that belongs to someone else."[16] Remembering in this way is not so concerned with textualizing history, but with reckoning with the *way* in which we remember the past. If our memory of the Movement is invoked by the visual image of the fisted hand, the play on the Dap, and the typical stance, it is also immediately transformed by its embodiment by the women and the way in which the choreography—the movement and the accompanying text—embeds it in celebrating, questioning, dissenting, delighting, clashing. The memory then does not stay locked in the specificity of a time and place in the past, but is activated and released into the present. The re-enactment of images from the past—information about which is culled from interviews, memoirs of those who were in the Movement, Zollar's own rememberings of this time, as well as other historical sources—is not so much a reiteration, but a creative refiguring of a collective memory that mediates the relationship between the past and the present.

Sections like this also coincide with the emphasis laid on artistic aspects of the black revolutionary movements in the sixties, highlighting the politics of cultural and creative production. The legacy of artists working to enhance the spirit of a political movement—which really gained momentum in the African American community in the sixties and seventies—marks an important strain in the history of black performance, and in that respect is certainly a valuable influence on Zollar's work. Imamu Amiri Baraka had predicted in 1966 that black music, especially R&B, would soon come to reflect the black desire for more self-consciously political lyrics. Indeed, this period was marked by songs like Aretha Franklin's "Respect" and James Brown's "Say It Loud, I'm Black and I'm Proud," with lyrical expressions about the uniqueness of black style and of black pride in general. For others yet, there was an unavoidable imperative to create art with a broadly formulated sense of political action. Brian Ward, writing about the impact of current politics on the work of musician Marvin Gaye, says, "He was prompted by a combination of his brother's letters from Vietnam and the ghetto riots to 're-evaluate [the] whole concept of what I wanted my music to say.' Gaye wondered, 'with the world exploding around me, how am I supposed to keep singing love songs?'"[17] This is the kind of question that rises from Zollar's work generally and from *Hands Singing Song* particularly, where political action springs from personal questions and a worldview permeated with consciousness about the greater context in which the work is situated.

Here we are also drawn to think about the value of an "interested" or "committed" historicizing. Here remembering the past is laden with possibilities for present mobilization, so that it remains alive, not monumentalized and remembered through souvenirs and empty nostalgia. This is significant at a time when photographed images of Angela Davis and other leaders find their way into the fashion industry in the style of "docufashion," which recycles the Afro hairstyle, the black jacket, typical markers of black militancy of that time, as part of the new aesthetic of revolutionary glamour. Davis argues that the commodification of these images empties them of their historical significance, reducing a politics of liberation to a politics of fashion: they are redeployed in the imagination of the newer generation of black peoples several years after her arrest in a "nostalgic surrogate for historical memory."[18] The piece takes up Davis's charge of finding ways of weaving images from black history into a sociocultural remembering that vitalizes the history of memories and also keeps them alive in the context in which they were engendered, such that their disruptive potential is not erased.

Moreover, as the piece unfolds, the different sections comment on each other, often asserting thematic correspondences and intersections and calling for renewed recognition of the interrelationships being articulated in this piece, such as the multiple inter-textings of women's relationships with violence, power, and sexuality. One of the most significant sections in this piece for me, one that forms a subtext for understanding all of the others and complicates their meaning substantially, is *My Female Hand.*

This is particularly true of the intersection of this section with the last, for instance. The asserting of female sexual desire in this context is doubly subversive because of the notorious sexism that dominated the movement despite the contribution of powerful women leaders. The claiming of sexual play for her own pleasure is subversive again when we remember that black women were urged to support the revolution by bearing and nurturing its future leaders and boosting the self-esteem of its current leaders, and generally sublimating their sexuality for the needs of the male-led movement. While it would be vulgar to generalize this comment, it is no doubt true that the comments of Chaka Walls of the Illinois Black Panther Party at the 1969 Convention of the Students for a Democratic Society reflected the problematic gender politics of most of the members of the movement. Here Walls declared that the role of women in the revolution was "for love and all that . . . for pussy power . . . The way women contribute is by getting laid."[19] And the celebration of self-generated ecstasy also blasts the heterosexism inherent even in several of the bastions of revolutionary thought.

Also, throughout the piece, we are pushed to rethink inherited notions of community. It is significant that the piece exists after the Anita Hill–Clarence Thomas hearings and their televised confrontations, an event that troubled the understanding of "community" in many black circles. The way the protagonists were positioned by the media ruptured the previous all-embracing notion of community that developed out of black history in this country, and many people sensed betrayal in having to "choose" between two black people held up under white scrutiny but placed in opposition. Angela Davis refers to this time:

> I grew up in a Southern black community where we always protected each other, no matter what. Community was racially all-embracing. That is why my mother, who identified with Anita Hill, also felt compelled to embrace and protect Clarence Thomas. That she finds herself in an untenable situation is a consequence of the historical obsolescence of the particular sense of community we once found so necessary.[20]

So facile notions of community based on certain taken-for-granted commonalities will no longer hold. But solidarity is vital for survival and for political struggles. If community can no longer be prefigured on the basis of some homogenous notion of race, then it has to be refigured, and once it is no longer a given, its construction necessarily involves questioning, confrontation and negotiation. That is why perhaps it is important to pay attention to the songs our hands sing: hands, immediately expressive parts of our body, identified with our labor, ways that we communicate and make contact with others, that more often than not actualize our feelings, of anger with a slap, of protest with the raised fist, of care with gentle touch— tell so much about the politics with which we live our lives. Community is built on the basis of shared politics that are anti-racist, anti-imperialist, anti-sexist, and resistant to hegemonic constructions: Sojourner Truth, who claimed her identity as black and female and as deserving of suffrage, is the first name on the list of ancestors in Scene I. And while the list names primarily African American leaders, it also names Chief Seattle and Sitting Bull, Cesar Chavez, and Nelson Mandela and Winnie Mandela among others. Community is built through identifiable political movements, but also through the work of artists like Ella Baker, Leonard Peltier, Bernice Johnson Reagan, and Katherine Dunham, and of educators like Nayo Watkins. This connects with the last few lines of the text that the dancers move to in the concluding section of the piece, where Zollar reminds us about the many individuals who are still on the frontline of the struggle but often go unnoticed. The vision of an organized movement against injustice and for human rights created through a broad base of coalition politics recalls June Jordan's inspirational and empowering dictum: freedom is indivisible.[21] It also reminds us that despite appearances and hegemonic rhetoric, the struggle of people of color and especially of black people in this country has never been completely squelched. Despite the heavy-handed ways in which most progressive movements led by people of color are stifled by bureaucratic manipulations, black resistance as well as other movements of people of color exist as a continuum, as a perpetual undertaking, in small quotidian ways or in larger, more organized ways: "many are working in quiet ways—in small ways—in spiritual ways—in artistic ways. Building multi-racial coalitions, embracing the leadership of women, embracing gay and lesbian participation and leadership, creating, working—in powerful ways, in positive ways, community building . . ."[22] Finally, identifying the politics of community formation feeds into and energizes the particular historicizing practices we have seen at work in this piece, like in so many resistance movements, and their mobilization as the cultural and political productions of a particular group of people sharing dreams, ideals, and values.

Hands Singing Song is a complex piece in which the collage of the five scenes creates complex commentary about black female identity. There is at once a claiming of the legacy of political aspiration and radical leadership created by women like Rosa Parks and others, and an understanding of the need to continue that struggle; the celebration of the healing and nurturing that black women have historically taken on; the acknowledgment of the violence that young women and girls are often thrust into in this sociocultural set-up; the assertion of female desire and self-fulfilled pleasure; and remembering and resuscitating of the energies of the past political projects, but with renegotations of the politics within such projects, and with the determination to create a broad-based fight against injustice. It is this insistence on shifting and differently accented formulations of identity and community, where different situations call for foregrounding of different aspects, and their location in a politics of shared and multifaceted struggles, that I see as a recurring theme in Zollar's current work, but thrown into sharp relief in this piece.

SRI (1990)
Feminist Visions for a Powerful Future

The lights coming up from downstage left pick up a group of six women
edging their way onto the stage from the diagonally opposite corner, their
spines stretched forward from their pelvises, backs jutting out to emphasize the broken line of the spine, knees flexed low, feet weighted to the
ground, arms held in rigid and lifeless lines at their sides, but their heads
still reaching searchingly forward. With their broken backs, they move
painstakingly, slowly: the heel of one foot rises almost imperceptibly and
drags the foot forward, the sole ever unable to dissociate itself fully from
the ground. The weight shifts forward with this arduous endeavor as the
body resigns itself onto the forward foot. Now the heel of the other foot
rises in a barely visible movement and drags the foot, yet unable to lift itself
from the ground, forward. The weight shifts one more time and another
step is inched on. And again, the heel of one foot rises almost imperceptibly and drags the foot forward, the sole ever unable to dissociate itself fully
from the ground. The weight shifts forward with this arduous endeavor as
the body resigns itself onto the forward foot. Now the heel of the other foot
rises in a barely visible movement and drags the foot, yet unable to lift itself
from the ground, forward. The weight shifts one more time and another
step is inched on. Each step speaks of weariness, pain, and a quest in spite
of that. One by one, the feet pull themselves forward and haul the body
across the stage in this terrifying, weighted effort. Still in a tight group, the
women move diagonally, reaching more than halfway across the stage. Suddenly, as if catching sight of some unseen attacker looming large in front of
them, they are halted in this journey. Their heads curve up a little, their
eyes rise; they acknowledge their arrested pathway and begin to retrace
their steps. One more time, their backs flexed over, the women drag their
broken bodies across to the corner they came from, still searching for their
spines, questing for recovery. One more time, the heel of one foot rises
almost imperceptibly and drags the foot backward, the sole ever unable to
disengage itself fully from the ground. The weight shifts backward with

this arduous endeavor as the body resigns itself onto the back foot. Now the heel of the other foot rises in a barely visible movement and drags the foot, still unable to lift itself from the ground, behind. The weight shifts one more time and another step is inched on. And again, the heel of one foot rises almost imperceptibly and drags the foot backward, the sole ever unable to disengage itself fully from the ground. The weight shifts backward with this arduous endeavor as the body replaces itself onto the back foot. Now the heel of the other foot rises in a barely visible movement and drags the foot, still unable to lift itself from the ground, behind. The weight shifts one more time and another step is inched on. And again. And again. This relentlessly repeated walk of silently searching women, inexorably covering the stage from corner to corner, gives the impression of an arduous exodus every step of which must be labored through.

This section from the third part of *Sri*, choreographed by Chandralekha in 1990, where the women move with their backs broken, creating the image of what happens to women under a patriarchal regime—of how, with their spines broken at base, their voices lost, their bodies weak, and their will to protest crushed, they are cowed into submission—lasts only about six minutes. But, in the unremitting cruelty and tension it builds up, it seems interminably long. It is followed by more images of the humiliation and degradation attendant upon women in contemporary society, though nowhere does the articulation of this emotional state take the form of sentimental or overtly emotional "realistic" gestures. As the women are gradually able to raise their backs upright, they continue to move, still huddled together in groups, in defined directions. But in unison, their heads turn over one shoulder and they direct the pupils of their eyes back to a certain point in the darkened auditorium. No other feature of the face moves, but the sheer power of that directed look, multiplied by being mirrored in the six pairs of eyes, spells the terror of pursuit and the possibility of assault. It is not safe to speak out yet.

Suddenly, one of the groups is splintered as one of the women's bodies splatters onto the floor, as if thrown off in an unprepared moment by an assailant. No loud crash attends the fall, no break in the musical score, no reaction in the other women: it happens matter-of-factly, as if it happens daily all the time. With great effort, she raises her pelvis in an endeavor to pick herself up, supporting herself by pressing her palms to the floor. Before she can rise fully, another woman drops, and another, and another. They fall on their faces, sometimes all the way to the floor, sometimes lurched over where their heads touch the ground, still on their feet, but almost always breaking from their pelvises as they fall: we see their spines thrown forward as they keel over. This sequence is followed by another where the women sink slowly to the floor to sit on their haunches, swiveling in semicircular motions on the balls of their feet, moving an arm in repeated, measured, rounded gestures, as if sweeping the floor. They move together, a mass of unacknowledged labor, never raising their eyes, continuing their work silently, part of their daily routine. This scene points to the invisibilization of women's work in general and echoes bell hooks's belief that for those women who *have* to work (as opposed to those who choose to work) the great claim of upper-class feminists that work is liberating is hardly comprehensible.[1]

Sri is unique for the depth of the feminist critique and commentary embedded in the fabric of the piece. More than in any other pieces in Chandralekha's repertoire, there is in *Sri* an embodied exploration of systemic gender oppression and its devastating consequences. In the drag walk scene, the women's spines, which would enable them to stand straight and independently, are broken. The spine here is metaphor for a sense of self understood on its own terms, which is a clear extension of its literal function in the body, its central stabilizing structure holding together so much of the muscular system, and guarding inside itself, the vital core of the nervous system. It is the way in which the weight of this system is literally taken on by the dancers' bodies, confronting us with images of haunting terribleness, that makes this section of *Sri* so powerful. The image of the broken spine is juxtaposed with images of internalized fear—the women halted in their journey by the unseen attacker, the look thrown over their shoulders—convincing us that they exist under perilous and destructive life conditions. Moreover, the idiom of the movement genre is itself transformed through such usage in a feminist context. The *sachi* or sideways glance of the Indian classical repertoire of eye movements, *drshtiveda*, for instance, which has a variety of expressive functions in different contexts, is transfigured as it is combined with a sharp head gesture in a look thrown over the shoulder and used to convey a specific mood unrecognized in the realm of classical performance: women's fear of imminent assault. The weight of the content and the politics is thus linked with a paradigmatic shift in the form of expression, and the prime agent of this articulation as well as the site of evidence for such shifts is the dancing body, which itself comes to be resignified through such choreography.

But *Sri* rejects a tragic and pathos-laden picture of women's victimization. Within each of these sequences there is a constantly emphasized pattern of resistance in the midst of utter humiliation. The women fall, but they pick themselves up again and again. Their backs are surely broken, but they reach toward recovery. It is as if feminist scholar Monique Wittig's insistence that women's consciousness of being oppressed, the very acts of their recognition and naming of oppression as such, changes the very definition of oppression, is brilliantly embodied and dramatized. In her essay "One Is Not Born a Woman," Wittig argues that

> when we discover that women are the objects of oppression and appropriation, at the very moment that we become able to perceive this, we become subjects in the sense of cognitive subjects, through an operation of abstraction. Consciousness of oppression is not only a reaction to (fight against) oppression. It is also the whole conceptual re-evaluation of the social world, its whole reorganization, with new concepts, from the point of view of oppression . . . call it a subjective, cognitive practice.[2]

Sri is permeated with a similar consciousness. In this piece, Chandralekha choreographs a quasi-teleology of gender relations to mark a steadily increasing domination over women through institutions devised by patriarchy and to chart a developmental pathway that mocks the rhetoric of "progress." But she also choreographs an intervention in that teleological line to make it circular: the piece begins with a powerful feminist vision and culminates with a compelling move toward reclaiming of lost strength. In this, the piece looks towards an epistemological overthrow, to a situation where the very structures of knowledge have changed radically. Reminiscent of Bhabha's characterization of "beyondness," a not-here, not-there, but somewhere in a presently unlocated zone, Chandralekha, especially in the prologue and the conclusion, beckons to a space "real-ly" unglimpsed at.

In this prologue Chandralekha herself dances, or, once again redefines the meaning of the concept of "dance" as it is currently understood in the Indian context, to evoke an image of Shakambari, the primordial force of natural vegetation, traditionally conceptualized as the herb-nourishing goddess. The curtains open to reveal Chandralekha herself in a shoulder stand in center stage, her white hair spread out around her head, her legs flexed at the knees and ankles again, held parallel and touching each other, resembling a pair of cranes with their beaks peaked forward. The spine, which grows out of the ground, energizes itself through that contact to sustain the body sculpture that grows from it. The arms are flexed thrice, the upper arms running perpendicular to the body along the ground, the forearms angling upward as the hands rest on the back supporting the body weight, creating synchronous architecture with the rest of the body. As the lights intensify, the structure reveals itself as dynamic: like the lips of the vulva, the two heels so far joined at the ankle separate and the toes flow out and in, touching, as if licking each other, in sensuous play. In continuous movement, the legs entwine each other, thrust toward the sky, stretch back and overhead with magnificent eroticism. They rotate at the hip joint to turn in the same direction, the knees pointing to one side cross, and the shins and feet billow out above, as if the branches and leaves of an abundant growth. The knees still touching, the shins move in different directions and the feet overlap as one foot places itself on the other. One leg straightens itself to extend directly above the body, and the other, slightly twisted before the straight leg, flexes at the knee, to snake up toward the other leg. The tips of the toes of the lowered leg reach up to touch the toes of the other foot, flexed down, again and again in marvelous play. Often in such "play," the legs register as if energized differently as they move in counterpoint to each other, one stretching to the other's flexion, one moving slowly and gently to the other's defined extension upward. In this play of differences, not only the body is animated by the dancing legs, but also the entire atmosphere, the circumambient space: each new space-shape sculpted between the differently playing legs is rendered alive and mobile as they merge into another new design and another. The richness of growth and movement, especially of natural vegetation, is evoked through these migratory shapes that are repeatedly created and moved into new ones.

There are moments, however, when the negative spaces are crushed out by the joining of the legs, which curve into the body and are depressed to the level of the floor, crouching into the forehead, motionless for a moment. Movement begins once again as the shins, still facing the floor, sway unevenly from side to side, and the legs stretch slowly to extend out above the head, which peeps out from between the legs. From this deep drop, life is renewed once again, as, charged with energy, the legs part as they rotate at the hips and flex at the knees in a perfect tilted mandala, rooted to the ground at base by the tips of the toes, invoking the opening of the *yoni* and the reawakening of sexual energy to create new life.[3] They sprout once more, splendid in their strength and slow, concentrated energy, rising to recreate the bodysculpture overhead. In a final unrushed opening, the legs branch out, turned out and the feet flexed to reach in different directions, once more evoking the lushness of growth. Finally, as the lights begin to fade slowly, the legs lower and the head rises: this opening segment darkens on the image of perhaps Shakambari herself sitting on the floor with her legs folded, her back to the audience, her arms planted directly to the floor behind her through her flattened palms, her spine tall, erect, and emitting waves of energy. It is significant that Chandralekha, who rarely performs in her own choreography and had not done so since *Angika* was produced five years ago, decided to perform this prologue herself. This move dissociates the power of growth and regeneration from categories of youthfulness. The image of her coming to sit with her back toward the audience, her white hair running down her spine and catching the lights sharply, is riveting: it refuses to conflate superficial notions of aging with a diminishing of powers and desires. Even from behind her, the sensual charge of the goddess-woman's body is evident: the opened *yoni* radiates her body and the atmosphere around. In a global context dominated by ageist exclusions and where "symbolic clitoridectomies" clamp down upon women's desires and sexualities everywhere, Chandralekha's asserting her sexual and creative powers makes a powerful statement.[4]

Let me briefly contextualize the understanding of Shakambari as fertility spirit here. The Shakambari figure, not a traditionally popular goddess in the high Hindu pantheon, is drawn from submerged layers of Indian histories and folk beliefs. This is not a romantic recalling of a fabled past: it is a picture conjured up from research, from evidence drawn from visual images from the prehistoric ruins of Mohenjo Daro and Harappa. However, in choreographic sections such as this, Chandralekha's work, rather than recalling glorious past times, an interpretation that a simplistic reading might yield, actually produces bodies that bear witness and recover subjugated knowledge, creates images that can sustain current struggles towards justice. Yet, reminiscent of the device of temporal movement through historicity in *Angika*, the postioning of this invocation of the Shakambari figure in a prologue to sections that will apparently chart the escalation of patriarchal power through time serves an important function. The long and historical presence of the herb goddess in the indigenous popular consciousness makes for a contested history, denaturalizing the development of male superiority and critiquing the direction of "civilization" through the establishment of a skewed power structure.

The particular way the Shakambari figure is performed calls for further reflection. Chandralekha is certainly celebrating the powers of the earth-goddess here, but not in a literal glorification of the birthing and nourishing powers of female body. Nor does she intend to repeat the problematic nature-culture opposition, which is why she creates her commentary through abstract and metaphoric images rather than by attempting realistic portrayal. She understands creativity as a principle of self-renewal and transformation, reflecting the innate regenerative qualities of natural forces such as air, water, light, earth, and life processes. It is not translatable into reproduction, the realistic propagation of life through progeny. In this, Chandralekha's perspective is radical:

> I am against nature that must fulfill itself through propagation. When I die, I want an absolute end for myself . . . There is no need for continuation through progeny; that too, a continuation of the man's line, his genes . . . This is something that Indian feminists have to understand, they have to question the understanding of this fulfillment. If a man does not need children to fulfill himself, why should a woman? My goal is like the great

prophets, I want self-realization for myself, I want to understand the meaning of being a woman, for I reject this understanding of the meaning of life through and for others.[5]

To understanding the meaning of being a woman, in this context, and on her own terms—this is a returning question in much of Chandralekha's work, artistic and activist. It is no doubt a quest that emerges from the historical dominance of male voices in philosophical discourse, such that it almost seems that "the search for self-realization has been a man's prerogative."[6] Oppositionally, it seems that women have had to tease value from their lives through fulfilling predetermined roles, such as a wife or a mother, convenient channels that fix them in nonthreatening grooves and prevent them from realizing their own potential. I believe Chandralekha's insistence on drawing a sharp distinction between creation and procreation is both stoked, and is particularly important in a context dominated, by a mythologization of motherhood that is then used to eclipse women's spaces for self-actualization. In fact, Chandralekha would typically argue that, socialized into believing that the fulfillment of their lives lies in nurturing their families and carrying on the great task of continuing the human race, women ultimately *allow* patriarchal society to harness their powers for its own needs. Motherhood is thus powerful in patriarchal systems, but only because it has come to imply a concomitant stasis and desexualization for women. This is a recurrent theme in much of Chandralekha's work and explored in great detail, for instance, in *Yantra*.

In Chandralekha's conception then, Shakambari is not the eternal mother, nature's goddess of propagation, but she is the very life force that energizes creation. Here, she draws on a figure from early rural animistic cults, outside the realm of scriptural reinforcement, to remind us of indigenous notions of empowerment that can serve as inspiration for contemporary women. These traditions are richly populated by earth goddesses, who, significantly, are neither married nor accompanied by children, but rule over the processes of life and growth, the life-sustaining forces in societies dominantly agricultural.[7] It is important then that this is a solo section: Chandralekha as Shakambari dances alone and for her own sake; the creative process is vitalized through the female principle alone. Moreover, unlike the conventions of Indian classical dance, the legs do not support the movement of the body or create patterns that can be reflected in the body: they dance by and for themselves and create an array of spatial patterns, one melting into the next, without building up to any narrative closure. This self-absorption, heightened through the nonpresentational mode of this scene—the dancing woman's upturned posture, her never facing the audience—echoes with a sharp, single-minded focus on the movement of the creative principle towards its own unraveling. This also enables Chandralekha to foreground herself as an intending subject, engaging fully with life and reshaping given terms and conditions to make meaning, resisting becoming an object of an overdetermined history. Here, too, the parallel between Chandralekha's abstract evocation of Shakambari and Wittig's notion about the subject coming into being through an "operation of abstraction," which entails a reconfiguration of the entire knowledge-frame within the subject's consciousness, is significant. Chandralekha's recasting of a traditional portrayal of the goddess where the creative and reproductive acts might be conflated, in terms of this energy field animated with life force, also brings to life Wittig's description of the journey of the female subject toward the actualization of her latent agency through a "subjective, cognitive practice."

The body of the piece, meanwhile, bears testimony to a history of increasing control and oppression for women. In a striking moment in the second section of *Sri*, Chandralekha dramatizes the institution of marriage, which ultimately becomes the cornerstone of patriarchy. With the chorus behind them, one man (Sridhar) and one woman (Padmini Chettur) emerge in relief in center stage, facing each other and in profile to the audience, executing a simple *taka dimi taka dimi* foot pattern in fast tempo.[8] The stage throbs with intimations of fire as, their feet still tapping out the incessant beat, their gazes fixed on each other, they advance to an electric closeness by mutual consent, their bodies a hair's breadth apart. The sounds of the stepping descend to a barely discernible whisper. Then, the spine of the man softens as he bends all the way down and touches the foot of the woman and pulls her toe gently forward and sets it down with tenderness. He looks up toward her with great regard while she accepts his gesture by a forward shift of her weight and continues to look ahead of her. The quiet beauty of this moment is brusquely ruptured by what follows. The man's entire body stance changes as he rises, and chest expanded, arms loosely fisted, and with an almost casual assertion of masculine prowess, he walks sure-footed to lead the woman by one hand in a circular pathway. In contrast, eyes lowering, head bending, her body no longer held as tall, the woman deferentially follows his every step as in a regular Hindu marriage ceremony, where the woman follows her husband in seven circles around the sacred fire to solemnize the marriage. This inaugurates a phase of institutionalized control over women's sexualities and desires, where their independence is increasingly curtailed, their knowledge of their own strengths gradually attenuated: here, we bear witness as the charged power of their erect spines and their confident footwork peters out.

The piece continues to explore more intensely the effect that the increasing force and the multiplying levels of oppression have on women as their voices are lost and their backs broken. Yet the women reassert themselves and arise one more time to create concluding images of immense beauty, defying the forces that would crush their creative and regenerative powers. *Sri* ends with an invocation to the future woman whom Chandralekha has visualized thus in a poster she designed. In the center, we see the impression of a woman's face, beneath whose large, fully opened eyes, stands a lotus in full bloom. On her forehead, just above the meeting point of her brows, is the red dot of *kumkum*.[9] In her hair, on either side of her head, are the sun and the moon, enhancing her already luminous face. Her face is drawn in red and black outlines against a white background, while the sun and moon are colored in with red and golden yellow paint. Framing this central motif are brilliant borders of red and golden yellow, colors generally regarded to be auspicious in the Indian aesthetic framework, intersected occasionally by lines of white and black. Above and below her picture are Chandralekha's words, scripted in black against a golden yellow background, the lines and periods marked in lines of red. Chandralekha's words read:

> She is radiant like the rising sun. Her beauty lights up the world. She wears sun and moon as her jewels. Her eyes are like fish and lotus and darting deer. Her face is fragrant like champaka, her hair like incense. She has capacities. She is active. She is aware. She is fearless. She is free.[10]

Particular and cosmic at the same time, this image of the ideal woman is as significant because of its striking aesthetic conception as its insistence on the intelligence and awareness that make up the quality of beauty. A similar picture of glorious strength, beauty, and sensuality, of multiple powers realized, is evoked in the last segment of *Sri* as five women gather together to stand in mandala position in a vertical line center-stage, one behind the other, such that we see the full figure of only the woman in front, but sense the volume of the collective behind her. As the dancer in front circles her hands to perform the *varabhaya mudra*, elbows flexed forward, one palm facing down to signify *abhaya*, dispelling fear, the other facing up to signify *vara* or blessing, the dancers behind her each raise their arms in different directions, each holding a different weapon or auspicious symbol. This powerful image evokes the ten-armed goddess, *dashabhuja durga*, who, according to Hindu mythology, was created by the joint efforts of all the gods, who, by themselves, were unable to combat the mighty demon *mahisasura* who had succeeded in routing them from their heavenly abode. Endowed with multiple powers and supported by the blessings of all, wielding different weapons in her ten hands, Durga alone is said to have subdued the powerful *asura* through skillful warfare and restored peace to the

Meera, Geetha, Jasmine, Krishna, Sujatha, Tripura, and Padmini, Chandralekha's *Sri*.
Photo © Dashrath Patel.

heavens. Chandralekha then pictures the future woman, like *dashabhuja
durga*: a woman who fully realizes her potential cosmic power and who is
able to combat the powers of evil that would threaten her. Importantly, however, this goddess spirit can only be imaged through a community of
women who collectively empower the concept.

The piece does not end with what might be read as this deification of
women in Hindu terms. Indeed, women's goddess-like powers are invoked,
the multiple dimensions of their powers and abilities remembered, and
then they are freed into dynamic movement. The goddess image is deconstructed as, one by one, each of the five women center their hands
before their chests and, with a jump, come to stand in a deep, turned out,
mandala, their feet wide apart. As they jump, they reach their arms out on
each side at shoulder level, the hands holding the *shikhara mudra*, where,
with the rest of the fingers folded into the fist, the thumb stands out, facing
up, signifying power. Still in a tight group, still in a deeply grounded *mandala*, maneuvering a continuous weight shift by shifting first the heel, then
the toes, forward, the women surge forward like mobilized life force.
Energy radiates out in all directions as the bodies move forward through
their outstretched arms, their turned out feet, their upward-pointing
thumbs, their flexed out knees, their flashing eyes. It is as if the women

revisit this mythical image momentarily by collectively embodying its several parts, and then internalize that power in order to move on with their struggle. *Sri* closes as it logically must, with intimations of this new beginning, with this magnificent coming-to-life.

I want to reflect briefly on the feminist implications of this piece. A complex female subjectivity unfolds as the piece progresses, and the site as well as the mode of this unfolding is the body. What is incredibly clear in the choreography is how the vicissitudes of a history of increasing oppression, internalized fear, and resistance are read through the changes registered by the dancing body. The very form of the body is produced by this history. I look askance at Judith Butler, askance because she is writing in a different context to rethink the production of gender and sexuality on and through the body, but the idea translates well here: the materiality of the body, its contours and fixities, can be rethought as the effect of power, "as power's most productive effect."[11] Let us look once more at the way the spine works in this piece. Drawing on the concept of the spine as the central location that can emanate empowerment and consciousness, in physical disciplines such as yoga and occult practices such as tantra, Chandralekha works exactly with the spine to create her palpable discourse on the patriarchal hegemony in place.[12] If the spine, along which the *chakras* (nervous centers) are located, is what enables us to hold ourselves straight up, it reads as a symbol of self-sufficiency and independence. The effects of an inequitable distribution of power shift the contours of the body by changing the shape and the force of the spine. It begins to cave in after the symbolic marriage ceremony even as the opposite phenomenon is seen in the male body: Sridhar's back flares out, expanding his chest, in a much more consciously rigid positioning just as Padmini's begins to curve in, her head beginning to droop. By the drag walk scene, the spine can no longer be straightened to hold itself up: it stays flexed forward, necessarily impeding mobility, making even the simple act of transfering weight from one to another foot arduous. History cycles around as, after a period of intense struggle, the women work up to unfurling their spines, a metaphor of their resistance and reaching toward empowerment. The body that is diminished in the way it approaches space, compressing itself and its movement, ultimately comes to claim space for itself as it mobilizes the image of the goddess, surging forward like waves. The shifting relations of power and the contrary relationship between notions of power and empowerment encode and restructure the body, reminding us of the negotiated material dimensions of the body.

It is also important to read the structuring of *Sri* in the context of Chandralekha's participation in the Indian women's movement. Discussing the future of the women's movement in India, Nandita Shah and Nandita

Gandhi wonder if the present sense of a lull in the dynamism and creativity of the movement is not attributable to the continued use of particular political practices and ideologies, and they suggest that women need to explore other methods, disciplines and perspectives. In this context they bring up the radical alternative proposed by Chandralekha when she asks women to go on strike and stop having children, endangering not only patriarchal necessities such as continuation of family line, but also large-scale industries focused on producing "kiddie" commodities:

> The question I ask is: Can we step outside the reality of family, marriage, religion, and law, step outside and look at ourselves? Difficult, because we are a product of this reality . . . To look at ourselves we will need to create a space, outside of these institutions. We will need to break up reality and recreate it afresh, in the way the painters, poets, writers, artists perceived realities through unusual perspectives.[13]

The creative process of deeply visionary artists is indeed radical because it effects an epistemological, ontological, and ethical reorientation. Such process produces alternative visions precisely because they "break up reality and recreate it," in other words, analyze the constitutive parts of the systematic management of society and figure possibilities of shaping oppositional frames from within the given situation. Obviously, there is no being "outside" the system, but there are continuously possibilities for resistance, and the challenge is to eke out perspectives that turn the current hegemonies on their heads. One is reminded of indigenous women's movements that have changed the face of history: the mass movements against deforestation through entirely nonviolent means, such as the Chipko resistance, or the Telengana and Tebhaga revolutions, where impoverished women risked every little bit they had to participate in a pitched struggle against landlords and colonial powers, and forces of capitalism generally.

The way Chandralekha imagines this reconfiguration also reminds one of bell hooks's notion of an oppositional aesthetic: an aesthetic that confronts the audience with its reorganization of the "real" or "truth" such that the individual audience member too is pulled into questioning her or his position in relation to this "reality." The artist's contribution lies in imagining an alternative reality, in conjuring up images that can inaugurate the possibility of alternatives. Chandralekha suggests, "We need dreams. By dreams, I don't mean the chronic nightmares we are familiar with . . . But a leap, a quantum jump, a flight into the future . . . We will need a fantasy that can cut across the oppressive reality of a system that has no exit, a system which is enclosed upon itself."[14] This concept of dream no doubt colors my reading of the last section of *Sri* and its evocation of an imminent future: not as images of a less-than-conscious mind, but as the vision of a deep desire, conjured up by an aware and searching imagination, realizing the full extent of one's creative powers, images that combat life-crushing forces to aspire to dimensions of life that currently seem to be beyond our reach.

The need for dreams fuels the choreography in many ways, particularly in the way it choreographs a feminist agenda. *Sri* insists that the resistance to struggle is not enough, that women need to work in positively creative ways in order to fully realize what they are capable of. This emphasis on self-actualization, both on an individual level (as in the Shakambari figure's self-absorption with her own processes) and a collective one (the multilayered and communal taking on of goddess-like powers), beyond the shared experience of struggle, to formulate themselves as subjects with agency to shape history, recalls the words of bell hooks. In a striking essay, "The Politics of Radical Black Subjectivity," hooks claims that "opposition is not enough. In that vacant space after one has resisted there is still the necessity to become—to make oneself anew."[15] The framing of the women's struggle by humanized and mobilized images of goddess figures signifies that reaching beyond the conditions of struggle in the present to herald the process of self-actualization. For me, these images function as what hooks, discussing how the photographs of artist Lorna Simpson name what is rarely articulated, calls "a technology of the sacred that rejoins body, mind, and spirit . . . Beyond the realm of socially imposed identity, the limitations of race and gender, one encounters the metaphysical."[16] This work of imagining and staging the "sacred" in ways that also refigure the ways in which this concept is understood, this willingness to invest in metaphysical dreams even as she documents the breaking of the women's spines in her work, is what imbues Chandralekha's vision with power, and urges a recognition of her as an artist committed to social change.

CREATING ALTERNATIVE COMMUNITIES
The Rewriting of the Gothic in Jawole Willa Jo Zollar's *Bones & Ash*
(1995)

In 1995, the Urban Bush Women Company premiered the evening length production *Bones and Ash*. Jawole Willa Jo Zollar collaborated with novelist Jewelle Gomez to adapt her novel, *The Gilda Stories*, as a dramatic script. She also worked with singer/song-writer Toshi Reagan, dramaturge Steve Kent, and a talented cast of company members and guest artists to recast the vampire of the Euro-American imaginary and create vital social commentary on notions of family, race memory, ancestorism, and women's relationships. All of these intersect the traditional myths about the struggle of good versus evil, and revise them, to create a complex scenario where traditional alignment of virtues is significantly upset and we are made to see things in a rather different light.

One of the most significant reversals has to do with how the notion of the Gothic is embodied and reworked to acquire almost the very opposite connotations that it has come to acquire, as a genre of Euro-camp in current discourse. While the piece is swathed in a general darkness, with lurking shadows, long and heavy curtains that keep out the impression of sunlight that the vampire figures cannot stand, we never see the typical makeup or most of the physical markers of the Gothic. Again, while there is sustained use of the principles of paradox and irony, often enough features of the Gothic imagination, in the choreographic and narrative structure, their usage in this context twists the archetypal Gothic narrative substantially. The Gothic sensibility and the dark, brooding atmosphere that characterizes the production interweaves a fantastical world with a historical one and the surreal world of Bird and Gilda, whose legacies are literally transported, intergenerationally, through different bodies, and intersects with the very specific realities of African American histories of oppression and resistance.

Of course African American vampire narratives, though not a hugely popular genre, have always marked themselves with a signal difference, in that they are haunted by considerations of racial difference. For instance, in one of the first black vampire films made in America, *Blacula* (1972), the primary vampire figure, played by William Marshall, begins as Prince Mamuwalde, an African leader who comes to the castle of Count Dracula in 1780 to ask his help to stop the slave trade from Africa. Count Dracula finds the idea preposterous and the discussion leads to an altercation whereby Mamuwalde is bitten by Dracula and shut up in a coffin in a locked basement, while his wife Luva is locked in the basement with him to starve to death. This sets the tone for the rest of the movie; Mamuwalde is awakened from his coffin in 1965 and plays out Dracula's curse, condemned to seek out blood and populate the world with vampiric creatures. Interestingly, in the sequel made a year later, *Scream Blacula Scream*, Blacula works with a voodoo priestess, Lisa, performing rituals that will rid him of his vampirism; but his efforts are thwarted by the police.

Even in the more clearly farcical film, *Vampire in Brooklyn*, we learn that Angela Bassett's mother, a highly qualified professor of anthropology in New York, loses her mind and dies because the man she fell in love with as she did her research in Haiti is deemed a "vampire" in the eyes of the western world. This is clearly a reference to the stigmatization of Africanist religious practices such as animal sacrifice and Voudun as dangerous and part of "devil worship." In fact she dies of a broken heart because she clearly understands that they cannot be together, though they have a child together in the "real" world. Again, when Eddie Murphy, the primary vampire figure in the movie, tries to convince Bassett to join him, he embarks on a rhetoric filled with exhortations to freedom, to not remaining caught up in the human world full of constraints.

The very different *Ganja and Hess* (1973) reroutes the fascination with blood through the obsession of the African queen of Myrthia whose call haunts the film. However, while it effects a unique translation of the Gothic genre into the black context, the film is deeply disturbing on several levels. Dr. Hess Green, a noted African American anthropologist and geologist who is stabbed to death by a stranger only to become immortal, is the primary vampire figure here. Clearly his desire and need for blood, deeply associated with high libido and sexual desire, belongs to the realm of the extraordinary, the unexplained myths from the "dark continent" that defy scientific rationality. Every time we see him thirsting for blood, we see the image of the Queen of Myrthia as if beckoning him or running through tall grasses, the long serpentine extensions from her elaborate headdress waving in the wind behind her. The appearance of the black Queen is always against a high-pitched soundscape, reminiscent of a continuous ululation, oddly syncopated, somewhat eerie. The several shots of the inscrutable expression on her face only heighten the many ways in which she is represented in stereotypical ways, fitting in with the exotica and "mystique" of Africa. Yet this strange power from the occult—seen mostly as a malady that possesses Hess—exists only to be vanquished by the shadow of the cross on his soul. I find this rather extra-ordinary narrative problematic primarily because it remains ensconced in the tropes of hetero-sexual excess and Christian dogma, while also reifying the rationality-exotic mystery binary of Europe-Africa.

However, while the vampire theme has not been so popular in African American cultural production, generally these few examples allow us to see that, from the beginning, the mapping of such representations on black bodies have made for narrativization and implications that are very differ-ent from their counterparts in Euro-American culture. The juxtaposition of the vampire figure with the history of demonization and hypersexualized stereotypes of black people, and the recurrent intrusion of police violence into black life based on charges of antisocial behavior, immediately lessens the possibilities for parody of the vampire figure: things are too close to home in a racist society to allow for metaphoric tweakings in this realm. However, most of these stories do not go far enough to tease out the full implications of this racialization, and it remains as a disturbance in the dominant codes of this typical story. What is significant about both Gomez's *The Gilda Stories* and Zollar's restaged performance of the literary narrative, *Bones and Ash*, is that they exceed and question the usual ways in which the vampire figure is routed through the history of race relations in America where the ultimate discrepancies in social relations are glossed over, and that they raise another complex set of questions that urge address-ing in contemporary times.

My analysis of the narrative refers primarily to the movement text, which has a shorter time span and a different sequence structure from the novel. Here Gilda (played initially by Deborah Thomas and later Pat Hall-Smith) is a biracial vampire, who has already lived for two hundred years at the time the action begins in 1850. She lives in New Orleans with her lover, Bird (played by Trinket Monsod), a Filipina woman in a previous life cycle-who has lived thereafter as a member of the Lakota Tribe. Importantly, they never draw on human blood to take life, but rather to sustain themselves only, and they always replenish these humans with energies, ideas, and dreams in return. They run a bordello called Woodard's, though interest-ingly enough, the sexual labor is completely played down in the perform-ance narrative. Further, in the version of the Urban Bush Women, all of the women in the bordello other than Bird are black, which gives an interesting twist to the story. A key individual bursts into the narrative close to the beginning: Girl (played by Christine King), a recently enslaved and or-phaned young black woman, originally from the Fulani tribe, fleeing after having stabbed the white overseer who was attempting to rape her. She finds a home with Gilda and Bird, and begins to learn history, reading, writing, and other practical and life skills with them.

Exhausted by the many wars she has seen in her lifetime, tired of the violence she has encountered, Gilda recognizes in Girl the potential to understand her extra-normative life. She transubstantiates into Girl, who becomes the new Gilda, and gives up her body. The next phase of the performance starts with GildaGirl's travels. *Bones and Ash* picks up on one of the sections of these travel stories, where GildaGirl is the owner of a hair salon in Boston's South End in 1955. This leads to her struggle with Fox (played by Kwame Ross), a vampire who is more in line with the Draculas of regular Gothic fiction, and who is on a killing spree. When confronted by Gilda previously, he had justified his violence by referring to all the brutality he has been exposed to as a black man in America, having experienced the assault, rape, abuse, lynchings of his people. Fox also holds in his power and abuses a young black prostitute, Toya (Maia Claire Garrison), who seeks GildaGirl's help to escape from him. In a fierce encounter, Gilda-Girl manages to kill Fox, and frees Toya from the terrible sexual bondage in which she had been laboring.

Obviously, even this cursory retelling of the "story" emphasizes that this is a vampire story with a signal difference, black or white. One of the first of the factors that makes for this difference is that the history of race relations in America is a persistent and vital subtext of this narrative. This story of two lesbian vampires of color is inaugurated by references to slavery and the sexual assault black women survived through these times— such as the conditions marking Girl's abrupt entry into their lives, fleeing from bondage and assault. Moreover, the progress of time from 1850 Louisiana, to 1955 Boston is marked through a slide show of the social protest movements that were part of the politics of the time: images from the Abolitionist movement, the black women's club movement, and the suffrage movement permeate this apparently fantastical narrative with a historical consciousness.

The consistent filtering of the performance of the Gothic mode through this consciousness shifts the terms of understanding of this genre. The slotting of these narratives into a historically and culturally specific framework means, for instance, that Gilda need not be cast in opposition to specific liberatory cultural practices associated with the black church in African American history. Hence, GildaGirl carries with her the metal cross that her mother gave her as a reminder of her personal history and legacy. This imbues her with cultural specificity and still functions in reclaiming the vampire genre from Christian and other dogmas. For the church here becomes distanced from the usual associations in the vampire genre with establishment and the codification and regulation of bodies and sexuality. It becomes instead a signifier of what has facilitated survival through the history of slavery, through the experiences of loss, pain, and struggle. It is this mode of distancing the usual connotations that have accrued to particular signifiers, and resituating these latter in other contexts that will re-signify differently, that we see in practice in *Bones and Ash* repeatedly, and what offers, for me, one of the most significant perspectives from which to read this performance text.

However, racial politics are complex here. For instance, Girl initially reads light-skinned Gilda as white, and only later comes to recognize her as Creole. We are reminded of the need for camouflage that a biracial, or black woman often engaged at that time, in order to operate as successful business entrepreneurs in the dominant white world. (I will revisit this concept of partial identifications in the conclusion.) We are also immediately reminded that race is not a fixed marker, but a construct whose significations shift as we migrate through different positionalities. Besides the ambiguity regarding the first Gilda's racial background, we also learn of Bird's shifting racial lineage through her different incarnations. She carries with her the memory of the decimation of her people in her previous life and connects with Girl's history of assault and persecution. The past and present overlap as the histories of the devastation of Native American peoples, the enslavement of African- Americans, and the later colonization of the Philippine Islands intersect in and through the bodies of these women. It is in the context of these histories of lives arbitrarily disrupted, cut short, lived partially, whether through enslavement or through police brutality, that I want to recall Zollar's comments when I asked her why she chose to dramatize this novel: "The concept of being able to *choose* to live for two hundred years seemed wonderful . . . unlike the characters of regular Gothic fiction, where the characters are obsessed with death, the characters here are obsessed with *life*."[1]

In coinciding the perennial "other" of Eurocentric society, lesbian women of color, with the typically European trope of othered sexuality, desire, and fantasy, the vampire figure, Gomez was motivated by her search for heroes, who, it seemed, most people need. "The women's movement showed us how much we want heroic figures. And I wanted to show that we already had them—in our families—and with some creative thinking they could be strategically placed within our culture."[2] She talks about researching the idea of prolonged life in several cultures, and realizing the importance of creating a mythology for her vampires that would place them within a "broader, more ancient cultural frame of reference" than the legacy of the Count.[3] So elements from Africanist traditions such as blood memory and ancestorism play into the narrative as Bird recounts stories from her previous life and as Girl transforms into Gilda, while the choreographic structure of Gilda's journey to her True Death reminds us of Africanist rituals surrounding death and mourning. All of this resituates the genre and renegotiates the terms on which it can operate within this context effectively, so that unlike most of the films I mentioned before, the concept of the vampire does not read like an ineffective experiment in transplants.

Moreover, the recasting of the vampire figures as women who still drink the blood of humans but do so in a mode of "fair exchange" makes of them something like healers. They finely puncture human flesh and enter human bodies to feed on the blood, but in the process remove negative impulses such as greed and anger, and painful feelings, while they fortify existing dreams and hope. For Nina Auerbach, this is a travesty of the female Gothic genre: according to her, it purges vampirism of aggression, conflict, and confrontation. Auerbach argues that *The Gilda Stories* are part of what she sees as the domestication leading to the death of the vampire genre, initiated by the onslaught of Reaganism and the large-scale spread of AIDS. As she says," If vampirism is a wasting disease like AIDS, its cure is a blessing, but if it contains immortality, secret strength, and forbidden identities, its domestication is a death more painful than Homer's."[4] Stuck in a binarized mode, she casts Gilda as the model of the good vampire versus the traditional bad vampire, the latter containing the potential for presenting a threat to established power through their infiltration of father-ruled households, and their dismantling of hierarchical authority through subversive intimacy with the daughters: "*Gilda* is clearly meant to be an enlightened response to the sexism inherent in the lesbian vampire tradition, but Gilda's virtue defangs her into another paralyzing stereotype: that of the good woman . . . Gomez's vampires are inhibited by their self-righteous decade, whose protests dissipate in piety."[5]

Thinking through Gomez's text, and with particular attention through Zollar's choreographic fabric, I find Auerbach's interpretation a rather simplistic reading of aggression, and her lack of attention to how race changes contexts and terms of analysis rather stultifying. Contrary to her argument, even as "good vampires" the images that this performance leaves us with call for a radical rethinking of dominant values and power relations that govern our lives, and are, in that sense, threatening to a stable, hegemonic social order. Besides, the simple good-bad bipolarity plainly does not hold in this case: Gilda and Bird are vampires and lesbians of color, who are aggressive about searching out what they need and desire and about pursuing their interracial relationship, and the way they live their lives redefines the given terms of social interaction in a hierarchically and prejudicially organized world. (I will talk more about my reading of Gilda and Bird as subversive subsequently.)

Moreover, we cannot read the vampire figure here as a trope of capitalistic exploitation as is a common Euro-American reading. It also seems equally limiting to read the vampire only as a source of erotic anxiety and corrupt desire, as it usually functions within a white heteronormative framework. It might be more profitable, in reading *Bones and Ash*, to shift our perspective to read the Gothic as a mode of resistance to hegemonic culture and its regulatory institutions of family and church, and as characterized by the insistence of the protagonists, who recognize themselves as "different" from humans, in pursuing what they desire and what sustains them. The subversive potential and reframing of issues in *Bones and Ash* can be argued to be typical of the Gothic subculture, even as the piece recirculates the terms and context of its dissidence.

Indeed, Miriam Jones has argued that the most radical transformation in *The Gilda Stories*, which self-consciously rewrites both the genre and the representation of the vampire figure, is the transformation of the metaphoric function of the vampire and vampirism. She invokes Gayatri Spivak's notion of the deconstructivist who narrates a displacement by using herself as a shuttle between the center/inside and the margin/outside in this discussion. She argues that the deconstructionist displacements in Gomez's narratives undertakes a series of negotiations: "1) from inside the genre itself, 2) in relation to contemporary reworkings of generic paradigms, and 3) within the broader context of political discourse and scholarship."[6] While Jones's is a significant reading of Gomez's narrative, I am more concerned with the nexus of issues raised in the intersection of a series of particulars that becomes more highly accented in the sensory immediacy of the performance: lesbian women of color who sustain themselves through the exchange of blood with other human beings, who live on the margins of established social relations, but from there redefine issues of community, family, and queer desire.

I want to call attention here to the figures of the Irissas, perhaps best described as the conscience of the narrative in *Bones and Ash*. Three women who begin and end the piece, moving as they speak, articulating some of the central questions of the piece, are not part of Gomez's novel, but were created for the performance specifically. They are archetypal spirits, the oldest of the vampires, described in the program notes as "teachers guiding their family." Their name derives from the root "iris," meaning rainbow, full of colors. The Irissas resonate as much with the Griot figure invested with the power of cultural memory as with the figures of the chorus in Greek tragedy entrusted with staking out the moral weight of

Christalyn Wright, Gacirah Diagne, Beverley Prentice, as the Irissas in Zollar's *Bones and Ash*. Photo by Cylla Von Tiedemann.

events and actions. Their opening words are about dreams: "We come here for the dreams/In the dreams we find ourselves/ . . . A world behind us/As large as the world ahead/In its arms lie questions/Leading to our path." These words are juxtaposed with movements that are heavy with breath and weighted in their relationship to the ground. The Irissas move with vocalized emphases, deep scooping movements of their arms emphasized by undercurves of the torso. This contextualizes the interpretation of the "dreams" they speak of, so that they land on us, not like airy escape moments, but as infused with the stuff of life, created by the leap of the imagination that enables us to survive through present crises and hold on to the vision of a world beyond them. This emphasis on dreams as that which nurtures life sets the tone for the understanding of the vampire figures in this piece, and highlights their abilities as healers, and thus those who facilitate and nurture life, enabling us to move on after pain.

I want to return to the question of violence and aggression, the toning down of which Auerbach reads as a move toward conformity, in relation to this search for dreams. Obviously women of color and specifically black women, who have been at the receiving end of long-range policy-based assault in this culture have a different relationship to violence than white women can generally have. What is in fact amazing about Gilda and Bird is that they have worked to keep from internalizing that violence, unlike Fox who has become part of that violent framework and is caught up in the repetitive cycle of senseless destruction. This resistance that these vampires exemplify—talking of dreams and striving to create meaningful lives even as they remember their histories—is, I suggest, threatening to a social order that is bent upon controlling or even erasing them through violence.

Joseph Andriano, talking of the fascination with feminine daemonology in the male Gothic tradition, points out that this "lady of Darkness," as he calls her, immediately signals a defiance of gender boundaries, for she is both sexually and intellectually aggressive.[7] Moreover, "she invades, inhabits, attempts to create change, which often occurs in spite of man's conscious will."[8] While Gilda and Bird do not so much invade and inhabit other bodies, their persistent use of their special powers to push for social change, for a world that is not gutted with senseless violence, can be seen as their rebellion against the "established" world order. In a world order that seems to be dominated by violence, it is resistance to being subsumed by that mode that reads as subversive.

Further, while their relationship with the human beings whose blood they drink is not sexual, the staging of lesbian interracial desire obviously reads as transgressive in a heteronormative world, ridden with anxieties about racial containment and miscegenation. Look at this section from the first act, for instance, where the first Gilda, weary of the violence around her, wants to take the True Death but hesitates to talk to her lover, Bird, about this decision. Bird is tender as she comes toward Gilda, and begins to hum softly "I know something about you . . . ," while the pauses in her song are filled in from the background by the Irissas who refrain, "open your heart to me." Bird, who has entered from behind Gilda, senses her

Deborah Thomas and Trinket Monsod as Gilda and Bird in Zollar's *Bones and Ash*. Photo by Cylla Von Tiedemann.

energies from behind and comes to stand close to her, reaching one arm out to Gilda's shoulder. Gilda responds immediately to the touch, turning around to take Bird in her arms. Holding each other, they turn each other around in a circle, each one slowly reaching into a backbend and then bending forward, depending on the other for support. Bird leans into Gilda, and they both play some with giving each other their weight completely, working with full body contact and the sureness of being shored up by the other. As their bodies yield in an embrace again, we witness a staging of queer desire that is neither sensational nor voyeuristic, but deeply moving in its sensitivity. How does this narrative about homosexual desire and exchange of bodily fluids work at a time when paranoia about AIDS has led to so much prejudice and violent exclusions of alternative sexualities? In a context when a disproportionate percentage of black people, and especially black women, are grappling with AIDS, and where, subsequently, queer sexuality and the open contact of orifices in the body have become stigmatized in an apparently inevitable relation to AIDS, the performance of both lesbian desire and vampiric activity as life-affirming is a positively resistive act.

What more does the vampire figure and the practice of blood exchange accomplish in this context? I think that the importance of the vampiric both for Gomez and for Zollar is in the linking of life to blood and the multiple metaphoric significance of blood. And it is how blood resonates through the histories shared by these women that imbue the feeding-on-blood with a light different from the usual vampire story. Traditional practices linking blood, especially menstrual blood, and semen or fertility, and the exchange of blood for blood as what sustains and renews life proliferate in several African societies. The memory of the large-scale spilling of blood, notions of memories that are secretly carried on through blood, rituals surrounding blood that is lost and gained in childbirth, are resonant ideas in African American history and culture. Blood recurs in multiple contexts as part of the symbolic framework of the lives of these women, and these resonances work to further the recontextualizing that Gomez and Zollar engage in. Further, there is the shared experience of menstruation, and as Gomez asks, "who would better understand the blood cycle than a woman? From puberty we're used to feeling the changes in our bodies because of the menstrual cycle. We know the uneasy feeling of being totally in our bodies and also adapting to the chemical changes that makes us feel alien to those bodies."[9] Such representation also defies patriarchal myths of menstruation, where the loss of blood is seen as a weakening experience, or as a reminder of women's procreative possibilities.

Here, then, the vampire is conceivable only in the image of women. And blood is the mode that establishes connections among women. In the staging of "The Hunt," where the two vampires search for blood, as Gilda and Bird approach two woman, who are evidently in pain though not in full consciousness, the Irissas hum from behind, ritualizing the moment of contact: "Your body speaks/The hunger comes . . . Reach inside/Feel what she feels/Reach inside/Need what she needs/Your body speaks/And she will answer." The mutuality of need and fulfillment is the vital link in the connection here. Moreover, the human scaling was also evident in the choreographic process for creating the scenes when Gilda and/or Bird feed on blood. Here the movement explorations focused on exercises of giving up and taking weight, trusting each other's support, and achieving openness in posture and body positioning. In performance, when Gilda and Bird approach the people who they will draw blood from, they come with gentleness, cradle the other's body in their arms, and then put their mouths on the other's body which has now relaxed into their supporting hold. This is more a performance of female intimacy than of violent or seductive vampiric penetration, but its calm embodiment is also no less threatening in the dominant homophobic context in which the piece is performed. I am reminded of Sue-Ellen Case's reimagining of the vampiric touch in her essay, "Tracking the Vampire": "What the dominant discourse represents as an emptying out, a draining away, in contrast to the impregnating kiss of the heterosexual, becomes an activism in representation."[10] This representational activism is focused on enabling a shift in the current homophobic perspective that conflates homosexual desire with the contamination of blood.

I want to invoke Amelia Jones's propositions that govern her reading of "unnatural" cultural production in this regard:

> Proposition one: it is the act (the in-process) and not the "fact" of unnaturalness that gives cultural manifestations power . . . Proposition two: the most disturbing acts are those that insistently perform bodies/selves in such a way as to activate spectatorial anxieties and/or desires, while at the same time calling into question what it might mean to call something "natural" (or, for that matter, "unnatural").[11]

It is in fact in the *distance* of this performance from the theatrical excess that marks Gothic's queer camp and its assumption of low-key "naturalness"—or we may say "humanness" here—that we can locate its deeply disruptive power. And it is also in its rejection of representational excess and the camp characteristics of queer Gothic, while it retains camp's strategy of reinscribing stigma as a survivalist strategy for "the subordinated, the excluded, the unnatural, the fake, or in Andrew Ross's phrase, 'history's waste'" that it resituates the genre to begin from a positioning in empowerment rather than an origin in lack or effortfully marked difference.[12]

Bones and Ash also performs significant commentary on current sociopolitical trends. The Irissas wind up the piece with a series of insistent questions: "How do we learn to love?/Where does our power come from?/ Is my family yours?/Who have we touched?/What have we built?" By the end of the piece, we have seen the nexus of the "family" and community shift repeatedly, so that any notion of a stable nuclear unit is undercut. Family and community are what are created by a group of black women, through their labor of love, care, and nurture, like the group of women at Woodard's, or Gilda and Bird, or Bird and Girl, or Gilda and her friends in the salon in Boston. The families, peopled primarily by women, are far from the traditional patrilinear, nuclear family. While matrilinearity has been a dominant trend in African American family organization, the political project of much black leadership since the Moynihan report as well as of the current times is marked by a recuperation of the family unit as defined through a typically patriarchal lens. Here I am reminded of Paul Gilroy's warnings against the "familialization" of current black politics that are based on essentialist and conservative understandings of family, race, and community. For Hall, this reads as a disaster for black feminist as well as alternative sexual politics: "the trope of the family is central to the means whereby the crisis we are living—of black social and political life—gets represented as the crisis of black masculinity. That trope of the family is there, also, in the way conflict, within and between our communities, gets resolved through the mystic reconstruction of the ideal heterosexual family."[13]

Steering away from the Anglo-American legacy of high individualism, *Bones and Ash* performs a kinship that is developed through desire, through music, through shared struggle, but also always in resistance to these dominant tropes of the ideal family. See, for instance, this section from the beginning of the second act where Bird and Gilda engage in a mutually enriching sharing process, just before Bird is about to leave this partnership. Working with Aikido movement, they dance to the clapping of hands. Arms swirl around, hands flexing up at the end of half-circles, as bodies swing, with pelvic undercurves, in low and wide pliés. Legs kick up high only to retract swiftly and pull the body along in the other direction. After a series of martial movements, bodies moving in concert with each other, the two come to face each other. With sharply vocalized breaths, they circle their torsos around, affirming their connections with mutually held gazes. It is significant that this connection of struggling and resisting together is affirmed even as Bird prepares to leave. Further, the extended communities at Woodard's as well as in Gilda's salon in Boston are neither nuclear nor fixed, for the protagonists constantly retain the choice to leave and seek their futures elsewhere. It is this renegotiation and remaking of family and home that resonates in Gilda's opening statement: "The shape of my life is motion, through fields, through time, through blood." This unmaking of fixed and normative organizing institutions in our lives and the tentative and fluxed restructurings of them constitute one of the significant commentaries embodied in *Bones and Ash*.

Ann Cooper Albright terms works like *Bones and Ash* and Bill T. Jones's *Uncle Tom's Cabin* the "New Epic Dance," particularly because they offer "a radical new vision of humanity" and retell the "ancestral blood memories" while they are historically meaningful.[14] I have attempted to expand upon and extend the radical vision that I too find embodied in Zollar's project. But the epical dimensions of *Bones and Ash* are as much about the larger vision embodied in it as about the critique and commentary of current social and political conditions upon which this vision is based. The epic dimensions are anchored to very local conditions, to the specificities of negotiations that these women engage in in order to live with the richness of dreams and desire. It is, in fact, the particularity of these negotiations that moves us to think of the larger sociopolitical scene. The epic dimensions are also in the ways in which the entire project asks us, the audience, to think about issues of performance and how it fractures the lens of normative representation for us, moving us to etch out more shifting, more complexly negotiated forms of identity.

It is useful to think of Jose Munoz's conception of disidentification in this context. Talking about minoritarian subjectivity, Munoz refers to the ways in which such subjects can often participate only partially with given modes of representation that are available through the circuits of majoritarian subject-formation. This makes for a disjunction between individual notions of identity and socially constructed narratives of self in which they are interpellated. "This collision is precisely the moment of negotiation when hybrid, racially predicated, and deviantly gendered identities arrive at representation. In doing so, a representational contract is broken; the queer and the colored come into perception and the social order receives a jolt that may reverberate loudly and widely, or in less dramatic, yet locally indispensable, ways."[15] A politics of disidentification works through a practice of intersectionality where each of the different co-ordinates that constitute identity are given their due weight and the interrelationships among these co-ordinates duly appreciated. Disidentification then, comes to be understood as resistance to normative ideology that dishes out select and partitioned slots for "others." It is a refusal to be assimilated into the spaces offered by dominant ideology and state policy: spaces which, like the check boxes on the diversity information sheets we fill out, and into which our identities must be partitioned, suppressed, and then channeled in draconian ways, can only be done at the cost of negating some aspects of minoritarian notions of self.

It is in this sense that Gilda and Bird, through their reformatting of notions of vampiric consciousness and selfhood and thus necessarily recasting typical associations of good and evil, practice disidentification. Unable to associate either with Coleridgian Christabels, Keatsian Dames sans merci, or Le Fanuvian Carmillas, because of the specificity of their histories and politics, or with the Blaculas because of their sexual preference, they understand their lives as queer women of color, but realize that as vampires they are imbued with the possibility of longer lives, of extra-ordinary powers. In this they necessitate understandings of identity negotiated between human and vampire, between traditions lived by black women and primarily white vampires. This practice of disidentification is obvious throughout the performance text, for instance, when Gilda uses the ambiguity about her racial background to facilitate her in running her business, when both women "pass" as men in their travels, or when they are out at night, for reasons of safety. But it becomes larger through the questions reiterated by the Irissas and the performance itself about identity and about making meaningful lives. Issues of migrancy, diaspora, hybridity are highlighted as we work our way through the shifting and renegotiated identities and communities of Gilda and Bird. We, especially as artists and cultural activists of color, are reminded about the larger project of carving out spaces for notions of selfhood that do not respond to the interpellating call of state-sponsored "safe" multiculturalism, but ask for recognition on our own, specific terms.

RAGA (1998) and *SLOKA* (1999)
Troubling Femininity

> The anti-terrorism bill has just been passed, exposing the violent authori-
> tarian premises of the democratic regime we live in, with its sanctioned
> systems of surveillance and punishment. Meanwhile, women's groups
> like RAWA have warned us repeatedly that life under a government
> formed by the Northern Alliance or any other political group, may not
> be that different for the women in Afghanistan unless models of power
> and governance are changed dramatically. Yet, despite many claims of
> "saving" the Afghan women, one of the justifications of the war, no atten-
> tion has been or will be paid to their needs as articulated by them, or to
> their resistances. This is entirely logical: very similar notions of power are
> at work here; power is entirely identified with military aggression and
> assault.*

The events of September 11, 2001, burned into our consciousnesses the
realization that notions of power are more than ever inalienably entangled
in notions of masculinity. In its incarnation in a context riddled with fundamentalisms, terrorism, and counter-attack agendas, masculinity is all about
brutish notions of maleness, and it is articulated through shows of military
strength, threats to "pulverize" and "crush," and exhortations to blood
revenge. Here, the paradigm of maleness is almost exclusively bloodthirsty
and destructive, and almost eclipses other ways of conceiving powerful
behavior. Concomitantly, femininity has come to occupy a space signifying
weakness, at the receiving end of male use, just like the women in Taliban-
ruled areas of Afghanistan are, in ignorance, supposed to be: veiled and
submissive. Recall, for instance, this statement by an army general from

---

*A different version of this chapter was presented as a paper at the plenary session of the CORD
conference at New York University in 2001. At that time, the paper had seemed extraordinarily
relevant, and I had begun with some preliminary comments about the situation of the world at
large. I add some of those remarks here, for they seem to me to contextualize the piece and re-
emphasize the urgency of such artwork.

Pakistan, published in an interview by Tariq Ali in *The Nation*: "Pakistan was the condom the Americans needed to enter Afghanistan . . . We've served our purpose and they think we can be just flushed down the toilet."[1] Of course, the outrage and anger the speaker feels at being used and discarded by the United States makes him see both Pakistan, facilitating male, or American, penetration, and Afghanistan, the site of entry, as trapped in a helplessly feminine position, penetrated and perhaps raped. These mappings of volatile political situations in gendered and sexualized terms are dangerous in many ways: I draw attention to them only to point to the widespread crass and polarized understandings of masculinity and femininity generated by such rhetoric.

It is in this context that I have come to value Chandralekha's work even more, especially the alternative notion of femininity that has long been a central concern in her work. *Raga* and *Sloka* in particular focus on a complex notion of femininity, and envision a world beyond compartmentalized gender distinctions that dominate contemporary configurations of identity and identification. In *Raga*, subtitled "In Search of Femininity," and where femininity is explored primarily by and in the bodies of men, and in *Sloka* as well, where the feminine is danced as the power of fertility and play, Chandralekha seems to be urging more complicated and less reified conceptualizations of masculine and feminine as energies and principles, not necessarily coincident with bodies marked male and female. In these two pieces, specifically, she wanted to explore the potential richness of the concept of femininity without ever romanticizing or sentimentalizing the experience of womanhood. Interestingly, while these works were often misread as emanating from "Western influence" and as being explorations of homoeroticism only, research will show that for her, this notion of femininity stems from beliefs and practices indigenous to her cultural context, and has been a long-standing concern with her. However, while this is a theme running through most of her work, it is with *Raga* that she names it explicitly as the principle of femininity, and focuses primarily on its articulations through bodies marked as male.

Interestingly, *Raga*, and to a lesser extent *Sloka*, have attracted the most criticism from the media and audiences in recent years. That notions of femininity have been hijacked by crass commercialization—whether it comes in the form of anatomically incorrect Barbie dolls, or the smiles on the faces of women who, in airline advertisements, welcome us to luxurious vacations in "exotic" lands—is obvious. So, no doubt, Chandralekha's revisioning of femininity as powerful life-energy would shift the frame of reference. But when I attended the U.S. premiere of this piece at Brooklyn Academy of Music in November 1998, for instance, I was taken aback at what seemed to be the very different reaction of a normally appreciative and

Shaji John and Sunny against the backdrop of Anish Kapoor's visual design, Chandralekha's *Raga*. Photo © Sadanand Menon.

progressive audience at this left-oriented space. After talking to several audience members picked randomly, I could only attribute the fact that several individuals had walked out during the performance of *Raga* to a central premise in this book: that Western audiences and critics often reject in the context of "other" cultures what seems "radical" in white/Western performance contexts, whether in terms of "excess" or as replicating what seems to be the exclusive possession of the Western avant-garde.

Chandralekha's focus was on femininity, but her work read as homoerotic. Further, neither did it create strong images of woman-power/Shakti, nor could it be read primarily as innovations in Bharatnatyam, which seemed to have been a prime expectation of the audience, and both of which have some popular currency in the art world now. This of course within the limits approved by a hegemony-driven marketplace. Indeed, critics here who had applauded her previous works, and appreciated the manipulations of the Bharatanatyam form and the powerful female imagery in the context of South Asian cultural traditions, found this work problematic. Of course, critics in India too misread the work, because of its plethora of homoerotic images, as being Western influenced. Interestingly, *Sloka*, which reverses the arrangement of scenes in *Raga* and flanks the no doubt shorter sections of homoeroticism with women-centered sections, was much more widely accepted. Certainly, it was applauded widely in a performance in Bangalore, India (2000), which I attended. It also ran to packed houses in Osaka, Japan (2000), where the work was presented as a collaborative piece with sets created by celebrated visual artist, Hiroshi Teshigahara.

In surveying these different reactions, one has to wonder about expectations specific sets of audiences have about specific artists, expectations that are obviously affected by racial, ethnic, or national identities. Performance that reads as homoerotic and associates men with femininity is likely to be problematic with mainly conservative audiences. This is obviously not the case with audiences in New York or most other North American metropolises, where there is a history of performance work focusing on alternative sexualities, the kind of work still rare in contemporary India. Detested by mainstream critics as the "gay Kamasutra," *Raga* still sparked lively audience debates in India.[2] On the other hand, progressive audiences at BAM, who were somewhat familiar with Chandralekha's work, found it difficult to fit *Raga* within the realm of their expectations. Anna Kisselgoff, for instance, who reviewed the work for the *New York Times*, deplored the work and its "bare-chested" male dancers: in particular, she was offended by the lack of "poetry" when "one man hugs the other's rump."[3] Had she thought about it, though, she might have realized that this image was an exploration in profile of the *lingam-yoni* theme that recurs in Chandralekha's work, one that brilliantly resituated the erotic symbol. And of course, male bare-chestedness is no novelty, either in the American dance scene or the Indian one, so one wonders what the objection was about.

In this context, it is interesting that many scholars and activists from the third world have critiqued their Western/white counterparts for claiming homosexuality as *their* radical resistance to the institutionalization of sexuality, and as a movement spearheaded and led by Euro-Americans. At any rate, while the images in these pieces can be read indubitably as homoerotic, they cannot be separated from the avowed intention of the choreographer, or from the entire fabric of the piece: the question, for instance, that is more meaningful to ask in this context seems to me to be, how do these images of homoeroticism read in the context of and in relation to the performance of femininity and fertility? It is interesting that a most progressive colleague, whom I respect a great deal, remarked to me that it was probably the slow unfolding of the piece that was difficult for audiences, not the homoeroticism. Of course, I had pointed out already that the slow unfolding, a typical feature of Chandralekha's work, had been acceptable to North American audiences in other pieces like *Sri, Yantra,* and *Mahakal* (1995). But the slow elaboration of movement that read as homoerotic on the bodies of two South Asian men, the physical intimacy of movements drawn from kalari massage sessions blending into erotic explorations, seemed too much.

In another rather problematic statement by Kisselgoff she faults the two men with not seeming professional dancers like the rest of the cast. It has precisely been the point of Chandralekha's work for a long time that physical disciplines like Kalari and yoga are deeply and historically connected to the dance and share understandings of the body and principles of movement. So while the two men are not indeed professional dancers, they are well-known practitioners of Kalari, no less professional than the dancers, and why that differentiation would matter so much in a nontraditional performance space such as BAM is still baffling to me. It is because of the widespread misreadings of the piece and problematic commentaries on it by leading dance critics that I want to offer another perspective on these works.

As a prologue to *Raga*, Chandralekha quotes the tenth-century poet from South India, Devaraja Dasamayiah: "If they see breasts and long hair coming, they call it woman, and if they see beard and whiskers, they call it man. But look, the sprit that hovers in between is neither man, nor woman." Interestingly, the choreography inspired by this comment about superficial ways of marking gender through overt bodily characteristics alone seems to invoke a power that is not-neither-man-nor-woman, but rather, that is man and woman at once. This both-ness, this refusal to subscribe to sharp binaries, creates a productive ambivalence that, by virtue of allowing for multiple locations, makes for greater agency. Possibilities and choices, with their associations of openings and new spaces, are integral to this concept of femininity.

At any rate, for Chandralekha, one of the most adequate ways to metaphorize her concept of femininity is through the principle of curvature, both in movement line and energy. She refers, for instance, to the Hindu concept of *pradakshina* that characterizes the moment of a devotee's encounter with the symbol of divinity. The devotee's line of vision is important here because, of course, the devotee is always inscribed in the feminine space, constantly reaching toward what she desires. It is never enough to view the image of the deity frontally only: one must walk around the shrine several times, encounter the image from various angles and perceive different aspects of the same symbol as that circular pathway is traced and retraced. Curvature is also intimately connected to life, for it rounds away to make room for itself. This concept is juxtaposed with the enduring and basic concept of the "geometry of the body" in her work,[4] and her idea that the dancing body in the cultural traditions of India is primarily a "continuous sequence of squares, circles, triangles, forming, dissolving, and blending . . . "[5] In this exploration of femininity through the geometric articulation of curvature and circularity, clarity of line is interwoven with its mobility. Both *Raga* and *Sloka* are marked by dancers creating overlapping curves through footwork, weaving in and out among each other, or perhaps standing in a circle and leaning their torsos sideways toward each other and then curving them back up toward the other side, marking figures-of-eight with the chest.

Interestingly, Chandralekha's concept of femininity is resonant with tantric beliefs and even pre- and early Vedic practices of goddess worship. Talking about the varied ways in which feminine energy has been conceptualized in early Indian rural cultures, Pupul Jayakar writes about the concept of the goddess, the symbol of ultimate and ideal femininity:

> The body of the goddess was a geometric abstraction as well as color. The appearance of the circle, the double-spiral, the cross, the square, the triangle, the svastika and the mystical diagram, constructed of an amalgam of mathematical figures, at the site of the Indus Valley and in the cave art of India, establishes an ancient worship of the female divinity in the form of hieroglyphs and simple geometric forms. Associations of the sacred feminine principle with pictorial abstraction are so deeply embedded in the Indian unconscious that the anthropomorphic form of the goddess never replaces the diagram, but continues to co-exist with it through the centuries.[6]

This is similar to the way the goddess-sign is conceptualized in Tantra: through the alchemy of color, sound, and geometric form that Jayakar also talks about. Indeed, the iconic imaging of the feminine principle in terms of verisimilitude with the human female body is certainly a later and often problematic development, deployed often to support the heteropatriarchal structuring of society. The setting up of a tradition of goddess-worship where goddess is invariably mother, and where feminine energy comes to be equated with nurturing, caring, and protecting, often functions in reactionary ways to subvert the very feminine energy that was to be adored, conflating women's sexualities with reproduction and their inevitable roles as self-sacrificing mothers.

At any rate, there is also evidence of other perspectives, that the overt symbols of such feminine power, female bodies, in fact often emanate this life force. Several ancient Hindu, and specifically tantric, texts such as the *Soundarya Lahari* tell us about the life-giving touch of different parts of the woman's body: the touch of her heel is supposed to send the Asoka tree into blossom, for instance. Vidya Dehejia, talking about the rich and erotic female iconography on the walls of temple sculptures in much traditional

Hindu art, points out how female bodies and feminine energy had traditionally been regarded as markers of auspiciousness and hence necessarily present in places of public worship, not as objects of the male artist's and patron's gaze, but as an integral part of a symbolic and aesthetic framework.[7] There is no doubt that there are associations of the female body and energy with possibilities of growth and fertility in traditional literature and art. In *Raga* and *Sloka*, however, Chandralekha avoids a dangerous coalescence of femininity with energies "naturally" found in female bodies. Instead, she works through abstract ideals of femininity as the creative principle that is necessary to energize the world to emphasize its deeply spiritual moving force. It is in the translation of early abstract notions of feminine power and its representative forms, from ideas to real bodies, from stilled images to moving and living articulations, extending and reformulating ideas that she had explored in *Yantra* for instance, that Chandralekha renegotiates their contemporary relevance, and both secularizes and broadens current understandings of femininity.

In *Raga*, the first two scenes are almost exclusively danced by women. In fact, the long middle section of the piece is bracketed off by shorter segments where the women, almost as if earth spirits, move with slow deliberation along the surface of the ground. As lights come up to the tapping of stones, patterning time in clear measures, we see three women sitting

Chandralekha Group, *Raga*. Photo © Sadanand Menon.

cross-legged on the floor, their heads bent over. In slow time, they come to sit straight up, then reach their spines down to the floor and curve their butts over, extending the legs beyond their heads, their toes touching the ground, in *halasana*, continuously in canon. As their legs move outward and then back in, they begin to raise themselves to sitting once again. The backdrop now begins to come alive—a large cylinder of bright red light, created by visual artist Anish Kapoor—illuminating the women before it in a different hue. As the piece progresses, this seemingly phallic shape is resymbolized through its association with color, light, and the performance of a feminine sensibility. Having thus set the tone for this search for femininity, the women now herald its awakening.

Three women run in, diagonally to the upstage left corner, their hands in *alapadma*, arms stretched out in front as if in beckoning, gazes fixed in the direction of the corner at which they have arrived. The music of the flute, long strains as if eking out the melody, fills the space as one woman enters from that corner which they have charged into life, bearing a long dry leaf flaming at one end, wide and deep *mandalas* carrying her into the space. The flame is in front of her as she turns with it, performs a series of kalarippayattu leg swings and extensions, and leans forward charging the flame to coax into life energies that are as yet beyond the realm of the visible. The three women emphasize this invocation with flat step–forced arch foot rhythms, *tei tei didi tei*, remarking that diagonal line they had etched on the stage earlier. The mobile flame, carried by the woman, infuses the space with palpable forces as she dances with it, reminding us of the intimate relationship of heat with energy and flow. The moving flame in the hands of the woman who seems as if to coax life into being with the long sweeping lines of her arms, is in fact sensuous, as it undercuts the neat lines of her movement with its waving and somewhat unruly existence. Here fire, too is resignified: its associations with sanctifying functions, celebrated in Indian rituals, specifically in Vedic and Hindu religious or cultural practices, are undercut and overlaid with more secular notions of energy and moving force.

One man runs in, carrying another across his chest and shoulders in the wake of their exit. Gently, he lowers this other man down in a bridge position on the floor. They fold into each other and end up lying in a long line across the front surface of the stage, parallel to the audience, head to head. Their chests arch up to look at each other, one leg swirls up and then around, below the other leg, dipping the body close to the floor and up. This series of movements, repeated in different ways, establishes their presence on stage, two bodies interacting, re-cognizing, focused on each other. For the first time, they now come to look directly at each other, and the space is filled with a woman's voice weaving classical melodies and

Shaji John and Sunny, Chandralekha's *Raga*. Photo © Sadanand Menon.

intensifying the concentration on stage. As the men turn their heads, look at the audience, and then return their gazes to each other, the women enter from the upstage right corner. Their goddess-like presence is heightened by the *varabhaya mudra*, images of blessedness, as they look at the men, turn and turn again, and then leave whence they had come. The articulation of femininity is now foregrounded as these two men move slowly across each other's bodies, exploring lines and energy circuits intersected occasionally with a different look of femininity as the women enter, comment on the men absorbed in their discovery of self and other.

From this moment until the end of the piece, the men never leave the stage, intent on weaving their own world. At one point, one, Sunny, stands facing the side, feet and hips parallel, knees bent, and elbows folding in from above his shoulders to hold his head. His partner Shaji stands before him and with calm purpose, flattened palms, traces the contours of his body, the curve in the spine, the long line of the torso, then he turns around and traces the rounded line of his butt, all the way down his legs to his feet. His hands now flatten on the floor, and from this squatting position, Shaji quickly flips his body up to hook his feet onto Sunny's shoulders, while his hands grip Sunny's ankles. The latter then encircles the other's hips with his arms, and curves down his upper body to behold Shaji's face, while the

Ramachandra Das, Meera, and Shaji John, Chandralekha's *Raga*.
Photo © Sadanand Menon.

latter curves up his head and torso as if to catch and return that look. As
Shaji returns to verticality, they stand facing each other. With a quick flick
of one leg typical to the kalarippayattu style, they sit with their butts resting
slightly on their upraised heels, legs turned out, one knee touching the
ground, the other up, arms out to rest the palms on the knees. From here
they slip their legs under themselves easily so that they lie on the floor on
their fronts, their torsos arching up close against each other, supported by
their arms. They take a moment to look intently at each other before they
raise their butts high off the ground and loop their sloping legs in and out
to weave a network of energies linking floor to air, as they move their
bodies together, in perfect harmony and ease.

    Into this self-focused world, where the one and the other draw cocoon-
ing movements around themselves, which dissolve even as they are being
formed to mark overlapping circles of exploration, there are occasional
interruptive possibilities, specifically in the form of the entry of the women.
They run into spaces demarcated by the men, intercutting them with sharp
rhythmic footwork patterns, often jumping in between the two male bodies
on the floor as they travel diagonally across the space. They pause in the
downstage left corner to look at the men, who are undeterred in their focus
on each other, and fixing their gazes on the men, they step downstage, leaning over the bodies of the men as they pass by them. At one point, Meera
runs in, easing herself in between the men. She jumps into the square

made by their intertwined shins, beating a quick succession of steps *digi-digi-digi-digi* on the balls of her feet, and then quickly folds her knees under to sit, inserting herself into that space between. From this space, she reaches out to relate to both men, leaning her head on one's shoulders to gaze at the other, even while they continue to move in relation to each other. At times, she is integrated into their world, such as this where their interactions create intersecting lines and relationships, and there are other moments of non-absorption, where her quick-moving, playful and naughty energy is oppositional and antithetical to their slowly curving movement.

Thus, even while the main focus of this piece is on the exploration of feminine energy through the curvilinear and un-bound yet precise lines of kalarippayattu, embodied by the men, there are constant reminders that femininity, which to Chandralekha is in fact about sensuality and the flow of life-energy, is also not a fixed "look" or form, but about many manifestations of the same force. There are also moments when the men take on the sharper, faster, occasionally more martial movements of Kalarippayattu, chasing Meera with the crocodile walk, which is a series of jumps with the horizontal body held in a close parallel to the ground with the toes and palms in a push-up position, so much so that she ultimately leaves the space. This aggressive accent is also seen momentarily in the last moments of the men's movement sequence, where they simulate the attack and

Sunny, Shaji, and Meera, Chandralekha's *Raga*. Photo © Sadanand Menon.

defense movement patterns of kalarippayattu. And what seems impossible to absorb into the idea of femininity so long explored, acts as foil to make stronger by contrast.

What is significant here is the unlatching of philosophy from biology in a necessary and concomitant relationship, the de-essentialized understanding of femininity. If femininity signifies life force, that which enables creativity, the philosophy of curvature, the energy of play, it is not anchored to female bodies, but inherent in all bodies. Neither is it articulated through movements typically indicative of female behavior, but rather through a wide range of movement qualitatively invoking these characteristics. What is also then integral to this understanding of femininity is fertility, understood as creative life force, not to be associated with ovarian or reproductive fertility. The intertwining of femininity with fertility in fact comes to signify the movement of life-energies toward the fulfillment of their own potential. Thus, while *Sloka* continues to explore femininity through male bodies, extending the thematic concerns of *Raga*, it also links it immediately to themes of fertility and the awakening of vital forces in female bodies. Moreover, *Sloka* continues in different ways to interweave the sense of play inaugurated in *Raga* with the auspicious energy of the feminine principle.

I want to refer briefly to the version of *Sloka* reworked by Chandralekha in a collaborative venture with visual artist, Hiroshi Teshigahara, and performed primarily in Japan. The artist created an uniquely beautiful set with green bamboo: a bamboo curtain downstage, running from stage left to the middle, another upstage, running from stage right corner to center, and a tunnel made from filings of the bark of the bamboo center stage. The pre-performance lighting scheme, created by Sadanand Menon, lit the bamboo tunnel set in center stage in rotating looks of ice and fire: one emphasized the cool green of the bamboo with an emphasis on blue, the other emphasized the full roundness of the tunnel shape with an emphasis on the ambers. The dancers and musicians interacted with the set constantly, weaving in and out of the bamboo curtains, running through the tunnel, highlighting both the theme of play and the theme of fertility and life-energies. The bamboo stalks swayed as the dancers moved through them and musicians tapped on them with their drumsticks, the loose ends of bamboo sheaves on the tunnel trembled with the wind caused by dancers' quick entrances and exits. The greenness of the bamboo, the inherent mobility of the set on stage, the suggestion of birthing in the shape of the tunnel, all emphasized the themes of Chandralekha's work.

Sloka begins with a half-hour-long scene mesmerizing in its slow and deliberate performance of eroticism if we understand the erotic in the sense of Audre Lorde, as power, as that movement which facilitates the realization of our sensuous potential. Chandralekha's allusion to "hidden

secrets in our bodies" in her introduction to the piece is no doubt somewhat problematic in the way it mystifies and renders esoteric the concepts
that inspire the piece. Perhaps it is more helpful to read the statement as
referring to ideas that were once important in the cultural framework but
have been suppressed as an increasingly intense patriarchal organization of
society became systemic. Certainly the poetic and metaphoric conceptualizations of the body as in yogic and tantric visualizations of nerve centers as
spiraled chakras and of life force as *kundalini shakti*, the coiled snake, seem
to exist primarily as specialized knowledge that has to be discovered,
though their piecemeal and commercialized popularity as exotic Eastern
kitsch in the Western cultural marketplace might suggest otherwise. That
such references to the tremendous creative potential of feminine energy
and sexuality should come to be suppressed in patriarchal contexts that
seek inevitably to weaken the inherent power of our sensuous and sexual
processes and render our bodies docile is of course not surprising. This
first act of *Sloka* then recalls such ideas through movement rich in
metaphoric images and tensile energy, incredibly patient in phrasing,
seeming to stretch the very boundaries of time and space without large
overt physicalities.

Against a soundscape of Caranatic Ragas sung intermittently by
Soundaram Krishnan, we see a woman, Padmini Chettur, sitting on the
ground. Silhouetted in the dark, the soles of her feet are together, her head
bent close to the floor. The increasing lights discover her slowly raising her
head and upper body. Rising onto the balls of her feet, sitting on her
haunches, she turns in her hips parallel to each other. As one knee places
itself on the ground before her, the other lengthens out behind her and
curves up behind her head. A series of quick swings in and out with that
leg. Ultimately she comes to sit, her butt on the floor, legs in parallel, feet
in front of her. Slowly, her arms reach out and her fingers clasp the big toes
of either foot, raise them from the floor to bring her body to a V-shape on
the floor, and then open the legs outward to either side. As the arms lower
to the floor, the legs come down as well to seat the body in a wide "second
position." Now, hands in *pataka*, the arms circle around the body and create
a series of *lingam-yoni mudras*, gestures signifying creativity and fertility,
close to the chest. Now the *pataka* hands join above the head to open into
alapadma, that symbol of the thousand-petalled lotus, the *sahasrara chakra*,
that lies dormant as the topmost *chakra* in our nervous system, waiting to
be energized into blossom and ultimate knowledge by the *kundalini shakti*,
the lowest energy center lying at the bottom of the spinal column, in the
sacral area. The *alapadma* rotates around itself so that the turning wrist
ultimately pulls the left elbow in, flexing in front of the face. The movements flow in an uncompromising *vilambit laya*, committed to fulfilling

Padmini Chettur, Chandralekha's *Sloka*. The pictures of *Sloka* in this book are from performances in India, not from the version which happened in collaboration with visual artist Hiroshi Teshigahara in Japan (which I write about). Photo © Sadanand Menon.

every line in the time and space that it seems to ask for.[8] The slowness of the energy evokes curvature, but though the process of performing the movement has only roundedness, the consummation of moving lines marks itself through geometricized positions that often have angular edges.

Now, the hands are in *pataka*, and one slides in front of the other as the fingers open wide creating the image of an opening, as a prologue for an awakening of potent spaces within the body, particularly those energy centers lying along the spine. The left elbow flexes up to face the hand, in *pataka*, forward. The right hand in *mukula*, symbol of a bud, rich in potential, rises from the ground along the surface of the body, and finding itself before the left palm, sprouts energetically into *alapadma*. The hands now come to the eyes, invoking vision, as the fingers cross into *kartarimukha* and trace the line of the open eyes. The eyes respond: the irises shift, carrying the gaze to the right, then to the left, up and then down; they flutter like the flame of a lamp that heralds the arousal of the goddess spirit; they circle around, energizing all direction within the lines of sight. Now the palms are together in the *matsya mudra*, the gesture of the fish, a traditional symbol of female sexuality, swimming down the chest to curve up. Now the arms, lifted above the head, curve backward to arch the torso and head to the floor. The arms come up, the hands in *yoni mudra*, to mark the chest, the stomach, and then dissolve into another sequence.

As she dances, this woman remarks the body through images that unravel the porous, sensory body: the salutation to the sun, the bow, the opening flower, the trident with the first and third fingers on the two eyes,

Padmini Chettur, Chandralakha's *Sloka*. Photo © Sadanand Menon.

and the middle finger on the "third" eye, that center of nervous and spiritual energy. This scene reads interestingly against the traditional representation of sexual play in much Indian classical performance, where the woman often describes the nail and teeth marks left on her body by her lover. Interestingly, the inversion of this also exists in some rare instances in folk and devotional literature, where the woman, in the intensity of her passion and desire, marks her lover's body. In the first scene of *Sloka*, however, the erotic marking of the woman's body is performed very differently, rewriting notions of eroticism, sensuality, desire, and pleasure as they are inscribed in the process of mapping the flow of feminine forces. Here, the autoerotic modality of this self-focused exploration in the search for femininity casts the body as the realm of energies that, once tapped, will generate pleasure, sexual and sensual power, life, and more energy. Further, in this search, the common hierarchical encoding of the body, where the feet are regarded as lower than the rest of the body, closest to the dust, is destabilized, for the erotic energy stretches from the toes to the brain and travels through the pores of the body as it extends, rotates, and encircles it. Sexuality, in this understanding, is integral to the flowing energy of femininity that energizes the entire body as erogenous zones, instead of being understood only in relationship to the sex act and specific related body parts.

As she rises slowly and comes to stand in a wide mandala, her hands now curve around on her breasts in *alapadma* gestures, and open out to either side of her body. Two men run in from either side swiftly and place themselves close beside her, standing in the "fish-tail" balance where the raised leg extends out sideways from the now composite image of the three bodies: the woman in center, her arms out to the side, her hands in *alapadma*; the men on either side, their bodies partly behind her, their chins in the hands that cup up and out wards as they open into the *mudra*, as if sprouting from her. As her arms extend out, the heads travel along to mark a semicircular pathway around them. She turns her head to return the look of the each of the men one by one, deliberate in their mutual beholding. Then lowering her arms, she circles her wrists and drops them into *dolahasta*, the gesture that is often seen on the image of Siva Nataraja as he dances in bliss or *ananda*, and then raises her arms above her head. Meanwhile the men ritually mark the four directions of the space with the typical sequence of movements that are used to invoke the sacred energies of a space in which kalarippayattu is to be practiced. With a jump, Padmini widens her stance to stand in a deep and wide mandala facing back this time, her arms out to either side, her hands in *shikhara mudra*, signifying, among other things, the *lingam* or the phallus. Now the men mobilized by the momentum of the large torso circles they have just drawn, slide their bodies onto the floor smoothly. Through the folds of her sari, from between her legs, we see the heads of the men emerge as they arch their torsos up from the floor. This image reminds of Chandralekha's idea in *Yantra* that "Men come from women's bodies," but as in that context, it invokes neither associations of motherhood nor sentimental notions of the woman as prime reproductive force. Rather, in this context, we sense the immediate

Padmini Chettur, Shaji John, and Sunny, *Sloka*. Photo © Sadanand Menon.

association of life force with the feminine principle, energies, movements, lines that confirm the flow of life, and metaphors of its tremendous power to generate life. We also see the mobilizing of the inner space of the mandala as it is intersected by these bodies that emerge from it.

The scene ends as the men lock arms under Padmini's *mandala* as if to form a seat on which she can sit. They lift her up to carry her forward, then back, and then finally run off the stage with her. Padmini is certainly here the operative sign of the feminine. The image reminds of the cultural practice of *bhashan*, common in the state of Bengal, where the goddess-spirit is called into an image created of clay and straw at the auspicious time of her worship. The goddess is invoked and adored, and then, at the end of the festival season, her image is immersed in water, where the sign of the divine dissolves into its constituent materialities and the stuff of our myths, and is washed along by the waters of the river. This kind of practice is much more typical of ceremonies of goddess worship than in the worship of male deities, though of course, Bengal is well-known for its strong tradition of *devi-puja* or goddess worship. This journey, carrying the goddess, is most significant: it is a time when the "feminine energy" is deeply manifest as much in the devotees, who participate in this recycling of energy and life-energy, as in the goddess-spirit.

There is also another moment of significance here. While devotees generally circumambulate the spaces where the deities are installed, these icons themselves sometimes repeat this gesture of the mobilized gaze. Local traditions often decree that deities be carried in procession from their seat in the temple or shrine to specific locations, generally within city limits. These processions, occasions of great sociocultural significance, are also mostly associated with the periodic reenactments of specific mythologies, more often than not linked to the ritual death and rebirth of the divinity. The dynamism of the deity allows for openings in the apparently structured space of the temple. Moreover, it mobilizes the gaze that beholds the devotee and, in the beholding, blesses many at the same time. Journeys and processionals, then, are of deep ritual significance in this cultural framework. Disallowing the ossification of sacredness in defined spaces, and replaying the endless drama of life, death, and rebirth ritualistically, they can be argued as suggesting understandings of divinity as feminized, characterized by movement and, unlike immanent godheads, subject to the cyclical energies of life.

In charting images for a viable contemporary vision of femininity, Chandralekha repeatedly refers to local customs and ideas that surround religious practice or operate in the realm of, or invoke dimensions of life that are larger-than-the-ordinary. Interestingly, she has always referred to alternative or at least lesser-known practices in her cultural framework, those that stand at a distance from what has been endorsed as Tradition. But it is in translating these images from a divine context to a human one, placing primacy on the female principle, and negotiating their relevance in a contemporary notion of femininity, which is routed through the body in all its sexual and sensual richness, that she secularizes and radicalizes them. Briefly tracing the genealogy of this idea of femininity ultimately helps to illuminate the specific context and relevance of pieces like *Raga* and *Sloka*.

For Chandralekha, the linking of this search for femininity with the process of self-realization, and its conceptualization as the force that invigorates the realization of the full potential of the self, has been part of a long search. Years ago, she collaborated with filmmaker G. Aravindan in making a film entitled *Sahaja* to be shown at the Women's Exhibition in Moscow in 1986. In particular, Chandralekha created the script for the film and also played an important role in the process of making it. The term *Sahaja* thought refers to the particular philosophy of the Bauls, followers of a wandering folk-religious group, known to advocate their philosophy through singing and dancing. In Sahaja and some other schools of thought in India, such as Tantra, the principle of femininity is revered as the ultimate route to salvation. Discussing this idea in the context of several Bhakti or devotional texts in India, Chandralekha emphasized that this is not to be understood as an advocacy of the equality of the two sexes, but rather as the primacy of the feminine mode of being, historically understood as the primary principle found in nature, humanity, and all manifestations of life: "The man prays to god to reveal the feminine in him so that he can be the undifferentiated, undivided being. He prays to god to take away the maleness from him so he can be *prakriti*, realize the principle of nature in himself."[9] In Tantra texts too, the man cries as he struggles to realize the nature of the female in him. Again, celebrating typical bhakti thought, Meerabai, the devotee queen, wrote many songs where all human beings are seen as Radha, forever yearning union with her lover-god, while divinity is seen as Krishna. In the Gaudiya and the Sakhi bhava sects of the Vaishnavaite devotional practice, male devotees identifying with the *gopinis*, cowherdesses who adore Krishna, is particularly common. Femininity is thus also a positioning, a force that carries the individual toward an embodied awakening and leads to an opening into self-realization.

To return to *Sahaja* the film: Here Chandralekha wanted to explore the ways in which the notion of femininity enriches traditional Indian performance, with particular reference to *abhinaya* or expressive modes of classical performance. Generally, in this mode, the performer focuses on becoming, as opposed to being, which might be understood as naturalistic and logistic verisimilitude, and the project offered Chandralekha opportunities of witnessing and documenting master performers and gurus, males, taking on female roles in the course of narrating a particular story, a strong tradition in Indian classical performance. She linked this performance of femininity with the concept of the *ardhanarishwara*, the male-female Shiva-Shakti intertwined deity. This however, proved annoying to the then minister of culture, who felt his manhood threatened by these implications of femininity and insisted that the film be withdrawn from the exhibition. Interestingly, the *ardhanarishwara* figure, danced by an exponent of the Mayurbhanj Chhau style, occasionally marking his way across the stage with the typically curvilinear movements of this style of dancing, had been part of *Raga* initially. But, by her own admission, Chandralekha felt ambiguous about his place in the highly metaphoric choreography and felt it was more a concession to her harsh critics rather than her own design, and edited these sections later.

It seems that while the feminine is generally celebrated in and as aspects of pre-colonial cultural production, the notion comes to be crystalized into a dominant characteristic inherent in some idea of Indianness, later, in contact with "other" cultures, particularly from the West. It is in fact with Western theorizings of Indian culture and religion that we begin to see how femininity, used as a distinction governing the relationality of east and west, comes to stand in for difference. It also when the philosophical and spiritual dimensions of femininity are eclipsed and it is collapsed into negative associations, where attributes previously celebrated are constructed in terms of lack. Here, femininity becomes the modus operandi of racialization and enables and structures relations of power in the colonial state. Annapurna Garimella, tracing the history of the reception of Indian art in the Western imagination, shows that with the beginning of Indology, we see a growing discomfort with this emphasis on the feminine, the necessarily embodied spirituality, and on the multiple centers of divine energy.[10] Western scholars like Hegel, Mill, and Cunningham, seeking to comprehend Indian and specifically Hindu art and religion through the grand organizing concepts of western aesthetics and philosophy, found Hindu art to be predominantly effeminate, lacking the masculine categories of rational thought, and concluded that India's racial consciousness was essentially feminine.[11]

The project of Indian nationalism took up this line of thinking, similarly choosing to be embarrassed by the lush female iconography and the feminized mode of knowing in Hindu thought, particularly with its emphasis on *maya* or play and illusion as creative principle. Earlier thought systems and practices came to be overwritten with the development of the virulent nationalism in the early twentieth century that exhort to "manliness" as the only antidote to colonial rule. One such example is the nationalist ascetic, Swami Vivekananda, who, though a disciple of Ramakrishna Paramahansa, reconstituted Hinduism through the masculinist characteristics of aggression in order to counter the devastation of Hinduism. On the other hand, his guru, the Kali-devotee Ramakrishna, repeatedly situated

himself through his songs and teachings as the feminine in this relationship of human and divine, even when understood through the dynamics of
a mother-son relationship.[12] The move to eradicate the "effeminacy" of the
Indian male, which had supposedly led "others" to power in the country,
while somewhat thwarted in the face of Gandhian philosophy, returned
with redoubled strength in contemporary times with the development of
religious fundamentalisms. This led to an overwhelming emphasis on
Advaita, or non-dualist philosophy, as "authentic" Hinduism, marginalizing
the indigenous polytheistic traditions and revoking the centrality of the
feminine principle. This does not mean that goddess worship and adoration of the feminine principle are not abundantly practiced in rural and
tribal popular culture, but just that they are deliberately "de-authenticated"
as tradition.

In light of this history, Chandralekha's work reads as a move toward
reimagining submerged and marginalized traditions within the cultural
context in which she is working, not in a vein of cultural revivalism and
premodern nostalgia, but in terms of refiguring tradition to make the most
sense of them in contemporary times. More importantly, her work reads as
resistance to contemporary fundamentalist claimings of Hinduism, deliberately coextensive with Indianness, as characterized by a need to recover
purusharth (valor, energy), lost through centuries of foreign domination that
has resulted in such "effeminacy" and "impotency." Culture and religion
here come to be narrowly wrapped around a concept of masculinity that is
constituted uniaxially, as social determinism. In this rhetoric a compulso-
rily aggressive action–orientedness and heterosexuality mark the ideal
Hindu subject, who can effect a slippage to pass as the ideal Indian subject.
It is the face of this heavy elitist embracing of Advaita philosophy, and the
consequent contemporary masculinization of Hinduism in fundamentalist
religious politics that Chandralekha's pieces must be read. Her exploration
of femininity primarily through the bodies of men, her linking of it with
abstract notions of fertility and her recasting of it as life force, is very largely
about resisting what she sees as the masculinist drive of current global politics and economy in the age of capitalist neocolonialism.

Reviewing the context in which these pieces are created and initially
performed highlights the resistive potential they are seeped in. Interestingly, while this is often read as rejection of "tradition," research also illu-
minates that it is indeed traditional cultural practices that are recalled and
activated in the choreography to emphasize ideas of mobility and openness,
the recycling of birthing and dying, creating and dissolving, in an ongoing
process of life, to set in motion images of femininity that can revitalize us.
Raga and *Sloka* bring into focus play, intimations of *maya* or *leela*, the illu-
sory yet creative principle that brings the world, as humans know it, into

being. The image of Meera running in to insert herself in between the two men in *Raga*, of Sunny suddenly running away from Shaji in *Sloka* as if tempting him to chase him, a game-like structure of catch between them, their torsos waving as they change direction running, the unstill shapes of the feminine life principle.

Such work also places in high relief the spiritual sensuality of bodies and spaces, and the vitalizing, opening-up of spaces within and without bodies. Witness for instance, the last scene of *Raga*: the women run in and sit in a triangular formation on stage, folding their legs to one side, each woman marking the different tips of the triangle. With their eyes they begin to energize the farthest reaches of the space before them as their gazes, slow and unwavering, travel from one corner and carve arches through space to reach the other corner. Suddenly, the lights come up to illuminate the two men standing high up, atop two ladders that are barely lit, facing each other, their arms extended up. As the women turn to sit facing them, the men move even closer to each other to stand, their legs crossing, intersecting the ground on which each man stands. Slowly, their arms descend and each man clasps the other around the waist. From their waists they bend backward, chests curving outward, pushing an opening out of the tip of the other vertical triangle they had at first seemed to mark with the women. The horizontal triangle of the women on the floor mobilizes itself simultaneously as they similarly curve their chests out and back, reminding one of the opening of the thousand-petalled lotus, the *sahasrara chakra*, that marks total spiritual awakening. The space darkens. As the lights come up one last time, we see the women once more on the floor, facing front, sitting calm and centered, earth women. Indeed, the dancers in *Raga* and *Sloka* are not divine beings. They are men and women intent in their search for the feminine principle of life-movement, exploring dynamic realms of feminine energy, working constantly with movement to reframe principles of creativity and sexuality in secular terms, dancing to throw the carefully ordered fundamentalist universe, that insists on partitioned energies and controlled bodies, in disarray.

DISLOCATIONS AND ROAMING ADDRESSES
Shelter (1988) and *Bitter Tongue* (1987)

Home, in the traditional sense of a place of inevitable return, typically connoting security, safety, and family, comes to be problematized, cherished
but often needing to be renegotiated, rent with disjunctions in much of
Zollar's work. Particularly in *Shelter* and *Bitter Tongue*, two apparently very
different pieces, the concept of home, and especially women's relationships
to home and home-making, the privileges and oppressions upon which
these relationships are predicated, are thrown into high relief.

Shelter, beginning from the image of a homeless woman on a piece of
cardboard, zooms out to ask larger questions about the location of home.
The individual story of one homeless woman draws our personal involvement, jeopardizing possibilities of objective distance as we are asked to consider the odds that this homeless woman could have been "you . . . you, any
of us";[1] we find ourselves looking back over our shoulders, imagining that
last look enslaved Africans stole at the disappearing coast of a native homeland as they sailed farther and farther away; we find ourselves scanning the
present, possibilities of mistakes that could force us to lose the homes we
have built up with so much effort; we find ourselves taken aback as we look
forward, faced with environmental depletion that has rendered so many
animals, birds, and other species homeless. This is not an apocalyptic
moment, but a vision of home that exceeds the physicality of a location and
instead invokes its emotional affect, the many interlocking circles of home,
and it insists on locating our responsibility and agency in keeping alive a
sense of "home." *Shelter*, created in 1988, is set to text by Hattie Gosset and
Laurie Carlos, while some of the sections work with percussion. Though I
will refer to the performances of the Urban Bush Women, because the
piece was initially created on and for them, I should mention that this piece
was also set on the Ailey Company by Zollar herself.

Even as the lights come up, six bodies lie huddled together on the
floor, a lifeless, drained, mass. In a voiceover, a woman begins to tell of
another homeless woman she would see as she walked from the subway

station to the office where she held a temp job, striking a strangely discordant note on the pavement of the plush upper East Side of Manhattan. The sound of the voice startles the pile of bodies: they wrench their bodies off the floor with quick, sharp, motions as they glance from side to side, as if watching out for some attacker. They rise to rush from one spot to another, their motions becoming increasingly alarmed as the voice reflects on the precarious edge on which so many of us live: she imagines herself making one wrong turn, which sets off a series of slips, causing her to lose her belongings and her rented apartment, and being trapped into the same situation as the homeless woman on the street. The movements of the women on stage become more and more frantic through this recounting, and as the voice rises to a crescendo to tell of the possibility of existing "at the intersection of reduced resources and reverberating rage," the women clump together in the center of the stage, suddenly stultified in their rushings about. The rage in the voice is now doubled in the movements of one woman (Beverley Prentice) who stands slightly apart from the group on stage left, in profile to the audience. Flexing her forearms forward, fisting her hands, she beats on the air repeatedly, striking her feet on the floor simultaneously: an image of utter desperation. One woman (Valerie Winborne) from the group staggers forward to fall to the floor, still glancing from one side to the other as if in fear, underwriting the other's fury with terror at its articulation. The unmoving silence of the other women in the group only underline the futility of their emotional testimony, but as they lend their bodies to catch the falling body of the woman who had moved in anger, they signal their understanding of her frustration and their support for her. Slowly, they all crumble to the floor.

Once more they rise, one by one, embarking on longer movement sequences marked by swirling turns, falls, difficult balances which ultimately ground themselves, as the voice repeats the text. As the others move, the one woman again separates out from the group to stand on upstage left corner, in profile to the audience. Her arms lasso around her body, hitting herself with fists that rebound back to swing around the body again and again, her head tossed around in a relentless non-rhythm. As the point of "reverberating rage" recurs, she gives up this frenzied rage for another, where she steps toward the group and beats one more time, with renewed fury, on the air with her fists. Once again, she falls and is caught by the network of hands that rise to bear her weight. One more time, they all engage in a series of increasingly frantic movements to gather in an angular formation on stage right. Suddenly, standing with feet wide apart and turned out, they flex their knees to stand in a deep, wide plié. Drawing her reflections to a logical conclusion, the voice locates the homeless woman in all of us: "it could happen to you too." With one sharp gesture, each woman raises an arm to shoulder level, pointing the index finger to one point in the darkened auditorium. Their heads turn to fix that point with their gazes. Rising slowly out of plié, they turn, tugged along by the finger that circles around, as if to point to the "'you," the "you," and the "you," the many "you's," and reinforce the easy juxtaposition of that one wrong turn with dwindling resources, disrespect, and the attendant attenuation of self-respect. The voice underlines the utter facility with which one—anyone really—can slide into the situation of the woman living on a piece of cardboard on the street corner: "Living on the streets, it's so easy. It could happen to you too."

Meanwhile, the women continue their revolution around to face the back. Then, each in her own time, eyes lowered, head bent slightly forward, begins, with very personal, intimate gestures, to touch herself. Their movements are quiet and small, but sharp, repeated several times. They wring despairing hands, they keep trying to brush something off, they shake their heads occasionally as if to push something off, they try to rub something off their bodies. Moving around themselves, they seem oblivious of their group location—each, as if locked into a terrible aloneness, embodies her frustration in a self-enclosed zone. The endlessly turning bodies of these women locked into self-contained spaces where they cannot register the closeness of each other, where not even eye contact is possible, bring home the shame, degradation, and humiliation of the situation and the stark isolation inherent in it. Slowly, one by one, they sink to the floor and lay down their bodies, as if exhausted with the weight of the realization.

They are allowed no rest. The drums suddenly break into the silence, sounding a rapid beat. Total panic breaks out onstage as the women jump up from the floor and scramble off in different directions, as if hounded by some unseen force. The anxiety does not subside as the women gradually fall into a fast movement sequence performed in canon. A jump with the body convexed over in a deep contraction is followed by a low run towards the downstage right corner. The run is lured into a stretch as one leg swings forward and hip high, pulling the pelvis off its center and forcing the upper body to lie out behind itself to maintain balance, while the arms to swing out to the side. This long extension in mid-air is crumpled with a quick, swirling descent into a series of rolls on the floor, and then again, with a series of shudders and convulsions that rack the women's bodies. It is as if the body, stretched to its limits in its frantic mobility that allows no moment for rest, finally reacts with a crumbling of its energy fields. This pattern is continued as each rolls through floor space in her own time, then suddenly scrambles onto her knees. Immediately, her torso is as if hurled up, her chest flung open, her head thrown back, arms rushed up. Her body drops from that momentary elevation to flop back to the floor, drained of

Treva Offut, Beverley Prentice-Ryan, Maia Claire Garrisson, Christine King, Valerie Winborne, Terri Cousar in Zollar's Shelter. Photo by Cylla Von Tiedemann.

energy. One more time, the women are shaken out of their search for a resting place, and they dart from side to side, trying to carve out a small niche for themselves. But they are condemned to a lifetime of rest/shelter–lessness, of moving on: these women's frantic movement sequences emphasize that there is hardly any opportunity to catch one's breath.

In a residency at the University of Minnesota, Zollar taught students, (myself included), some of this section of the piece. To execute the choreography with clarity at tempo proved to be extremely challenging, with all the rapid level changes, directional shifts, and detailed isolations that constituted the particular flavor of the piece. But embodying it made me realize even more clearly how the choreography was driven by the permanence of interruption, the continuous disruption of "home," or a resting place.

The pattern of frenzied, rushing movement now begins to be interrupted more routinely and substantially as if the resources of the body are gradually being depleted along with the draining of other resources. As the unsheltered body's capacity to resist and even to flee from the forces that chase after it become diminished, we see an uneven movement pattern where the women run from corner to corner, then suddenly give in and sink to the floor to lie down for a moment. As the drums intrude one more time upon their numbed senses, their bodies, lying sideways and facing the audience, begin to shudder and convulse, as if in the grip of an excruciating seizure. They roll onto their backs through the convulsions. The percussive spasms of arms and legs, which throb flexed up in the air, remind us of the utter rootlessness they have been forced into, while the rude overtaking of their bodies by external forces that condemn them to paroxysms of anguish comment on this dehumanizing experience, systemically produced. The terror, deprivation, and despondency of this situation have gnawed away at the rage and stubborn fortitude that had marked their earlier reactions: their helplessly flailing limbs and torsos are witness to their broken-down resistance.

Yet, it is these women, even as their drooping bodies give evidence of flagging wills and depleted energies, who once again muster their remaining strength to confront us with questions and perform a commentary on the situation and its global implications. As the piece draws to an ending, its perspective broadens out from this apparently commonplace tragic situation to evoke a wider conception of "home." Moments of uncanny déjà vu: the contemporary story of the woman on the East Side street corner weaves in and out of history as the piece embarks upon the Middle Passage section. Performed to Laurie Carlos's poem "Belongo . . . a long long time ago," the section is rife with the painful affect of lost home, experienced on multiple levels: reaching toward a disappearing hope, the swinging between lament and remembering, between despairing resignation and determination to resist, intercut with images of a rocky journey across the waters, the confinement to a narrow piece of wood aboard the crowded slave ship. Series of rolls on the floor, which come up to suspend momentarily and then fall again. In all the movement, searching eyes, intensely seeking for something to hold onto. Remembering catapults the dancers into the Warrior section, in an uncanny coalescing of time frames: is the fight for home a reflection of African American history? Is it that of a black woman caught "between a hard place and a rock, at the intersection of reduced resources and reverberating rage" in a capitalist system? This linking of homelessness to the lost home of enslaved Africans enables a critical shift: those who had been mentioned earlier as regarding the woman on the upper East Side street with fear and disgust might have placed the responsibility for her state solely on her. However, the piece makes clear that this is a misreading that results from a lack of analysis of how capitalism works, of how class society inevitably penalizes those who do not commit to the kind of aggressive financial strategizing that forms its condition of success. Moreover, comfortable and distanced viewing of the fear, rage, pain, and resistance of another unfortunate homeless woman has already been destabilized as the dancers have repeatedly implicated each of us in the possibility of that location; it could happen to you. Now, recalling history, we realize that loss of home is often the result of others' explicit greed and exploitation.

Zoning into contemporaneity once again, the piece beckons the future as it calls on us to pay attention to the environmental crisis that is threatening global well-being and as it reframes questions of responsibility and agency one more time. Now, as the voice enters the piece one more time, it implicitly tells *you* and *you* and *you*, all of us, that our homes, our shelter, are in fact being corroded away, every minute, through phenomena like "population growth, poverty, ill-advised policies, and simple greed." Meanwhile, the women, who have just performed a dance sequence of seething power and passion to the relentless rhythm of the drums, now once more come together in a group center stage. Once more, they move slowly, sliding into low, wide, pliés, their torsos swinging around in half-circles. Then, each woman begins to move in her own time and rhythm, each turning around herself with individual arm and body movements. Each is like a discrete life form, exploring her own energy circuit: together they recall the "diversity of life" that, we are told, this earth teemed with before humanity began its war with the plants and animals that share the planet with it. At every point, the choreography has multiple import. The shrinking diversity of life forms cannot but recall an Orwellian vision of standardized mechanization where everyone is subjected to a specified routine. Moreover, we are forced into a realization of the macrocosmic duplication of the situation of the homeless woman, her resources gradually petering out as we hear the ominous words: "The earth is suffering the decline of entire ecosystems. The nurseries for new life forms are dying. We are now experiencing the death of earth." One by one, the women filter off stage, revolving circuits of meaning as if to emphasize the inevitable, slow extinction of life forms.

In a world of increasing military domination and nuclear resources for destruction, we are all ultimately, like the snow leopard, the bald eagle, like "black children living in America," endangered species. Finally, as the lights dim on the last few women winding their way offstage, confronting the audience with their full gazes and their extended arms, as they turn front, one question weaves into another: "Tell me, where we all gonna call home? Tell me, where we all gonna go? Tell me, what we all gonna do?" This series of questions effects a broadening of the boundaries of home so that it becomes about collective, not individual, responsibility. It redefines social and civic accountability even as it critiques the myth of individual agency that is the corner of capitalist expansion, and as it reflects on the multiple meanings of home.

Home—constructed as a place of origination, where we return at the

Treva Offut, Beverley Prentice-Ryan, Maia Claire Garrisson, Christine King, Valerie Winborne, Terri Cousar in Zollar's Shelter. Photo by Cylla Von Tiedemann.

end of the day, which confers on us identity—is also troubled in *Bitter Tongue*. Very different from *Shelter* in apparent theme and context, the piece resonates with similar concerns and questions, and larger political-historical connotations. Clearly, there is a disjunction between the cartographed location of home and its cultural-political affect, a result of continued Western imperialism in "developing" and "underdeveloped" countries in the third world. Of course, the migration of populations to different parts of the world often has a typical gender bias, and differences and conflicts about values arise with those who are left at "home." These latter, most often women, most often charged with the responsibility of embodying and ensuring the continuity of "tradition," in opposition to Westernization, as well with the responsibility of home-making in accordance with patriarchal normativity, then find themselves in double jeopardy. For the legacy of domination and colonization by the West also ensures that it becomes an important locus of desire. The violation experienced by women in contemporary society, where they are first expected to retain tradition and then relegated outside the zone of desire precisely because of the role they have been commanded to play, is the underlying theme of *Bitter Tongue*.

Once again, the personal story of a woman is choreographed such that it reflects on global issues, in particular, like *Shelter*, on the issues of women and their relationship to and loss of "home." Program notes tell us about a woman whose husband goes from their native Uganda to Europe and returns having imbibed Europeanized culture and practices. Suddenly, the traditional ways represented by his wife are unsuitable for him. Zollar's conceptualization of this scenario is not based on a simplistic representation of the pain of the woman who feels rejected. It is more a trenchant and layered critique of the global reach of Europeanization, the subsequent devaluation of indigenous cultures, and the inevitable separation and hierarchizing of the realms attributed to men and women in such societies where the postcolonial colludes with the neocolonial. The piece is unique in its foregrounding of a radical womanist consciousness such that critiques of and resistance to these larger econo-political schemes are formulated and performed by women from the indigenous/traditional/third-world societies. Like the women in *Shelter*, who force a recognition of the complex processes implicit in homelessness and perform a critique of capitalism, these women from Uganda are vocal in their critique: it is they who confront the situation, not as victims, but as agents who are unaccepting of it. Ultimately, of course, it is Zollar who imagines both African American women and Ugandan women in this revolutionary mode. In this is implicit another critique: that of the hijacking of any notion of feminism by the agenda and leadership of Western Anglo-American women. By resituating the issues and location of women's resistance, she dislodges hegemonic notions of a feminist movement and claims a more diverse and transnational framework for it.

Yet, Zollar does not "simplify" the situation and trivialize the complex emotional negotiations by which the women finally arrive at that mental state that marks the conclusion of the piece. The piece begins with a sense of unease: in full light and to the drumming of the live percussionist, a woman (initially danced by Zollar herself) enters from stage left, crouching, and moving forward on flat feet, in that low position. One hand jumps up to her face, covering her nose and her mouth with her out-facing palm, while her head jerks around to look diagonally across. It is a startled moment of arrest that spells fear and shock. The pattern of movement arrested recurs as she rises and moves, initially in slow, soft, rounded phrases, and then in faster, more percussive segments. Always the flow of her dancing is undercut by violent, spasmic movements—an arm circle generously supported by the rounding body is immediately followed by a couple of jumps where the legs are parallel and wide apart, the body curved over, the hands splaying out as the body is lifted and lowered. Pauses punctuate this already disrupted flow, catching the body at what seems to be uncomfortable moments in the movement, enhancing the sense of dis-ease and dis-orientation in which this woman seems to be trapped. As she

Jawole Willa Jo Zollar, *Bitter Tongue*. Photo by Cylla Von Tiedemann.

dances slightly off-center toward stage right, her movements contrast with those of the three women who enter slowly from stage left and remain more or less clustered together near that corner. Their movements are marked by undulating torsos, spines extending long, arms gliding to reach behind the body. The flow, which is so interrupted in her, is clearly articulated in their bodies as they dance with the smooth course of breath, enhancing the sense of isolation she performs.

The following section heightens the disjunction and anger experienced by the women in a different way as they take on the critique embedded in the piece. The three women are now joined by the rest of the ensemble, and they clump together in a circular formation at stage center. The woman who began the piece stands a little apart and inaugurating a series of sharp incisive movements which still, as if deliberately, remain grounded, sings out in jagged tonalities: "My husband's tongue is bitter!"[2] Interestingly, in later performances of the piece, this line, which is repeated fully or in fragments through the rest of the piece, has come to be performed as a more confrontational questioning: "Why, Why, Why! is your tongue so bitter!" The pain and frustration of this lone woman is externalized in the group, as with their hands fisted and forearms flexed to point directly forward, they heave their chests, leaning over to one side, and echo the words sung out by her. The lone woman herself repeatedly enacts a circle around herself: one foot remains fixed, pivoting around itself as the other foot hits the ground in a wide parallel stance, turning the body in a circle, convulsing the torso with every step stamped. One hand slaps the air flat as the voice rings out a "my . . . my . . . my . . . my" obsessively against the group's enunciation of the entire line of the song. Ironically revelatory of her complex positionality, she is at once center and margin of the space she inhabits. At a slight distance, the chorus, with their unison movement—a complex choreography of shaking fists, bent over torsos, pronounced exhalations—dance as if in ritual mourning.

A sudden freezing of all movement. Silence. The entire group is together now; the lone woman is not by herself, but integrated into the community of women. A shiver arises among the group and subsides. Slowly, in unison, the women edge their feet away from each other to stand in a wide parallel, their chests reaching forward, their eyes focused in front. Forearms once again flexed forward to face the audience with fisted hands, the women raise and drop one heel after another in place, pounding the floor with force. Beginning as a murmur, the movement grows bigger and bigger, until the pulsating bodies come to pummel the floor with tremendous grounded power. This leads to larger movement phrases where high flexed-foot kicks are used to swivel the body around, stamping walks carry the body back and forth, culminating ultimately in a frantic pitch of motion. This movement section rearranges the women to position them in a diagonal line across the stage, and they pause for a moment, as if marking the lull between two storms. One more time, the shiver arises, the trembling bodies give way to throbbing, resonating, thudding feet. This time, the women weave in phrases of stamped rhythms where shoulders swing loosely with turning bodies and slapping hands emphasize occasional steps. Their dance of resistance and self-assertion is underscored by their periodically shaking heads in gestures of nonacceptance. As a regular rhythm pattern is established, the woman at the tip of the line pivots herself around, with a stepping pattern that counterpoints the rhythm of the group, cutting into its silences. As she turns, she drops her fisted hands almost with a vengeance and shaking her upper body loose, marches off stage. The drums, which had been quiet in this second section that is musicalized by breath patterns, claps, and stamps, now pick up the rhythm and grow louder and louder in the background. One by one, the women create gestures of defiance and free themselves from the dance as they march off stage, knocking the floor with their heels in their exit.

More than any other piece, *Bitter Tongue* implicitly invokes and critiques the two phenomena that occur repeatedly in third-world societies or among populations of color who are struggling to emerge from the onslaught of European colonization or slave trade, and are still in the throes of a fervent nationalism. One is the inevitable conflation of modernization and "progress"—which come to be seen as highly desirable and more or less inevitable—with Westernization. The other is the modernist politics of essentializing notions of national, racial, and traditional identities, constructed on the female body. However, what is striking about what Zollar accomplishes is that she manages to communicate the complexity with which she obviously reads the situation: the structure of the piece highlights not only that these ideologies are mobilized on and through the bodies of these women, and at their expense, for which they pay a terrible price, but also that, at the same time, they mark a site of little-publicized struggle and resistance, refusing to submit passively to their victimization.

As usual, the movement idiom in *Bitter Tongue* is marked by a combination of Africanist and modern dance styles, but the movements are refigured in keeping with the mood of the piece. The rejection of the "traditional" or "indigenous" female body as undesirable in the gaze of a Europeanized aesthetic, shocks and pains: the woman reacts with confusion, performing broken-off movement phrases, jolted into sudden jumps, halted in mid-sequence. In contrast to the dancing of the three women in the first section where the entire body is integrated into the movement, their dancing in the following section is marked by isolations and jerkiness that emphasize the complex psychological experience. Here the body is as if splintered between pain (heaving torsos, heavy exhalations), anger (raised fists, stamping feet), and frustration (the circle that keeps turning on itself without going anywhere, the repeating of the possessive pronoun only from "My husband's tongue is bitter"). Clearly, however, there can be no simplistic rejection, for the two are in an intimate relationship; metaphorically, at least, they are husband and wife. Initially, there is a sense of loss, disempowerment and dis-ease, the body racked in pain. Yet, the community of women seek out other meaningful partnerships, revitalize themselves and become their own source of power: they shake off the impact of the bitter words, and refuse to be thwarted by their rejection, walking off the stage with the lights fully on. They find and establish their own rhythm as they articulate strong movement sequences. Their protest also recalls the critique of what Spivak calls "internal colonization," and resists the way "metropolitan countries discriminate against disenfranchised groups in the midst," and points to and protests against the internalization of Euro-American hegemonies.[3] Home is here wrapped up in the politics of nation-making and its gendered hierarchies, and neocolonialism in the name of globalization.

This piece in particular, and a discussion of Zollar's choreography in general, reminds one of Cornel West's articulation of the three particular modes of resistance deployed in black cultural practices: kinetic orality, passionate physicality, and combative spirituality.

> By kinetic orality, I mean dynamic repetitive and energetic rhetorical styles that form communities, e.g., antiphonal styles and linguistic innovations that accent fluid, improvisational identities and that promote survival at any cost. By passionate physicality, I mean bodily stylizations of the world, syncopations and polyrhythms that assert one's somebodiness in a society in which one's body has no public worth, only economic value as a laboring metabolism. And by combative spirituality, I mean a sense of historical patience, subversive joy, and daily perseverance in an apparently hopeless and meaningless historical situation.[4]

It is indubitable that such resistive modes have marked black cultural practice from the time of the landing of the slave ships on the coasts of America and continue into the present. What I find interesting about the work of a choreographer like Zollar is how these modalities intersect and layer each other, how they work together to emphasize the immediacy of the artistic and cultural as political practice, with particular emphasis on the articulate body.

Though choreography and movement are the genres in which Zollar's work is normally categorized, she works most often in an interdisciplinary way, melding different performance modes. And it is through this rich deployment of multiple bodily resources that West's modalities are reinterpreted. I find kinetic orality—the "dynamic repetitive and energetic rhetorical styles that form communities"—energizing the text that is used, each repetition being uttered, sung, or shouted with a slight alteration of words, accent, or tonality. Indeed, the way the title statement, "My husband's tongue is bitter," doubles and redoubles as question, accusation, and critique, signaling the mobility in the growing organization and empowerment of the women, offers a fine way to think about the notion of kinetic orality. But I also see it in the splintering of the "why . . . why . . . why" through which the group of women return to the central question-statement in the piece as a motif, layered by the unison movement of jutting-out elbows, fisted hands, and stamping feet. Typically, in fact, this vocalization is layered with movement, the choreography re-emphasizing the principle of dynamic and energetic repetition. In the central segment of *Bitter Tongue*, for instance, the women, positioned in wide stances, turned out, and flexed at the knees, reach their arms forward, and sing, the tones and the tune echoing the harshness of the situation: "Why is your tongue so bitter!" The last word is almost spat out, and the hands of the women gesture percussively as they enunciate the word, punching the air with their fists or stabbing the air sharply with pointing fingers, enacting the bitterness in the words of the husband. The repeatedly asked question splits as a couple of the women continue to enact it in the same way as before. Others begin with a new movement phrase and begin their questioning in the middle of it, singing at a different pitch from the other group. One woman, slightly away from the group, obsessively repeats "Why! Why! Why! Why!" turning around herself again and again, one foot fixed in the center and the other stamping the ground repeatedly, one hand slapping the air as the body circles round and round. The fragmentation of the initial question, the differing structures of the repetition, the juxtaposition of various rhythms and tonalities are multiple manifestations of the principle of kinetic orality. A characteristic feature of Zollar's technique is such realization of West's modalities in a uniquely intertexted way: the physicality in the movement is not only passionate; it is also combative and kinetic.

The scene from *Bitter Tongue* just described, marked as it is by polyrhythms and syncopations, not only in movement, but in the vocalization as well, also gives evidence of West's "passionate physicality." Clearly, the body is not here a "laboring metabolism" where labor is all about working to create surplus value for others, but engaged in aesthetic-political-cultural signification on its own terms, asserting "somebodiness" as it asks vital questions about happiness and value. Combative spirituality channeled through this work evidences itself somewhat differently; here, the patience is in the insistence on self-respect and happiness, while the perseverance insists that life has to be more than survival, than a somehow living through days despite unhappiness. Zollar imbues performance with an indomitable spirit of resistance that relocates agency and the possibilities of self-definition—witness, for instance, the conclusion of *Bitter Tongue*, where the women stomp off stage, one by one, each in her own time, tempo, and rhythm, marking their indignant rejection of a system of values that would relegate them to a position of passivity and subservience.

So, what's home got to with it? It is the ungendering of the home-making that is significant, for instance, as much as the questioning of its associations of stability and safety, and of its constitution as a socially necessitated, individual and individuating institution. And this questioning has as much to do with postmodern fragmentation as with historical circumstance, legacies of political and economic exploitation, and through it emerge acutely articulated critiques of broader sociocultural phenomena. Ultimately this points to the multiple valences of home and leads us to rethink its location in our desire. On the one hand, in *Shelter*, the women are robbed of their homes by a capitalist exploitative system, but they point to universal responsibility in arresting the debilitation of the resources of what functions as our "home" in the larger sense. Home here is a positive, it is shelter, conferring a sense of roots, it is what we desire and all deserve in an ideal world. On the other, while the fracturing of the home as a place of intimacy with one's family is painful in *Bitter Tongue*, it is the insistence that it be renegotiated, even if what was previously built with so much care has to be rejected, its disfunction exposed, that is significant. Here, too, home confers roots, but when those roots, carefully nurtured by one group of people, is devalued and rejected by another whose participation is central to its continuity as such, the former rebel against such a notion of home-making: the women stomp off the very space they have designated through their performance as the home space, at the end of *Bitter Tongue*. Home is jeopardized here too by the politics of the larger world, but the women refuse to be tied up in home-making as their only arena of work and authority. Of course home is caught up in the multiple significances such as culture, community, country, as much as it signifies a basic kind of shelter. And in this understanding of home as a series of expanding, often conflicting, intercutting circles, it also becomes a space where resistance can begin. Importantly, too, because home in this last sense is created repeatedly through the labor of a group of women who support and sustain each other, the compulsory heteronormativity in the dominant notion of "home" is also dislodged.

As I think through these pieces now in a last editorial attempt, I cannot but think of the vital significance of these pieces, the dangers they highlighted and foreshadowed in the complexity of their conception. The shrinking diversity of life forms, the warning that ends *Shelter*, in fact emphasizes the danger of notions of home built on enforced uniformities. I am drawn to think of the dubbing of nations as "homeland" and the terrible waves of "ethnic cleansing" that, despite the learned lessons from the Holocaust on, have littered our recent world history. It is also impossible not to remember the Israeli-Palestinian crisis in thinking about the shifting connotations of "home": home to one is "occupied territory" to the other. *Bitter Tongue* disrupts the naturalized dangerous conflation of "nation" and "home," even as both pieces implicate us all in the sociopolitical responsibility of maintaining home-ness for all communities and push us to rethink the volatile shifts, silencings, and violences implicit in powerful signifiers such as "home" and "community."

Thinking over what this project has meant to me, I realize that I have followed the work of Jawole Willa Jo Zollar and Chandralekha for about eight
years by this time. And I will continue to do so. Their work is inspiring for
me in many ways: artistically, politically, discursively. Their choreographies
have pushed me to think about what it really means to make dances with
deep political engagement, about remaining deeply committed to cultural
specificity even as they articulate an oppositional aesthetic, to forge form
and structure through the welter of complex ideological and political theorizations and tensions.

I have also learned, in my own work, to resist the ghettoization that
typically happens to work produced by some artists of color in the United
States: these artists, who insist on working through "difference," often find
that they cannot fit their artistic vision into the set modules of performances, workshops, marketing that have come to be functional in mainstream cultural production. Thus artists of color often find themselves
being dubbed as doing "community work," which is quite often an anomaly
because a certain kind of engagement with issues that arise from local contexts is an integral part of the artistic framework of these artists, not super-
imposed from above, and this label in fact reflects divergent notions of
artists and their world-views. Concomitantly, these artists can hardly lay
claim to the kind of resources, focus, and acknowledgment that might
seem only "natural" in the case of artists whose works are considered individual "masterpieces," part of an undeclared canon: artistic excellence or
production quality, it is often argued, is not quite the norm here, it is the
presence of folks from the "community." This is a heinous split, and I
struggle with it in my own work. Yet, I know that along with some other
artists, Chandralekha and Zollar are exceptional in the high standards of
professionalism they uphold—making sure first that they lay out the terms
of a "professionalism" that is acceptable to them, one which, for instance,
does not entail the separation of artist from relationships with local context—and in demanding high standards of technical and professional production assistance and insisting on delivering artistic excellence. In other
words, their leadership has been vital in mobilizing systemic changes,

opening up key concepts in a global performance circuit, such as "mainstream," "artistic excellence," and "professionalism" for reformulation.

It has been my aim, through the "readings" of different pieces, to show the many processes at work in the formation of resistant aesthetics in the work of these two artists. All of this work is also instrumental in triggering the changes in context that I have referred to, and I hope that work such as mine, theorizing the cultural politics in such work, contributes towards consolidating such changes. I have been able to discuss in detail only five pieces of Chandralekha's work and six of Zollar's. There are some others that I have referred to but have not been able to "read" in so much detail. What was at stake for me in the choices I made about the pieces I would work through is clear from the theoretical claims I put forward in the earlier chapters, especially chapters 4 and 5. It is not that the other pieces might not yield equally rich analyses, but rather that I chose the pieces that would help me articulate most strongly what I saw in their work. Chandralekha's *Lilavati* (1989), structured through a playful mathematical riddle, for instance, would make for an exciting critique of the conventional uses of Bharatanatyam and extend the boundaries of "tradition" by foregrounding a female consciousness engaged in intellectual—indeed mathematical, not romantic or devotional—artistry. But its power is subtle and it is the one piece that has been accepted by conservative audiences who can still appreciate the minimalist aesthetic that does not insist on producing itself as anti-aesthetic. The point is made in stronger and different ways, however, by *Angika*, for instance, which I found essential to work with in detail in order to theorize the kind of disruptions it accomplished. Moreover, in following the artists' work over time, I have noticed the changes in their aesthetic and artistic philosophy and have preferred to work more with recent pieces, particularly those that I have been able to see in rehearsal and performance several times, and have talked to the choreographers about these pieces when these were constantly present in the repertoire.

This project has not ended for me. I bring the book to a close because logistically, I have to. But I believe this is one of the first of subsequent works that will attempt to theorize dancing bodies in the works of other artists, choreographers whose works I find incredibly valuable as cultural-political articulations. Indeed, this project has inspired me to continue working through a fine balance of understanding the choreographers' "intention" and vision, my own interpretations of the work-in-context, and in-depth embodied research, in order to insist on the immediate preciousness of danced "texts." While working with other artists is important to bust the canonical or masterpiece model that might threaten to sneak in when working with specific artists, this research model also provides me an extraordinary opportunity to engage with work that is inspiring and rewarding, to dance as much as to write, to embody as much to theorize, and to thoroughly enjoy the entire process of scholarly activity. This also because *Butting Out* has constantly opened up other questions for me, about gender and sexuality in cultural production, for instance, and about the drastic changes in global contexts that are demanding urgently that artistic work be "read" in other and vital ways as well. The possibilities of artistic production have also changed dramatically since I began to write this book, and I have, in the process of its researching, found myself caught up in considering these questions in the work of other artists whose work poses very different challenges. Instead of marking a closure in these pages then, I find myself committing to a continuation: the extension of this journey into several other journeys that promise to be as rich and complex as this one.

Notes

Premises and Locations

1. While this no longer needs substantiation after 9/11, it is important to recognize that 9/11 marked an intensification, not the emergence, of discriminatory behavior by immigration and travel officials toward citizens of third-world countries.

2. Here I am referring to the crucial distinction between "cultural difference" and "cultural diversity" theorized most brilliantly by Homi Bhabha in his essay, "The Commitment to Theory" published in *New Formations* 5, in 1988. Here Bhabha argues that "cultural diversity is an epistemological object—culture as the object of empirical knowledge . . . cultural difference is a process of signification through which statements of culture or on culture differentiate, discriminate, and authorize the production of fields of force, reference, applicability and capacity" (p. 18).

3. The reference is to Jacqui Alexander's keynote speech at *Removing the Veil*, a conference focusing on issues of third-world women and women of color, at the University of Pennsylvania, Philadelphia, March 20, 1998.

4. Cornel West, "The New Cultural Politics of Difference," in Russell Ferguson, Martha Gever, Trinh T. Minh-ha and Cornel West, eds., *Out There: Marginalization and Contemporary Culture.* (New York, N.Y. and Cambridge, Mass.: New Museum of Contemporary Art and MIT Press, 1990), pp. 34–35.

5. Brenda Dixon-Gottshild, *Digging the Africanist Presence in American Performance* (Westport, Conn., and London: Praeger, 1996), pp. 3–4. In her introduction to the book, Dixon-Gottschild cites the influence of usage of contemporary African American scholars, Joseph Holloway and Toni Morrison, in her work, to suggest much more an interactive process of presencing rather than an achieved product.

6. This of course reflects the problematic conflation of the category of the "primitive," a concept loaded with notions of crudity, rawness, and such, with notions of "primeval" or chronological descriptors of being early in time. This unnecessary connection of qualitative and quantitative descriptors, this conflation is of course the central concept at work in the deployment of modern as an oppositional category to the primitive.

7. This, in fact, is the same trajectory of "progress" that can be argued to have changed, only if superficially, the material face of a great part of the urban centers through earlier colonial, and later capitalistic and incorporation, endeavors. Such projects seem to have rendered lived conditions of "modernity" and "postmodernity" imaginable in the least—through the apparently uniform availability of commodities like Pepsi, Revlon lipsticks, and washing machines—in locations where these conditions still read as "Western" imports, responding to created needs. But in reality, the fitting on of socioeconomic structures developed elsewhere have only deepened the neoimperialist hold of the Euro-American bloc over third-world markets and deepened the rift between urban and rural.

8. Dixon-Gottschild, p. 41.

9. Deborah Jowitt, "Rich and Strange: Three Women Ignite Asian Traditions," *The Village Voice* 43 (1 December 1998), pp. 48, 141.

10. Ibid., p. 48.

11. Ibid., p. 141

12. Ibid., p. 141.

13. Bhabha, Ibid., p. 7. This essay was, in fact, a response to the some of the debates that emerged during the 1986 conference on "Third Cinema" organized by the Edinburgh International Film Festival.

14. Ananya Chatterjea, "Theorizing As If Race Matters," Unpublished paper presented at Stanford University, 10–11 April 2002.

15. bell hooks, "Choosing the Margin As a Space of Radical Openness," in *Yearning: Race, Gender, and Cultural Politics.* (Boston: South End Press, 1990), p. 145 and 152, respectively.

16. St. Mark's Church Home Page *<http://www.saintmarkschurch.org/>*. Dance Theater Workshop Home Page *<http://www.dtw.org/>*. Brooklyn Academy of the Arts Home Page *<http://www.bam.org/>*. Joyce Theater Home Page *<http://www.joyce.org/>*. Jacob's Pillow Home Page< http://www.jacobspillow.org/>.

17. Trinh T. Minh-ha, "Not You/Like You: Post-Colonial Women and the Interlocking Questions of Identity and Difference," *Inscriptions* 3/4 (1988), pp. 71–78.

18. Ibid., p. 73.

19. Bhabha elaborates on his distinction between difference and diversity, which is key to understanding his comments on cultural change and transformation, in an interview with Jonathan Rutherford, published in *Identity: Community, Culture, Difference,* Jonathan Rutherford, ed. (London: Lawrence & Wishart, 1990), p. 208.

20. Ibid., p. 209.

21. Homi Bhabha, "Introduction: Locations of Culture," *The Location of Culture* (New York & London : Routledge, 1994), p. 1.

22. Darcy Grigsby, "Dilemmas of Visibility: Contemporary Women Artists' Representation of Female Bodies," in Laurence Goldstein, ed., *The Female Body: Figures, Styles, Speculations* (Ann Arbor: Univ. of Michigan Press, 1991), pp. 99–100.

23. Zollar, personal communication with author, 1993.

24. Noel Caroll, "Air Dancing." *Drama Review* 19:1 (March 1975), pp. 6–7.

25. Howard Gardner, *Frames of Mind: The Theory of Multiple Intelligences* (New York: BasicBooks, 1993), p. 206.

26. Foster, Susan Leigh, *Reading Dancing: Bodies and Subjects in Contemporary American Dance* (Berkeley: Univ. of California Press, 1986), p. 46.

27. Ibid., p. 43.

28. Hortense Spillers, "Mama's Baby, Papa's Maybe," *Diacritics* 17:2 (Summer 1987), p. 71.

29. Bhabha, 1988, p. 16.

30. Of course, notations of pieces may be argued to be choreographic "texts" of some sort, but clearly this recording of the grammar of the piece is vitally different from the way the piece lives in dancers' kinesthetic memories and how it is reconstituted through their live interaction.

31. Trinh T. Minh-ha, *Woman, Native, Other: Writing Postcoloniality and Feminism* (Bloomington: Indiana Univ. Press, 1989), p. 22.

32. The comments of Henry Louis Gates, Jr. in his introduction to *"Race," Writing and Difference,* also edited by him, are particularly pertinent here, raising questions about the possibilities of transforming an "expressive" modality that is by definition

predicated upon certain kinds of erasures (Chicago: Univ. of Chicago Press, 1986), p. 12.

33. Ibid.

34. Toni Morrison, "Unspeakable Things Unspoken," *Michigan Quarterly Review* (Winter 1989, pp. 1–34).

35. Peggy Phelan, Introduction, in Phelan, Peggy and Lynda Hart, eds., *Acting Out: Feminist Performances* (Ann Arbor: Univ. of Michigan Press, 1993), p. 15.

36. Patti Lather talks about these ideas in her seminal essay, "Research As Praxis," *Harvard Educational Review* 56: 3 (August 1986).

37. Ibid.

CHAPTER 2 **By Way of Introductions**

1. The *arangetram* is one of the most significant moments in the career of a professional classical dancer. After having spent years under the tutelage of a guru learning the art, the student is finally presented by the guru as an artist. This marks the artist's entrance onto the performance stage and the formal beginning of her career as dancer.

2. Chandralekha, "Contemporary Relevance in Classical Dance—A personal note," *NCPA Quarterly Journal* XII: 2 (June 1984), pp. 60–64.

3. Chandralekha, "The Search is One: Anees Jung Talks to Susanne Linke, Chandralekha, and Georg Lechner," *NCPA Quarterly Journal* XII: 2, (June 1984), pp. 52–55.

4. bell hooks, "An Aesthetic of Blackness: Strange and Oppositional,"in *Yearning: Race, Gender, and Cultural Politics* (Boston: South End Press, 1990), p. 111.

5. Rusom Barucha, *Chandralekha: Woman, Dance, Resistance* (New Delhi: Harper-Collins, 1995), p. 275.

6. Chandralekha, personal communication with author, 1994.

7. Chandralekha, *One More News* (Madras: Skills, 1987), n.p.

8. Zollar, quoted by Patricia Charmaine Warren, "Urban Bush Women 'Cooking' with Dance, Music at The Kitchen," *Amsterdam News* 84: 19 (8 May 1993, n.p.).

9. Cornel West, "Black Culture and Postmodernism," in Barbara Kruger and Phil Mariani, eds., *Remaking History* (Seattle, Wash.: Bay Press, 1989), p. 93.

10. Zollar, personal communication with author, 1994.

11. Urban Bush Women, *Divas on the Road* (Newsletter. UBW, Inc.) Dec. 1992, p. 2.

12. This project is currently being researched and discussed by performance scholar Nadine George.

13. As I have said earlier, the structure of this section is necessarily determined by the different ways in which the two choreographers work. It is also important to mention that Chandralekha does not train her dancers through daily classes; rather, she expects them to continue their training outside of their work with her. The training they undergo with her consists primarily of working through sequences and movements that she describes and directs, of searching for ways to articulate her ideas under her direction. Zollar, on the other hand, begins with company class and thereafter moves on to choreography, something also made possible by the fact that she works with a structure of a professional company where the dancers work with her for full days, and rehearsal directors and stage managers are around to facilitate the process. While this kind of structure for dance companies has so far not been

possible in India for many reasons, it is also true that the different kinds of dance forms that the dancers work with require different kinds of training systems. I have talked more about the ideological base for the kind of choices that Chandralekha has made with regard to consolidating her idiom, while with Zollar, I have been able to give more details about ways specificities of technique work in the choreography.

14. Chandralekha, personal communication with the author, 1994.

15. Chandralekha, opening comments, The Other Festival, 1999.

16. Chandralekha, "Choreography in the Indian context," *Indian and World Arts and Crafts* (April 1991), p.3.

17. Chandralekha, "Contemporary Relevance in Classical Dance—A Personal Note," *NCPA Quarterly Journal* XII: 2 (June 1984), pp. 60–64.

18. Ibid.

19. Zollar, personal communication with author, 1993.

20. Zollar, quoted in Ntozake Shange, "Urban Bush Women: Dances for the Voiceless," *New York Times*, Dance section (8 September 1991).

21. Zollar, quoted in Andrew Dreyfus, "In 'Praise' of Revelations," *Boston Herald* (1 January 1991), pp. 49–50.

22. Shange, Ibid.

23. Deborah Jowitt, "Interior Itch," *The Village Voice*, (31 May 1994).

24. Bourdieu discusses his notion of the heterodoxical, located in between the states of orthodox and paradox, in *The Logic of Practice* (1990), pp. 52–65.

25. Chandralekha Group, Program Notes, *Bhinna Pravaha* (1993).

26. *Chhau* is a semiclassical dance form from the eastern part of India, which has developed to a large extent from the practice of martial arts. There are three major schools of Chhau, Mayurbhanj and Seraikella styles (from Orissa), and the Purulia style (West Bengal), this last being a masked form. Ileana Citaristi is an exponent of the first style of Chhau.

27. The U.S. premiere of this piece happened in conjunction with the first international conference on Bharatanatyam in this country, held in Chicago, 6–9 September 2001. All sessions, showcases, and performances happened in the Dance Center of Columbia College. I have also referred to this conference in Chapter 4. However, this piece has been performed later by other dancers, primarily with Sruti Das and Tishani Doshi replacing Padmini Chettur.

28. Yashodhara Dalmia, Interview of Chandralekha: "Is Indian Dance Decadent?" *Times of India* (19 October 1975), pp.10–11.

29. Jochen Schmidt, "Indische Tanzverwandhingen"(translated and reprinted in) *Sruti* 132 (September 1995), p. 22.

30. Chandralekha, personal communication with author, 1995.

31. Ibid., 1994.

32. Shange, 1991.

33. Zollar in Osumare and Lewi-Fergusson (1991, pp. 74–75). Importantly, what is built into Zollar's comment but not made explicit here is the understanding of the black church as a forum for community building and resistive spirituality, and as an important site for the development of cultural forms.

34. I am referring to Houston Baker's notion of conjure that I elaborate on in Chapter 5: a power of spiritual transformation that dissolves formal boundaries and works through a continuity of flow.

35. bell hooks, *Outlaw Culture: Resisting Representations*. (London and New York: Routledge, 1994), p. 37.

36. Author's notes from rehearsal.

37. Cornel West, "Black Culture and Postmodernism," in Barbara Kruger and Phil Mariani, eds., *Remaking History*, (Seattle: Bay Press, 1989), pp. 87–96.

38. Ibid.

39. Zollar, personal communication with the author, 2001.

CHAPTER 3 **The Body Mobile, Mobilized, Mobilizing**

1. *Vrkshasana* is the second asana of the repertoire of standing asanas, with which series one begins one's practice, according to the Iyengar system of Hatha Yoga. The word *vrksha* means tree, and the asana is practiced in a balance with the standing leg in a steady parallel, as if like a tree trunk, the other folded in on it, and the arms extended overhead.

2. Odissi is one of the forms of Indian classical dance, originally practiced in the state of Orissa. *Tarijham* is a typical syllabic accompaniment for the thrice-repeated phrase that marks a climax or break in a piece. *Tribhangi* is a body position that is unique to and typical of Odissi. It is a thrice-bent position, with the weight resting on one foot, and the hip deflected to one side.

3. Michael Feher, Ramona Nadaff, and Nazia Tazi, eds., *Fragments for a History of the Body*, Parts 1, 2, and 3 (New York: Zone, 1989).

4. Simone de Beauvoir. *The Second Sex*, H. M. Parshley, tr. (London: Jonathan Cape; New York: Knopf, 1953), p. 13, 273.

5. Helene Cixous, "The Laugh of the Medusa" (1975), in Robin Warhol and Diane Herndl, eds., *Feminisms* (New Brunswick, N.J.: Rutgers Univ. Press, 1991), p. 334.

6. Typical of the strategic moves of the French feminists that highlighted difference and urged structural reconsiderations, Cixous uses the metaphor of the dark continent to suggest gendered alterity in "The Laugh of the Medusa," while Luce Irigaray refers to both creative and sexual dimensions of women's pleasure through the sexual imagery of the "two lips." See her groundbreaking essay "This sex which is not one," initially published in 1974 and reprinted in Warhol and Herndl, *Feminisms*.

7. The Fall 1991 issue of the feminist journal *Hypatia* (6:3), entitled *Feminism and the Body*, was a special issue dedicated to these discussions. Vicky Kirby, who has also written elsewhere on the importance of taking into account the material body in feminist theorizing, writes specifically in her essay, "Corporeal Habits: Addressing Essentialism Differently," that the fear of essentialism has led to a kind of "somatophobia." I find useful her suggestion that while "woman" is the embodiment of phallocentric constitutive essentialisms, the female body also exceeds essentialism because it sites too many unresolved questions. Kirby concludes by evoking the notion of a space, literal and figural at the same time, created through an intricate imbrication of discourse and referent, which is the locus of the female body.

8. See, for instance, Ann Daly's essay on the possibilities of such interdisciplinarity, "Dance and Feminist Analysis: An Unlimited Partnership" published in *Dance Research Journal* 23: 1 (Spring 1991).

9. Rajeswari Sunder Rajan, *Real and Imagined Women: Gender, Culture, and Postcolonialism*, (New York and London: Routledge, 1993).

10. *Sati*: Here the term refers to the practice of immolation of women on the funeral pyres of their husbands, an area of heated controversy since colonial times, and strongly exacerbated by colonial intervention in the name of civilizing missions.

11. Audre Lorde, ""The Uses of the Erotic: The Erotic as Power," *Sister Outsider* (Freedom, Calif.: The Crossing Press, 1984).

12. bell hooks, "Being the subject of art," *Art on My Mind: Visual Politics* (New York: The New Press, 1995), p. 133.

13. Ibid., pp. 135–137.

14. Judith Butler, *Bodies That Matter: On the Discursive Limits of Sex* (New York and London: Routledge, 1993), p. ix.

15. Frantz Fanon, *A Dying Colonialism* (New York: Grove Press, 1967).

16. Frantz Fanon, *Black Skin, White Masks* (London: Pluto, 1986).

17. Ibid., pp. 110–12.

18. Malek Alloula, *The Colonial Harem* (Minneapolis: Univ. of Minneapolis Press, 1986).

19. Ibid., p. 122.

20. Gayatri Chakravorty Spivak, trans., "'Draupadi' by Mahasweta Devi" and "'Breast-Giver' by Mahasweta Devi," *In Other Worlds: Essays in Cultural Politics* (New York and London: Routledge,1988).

21. Ibid., p. 196

22. Ibid., p. 257

23. See, for instance, Judith Lynne Hanna's book, *The Performer-Audience Connection: Emotion to Metaphor in Dance and Society* (Austin: Univ. of Texas Press, 1983), where she traces audience reactions to the complex symbology of dance. While it is obvious in the writing that perception and recognition of symbols are dependent on cultural specificity, as well as factors of racial, gendered, class-based locations, the complexity of "seeing" or interpreting hardly comes across in the book. The same is true of understandings of the body, and the political location of the dancing body is hardly realized through the descriptions of movement and cultural contexts. Very different is the work of Sally Ann Ness, where through a continuous self-reflexivity, she locates and politicizes the acts of "seeing" and "showing," and shifts the model of research in this field in interesting ways. See, for instance, her essay "Dancing in the Field: Notes from Memory" in the anthology *Moving History-Dancing Cultures*, ed. Ann Dils and Ann Cooper Albright (Middletown, Conn.: Wesleyan Univ. Press, 2001).

24. Louise Steinman, *The Knowing Body: Elements of Contemporary Dance and Performance* (Boston: Shambala Press, 1986).

25. Susan Leigh Foster, ed., *Corporealities: Dancing Knowledge, Culture, and Power.* (New York and London: Routledge, 1996), p. 10.

26. Ibid., pp. 15–16

27. Ibid., p. 15

28. Ibid., p. xi; emphases mine.

29. Barbara Browning, *Samba: Resistance in Motion* (Bloomington: Indiana Univ. Press, 1995); Ann Cooper Albright, *Choreographing Difference: The Body and Identity in Contemporary Dance* (New London, N.H.: Univ. Press of New England-Wesleyan Univ. Press (1997); and Amy Koritz, "Dancing the Orient for England: Maud Allan's the Vision of Salome," in Jane Desmond, ed., *Meaning in Motion*, (Durham, N.C.: Duke Univ. Press, 1997).

30. Susan Foster, *Reading Dancing: Bodies and Subjects in Contemporary American Dance* (Berkeley: Univ. of California Press, 1986).

31. Brenda Dixon-Gottschild, *Digging the Africanist Presence in American Performance* (Westport, Conn. and London: Praeger, 1996).

32. Jane Desmond, "Embodying Difference: Issues in Dance and Cultural Studies," in Jane Desmond, ed., *Meaning in Motion: New Cultural Studies of Dance* (Durham, N.C.: Duke Univ. Press, 1997).

33. Jane Desmond, "Making the Invisible Visible: Staging Sexualities Through Desires," Introduction, *Dancing Desires* (Madison: Univ. of Wisconsin Press, 2001), p. 3.

34. Randy Martin, *Critical Moves: Dance Studies in Theory and Politics* (Durham, N.C.: Duke Univ. Press, 1998), p. 182.

35. Ibid., pp. 182–83.

36. Ibid., p. 109.

37. Halifu Osumare, "Global Break Dancing and the Intercultural Body," *Dance Research Journal* 34: 2 (2003). Initially presented as conference paper in October 2001, CORD Conference, NYC.

38. Ann Daly, "The Balanchine Woman: Of Hummingbirds and Channel Swimmers," *The Drama Review* 31:1 (Spring 1987).

39. Ann Daly, *Done into Dance: Isadora Duncan in America* (Bloomington: Indiana Univ. Press, 1995).

40. Susan Manning, *Ecstasy and the Demon: Feminism and Nationalism in the Dances of Mary Wigman* (Berkeley: Univ. of California Press, 1993).

41. Ibid., p. xiii.

42. Ann Cooper Albright, 1997, p. 13.

43. In her essay "A final yearning," a conversation with herself, bell hooks talks about her notion of "polyphonic vocality" as the movement between different positionalities that emerges typically from a postmodern social context, and from the recurrent postmodern conditions of "homelessness, displacement, rootlessness, etc.," in *Yearning*, p. 229.

44. Foster, 1996, p. xi. Quoted in more detail earlier in the chapter.

45. Christy Adair, *Women and Dance: Sylphs and Sirens* (New York: New York Univ. Press, 1992).

46. For an example of this, see for instance, Susan Glazer's essay "Political Issues of Jawole Willa Jo Zollar, Artist/Activist" in *Dancing Female*, a series of essays on different choreographers, edited by Sharon Friedler and Susan Glazer (Amsterdam: Harwood Academic Publishers, 1997).

47. Rustom Barucha, *Chandralekha: Woman, Dance, Resistance* (New Delhi: HarperCollins, 1995).

48. Veta Goler. "Dancing Herself: Choreography, Autobiography, and the Expression of the Black Woman Self in the Work of Dianne McIntyre, Blondell Cummings, and Jawole Willa Jo Zollar" (Emory University, unpublished dissertation, 1994).

CHAPTER 4 **Danced Disruptions**

1. *Mandala* refers to the basic position of the body in dance, specific to each dance style, but always a grounded and centered position. Generally, the conception of the *mandala*, the starting point of movement, also reflects the philosophy of the body-in-the-world that energies the dance. *Mudras* are hand gestures that are a vital part of conveying meaning in classical dance and also important in ritualistic and general aesthetic articulation.

2. Fredric Jameson talks about these ideas in his classic text of postmodern theory, *Postmodernism, or, The Cultural Logic of Later Capitalism* (Durham: Duke Univ.

Press, 1991). Interestingly, he describes an "aesthetic of cognitive mapping" as the marking characteristic of new cultural forms of the postmodern, where models of political culture necessarily work with spatial issues as a "fundamental organizing concern" (p. 51). Yet, it seems to me that the understanding of "space" still remains limited here, and what could have been a potentially rich analytical mode in postmodern theory remains, through the work of postmodern scholars in the West who have discussed these ideas again and again, invested with a strong sense of center, particularly in terms of cultural production, even when critiques of political and economic domination are strong and complex.

3. Alan Moore, "I Lost It at the Auction." <http://www.artnet.com> (2001). Also see Tricia Rose, who talks about how the ultimate interest of the downtown arts scene, in "providing the graffiti artists with fleeting legitimacy," was really about "an investment in their own 'cutting-edge image'" (1994, p. 46).

4. Working through transcripts of talk shows and commercials on the now widespread availability of colored contact lenses, Bordo points to the construction of all cosmetic changes as having "equal political valence . . . and the same cultural meaning" (p. 253). This to me is one of the most significant parts of her argument in *Unbearable Weight: Feminism, Western Culture, and the Body* (Berkeley: Univ. of California Press, 1993), theorizing the problematic collusion of postmodernity and capitalism from a feminist perspective.

5. Kobena Mercer, "Black Hair/Style politics," in *Welcome to the Jungle: New Positions in Black Cultural Studies* (New York and London: Routledge, 1994), p. 125.

6. Chutney Soca is the typical descriptor of music produced in the diasporic Indo-Caribbean communities, a unique blend of South Asian and West Indian rhythms and melodies. This is reflected in the name itself, Chutney being a form of singing that evolved among the Indian communities in the West Indies, and Soca, the familiar Carnival party music, is a blend of Soul and Calypso. A popular calypso, *Brotherhood of the Boar*, describes this hybrid form thus: "No more Mother Africa, no more Mother India, just Mother Trini" <http://www.caribana.com/glossary>. Interestingly, though now accompanied by Bollywood-influenced dancing blended in with local club styles, chutney singing initially evolved among the women and then became a larger phenomenon. For more on this, see for instance, the article, "The Chutney-Soca Confusion," by Phoolo Danny <http://southex.co.tt/chutney> (May 4, 2001). I am making a distinction here between practices that in their politics might call for understanding as postmodern even when in the most obvious terms they read as traditional. I am thinking of Arthur Mitchell's work for instance, bringing ballet into the working-class communities of Harlem and creolizing ballets like *Giselle* and *Swan Lake*. These acts of translation, and in effect contamination, of mainstream classics, push me to think about the politics in his work even though overtly he is working with the idiom of ballet and in the United States.

7. Guillermo Gomez-Pena, "Bilingualism, Biculturalism, and Borders" (Interview with Coco Fusco) in Coco Fusco, *English is Broken Here: Notes on Cultural Fusion in the Americas*, New York: The New Press, 1995), pp. 148–49).

8. Angelika Bammer, ed., *Displacements: Cultural Identities in Question* (Bloomington: Indiana University Press, 1994).

9. Fredric Jameson, "Modernism and Imperialism," in Terry Eagleton, Fredric Jameson, and Edward Said, eds., *Nationalism, Colonialism and Literature* (Minneapolis: Univ. of Minnesota Press, 1990), p. 51.

10. Ibid.

11. Salman Rushdie, *Imaginary Homelands: Essays and Criticism 1981–1991* (New York: Viking, 1991), p. 13.

12. Ibid., p. xiii.

13. Bammer, 1994, p. xiv.

14. Stuart Hall, *Identity: Experience of Migration from Colonial Periphery to Postimperialist Metropolis* (London: ICA, 1987).

15. Gus Solomons, Jr., personal communication with the author, May 2002.

16. Susan Leigh Foster, *Dances that Describe Themselves: The Improvised Choreography of Richard Bull* (Middletown, Conn.: Wesleyan Univ. Press, 2002). In this recently published book, Foster begins with tracing the development of improvisational structures in choreography, and her first chapter is called "Genealogies of Improvisation." The complex discussion that continues through the book interweaves layers of information and influences to create a picture that necessarily complicates the previous historicizations of postmodern dance.

17. Sally Banes, *Writing Dancing in the Age of Postmodernism* (Hanover, N.H.: Univ. Press of New England/Wesleyan Univ. Press, 1994), p. 303.

18. Ibid., p. 333.

19. Ibid., p. 304.

20. Sally Banes, *Terpsichore in Sneakers* (Middletown, Conn.: Wesleyan Univ. Press, 1977, 1987), p. xxii. Of course, this marker too could be questioned by a work such as Eleo Pomare's *Narcissus Rising*, danced by Pomare himself to a collage of traffic sounds, roaring motorcycles, and police sirens, a reflection of the highly sexualized and hypermasculinized symbolism of leather-and-motorcycle men. For details, see Arthur Theodore Wilson, "Eleo Pomare: "Pomare Power!" in *African American Genius in Modern Dance* (American Dance Festival, 1994).

21. Yvonne Rainer, in conversation with Sally Banes, Talking Dance Series, Walker Arts Center, Minneapolis, 2001.

22. Marcia Siegel, "Is It Still Postmodern? Do We Care?" in Ann Daly, "What Has Become of Postmodern Dance?" *The Drama Review* 36:1 (Spring, 1992), p. 51.

23. The reference here is to Arthur Mitchell's Dance Theater of Harlem, a black ballet company and training school, established in New York City's Harlem area in 1969, following the death of Martin Luther King, Jr.

24. *Negro Digest*, an important mouthpiece for the protagonists of the Black Arts Movement, was initially published in 1964. It was later renamed *Black World*.

25. Sally Banes, "Is It All Postmodern?" in Ann Daly, "What Has Become of Postmodern Dance?" *The Drama Review* 36:1 (Spring, 1992), p. 58.

26. Yvonne Rainer, in conversation with Sally Banes, Talking Dance Series, Walker Arts Center, Minneaoplis, 2001.

27. John Martin, *The Book of the Dance* (New York: Tudor Publishing, 1963), p. 179.

28. Michelle Wallace, "Reading 1968 and the Great American Whitewash," in Barbara Kruger and Phil Mariani, eds., *Remaking History* (Seattle: Bay Press, 1989), p. 106.

29. All these conversations were held informally after a performance at Bielefeld, Germany, in 2001.

30. Jochen Schmidt, "Indische Tanzverwandhingen," translated and reprinted in *Sruti* 132 (September 1995), p. 22.

31. Ibid.

32. Ibid.

33. Ibid.

34. Gayatri Chakravorty Spivak, *The Post-Colonial Critic: Interviews, Strategies, Dialogues*, ed. by Sarah Harasym (New York and London: Routledge, 1990), p. 8. A particularly poignant instance of this phenomenon is of course Anna Pavlova's refusal to teach Uday Shankar the "western" dance forms which he so desired to learn, encouraging him instead to learn the traditional dance forms of his "own" culture.

35. Sally Banes, 1994, p. 327.

36. Ibid., p. 333.

37. Ibid.

38. Michael Kirby, "Post-Modern Dance Issue: An Introduction," *The Drama Review* 19: 1 (March 1975), p. 3.

39. Ibid.

40. Susan Foster, *Reading Dancing*, 1986.

41. See Banes, p. xvii, "a catalogue of uninflected movements, time was flattened and detheatricalized"; p. xvii, choreographers' search for "the 'natural' body"; p. xix, "simple acts of walking and running"; p. xx, a "reductive, factual, objective and down-to-earth" style; p. xxii, "a heroism of the ordinary"; p. xxvii, the choreographers' refusal "to differentiate the dancer's body from an ordinary body"; p. 17, how the postmodern choreographers conceptualized "natural" movement, which is movement "undistorted for theatrical effectiveness, drained of emotional overlay, literary reference, or manipulated timing." These are some of many references.

42. Yvonne Rainer, chart from "A Quasi Survery of some 'minimalist' tendencies in the quantitatively minimal dance activity midst the plethora, or an analysis of *Trio A*," in *Work, 1961–73* (Halifax and New York: The Press of Nova Scotia College of Art and Design and New York University Press, 1974), p. 63. This is somewhat corroborated in Banes's assertion that, for these postmodern choreographers, a dance was one "not because of its content but because of its context—i.e., simply because it was framed as a dance" (1987), p. xix.

43. This is particularly substantiated when we read reviews and discussions of *O Rangasayee*. See Joan Acocella, *Mark Morris* (New York: Farrar, Straus, & Giroux, 1993).

44. Jowitt, 1998, p. 48.

45. Yvonne Rainer, "Indian Journal"(1971), in *Works* (1974), p. 180.

46. Ibid., p. 187.

47. Generally the repertoire of classical dance forms include pieces that are *nrtta*, pure dance, elaborating an aesthetic framework, without an narrative intent; and *nritya*, or expressive dance, articulating an emotional landscape, for instance, and working through role-playing. This genre of dance, with some kind of narrative intention, is also known *abhinaya* and works through several forms of expressivity. One of the primary of these forms is *angika abhinaya*, or expression through bodily movements, with a rich repertoire of movements for different parts of the body. An important part of *angika abhinya* is the use of *mudras* or hand gestures. While *mudras* are used in *nrtta* sections as an inherent part of an abstract aesthetic, they are vital for *abhinaya*, for they carry immense possibilities for expressivity: *mudras* signify differently depending upon manner of usage and context, which is referred to as *biniyoga*.

48. Rainer, 1974, p. 181.

49. Ibid., p. 185.

50. Ramsay Burt, "Yvonne Rainer and Andy Warhol: Some Points of Compari-

son," unpublished paper presented in Dancing at the Millenium Conference, Washington, D.C., 21 July 2000.

51. Artservices archives, Grand Union Episodes, author unknown, np.

52. Dixon-Gottschild, 1995, p. 55.

53. Fredric Jameson, *Postmodernism, or, The Cultural Logic of Late Capitalism* (Durham: Duke Univ. Press, 1991), p. i.

54. Ibid.

55. Sally Banes, *Greenwich Village 1963*, Durham, N.C.: Duke Univ. Press, 1993), p. 193.

56. Ibid.

57. Ibid.

58. Ibid., p. 204.

59. Ibid., p. 206.

60. bell hooks, "In Our Glory: Photography and Black Life," in *Art on My Mind* (New York: The New Press, 1995), p. 64.

CHAPTER 5 **The Historic Problem**

1. Dipesh Chakrabarty, "Postcoloniality and the Artifice of History," in *The Subaltern Studies Reader, 1986–1995*, edited by Ranajit Guha (Minneapolis: University of Minnesota Press, 1997), p. 264.

2. Ajay Skaria, *Hybrid Histories* (Delhi: Oxford Univ. Press, 1999), p. 1

3. In his essay, "Strictures on Structures: The Prospects for a Structuralist Poetics of African Fiction," Appiah urges the importance of assessing cultural production in terms of contextual and cultural specificities, of using particular ideas and methodologies evolved in other contexts, ostensibly the West here, in ways that simultaneously and specifically subvert the supposed universality of Western categories. Appiah argues: "It is not necessary to show that African literature is fundamentally the same as European literature in order to show that it can be treated with the same tools . . . nor should we endorse a more sinister line . . . show that African literature is worthy of study precisely (but only) because it is fundamentally the same as European literature." in Henry Louis Gates, Jr., ed., *Black Literature and Literary Theory* (New York: Methuen, 1984), p.146.

4. Dipesh Chakrabarty, *Provincializing Europe: Postcolonial Thought and Historical Difference* (Princeton: Princeton Univ. Press, 2000).

5. Lisa Lowe and David Lloyd, eds., Introduction, *The Politics of Culture in the Shadow of Capital* (Durham, N.C.: Duke Univ. Press, 1997), pp. 9–10.

6. Ranajit Guha, "The Small Voice of History" in Shahid Amin and Dipesh Chakravorty, eds., *Subaltern Studies IX*, 1–12 (Delhi: Oxford Univ. Press, 1996), p. 1.

7. Ibid., p. 3.

8. Ibid., p. 3; p. 11.

9. *Devadasis* are women dedicated to the service of the gods, according to longstanding practices in Hindu temples. They were vital parts of temple rituals and were importantly, the first professional dancers and singers in the community. This practice is discussed in detail later in the chapter.

10. *Sadir nac* was the vernacular name for Bharatnatyam, which came to be regarded as debased. Initially renamed as *Dasi Attam*, it came to be reincarnated as Bharatanatyam, a name with nationalist implications, during the cultural revival

movement of the 1940s. This process will be discussed in greater detail later in the chapter. The *Natyashastra* is the ancient scripture of performances that establishes the codes and rituals for classical performance, written by the sage Bharata sometime between the third and fifth centuries. This text has become increasingly significant in constructing a sense of a pan-Indian classical performance aesthetic, and in legitimizing claims for long traditions of classicism in the performance arts of India.

11. Veve Clark, Introduction, in Veve Clark and Margaret Wilkerson, eds., *Kaiso! Katherine Dunham: An Anthology of Writings* (Berkeley: Institute for the Study of Social Change and CCEW Women's Center, UCLA, 1978), p. 3.

12. This comment of course refers to general scholarship and popular opinion. Moreover, no doubt scholars of color working in racially over-determined situations have often found it strategically necessary to prioritize discussions of these artists' work with tradition and in creating choreographic works, over issues such as negotiations of sexual identities, which might often be misinterpreted to reinforce pre-existing stereotypes. This is constantly refuted through the work of scholars such as Brenda Dixon-Gottschild, Thomas deFrantz, and others.

13. While this project is beyond the scope of my book, I want to suggest that there might be much to be gained by examining, from different perspectives, the works of women such as these—whose bodies were the very "modern" dancing bodies in these cultural contexts that changed the direction of dance history—in the service of constructing alternative historical narratives and structuring "different" models and methodologies of dance history, populated by diversely raced, classed, gendered, and sexualized bodies, dancing different politics.

14. Deborah Jowitt, "Interior itch," *The Village Voice*, (31 May 1994).

15. Ibid.

16. Ibid.

17. Program Notes, *Nyabinghi Dreamtime*, Archives, Urban Bush Women, Inc.

18. The revival of Bharatanatyam was in full force in the 1940s and reached a climax with the establishment of Rukmini Devi's institution, the Kalakshetra College of Dance and Music in Madras in 1936. It is true that Kathakali was going through a period of revival simultaneously, with the poet Vallathol establishing the Kerela Kalamandalam in 1930 on a small scale, and then creating a larger institutional structure for it in 1937 for sustained training in this dance form. However, an elaborate dance-drama form, Kathakali is still danced primarily by men, with female roles being played in drag, hence it did not have to work its way through the slur of impropriety that the other dance forms, where most of the dancers were female, had to.

19. *Nautch*, a term that came into being in the colonial era, is the British mispronunciation of the local vernacular *naach* (in several language like the Hindi, Bengali, the word is the same or similar), meaning dance. Initially, the term nautch-girl was used to refer to traveling entertainers, but both because the British did not care about making distinctions between these traveling performers and the temple dancers, and also because the distinction between them was slowly eroding due to financial and sociocultural crises, the term ultimately came to refer to all dancers.

20. Quoted in D. N. Patnaik, *Odissi dance* (Bhubaneshwar: Orissa Sangeet Natak Akademi, 1990).

21. For more details, look, for instance, at Radha Kumar, *The History of Doing* (Delhi: Kali for Women, 1993).

22. It is important to remember that both E. Krishna Iyer and Rukmini Devi,

architects of this revival, were Brahmins from educated, highly cultured and influential circles. Rukmini Devi besides had the approval and express encouragement of British circles, specifically of her husband, Lord Arundale, and of her mentor, the founder of the Theosophical Society, Annie Besant.

23. While I came to know this story from word of mouth, Bala herself tells the story in an interview by Pattabhi Raman and Anandhi Ramachandran. "T. Balasaraswati: The Whole World in Her Hands," *Journal of the Sangeet Natak Akademi* 72–3 (April–September 1984), 15–54.

24. *Apsaras* are the nymphs of heaven, semi-divine, semi-human, women who were celebrated for their beauty and performance skills.

25. Frantz Fanon, *The Wretched of the Earth* (New York: Grove Press, Inc., 1966), p. 181.

26. Ibid., p. 191.

27. Sadanand Menon, informal address, "Bharatanatyam in the Diaspora," Chicago, 9 September 2001.

28. Richard Shechner, *Between Theater and Anthropology* (Philadelphia: Univ. of Pennsylvania Press, 1985), p. 65.

29. Sterling Stuckey, *Slave Culture* (New York and Oxford: OUP, 1987), p. 11.

30. Veve Clark, "Katherine Dunham: Method Dancing or Memory of Difference," *African American Genius in Modern Dance* (Durham, N.C.: American Dance Festival, 1994), p. 5.

31. Houston Baker, *Modernism and the Harlem Renaissance* (Chicago: Univ. of Chicago Press, 1987), p. 50.

32. Ibid., p. 50–51.

33. For more details on how black dancers began to make their way slowly into the field of concert dance, especially of modern dance, in the late 1920s and 30s, and worked with keen observation to pick up on the new trends in the field, see John. O. Perpener III, *African-American Concert Dance* (Urbana: Univ. of Illinois Press, 2001).

34. Perpener, 2001, p. 163.

35. Baker, 1987, pp. 51–52).

36. John Martin, "Negro Dance Art Shown in Recital," *New York Times*, (19 February 1940), p. 21.

37. Edith Segal, "Pearl Primus Thrills Broadway," *Daily Worker*, (7 October 1944), n.p. Also, see, for instance, John Martin, "The Dance: A Negro Art," *New York Times*, (25 February 1940), sec. IX, p. 2.

38. Joe Nash, in Halifu Osumare and Julinda Lewis-Ferguson, eds., *Black Choreographers Moving: A National Dialogue* (Berkeley: Expansion Arts, 1991), p. 163.

39. I am aware that my argument reflects the hierarchization of concert dance over social and vernacular modes. While there is no denying the creative richness that marked all of these performance modes and genres, there are clearly ways in which, through venues and marketing and differences in audiences, the former come under the consideration of "serious art" while the latter are usually located in conversations about technical virtuosity and entertainment. I believe that these early African American moderns fully recognized that the generic associations of black dance with folk/social/vaudeville ultimately limited recognition of the layered cultural and political resonances and artistic merit of their work, and that they would have to enter the field of mainstream modern dance, a.k.a. serious art, in order to demand different ways of looking at their choreographies. They also recognized that this had serious implications for the propagation of black dance forms and that for-

malizing and institutionalizing culturally specific modes of modern dance in training, as Graham and Cunningham had been able to do, would ensure and support this status.

40. Isadora Duncan, "I See America Dancing," in *The Art of the Dance* (New York: Theater Arts Books, 1928), pp. 48–49; Reprint, Sheldon Cheney, ed., 1969.

41. There can be another very interesting way of reading this phenomenon, one articulated by Eleo Pomare as he comments on Ailey's typical strategy. In his essay "Eleo Pomare: "Pomare Power!" Arthur Wilson notes that Pomare admitted to having "analyzed the work and realized that Ailey had wisely manipulated every colonial motif to incite acceptance of 'Black Culture' as entertainment rather than as the raw messages inherent in 'Negro Spirituals': a tattoo and scream against slavery and bigotry," in *African American Genius in Modern Dance* (Durham, N.C.: American Dance Festival, (1994), p. 24.

42. Brenda Dixon-Gottschild, "Stripping the Emperor: The Africanist Presence in American Concert Dance," in David Gere et al., eds., *Looking Out: Perspectives on Dance and Criticism in a Multicultural World* (New York: Schirmer, 1995), pp. 5–6.

43. Sally Banes, *Terpsichore in Sneakers*, 1987, p. xxii.

44. Going by Solomons's own descriptions, these pieces seem to work well within the typical postmodern dance aesthetic of that time: "*Neon* is a solo, set to James Brown music, electronically altered. *Bone Jam* is a nonlinear narrative in which the dancers start in big trench coats and gradually disrobe throughout the piece until they're in their underwear." Personal communication with the author, 25 June 2002.

45. Kwame Anthony Appiah, "New Literatures, New Theory?" in Raoul Granquist, ed., *Canonizing and teaching of African literatures* (Amsterdam: Editions Rodopi B.V., 1990), p. 69.

46. Chuck Davis was one of the conveners of the Dance Africa Festival at Brooklyn Academy of Music, and the artistic director of the Chuck Davis Dance Ensemble. I am quoting from his remarks made at the performance held on 5 June 1988.

47. I am here referring to the announcements made by Davis. According to my personal research Guirard's company is based in Cote d'Ivoire, and has been so since the 1960s.

48. Comments made by Chuck Davis, 5 June 1988.

49. Afropop Worldwide Home Page. <*http://www.afropop.org*>, accessed 20 June 2002.

50. Interestingly, Sister Rose introduced some of the dances by saying that even though they were "choreographed," each step is "as it should be because each step means something." For her, dancing and working in contemporary Africa, this is not a conflicted notion, but more a matter of adapting to the global phenomenon of urbanization, which of course cannot be dissociated from Europeanization.

51. Comments made by Chuck Davis, 5 June 1988.

52. Zollar, for instance, talks about the surprised reaction of several African and Jamaican dancers on seeing her company perform: "You really dance hard!" (Zollar, 1993), a comment that goes beyond marking the typical "attack" in the style characteristic of Zollar and her dancers. This comment about the "dancing hard" of African American dancers in contrast to the "softer" energies of these dancers from Africa and the Caribbean, remind us to pay attention to this kind of cultural specificity, the nuances of difference, even as we locate continued practices.

53. Marilyn Tucker, in Osumare and Lewis-Ferguson, 1991, p. 69.

54. Langston Hughes, "The Negro Artist and the Racial Mountain," *The Nation* (23 June 1926), p. 72.

55. Lula Washington, in Osumare and Lewis-Ferguson, 1991, pp. 41–42.

56. Zita Allen, "What Is Black Dance?" in Gerald Myers,ed., *The Black tradition in American Dance* (Durham, N.C.: American Dance Festival, 1988), p. 22.

57. Stuart Hall, "Cultural Identity and Diaspora," in Patrick Williams and Laura Chrisman, eds., *Colonial discourse and post-colonial theory* (New York: Columbia Univ. Press, 1994), p. 394.

58. Jawole Willa Jo Zollar, in Osumare and Lewis-Ferguson, 1991, p. 79.

59. Both examples are from *Womb Wars*, created in 1992.

60. Hall, 1994, p. 395.

61. Hall, 1994, p. 399.

62. My impressions of this struggle are once again gleaned from the valuable research done by Amrit Srinivasan and Avanthi Meduri.

63. Somnath Zutshi, "Woman, Nation and the Outsider in Contemporary Hindi Cinema," in Tejaswini Niranjana, P. Sudhir, and Vivek Dhareshwar, eds., *Interrogating Modernity: Culture and Colonialism in India* (Calcutta: Seagull Press, 1993), p. 100, 102.

64. Ibid., p. 108.

65. Quoted in Anandhi S, "Representing Devadasis: 'Dasigal Mosavalai' As a Radical Text," *Economic and Political Weekly* Annual (March 1991), pp. 739–746.

66. Amrit Srinivasan, "Reform or Continuity? Temple 'Prostitution' and the Community in the Madras Presidency," in Bina Agarwal, ed., *Structures of patriarchy* (Delhi: Kali for Women, 1988), p. 198.

67. Homi Bhaba, "DissemiNation: Time, Narrative, and the Margins of the Modern Nation," in *Nation and Narration* (New York and London: Routledge, 1990), p. 301.

68. Michael Borshuk, for instance, has also argued that Baker further challenged the stereotypes foisted upon her through exaggerating to an incredible excess the primitivism and sexual threat she was supposed to embody. Michael Borshuk, "An intelligence of the body: Disruptive parody through dance in the early performances of Josephine Baker," in Dorothea Fischer-Hornung and Alison D. Goeller,eds., *Embodying Liberation* (Munster, Hamburg, and London: Lit Verlag, 2001).

69. Baker, 1987, pp. 45, 47.

CHAPTER 6 **Subversive Dancing**

1. Notes taken from a video of Urban Bush Women performances 13 February 1998, Aaron Davis Hall, Harlem, New York City.

2. Deborah Jowitt, "Interior Itch," *The Village Voice* (31 May 1994).

3. Jennifer Dunning, "Ritual and Commentary by Urban Bush Women," *New York Times* (12 May 1994).

4. Janice Berman, "A Unique Power of Sheer Womanpower," *New York Newsday*, (12 May 1994).

5. Susan Tenaglia, "Urban Bush Women," *Dance Pages* (1994, UBW Archives).

6. Sander L Gilman. "Black Bodies, White Bodies: Toward an Iconography of Female Sexuality in Late Nineteenth-Century Art, Medicine, and Literature," in Henry Louis Gates, Jr., ed., *"Race," Writing, and Difference* (Chicago: Univ. of Chicago Press, 1986), pp. 223–261.

7. Anne Fausto-Sterling, "Gender, Race, and Nation: The Comparative Anatomy of "Hottentot" Women in Europe, 1815–1817," in Jennifer Terry and Jacquelyn Urla, eds., *Deviant Bodies* (Bloomington: Indiana Univ. Press, 1995), p. 22.

8. Gilman, 1986, p. 232.

9. Cornel West, "The New Cultural Politics of Difference," in Rusell Fergusson, Martha Gever, Trinh T. Min-ha, and Cornel West, eds., *Out There: Marginalization and Contemporary Culture* (New York: New Museum of Contemporary Art, 1990), p. 27.

10. Stuart Hall, "Cultural Identity and Diaspora," in Patrick Williams and Laura Chrisman, eds., *Colonial discourse and post-colonial theory* (New York: Columbia Univ. Press, 1994), pp. 392–403.

11. bell hooks, "Subversive Beauty: New Modes of Contestation," *Art on My Mind*. (New York: The New Press, 1995), p. 50.

12. Richard Farris Thompson, *African Art in Motion* (Washington, D. C.: National Gallery of Art, 1974), p. 22.

13. Geneva Smitherman, *Talking and Testifying: The Language of Black America* (Boston: Houghton Mifflin, 1977), p. 118.

14. Samuel Floyd, Jr., "Ring Shout! Literary Studies, Historical Studies, and Black Music Inquiry," *Black Music Research Journal* (Fall 1991), pp. 11, 8.

15. Ibid., p. 8.

16. Ibid., p. 10.

17. bell hooks, "Selling Hot Pussy," in *Black Looks: Race and Representation* (Boston: South End Press, 1992), p. 63.

CHAPTER 6 *Angika* (1985)

1. In Rustom Barucha, *Chandralekha: Women, Dance, Resistance* (Delhi: Harper-Collins, 1995), p. 168. I am indebted to Rustom Barucha's descriptions of this piece, which sometimes helped me fill in the gaps in my recollections of a piece I had seen long ago, and the only available video recording of which is of rather poor quality, shot from far away, and hence difficult to distinguish.

2. A *varnam*, which is the most elaborate interpretive piece in the piece, marks the dancer's skills in *abhinaya*, not just her ability to narrate a story through her deployment of the grammar of the technique, but also the depth of her poetic imagination in interpreting the many metaphoric levels of each line of the lyrics. A *tillana*, on the other hand, a pure dance piece, is final proof of the technical skills of the dancer, marking the culmination of the performance, and thus offering these brilliantly polished skills to divinity.

3. In Barucha, 1995, p. 151. In the *Swastika Banda* gesture, the arms are crossed at the wrists before the chest.

4. Program Notes, *Angika*, Chandralekha's archives.

5. Ibid.

CHAPTER 6 *Womb Wars* (1992)

1. Quoted phrases are taken from the spoken text of Zollar's performance of *Womb Wars*. I have adhered to the text in a recorded version of the piece, performed in The Kitchen, in New York City, in 1988.

2. Ibid.

3. In Angela Davis, *Women, Race and Class* (New York: Vintage Books, 1983), p. 205.

4. Peggy Phalen's argument is in her essay "White Men and Pregnancy," published for instance in her book, *Unmarked: The Politics of Performance* (New York and London: Routledge, 1993).

5. Condit, Celeste Michelle, *Decoding Abortion Rhetoric* (Urbana: Univ. of Illinois Press, 1990).

6. *Womb Wars* performance text, 1988.

7. Ibid.

8. Ibid.

9. Ibid.

10. In his book *The Famished Book* (London: Jonathan Cape, 1991), Ben Okri speaks about the Abiku, the spirit-children of the Yoruba world thus: "We were the ones who kept coming and going, unwilling to come to terms with life. We had the abilities to will our deaths . . . We are the strange ones, with half of our beings always in the spirit world" (p. 4).

11. *Womb Wars*, performance text, 1988.

12. Ibid.

13. Ibid.

14. Elaine Scarry, *The Body in Pain* (New York and Oxford: OUP, 1985), p. 64.

15. Such excess precisely marks, for instance, the *New York Times'* representations of Roop Kanwar, a woman who burned to death in India in 1987, and their articles on and pictures of genital mutilation of young black women in 1996, highlighting with the curious fascination shameful things that happen to women "elsewhere." Especially for the latter, refer to the *New York Times* issue of 5 October 1996, where the article on circumcision in Kenya is accompanied by a large picture of a young woman undergoing the ritual, with the caption beneath the picture emphasizing her agony: "'Just finish it,' the girl muttered. 'Just finish it.'" Other, often more gruesome, images are plentiful in the media, especially on television. For an excellent discussion of the difficulty of such representations, look at Rajeshwari Sunder Rajan's *Real and Imagined Women* (New York and London: Routledge, 1993), with particular attention to pages 27–30. Referring to the well-known picture of three sisters who hung themselves from a ceiling fan, in despair and frustration over the dowry system, in Kanpur, India, and analyzing media representations of pain, Rajan argues, "The photograph is a poignant and powerful one and stirred strong feelings of anger and pity all over the country. But its currency has something at least to do with its aesthetic quality: the composition of the three bodies gracefully swinging outwards from a central point, one girl facing obliquely away from the camera, her beautiful face drooping like a flower broken on a stalk, the expression calm, tragic, painless" (p. 27).

16. Obviously, I have used Scarry's thesis partially to move on to other arguments, largely to argue that the embodied representation of pain, unknowable outside of the boundaries of the suffering body, can still work through memory, imagination, and empathy, to effect significant shifts in understanding. In this, I am more in line with Rajan's argument, but I want to acknowledge the importance of Scarry's focus on the body and on the problematic ontology of physical pain. Not being immediately translatable into language does not mean something is beyond representation or beyond comprehension: my objection is to the emphatic logocentrism of the argument. What causes the audience to flinch in successful perfor-

mative representations of pain is the imaginative identification with the body-in-pain, *as if they were feeling it,* even though the exact knowledge of the sensation of pain is absent. And this is what "moves," often induces further thought and action.

17. Rajan, 1993, p. 22.

18. Womb Wars, performance text, 1988.

19. Ibid.

20. Davis, 1983, p. 210.

CHAPTER 6 *Yantra* (1994)

1. Jane Desmond, introduction to *Dancing Desires* (Madison: Univ. of Wisconsin Press, 2001), p. 3.

2. Mary E. John and Janaki Nair, introduction to *A Question of Silence?* (New Delhi: Kali for Women, 1998), p. 1.

3. Ibid., pp. 1–2.

4. Program Notes, *Yantra,* 1992.

5. *Kadamba* is a tree with lush green foliage and large, round, fragrant flowers.

6. Author's notes from the U.S. premiere of *Yantra,* St. Mark's Space, New York City, 1993.

7. Chandralekha, personal communication with the author, 1994.

8. Pupul Jayakar, *The Earthern Drum* (Delhi: The National Museum, 1980), p. 252.

9. *Alidha pada* is a body position where the legs are flexed deeply at hips, knees, and ankles, and turned out, and where the right foot is placed slightly forward of and away from the left foot, so that the weight of the body falls primarily on the back foot.

10. The image of the lamp is interesting here, because the hand gesture used to symbolize it, the *pradeepa mudra,* can look similar to the *lingam-yoni mudra,* for here too one palm is horizontal and the other vertical. In the former mudra, the flattened or cupped palm represents the lamp, and the other palm, which rises from the edge of the horizontal palm, at its wrist, represents the flame. Unlike the flame, which rises from the tip of the lamp, the lingam is surrounded on all sides by the yoni, but like the flame, which needs the lamp and its oil to exist, the lingam needs to exist thus encircled by the yoni in order to fulfill its own destiny.

11. Though I have written briefly about Tantra in the Notes to *Sri,* I want to refer to it in a little more detail here because the conceptualization of the piece, its structure and many of the images, are based on the Tantra philosophy. This non-mainstream Hindu spiritual practice, which is a unique synthesis of *bhoga,* enjoyment, and *yoga,* liberation. Tantra also holds that the body is the seat of truth, so that the man/woman contains in microcosm within his/her own body the truth of the entire universe. Thus, the body, with its uniquely designed physiological and physical structure and processes is the perfect vehicle to attain liberation. Tantra further believes that the human body is organized in terms of several centers of energy, *chakras,* endowed with latent psychic powers. Simultaneously activated, the chakras can release a human being into the plane of cosmic awareness. While all the seven main chakras are located in the vertebral column, the first, muladhara chakra is located specifically at the base of the spine, and the seventh, sahasrara chakra, is located four fingers above the cerebral cortex. The former is said to be the seat of kundalini shakti, the cosmic energy, the primal female energy, which lies coiled three and a half times, snake-like, inside the chakra. The sahasrara chakra, visual-

ized as a thousand-petalled lotus, is the abode of Shiva, the cosmic consciousness, the primal male energy. Ultimate bliss is realized when the kundalini uncoils to rise along the spinal passage, arousing, energizing, and transforming each center in the path of its flow, to unite with the Shiva Shakti.

12. Chandralekha, personal communication with the author, 1994.

13. Rustom Barucha, *In the Name of the Secular: Contemporary Cultural Activism in India* (Delhi: Oxford Univ. Press, 1998), p. 101.

14. Audre Lorde, "The Uses of the Erotic: The Erotic as Power," *Sister Outsider* (Freedom, Calif.: The Crossing Press, 1984), p. 56.

15. Ibid., p. 57.

CHAPTER 6 **Metonymy Mining History**

1. Zollar, personal communication with the author, 2001.

2. Audre Lorde, "The Transformation of Silence into Language and Action," *Sister Outsider* (Freedom, Calif.: The Crossing Press, 1982), p. 42.

3. Zollar, notes from her interviews with Abiodun Oyewole.

4. Ibid.

5. Toni Morrison, *Sula* (London: Chatto & Windus, 1980), p. 48.

6. Zollar, personal communication with the author, 2001.

7. Hazel Carby, "It jus be's dat way sometime: The sexual Politics of Women's Blues," in Robyn E. Warhol and Diane Price Herndl, eds., *Feminisms: An Anthology of Literary Theory and Criticism* (New Brunswick, N.J.: Rutgers Univ. Press, 1999), p. 756. Originally printed in *Radical America*, 20: 4 (1986), pp. 9–24.

8. Luce Irigaray, "This Sex Which Is Not One," in Warhol and Price Herndl, *Feminisms*, p. 354. The first English translation of this classic text (trans. Claudia Reeder) was published in Elaine Marks and Isabelle de Courtivron, eds., *New French Feminisms* (New York: Schocken Books, 1981). The other text referred to here is Helene Cixous's classic, "The Laugh of the Medusa," published in 1975.

9. Michael Wimberly, interview with author, 2001.

10. Zollar, notes from score.

11. Michael Wimberly, interview with author, 2001.

12. Zollar, notes from score.

13. Paul Gilroy, informal talk at Race, Ethnicity, and Migration Center, University of Minnestoa, 12 April 2000.

14. Angela Davis, "Black Nationalism: The Sixties and the Nineties," in Michelle Wallace and Gina Dent, eds., *Black Popular Culture* (New York: The New Press, 1983), p. 320.

15. Elaine Brown, *A Taste of Power* (New York: Random House, 1992), p. 358.

16. Toni Morrison, *Beloved* (London: Chatto & Windus, 1987), p. 136.

17. Brian Ward, *Just My Soul Responding* (Berkeley: Univ. of Calif. Press: Berkeley, 1988), pp. 367–8.

18. Angela Davis, in Monique Guillory and Richard C. Green, eds., *Soul: Black Power, Politics, and Pleasure* (New York: New York University Press, 1998), p. 28.

19. Quoted in Brian Ward (1988), p. 382, from Caute D., *Sixty-Eight* (London: Hamish and Hamilton, 1988).

20. Angela Davis, "Comments in Discussion," in Wallace and Dent, *Black Popular Culture*, p. 328.

21. June Jordan, "A New Politics of Sexuality," *Technical Difficulties* (New York:

Pantheon, 1992), p. 191. This essay was adopted from her keynote address at the Bisexual, Gay, and Lesbian Student Association at Stanford University on 29 April 1991.

22. Zollar, notes from score.

CHAPTER 6 *Sri* (1990)

1. bell hooks, *Feminist Theory: From Margin to cCenter* (Boston: South End Press, 1984).

2. Monique Wittig, "One Is Not Born a Woman," *Feminist Issues* 2 (Winter 1981), p. 52.

3. In Sanskrit, the vagina is referred to as the *yoni*, while the phallus is referred to as the *lingam*. However, these terms are much more than anatomical nomenclature and are associated with the metaphoric coupling of male and female forces. Together, they also symbolize the union of Shiva and Shakti, and, more generally, the fountain of life. In performance and in ritual, the yoni is signified through the hand gesture where the thumbs of the two hands, each open at right angles to the rest of the hand, touch other at their tips. The index fingers of the two hands also join, enclosing a square space between them.

4. Gayatri Chakravorty Spivak, in *The Post-Colonial Critic: Interviews, Strategies, Dialogues*, Sarah Harasym, ed. (New York and London: Routledge, 1990), p. 10.

5. Chandralekha, personal communication with author, 1995.

6. Ibid.

7. For detailed discussions on this, read, for instance, D. D. Kosambi, *Culture and Civilization of Ancient India in Historical Outline* (Delhi: Vikas Publications, 1970).

8. *Taka dimi* is the basic four-unit (ta ka di mi) syllabic accompaniment to foot-work used in Bharatanatyam.

9. *Kumkum* is a vermillion powder made from natural ingredients and is used by Indian women to draw a motif in the center of their foreheads. The initial inspiration behind this practice was to cover the spot of the third eye, a particularly sensitive pressure point for women, from the rays of the sun. Now, however, it is primarily regarded as part of the cultural aesthetic.

10. Chandralekha, Skills postcard (1985).

11. Judith Butler, *Bodies that Matter: On the Discursive Limits of Sex* (New Yirk and London: Routledge, 1993), p. 2.

12. Tantra, a lesser known branch of Hinduism, insists on a very embodied rout-ing of spiritual journeys towards self-realization. Here the male and female in coitus symbolize the coming together of forces within the body, the release of powerful energies from different nervous centers in search of self-actualization. However, while Tantra believes in sexual union as a way of achieving enlightenment, this union must be practiced with extreme restraint and within certain ritual delimita-tions of time, space, and bodily condition. Ultimate control must be exerted while engaged in a copulation pose, for instance, and orgasm, distracting the mind and rendering the enjoyment purely physical, must not be achieved. For more details on tantric beliefs, see, for instance, Ajit Mookerjee, *Tantra Asana: A Way to Self-Realiza-tion* (Paris and Delhi: Ravi Kumar, 1981).

13. Nandita Shah and Nandita Gandhi, *The Issues at Stake: Theory and Practice in the Contemporary Women's Movement in India* (Delhi: Kali for Women, 1992), p. 333.

14. Ibid.

15. bell hooks, "The Politics of Radical Black Subjectivity," *Yearning: Race, Gender, and Cultural Politics* (Boston: South End Press, 1990), p. 15.

16. bell hooks, "Facing Difference," *Art on My Mind: Visual Politics* (New York: The New Press, 1995), p.100.

CHAPTER 6 **Creating Alternative Communities**

1. Zollar, personal communication with the author, 2001.

2. Jewelle Gomez, "Recasting the Mythology: Writing Vampire Fiction," in Joan Gordon and Veronica Hollinger, eds., *Blood Read: The Vampire as Metaphor in Contemporary Culture* (Philadelphia: Univ. of Pennsylvania Press, 1997), p. 87.

3. Ibid., p. 88.

4. Nina Auerbach, *Our Vampires, Ourselves* (Chicago: Univ. of Chicago Press, 1995), p. 192.

5. Ibid., pp. 185–6.

6. Miriam Jones, "*The Gilda Stories*: Revealing the Monsters at the Margins," in Gordon and Hollinger, *Blood Read*, p. 153.

7. Joseph Andriano, *Our Ladies of Darkness: Feminine Daemonology in Male Gothic Fiction* (University Park: Penn. State Univ. Press, 1993), p. 6.

8. Ibid.

9. Gomez, 1997, p. 91.

10. Sue-Ellen Case, "Tracking the Vampire," *Differences* 3:2 (1991), p. 15.

11. Amelia Jones, "Acting Unnatural: Interpreting Body Art," in Sue-Ellen Case, Philip Brett, and Susan Leigh Foster, eds., *Decomposition: Post-disciplinary Performance* (Bloomington: Indiana Univ. Press, 2000), pp. 10–13.

12. Fabio Cleto, "Introduction: Queering the Camp," in Fabio Cleto, ed., *Camp: Queer Aesthetics and the Performing Subject* (Ann Arbor: Univ. of Michigan Press, 1999), p. 8.

13. Paul Gilroy, "It's a Family Affair," in Wallace and Dent, *Black Popular Culture*, p. 313.

14. Ann Cooper Albright, *Choreographing Difference: The Body and Identity in Contemporary Dance* (Hanover, N.H.: Univ. Press of New England/Wesleyan Univ. Press 1997), pp. 172, 151.

15. Jose Esteban Munoz, *Disindentifications: Queers of Color and the Performance of Politics* (Minneapolis: Univ. of Minnesota Press, 1999) p. 6.

CHAPTER 6 *Raga* (1998) and *Sloka* (1999)

1. ——— (Unnamed Pakistani army general). Quoted by Tariq Ali, "A political solution is required: Special Comment," *The Nation*, 1 October 2001 (posted 18 September 2001) <*http://www.thenation.com/doc.mhtml?I=20011001&5=ali_wtc_20010917*>.

2. S. Kalidasa, "Gay Kamasutra," *India Today* (9 November 1998), p. 84.

3. Anna Kisselgoff, "A hovering self, not man or woman," *New York Times* (20 November 1998), p. E6. Interestingly, the points I made earlier in Chapter 3 about the misreadings, incomplete understandings of context, and ownership about radical art making, are once again manifested in this review. With little attention to the differences and constant evolution of dance in India, Kisselgoff aligns Chandralekha's minimalist postmodern choreography with the work of Uday Shankar and Ram

Gopal, who she describes as "the pioneers" but whose work is very different, and is best understood as part of the neoclassical modern in India, often strongly Orientalist in aesthetic. Once again, she talks somewhat patronizingly about "hip young choreographers from India weaving tradition with Western postmodern ideas." I have already argued against such claims, so at this point I only want to quote Sadanand Menon, who critiqued Kisselgoff's review in a letter to the editor, which of course was never published. Referring to what he finds to be a rather prejudiced review, whereby *Raga* could only be reviewed with reference to Kisselgoff's ideas of what Indian dance should be or look like, and where the West has the prerogative of defining the postmodern, he deplores this "Macdonaldization of dance," and points out that "the West arrived at postmodernism; the East was living it."

4. Chandralekha, personal communication with author, 1996.

5. Chandralekha and Dashrath Patel, "The Hindu Temple," *Rediscovering India: Places of Worship* (Discovery of India Museum Project, 1979–80), p. 18.

6. Pupul Jayakar, *The Earthern Drum* (Delhi: The National Museum, 1980), pp. 38–39.

7. Vidya Dehejia, "Issues of Spectatorship and Representation", in Vidya Dehejia, ed., *Representing the Body: Gender Issues in Indian Art* (New Delhi: Kali for Women, 1997).

8. *Laya* is literally *tempo*, and in classical performance there are typically three ways of dividing the time within each cycle of a rhythmic pattern, or tala: *drut* or fast, *madhyam* or medium, and *vilambit* or slow. In *vilambit*, for instance, all the counts of a bar in a 4-count tala cycle might signify 1, while in *drut*, each count of this cycle might be performed as a quarter or half beat.

9. Chandralekha, personal communication with the author, 2000.

10. Annapurna Garimella, "Engendering Indian Art," in Vidya Dehejia,ed., *Representing the Body* (New Delhi: Kali for Women and Book Review Literary Trust, 1997), pp. 22–41.

11. A. L. Basham, *The Wonder That Was India* (Bombay: Rupa Co., reprint, 1987), p. 301.

12. For a detailed discussion on this and how certain forms of the feminine, emphatically non-sexual, are mobilized by these spiritual leaders, see, for instance, Parama Roy, "The Master As He Saw Her,"in *Cruising the performative: Interventions into the representation of ethnicity, nationality, and sexuality*, Sue-Ellen Case, Philip Brett, and Susan Leigh Foster, eds. (Bloomington: Indiana Univ. Press, 1995).

CHAPTER 6 **Dislocations and Roaming Addresses**

1. Quoted spoken phrases are from my notes taken from the score of *Shelter*, from a video recording, Playhouse 91, NYC, 11 December 1995.

2. Quoted spoken phrases are from my notes taken from a video recording of *Bitter Tongue*, Dance Africa Festival, BAM, 1988.

3. Gayatri Chakravorty Spivak, "Who Claims Alterity?" in Barbara Kruger and Phil Mariani, eds., *Remaking History* (Seattle: Bay Press, 1989), p. 274.

4. Cornel West, "Black Culture and Postmodernism," in Kruger and Mariani, *Remaking History*, p. 93.

Bibliography

Accocella, Joan. *Mark Morris*. New York: Farrar, Straus, & Giroux,1993.

Adair, Christy. *Women and Dance: Sylphs and Sirens*. New York: New York University Press, 1992.

Afropop Worldwide Home Page. <*http://www.afropop.org*>. Accessed 20 June 2002.

Albright, Ann Cooper. *Choreographing Difference: The Body and Identity in Contemporary Dance*. Hanover, N.H.: Univ. Press of New England/Wesleyan Univ. Press, 1997.

Alexander, Jacqui. "Keynote Speech." Unleashing Our Legacies Conference. Houston Hall, University of Pennsylvania. Philadelphia, 20 March 1998.

Ali, Tariq. "A Political Solution is Required: Special Comment." *The Nation*, 1 Oct. 2001. (posted 18 Sept. 2001) <http://www.thenation.com/doc>.

Allen, Zita. "What Is Black Dance?" In Gerald Myers (ed.), *The Black Tradition in American Dance*. Durham, N.C.: American Dance Festival, 1988.

Alloula, Malek. *The Colonial Harem*. Minneapolis: University of Minnesota Press, 1986.

Anandhi S. "Representing Devadasis: 'Dasigal Mosavalai' As a Radical Text." *Economic and Political Weekly* Annual, March 1991.

Appiah, Anthony Kwame. "New Literatures, New Theory?" (In) Raoul Granquist (ed.), *Canonizing and Teaching of African Literatures*. Amsterdam: Editions Rodopi B.V., 1990.

Appiah, Anthony Kwame. "Strictures on Structures: The Prospects for a Structuralist Poetics of African Fiction." (In) Henry Louis Gates, Jr., (ed.) *Black Literature and Literary Theory*. New York: Methuen, 1984.

Auerbach, Nina. *Our Vampires, Ourselves*. Chicago: University of Chicago Press, 1995.

Baker, Houston A. *Modernism and the Harlem Renaissance*. Chicago: University of Chicago Press, 1987.

Bammer, Angelika, ed. *Displacements: Cultural Identities in Question*. Bloomington: Indiana University Press,1994.

Banes, Sally. *Greenwich Village 1963: Avant-Garde Performance and the Effervescent Body*, Durham, N.C.: Duke University Press, 1993.

———. "Is It All Postmodern?" In Ann Daly, "What Has Become of Postmodern Dance?" *The Drama Review* 36:1, Spring 1992.

———. *Terpsichore in Sneakers*. Middletown, Conn.: Wesleyan University Press, 1977, 1987.

———. *Writing Dancing in the Age of Postmodernism*,. Hanover, N.H.: University Press of New England/Wesleyan Univ. Press, 1994.

Bartky, Sandra. *Femininity and Domination: Studies in the Phenomenology of Oppression*. New York and London: Routledge, 1990.

Barucha, Rustom. *Chandralekha: Woman, Dance, Resistance.* New Delhi: Harper-Collins, 1995.

———. *In the Name of the Secular: Contemporary Cultural Activism in India.* Delhi: Oxford University Press, 1998.

Basham, A. L. *The Wonder That Was India.* Bombay: Rupa Co. (reprint) 1987.

Beauvoir, Simone. *The Second Sex.* Trans. H. M. Parshley. London and New York: Jonathan Cape, 1953.

Berman, Janice. "A Unique Power of Sheer Womanpower." *New York Newsday,* 12 May 1994.

Bhabha, Homi. "The Commitment to Theory." *New Formations* 5, 1988.

———. *The Location of Culture.* New York and London: Routledge, 1994.

———. "DissemiNationa: Time, Narrative, and the Margins of the Modern Nation." *Nation and Narration.* New York and London: Routledge, 1990.

Bordo, Susan. *Unbearable Weight: Feminism, Western Culture, and the Body.* Berkeley: University of California Press, 1993.

Borshuk, Michael. "An Intelligence of the Body: Disruptive Parody Through Dance in the Early Performances of Josephine Baker." In Dorothea Fischer-Hornung and Alison D. Goeller (eds.), *Embodying Liberation.* Munster, Hamburg, London: Lit Verlag, 2001.

Bourdieu, Pierre. *The Logic of Practice.* Trans. Rich Nice. Palo Alto, Calif.: Stanford University Press, 1990.

Brooklyn Academy of the Arts Home Page. <http://www.bam.org/>.

Brown, Elaine. *A Taste of Power.* New York: Random House, 1992.

Browning, Barbara. *Samba: Resistance in Motion.* Bloomington: Indiana University Press, 1995.

Burt, Ramsay. "Yvonne Rainer and Andy Warhol: Some Points of Comparison." Paper presented at Dancing in the Millenium Conference. Washington, D.C., 2000.

Butler, Judith. *Bodies That Matter: On the Discursive Limits of Sex.* New York and London: Routledge, 1993.

Carby, Hazel. "It Jus Be's Dat Way Sometime: The Sexual Politics of Women's Blues." *Radical America* 20:4, 1986.

Caribana Home Page. <http://www.caribana.com>

Carroll, Noel. "Air Dancing." *The Drama Review* 19:1, March 1975.

Case, Sue-Ellen. "Tracking the Vampire." *Differences* 3:2, 1991.

Case, Sue-Ellen, Philip Brett, and Susan Leigh Foster, eds., *Decomposition: Post-disciplinary Performance.* Bloomington and Indianapolis: Indiana University Press, 2000.

Chakrabarty, Dipesh. "Postcoloniality and the Artifice of History" In Ranajit Guha, Ed., *Subaltern Studies Reader, 1986–1995.* Minneapolis: University of Minnesota Press, 1997.

———. *Provincializing Europe: Postcolonial Thought and Historical Difference.* Princeton, N.J.: Princeton University Press, 2000.

Chakravorty Spivak, Gayatri. *In Other Worlds: Essays in Cultural Politics.* New York and London: Routledge, 1988.

———. *The post-Colonial Critic: Interviews, Strategies, Dialogues.* Ed. by Sarah Harasym. New York and London: Routledge, 1990.

Chandralekha and Dashrath Patel. "The Hindu Temple." In "Rediscovering India: Places of Worship." Discovery of India Museum Project. Unpublished manuscript. 1979–80.

Chandralekha "'68 Poems" Unpublished collection of previously published poems. 1968.

———. "Contemporary Relevance in Classical Dance—A Personal Note." *NCPA Quarterly Journal* XII: 2, June 1984a.

———. "The Search Is One: Anees Jung talks to Susanne Linke, Chandralekha, and Georg Lechner." *NCPA Quarterly Journal* XII: 2,June 1984b.

———. Skills Postcard, 1985.

———. *One more news.* Madras: Skills, 1987.

———. "Choreography in the Indian Context." *Indian and World Arts and Crafts,* April 1991.

———. Personal Interviews. 1994, 1995, 1996, 2000.

———. Inaugural Talk at The Other Festival, Chennai, 1 December 1999.

Chandralekha Group. *Angika* Program Notes. Chandralekha's Archives.

———. *Bhinna Pravaha* Program Notes, 1993.

———. *Yantra* Program Notes, 1992.

Cixous, Helene (1975). "The Laugh of the Medusa."In Robyn Warhol and Diane Price Herndl, eds. *Feminisms.* New Brunswick, N.J.: Rutgers University Press, 1991.

Clark, Veve. "Katherine Dunham: Method Dancing or Memory of Difference." *African American Genius in Modern Dance.* Durham, N.C.: ADF, 1994.

Clark, Veve and Margaret Wilkerson, eds. *Kaiso! Katherine Dunham: An Anthology of Writings.* Berkeley: Institute for the Study of Social Change and CCEW Women's Center, UCLA, 1978.

Cleto, Fabio, ed. *Camp: Queer Aesthetics and the Performing Subject.* Ann Arbor: University of Michigan Press, 1999.

Condit, Celeste Michelle. *Decoding Abortion Rhetoric.* Urbana: University of Illinois Press, 1990.

Coomaraswamy, Ananda. *The Dance of Shiva.* New York: Noonday Press, 1957.

Cooper Albright, Ann. *Choreographing Difference: The Body and Identity in Contemporary Dance.* Hanover, N.H: University Press of New England/Wesleyan University Press, 1997.

Dalmia, Yashodhara. Interview with Chandralekha: "Is Indian Dance Decadent?" *Times of India,* 19 October 1975, pp. 10–11.

Daly, Ann. "Dance and Feminist Analysis: An Unlimited Partnership." *Dance Research Journal* 23: 1, Spring 1991.

Daly, Ann, ed. "What has become of postmodern dance?" *The Drama Review* 36:1, Spring 1992.

Daly, Ann. "The Balanchine Woman: Of Hummingbirds and Channel Swimmers." *The Drama Review* 31:1, Spring 1987.

———. *Done into Dance: Isadora Duncan and America.* Bloomington: Indiana University Press, 1995.

Dance Theater Workshop Home Page. <http://www.dtw.org/>.

Danny, Phoolo. "The Chutney-Soca Confusion." Southex Home Page (4 May 2001). <http://southex.co.tt/chutney>.

Davis, Angela. *Women, Race and Class.* New York: Vintage Books, 1983.

Davis, Chuck. Dance Africa Festival. Brooklyn Academy of Music, New York, 5 June 1988.

Dehejia, Vidya. "Issues of Spectatorship and Representation." In Vidya Dehejia (ed.), *Representing the Body: Gender Issues in Indian Art.* New Delhi: Kali for Women, 1997.

Desmond, Jane, "Making the Invisible Visible: Staging Sexualities Through Desires." Introduction. *Dancing Desires*. Madison: University of Wisconsin Press, 2001.

Desmond, Jane, ed. *Meaning in Motion: New Cultural Studies of Dance*. Durham, N.C.: Duke University Press, 1997.

Dipesh, Chakrabarty. *Provincializing Europe: Postcolonial Thought and Historical Difference*. Princeton, N.J.: Princeton University Press, 2000.

Dixon-Gottschild, Brenda. *Digging the Africanist Presence in American Performance*. Westport, Conn. and London: Praeger, 1996.

———. "Stripping the Emperor: The Africanist Presence in American Concert Dance." In David Gere et al. (eds.), *Looking Out: Perspectives on Dance and Criticism in a Multicultural World*. New York: Schirmer, 1995.

Dreyfus, Andrew. "In 'praise' of revelations." *Boston Herald*, 1 January 1991.

Duncan, Isadora. *The Art of the Dance*. New York: Theater Arts Books., 1928. Reprinted 1969, Sheldon Cheney, ed.

Dunning, Jennifer. "Ritual and Commentary by Urban Bush Women." *New York Times*, 12 May 1994).

Fanon, Frantz. *A Dying Colonialism*. New York: Grove Press, 1967.

———. *Black Skin, White Masks*. London: Pluto, 1986.

———. *The Wretched of the Earth*. New York: Grove Press, 1966.

Feher, Michael, Ramona Nadaff, and Nazia Tazi, eds. *Fragments for a History of the Body*, Parts 1, 2, and 3. New York: Zone, 1989.

Fergusson, Rusell, Martha Gever, Trinh T. Min-ha, and Cornel West, eds. *Out There: Marginalization and Contemporary Culture*. New York: New Museum of Contemporary Art, 1990.

Floyd, Samuel, Jr. "Ring Shout! Literary Studies, Historical Studies, and Black Music Inquiry." *Black Music Research Journal*. Fall 1991.

Foster, Susan Leigh. *Dances That Describe Themselves: The Improvised Choreography of Richard Bull*. Middletown, Conn.: Wesleyan Univ. Press, 2002.

Foster, Susan Leigh, ed. *Corporealities: Dancing Knowledge, Culture, and Power*. New York and London: Routledge, 1996.

———. *Choreographing History*. Bloomington: Indiana University Press, 1995.

Foster, Susan Leigh. *Reading Dancing: Bodies and Subjects in Contemporary American Dance*. Berkeley: University of California Press,1986.

Friedler, Sharon, and Susan Glazer. *Dancing Female: Lives and Issues of Women in Contemporary Dance*. Amsterdam: Harwoord Academic Publishers, 1997.

Fusco, Coco. *English Is Broken Here: Notes on Cultural Fusion in the Americas*, New York: The New Press, 1995.

Gardner, Howard. *Frames of Mind: The Theory of Multiple Intelligences*. New York: Basic Books, 1993.

Garimella, Annapurna. "Engendering Indian Art." In Vidya Dehejia (ed.), *Representing the Body*. New Delhi: Kali for Women and the Book Review Literary Trust, 1997.

Gates, Henry Louis, Jr., ed. *"Race," Writing and Difference*. Chicago: University of Chicago Press, 1986.

———. *Black Literature and Literary Theory*. New York: Methuen, 1984.

Gilroy, Paul. Informal talk. Race, Ethnicity, and Migration Center, University of Minnesota, 12 April 2000.

Glazer, Susan. "Political Issues of Jawole Willa Jo Zollar, Artist/Activist." In Sharon Friedler and Susan Glazer, eds., *Dancing Female*. Amsterdam: Harwood Academic Publishers, 1997.

Goler, Veta. "Dancing Herself: Choreography, Autobiography, and the Expression of the Black Woman Self in the Work of Dianne McIntyre, Blondell Cummings, and Jawole Willa Jo Zollar." Emory University, unpublished dissertation, 1994.

Gordon, Joan, and Veronica Hollinger, eds. *Blood Read: The Vampire as Metaphor in Contemporary Culture.* Philadelphia: University of Pennsylvania Press, 1997.

Grand Union Episodes. Artservices archives.

Grigsby, Darcy Grimaldo. "Dilemmas of Visibility: Contemporary Women Artists' Representation of Female Bodies." In Laurence Goldstein (ed.), *The Female Body: Figures, Styles, Speculations.* Ann Arbor: University of Michigan Press, 1991.

Guha, Ranajit. "The Small Voice of History" In Shahid Amin and Dipesh Chakravorty (eds.), *Subaltern Studies IX,* 1–12. Delhi: Oxford University Press, 1996.

Guillory, Monique, and Richard C. Green, eds. *Soul: Black Power, Politics, and Pleasure.* New York: New York University Press, 1998.

Hall, Stuart. "Cultural Identity and Diaspora." In Patrick Williams and Laura Chrisman (eds.), *Colonial Discourse and Post-Colonial Theory.* New York: Columbia University Press, 1994.

———. *Identity: Experience of Migration from Colonial Periphery to Postimperialist Metropolis.* London: ICA, 1987.

Hanna, Judith Lynne. *The Performer-Audience Connection: Emotion to Metaphor in Dance and Society.* Austin: University of Texas Press, 1983.

Hess, Ron. *Given to Dance: Orissa's Dance Traditions.* Videotape produced by Wesleyan University, 1985.

hooks, bell. *Art on My Mind: Visual Politics.* New York: The New Press, 1995.

———. *Outlaw Culture: Resisting Representations.* New York and London: Routledge, 1994.

———. *Black Looks: Race and Representation.* Boston: South End Press, 1992.

———. *Yearning: Race, Gender, and Cultural Politics.* Boston: South End Press, 1990.

———. *Feminist Theory: From Margin to Center.* Boston: South End Press, 1984.

Hughes, Langston. "The Negro Artist and the Racial mountain." *The Nation,* 23 June 1926.

Irigaray, Luce. 1974. "This Sex Which Is Not One." In Robyn Warhol and Diane Price Herndl (eds.), *Feminisms.* New Brunswick, N.J.: Rutgers University Press, 1991.

Jacob's Pillow Home Page. <http://www.jacobspillow.org/>.

Jameson, Fredric. *Postmodernism, or, The Cultural Logic of Late Capitalism.* Durham, N.C.: Duke University Press, 1991.

———. "Modernism and Imperialism." In Terry Eagleton, Fredric Jameson, and Edward Said (eds.), *Nationalism, colonialism and literature.* Minneapolis: University of Minnesota Press, 1990.

Jayakar, Pupul. *The Earthen Drum.* Delhi: The National Museum, 1980.

John, Mary E., and Janaki Nair. *A Question of Silence?* New Delhi: Kali for Women, 1998.

Jordan, June. *Technical Difficulties.* New York: Pantheon, 1992.

Jowitt, Deborah. "Rich and Strange: Three Women Ignite Asian Traditions." *The Village Voice* XLIII: 48, 141, 1 December 1998.

———. "Interior itch." *The Village Voice,* 31 May 1994.

Joyce Theater Home Page. <http://www.joyce.org/>.

Kalidasa, S. "Gay Kamasutra." *India Today,* 9 November 1998).

Kirby, Michael. "Post-Modern Dance Issue: An Introduction." *The Drama Review* 19: 1, March 1975.

Jung, Daryl. "Tough Troupe Traces Cultural Connections" *Now* (Toronto), (10–16 February 1994.

Kirby, Vicki. "Corporeal Habits: Addressing Essentialism Differently." *Hypatia* 6: 3, Fall 1991

Kisselgoff, Anna. "A Hovering Self, Not Man or Woman." *New York Times* 20 November 1998.

Koritz, Amy. "Dancing the Orient for England: Maud Allan's The Vision of Salome." In Jane Desmond (ed.), *Meaning in Motion*. Durham, N.C.: Duke University Press, 1997.

Kosambi, D. D. *Culture and Civilization of Ancient India in Historical Outline*, Delhi: Vikas Publications, 1970.

Kruger, Barbara, and Phil Mariani, eds. *Remaking History*. Seattle: Bay Press, 1989.

Kumar, Radha. *The History of Doing*. New Delhi: Kali for Women, 1993.

Lather, Patti. "Research As Praxis." *Harvard Educational Review* 56: 3, August 1986.

Lorde, Audre. *Sister Outsider*. Freedom, Calif.: The Crossing Press, 1984.

Lowe, Lisa, and David Lloyd, eds. *The politics of culture in the shadow of capital*. Durham, N.C.: Duke University Press, 1997.

Manning, Susan. *Ecstasy and the Demon: Feminism and Nationalism in the Dances of Mary Wigman*. Berkeley: University of California Press, 1993.

Marks, Elaine, and Isabelle de Courtivron, eds. *New French Feminisms*. New York: Schocken Books, 1981.

Martin, John. *The Book of the Dance*. New York: Tudor Publishing, 1963.

———. "The Dance: A Negro Art." *New York Times*, 25 February 1940, sec. IX.

———. "Negro Dance Art Shown in Recital." *New York Times*, 19 February 1940.

Martin, Randy *Critical Moves: Dance Studies in Theory and Politics*, Durham, N.C.: Duke University Press, 1998.

Menon, Sadanand. Comments at Conference, Bharatanatyam in the Diaspora: Chicago, 9 September 2001.

Mercer, Kobena. *Welcome to the Jungle: New Positions in Black Cultural Studies*, New York and London: Routledge, 1994.

Mookerjee, Ajit. *Tantra Asana: A Way to Self-Realization*. Delhi: Ravi Kumar, 1981.

Moore, Alan. "I Lost It at the Auction." <http://*www.artnet.com*>, 2001.

Morrison, Toni. "Unspeakable Things Unspoken." *Michigan Quarterly Review*, Winter 1989.

———. *Beloved*. London: Chatto & Windus, 1987.

———. *Sula*. London: Chatto & Windus, 1980.

Munoz, Jose Esteban. *Disindentifications: Queers of Color and the Performance of Politics*. Minneapolis: University of Minnesota Press, 1999.

Okri, Ben. *The Famished Book*. London: Jonathan Cape, 1991.

Osumare, Halifu. "Global Break Dancing and the Intercultural Body." *Dance Research Journal* 34: 2, 2003.

Osumare, Halifu, and Julinda Lewis-Ferguson. *Black Choreographers Moving: A National Dialogue*. Berkeley: Expansion Arts, 1991.

Patnaik, D. N. *Odissi Dance*. Bhubaneshwar: Orissa Sangeet Natak Akademi, 1990.

Perpener, John E. *African-American Concert Dance*. Urbana: University of Illinios Press, 2001.

Phelan, Peggy. *Unmarked: The Politics of Performance*. New York and London: Routledge, 1993.

Phelan, Peggy, and Lynda Hart, eds. *Acting Out: Feminist Performances*. Ann Arbor: University of Michigan Press, 1993.

Rainer, Yvonne, and Sally Banes. Author's notes from "Talking Dance." Walker Arts Center, Minneapolis, 2001.

Rainer, Yvonne. *Work, 1961–73*, Halifax and New York: The Press of Nova Scotia College of Art and Design/New York University Press, 1974.

Rainer, Yvonne, interview with William Coco and A. J. Gunawardana. "Responses to India." *The Drama Review* 15: 3, 139–42, Spring 1971.

Rajan, Rajeswari Sunder. *Real and Imagined Women: Gender, Culture,and Postcolonialism*. New York and London: Routledge, 1993.

Raman, Pattabhi, and Anandhi Ramachandran. "T. Balasaraswati: The Whole World in Her Hands." *Journal of the Sangeet Natak Akademi* 72–3, April–September 1984.

Rose, Tricia. *Black Noise: Rap Music and Black Culture in Contemporary America*. Middletown, Conn.: Wesleyan University Press, 1994.

Roy, Parama. "The Master As He Saw Her." In Sue-Ellen Case, Philip Brett, and Susan Leigh Foster (eds.), *Cruising the Performative: Interventions into the Representation of Ethnicity, Nationality, and Sexuality*. Bloomingtion: Indiana University Press, 1995.

Rushdie, Salman. *Imaginary Homelands: Essays and Criticism 1981–1991*. New York: Viking, 1991.

Rutherford, Jonathan, ed. *Identity: Community, Culture, Difference*. London: Lawrence & Wishart, 1990.

Scarry, Elaine. *The Body in Pain*. New York and Oxford: Oxford University Press, 1985.

Schechner, Richard. *Between Theater and Anthropology*. Philadelphia: University of Philadelphia Press, 1985

Schmidt, Jochen. "Indische Tanzverwandhingen." Translated and reprinted in *Sruti* 132, September 1995.

Segal, Edith. "Pearl Primus Thrills Broadway," *Daily Worker*, 7 October 1944.

Shah, Nandita, and Nandita Gandhi. *The Issues at Stake: Theory and Practice in the Contemporary Women's Movement in India*. Delhi: Kali for Women, 1992.

Shange, Ntozake. "Urban Bush Women: Dances for the Voiceless." *New York Times* Dance Section, 8 September 1991

Siegel, Marcia. "Is It Still Postmodern? Do We Care?"In Ann Daly, (ed.), "What Has Become of Postmodern Dance?" *The Drama Review* 36: 1, 48–69, Spring 1992.

Skaria, Ajay. *Hybrid histories*. Delhi: Oxford University Press, 1999.

Smitherman, Geneva. *Talking and Testifying: The Language of Black America*. Boston, Houghton Mifflin, 1977.

Solomons, Jr, Gus. Personal Interview, May–June 2002.

Spillers, Hortense. "Mama's Baby, Papa's Maybe," *Diacritics* 17:2, Summer 1987.

Spivak, Gayatri Chakravorty. *The Post-Colonial Critic: Interviews, Strategies, Dialogues*. Sarah Harasym, ed. New York and London: Routledge, 1990.

———. "Who Claims Alterity?" In Barbara Kruger and Phil Mariani (eds.), *Remaking History*. Seattle: Bay Press, 1989.

———. *In Other Worlds: Essays in Cultural Politics*. New York and London: Routledge, 1988.

Srinivasan, Amrit. "Reform or Continuity? Temple 'Prostitution' and the Community in the Madras Presidency." In Bina Agarwal (ed.), *Structures of Patriarchy*, New Delhi: Kali for Women, 1988.

St. Mark's Church Home Page. <*http://www.saintmarkschurch.org/*>.

Steinman, Louise. *The Knowing Body: Elements of Contemporary Dance and Performance.* Boston & London: Shambala, 1986.

Stuckey, Sterling. *Slave Culture.* New York and Oxford: Oxford University Press, 1987.

Sunder Rajan, Rajeswari. *Real and Imagined Women.* New York and London: Routledge, 1993.

Tenaglia, Susan. "Urban Bush Women." *Dance Pages.* UBW Archives, 1994.

Terry, Jennifer, and Jacquelyn Urla, eds. *Deviant Bodies.* Bloomington: Indiana University Press, 1995.

Thompson, Richard Farris. *African Art in Motion.* Washington, D.C.: National Gallery of Art, 1974.

Trinh, Min-ha T. *Woman, Native, Other: Writing Postcoloniality and Feminism.* Indianapolis: Indiana University Press, 1989.

————. "Not You/Like you: Post-colonial Women and the Interlocking Questions of Identity and Difference." *Inscriptions* 3/4, 1988.

Urban Bush Women. *Divas on the road.* Newsletter. UBW, Inc., December 1992.

Wallace, Michelle, and Gina Dent, eds. *Black Popular Culture.* New York: The New Press, 1983.

Wallace, Michelle. "Reading 1968 and the Great American Whitewash." In Barbara Kruger and Phil Mariani (eds.), *Remaking History.* Seattle: Bay Press, 1989.

Ward, Brian. *Just My Soul Responding.* Berkeley: University of California Press, 1988.

Warhol, Robyn E., and Diane Price Herndl, eds. *Feminisms: An Anthology of Literary Theory and Criticism.* New Brunswick, N.J.: Rutgers University Press, 1999.

Warren, Charmaine Patricia. "Urban Bush Women 'Cooking' with Dance, Music at The Kitchen." *The Amsterdam News* 84: 19, 8 May 1993.

West, Cornel. "Black Culture and Postmodernism." In Barbara Kruger and Phil Mariani (eds.), *Remaking History.* Seattle: Bay Press, 1989.

————. "The New Cultural Politics of Difference," In Russell Ferguson, Martha Gever, Trinh T. Minh-ha and Cornel West (eds.), *Out There: Marginalization and Contemporary Culture.* New York and Cambridge, Mass.: The New Museum of Contemporary Art/The MIT Press, 1990.

Williams, Patrick, and Laura Chrisman, eds. *Colonial Discourse and Post-Colonial Theory.* New York: Columbia University Press, 1994.

Wittig, Monique. "One Is Not Born a Woman." *Feminist Issues* 2, Winter 1981.

Young, Iris. *Throwing Like a Girl and Other Essays in Feminist Philosophy and Social Theory.* Bloomington: Indiana University Press, 1990.

Zollar, Jawole Willa Jo. Comments are part of panel "The Black Aesthetic, the Critic, and Racism." In Halifu Osumare and Julinda Lewis-Ferguson (eds.), *Black Choreographers Moving: A National Dialogue.* Berkeley, calif.: Expansion Arts, 1991.

Zutshi, Somnath. "Woman, Nation and the Outsider in Contemporary Hindi Cinema." In Tejaswini Niranjana, P. Sudhir, and Vivek Dhareshwar (eds.), *Interrogating Modernity: Culture and Colonialism in India.* Calcutta: Seagull Press, 1993.

Index

Page numbers in *italics* represent illustrations.

Bassett, Angela, 276
Batty Moves, 180–92; Africanist elements of, 187, 188; ballet compared with, 181, 188, 189–90; classical and dialectical bodies intersecting in, 133; concert dance as context of, 184; double-bodied choreography of, 189–90; feminist reclaiming of black female bodies in, 131, 184–86, 191; juxtaposition of high and low in, 188; mainstream reviews of, 180–82; and modern dance, 188, 189, 191–92; on politics of aesthetic preference, 181; returned gaze in, 131; "scoot forward" in, 182, 184, 185–86, 187, 190; as subversive, 180, 188–89; Zollar's intention in creating, 180, 182
Bauls, 307
Bayadere, La, 1
Beatty, Talley, 160
Beauvoir, Simone de, 77
Beloved (Morrison), 257
Berman, Janice, 181
Besant, Annie, 142, 151, 175, 341n.22
Beyondness, 21–22
Bhabha, Homi, 2, 12, 16–17, 21–22, 27–28, 265, 329n.2, 330n.13
Bharata, 48, 202, 204
Bharatanatyam: acceptance by official culture, 7; Rukmini Devi Arundale, 142–43, 144, 151, 175; Balasaraswati, 142, 143, 144, 146, 152; basic elements of, 46–47; in *Bhinna Pravaha*, 57–58; Chandralekha moving away from, 10, 36, 44; Chandralekha's *Angika* and, 194, 195, 196–97, 200, 203, 209; and Chandralekha's *Raga* and *Sloka*, 291; commercialism of, 10, 44, 45, 48; criticism of Chandralekha's use of, 61, 116–17, 132, 156; international conference on, 155–57, 332n.27; kinesthetic intelligence and, 25; *nattuvanar*, 45; radical avant-garde working with, 133; revival of, 149–57, 206, 340n.18; as *sadir nac*, 142, 152, 205, 339n.10; specific kind of dancing body produced by, 48. See also *Devadasis*
Bhashan, 306

Bhinna Pravaha, 57–58
Bicultural identities, 119–20
Birth control movement, 224
Bitter Tongue, 311–25; and black resistive practices, 322–24; progress and essentialism critiqued in, 321
"Black," 5–6
Black Americans. *See* African Americans
Black Arts Movement, 115, 252
Black Choreographers Moving Conference (1989), 167–68
Black church, 63, 65, 332n.33
"Black dance" aesthetic, 164–70
Black music: female blues singers, 251; hip-hop, 41, 63, 90, 91, 103, 255; jazz, 114, 162; and politics of the sixties, 258
Black Panthers, 112, 115, 256, 259
Black Power Movement, 247, 253, 254–57
Black Skin, White Masks (Fanon), 81
Blackwell, Emery, 93
Blacula (film), 276
Blainville, Henri de, 185
Blood, 284–85
Blues singers, 251
Bodies That Matter (Butler), 80
Body, the: academic literature on, 73–76; blood, 284–85; Chandralekha on recovery of, 45–46; circuits of energy of, 227, 232, 235, 236–38; of colonial women, 80–82; composite body, 90–91; corporeality, 85, 87, 88, 89, 94; cultural specificity of movements of, 74–75; dance as generating awareness of, 37; the dancerly body, 50; dance studies on, 82–93; disabled bodies, 92–93; Europeanist reification of, 86; as historically charged, 228; as intelligent and multivalent, 25; intercultural body, 91; kinesthetic intelligence of, 23–25, 83–84; as locus of ideological commentary, 25–26; mind-body dualism, 74; *Natyashastra* on, 151, 153, 194, 196, 202–3; the "other" associated with, 28; pain, 214, 221–23, 345n.16; performativity of, 80; the spine, 37,

Condit, Celeste Michelle, 214
Conference of the Congress of Research on Dance (2001), 1
Contact improvisation, 51
Contagious Diseases Act of 1864, 150, 174
Contrapuntal narratives, 138
"Cool" attitude, 8, 163
Coomaraswamy, Ananda, 154
Coq Est Mort, Le, 115–16
Corporealities (Foster), 87
Corporeality, 85, 87, 88, 89, 94
Cousar, Terri, *314, 317*
Cubism, 8
Cultural difference: commodification of, 119; cultural diversity versus, 16–17, 329n.2; Eurocentric theory leaving no room for the "other" in, 27–28; understanding horizontally as well as vertically, 95; West on new politics of, 6
Cultural diversity, 16–17, 329n.2
Cultural studies, 75, 84, 88, 94
Cummings, Blondell, 96, 110
Cunningham, Alexander, 308
Cunningham, Merce, 87
Curvature, 293–94
Cuvier, Georges, 185

Dafora, Asadata, 158, 159
Daly, Ann, 87, 91–92
Dance: academics not taking seriously, 93; African dance, 165–67; "black dance" aesthetic, 164–70; choreographies as not texts, 28, 330n.30; cultural activism associated with, 145; the dancerly body, 50; female bodies overrepresented in, xii; as generating awareness of bodies, 37; high and low art in, 41, 42; literature on, 108; non-normative sexualities in, 89; and politics, 143–44; reading, 26–27, 89; social dance, 2, 49, 50, 160; specialization and commodification of, 195; street dance, 41, 49, 88, 114, 126; visual immediacy of, 26–27; Western historiography of, 1–3, 7–8; "World Dance," 112. *See also* Choreographers of color; Concert dance;

Dance studies; Postmodern dance; Technique
DanceAfrica festivals, 165–66
Dance criticism, 15
Dance of Rebirth, 8
Dance of Shiva, The (Coomaraswamy), 154
Dance of the Red and Gold Sari, 2
Dance saris, xii
Dances that Describe Themselves: The Improvised Choreography of Richard Bull (Foster), 337n.16
Dance studies: intention in, 28; intersecting with other disciplines, 94; logocentric still privileged in, 86; marginalization of, 88, 93–94; scope of, 84; writing on the body, 82–93
Dance Theater Workshop, 14
Dance therapy, 83
Dancing Herself: Choreography, Autobiography, and the Expression of the Black Woman Self in the Work of Dianne McIntyre, Blondell Cummings, and Jawole Willa Jo Zollar (Goler), 96–97
Daniel, Lloyd, 43
Danse Actuelle, 112
Dap, 247, 256
Das, Ramachandra, *298*
Das, Sruti, 332n.27
Dasamayiah, Devaraja, 293
Dashabhuja durga, 270–71
Davis, Angela, 214, 242, 256, 258, 259
Davis, Chuck, 164, 165–66, 342n.46
Dean, Laura, 110, 114, 122
Death of the author, 28
Decolonization, 101, 114, 116, 155
De Flor, 9
Deformation of mastery, 159–61
Dehejia, Vidya, 294–95
Desmond, Jane, 85, 87, 88–89, 225
Devadasi, 193
Devadasi Abolition Bill, 173
Devadasis, 149–50, 339n.9; anti-nautch movement, 173–76; in Bharatanatyam, 142, 148, 151–52, 205, 206; and Chandralekha's *Angika*, 204; marginalization of, 206
Development, 4, 7–8, 107, 138
Devi, Mahasweta, 81–82

Ethnicity: commodification of, 123; ethnic cleansing, 324; "other" artistic production associated with, 139

Euro-American culture. *See* Western (Euro-American) culture

Evans, Minnie, 63, 65

Fagan, Garth, 93, 111

Family structure, African American, 286

Fanon, Frantz, 80–81, 155–56

FBI, 254

Feher, Michael, 76

Female blues singers, 251

Female genital mutilation, 216, 224, 345n.15

Female trickster figures, 40

Femininity: associated with curvature by Chandralekha, 293–94; in Chandralekha's *Raga* and *Sloka*, 289–310; commercialization of, 290; constructed in terms of lack, 308; de-essentializing, 300; as liberatory, 56, 293; as life force for Chandralekha, 299, 300, 305, 306; self-realization associated with, 307; as standing in for difference, 308; weakness signified by, 289–90

Feminism: approach to performance studies of, 31; black women and, 256; Chandralekha's interaction with Indian, 36–37; of Chandralekha's *Sri*, 264, 272–74; Chandralekha's use of Hindu iconography affected by, 56; essentialism attributed to, 77, 333n.7; French, 30, 251, 333n.6; Indian women's movement, 36–37, 57, 272–73; Cardinal O'Connor's critique of, 216, 217; radical, 37–40; reclaiming of black female bodies, 131; women of color and, 172; and writing, 30; writing about the body, 75, 76–80; Zollar and Chandralekha's choreography embodying, 11, 171

Fertility, 208, 290, 295, 300, 301, 309

Fetus, images of the, 214

First world: and globalization, 4; irreducible differences between third world and, 2–3, 4–5; third-world immigrant communities in, 103–4. *See*

also Western (Euro-American) culture

Fist, raised, 253, 255, *255*, 256, 257

Floyd, Samuel, A., Jr., 190, 191

Foregger, Nikolai, 122

Forti, Simone, 122

Foster, Susan: on African American choreographers, 108; on body as endowed with symbolic meaning, 26; on body as locus of ideological commentary, 25; on body in dance history, 85–88; *Choreographing History*, 85–87; *Corporealities*, 87; on corporeality, 85, 89, 94; *Dances that Describe Themselves: The Improvised Choreography of Richard Bull*, 337n.16; modern and postmodern dance contrasted by, 122–23; *Reading Dancing: Bodies and Subjects in Contemporary American Dance*, 87–88

Foucault, Michel, 25–26, 28, 86

Fragments for a History of the Body (Feher, Nadaff, and Tazi), 76

Franklin, Aretha, 258

Franko, Mark, 87

Freud, Sigmund, 76

Fuller, Loie, 2

Fusco, Coco, 120

Games, 52

Gandhi, Mohandas, 173, 309

Gandhi, Nandita, 272–73

Ganja and Hess (film), 276–77

Garcia, Carolina, 70, 245, *245*, 249

Gardner, Howard, 24–25

Garimella, Annapurna, 308

Garrison, Maia Claire, 180, 278, *314*, *317*

Gates, Henry Louis, Jr., 30, 190, 330n.32

Gaudiya sect, 307

Gaye, Marvin, 258

Gaze, the, 22–23; Baker and, 177, 178; doubled in Chandralekha's *Angika*, 129, 205; Dunham guarding against, 144; Fanon on colonial, 81; mobilized gaze in icons, 306; nationalists and conservatives colluding with Western, 116; returned in Zollar's *Batty Moves*, 131; Wigman and, 92

Gender: bias in migration, 317; efferves-
cent body mixing genders, 132; in
Indian classical dance, 193–94;
marking through overt bodily characteristics, 293; masculinity, 289, 309;
polarized understandings of, 290; si-
lencing of issues of, 11. *See also* Femi-
ninity; Sexuality; Women
Genital mutilation, 216, 224, 345n.15
Gherao, 90
Gilda Stories, The (Gomez), 275, 277,
280, 281
Gilman, Sander, 184–85
Gilroy, Paul, 2, 255–56, 286
Ginzel, Andrew, 61
Glazer, Susan, 335n.46
Globalization: flattening process of, 4–5,
12; hierarchies created by, 4; Hindi
film dance as, xi–xii; "others" and,
108; and "World Dance," 112
Goddess-worship (*devi-puja*), 231–32,
294, 306
Goler, Veta, 96–97
Gomez, Jewelle, 275, 277, 279, 280, 281
Gomez-Pena, Guillermo, 103–4
Gonzalez-Torres, Felix, 186
Gopal, Ram, 349n.3
Gopinis, 307
Gordon, David, 110, 122
Gosset, Hattie, 311
Gothic, the, 275, 278, 281, 283, 285
Graffiti, 102
Graham, Martha, 8, 17, 20, 48, 74, 87,
114, 159
Grand Union, 88, 112
Grigsby, Darcy, 22
Grotesque body, 132–33
Guergue, Margarita, 9
Guernsey's auction house, 102
Guha, Ranajit, 141
Guirard, Rosemarie (Sister Rose),
165–66, 342n.50
Gundecha brothers, 58

Haigood, Joanna, 164
Hall, Stuart, 106, 167, 168–69, 170, 186
Hall-Smith, Pat, 277
Hanayagi, Suzushi, 109

Handshake, 246, 247
Hands Singing Song, 241–61; game ges-
tures in, 244–46; "give your hands to
struggle," 241–44; "hands singing
Hallelujah," 251–52; "hand to fist,"
252–58; as mining history, 241; "my
female hand," 249–51, 258–59; "on
the black hand side," 246–49
Hanna, Judith Lynne, 334n.23
Hansbury, Lorraine, 242
Harlem walk, 247–48
Hay, Deborah, 87
Hegel, Georg Wilhelm Friedrich, 308
High art, 41, 42, 103, 111, 153, 159, 188
Hilfiger, Tommy, 102
Hill, Anita, 259
Hill, Constance Valis, 161
Hindi film dance, xi–xii
Hinduism: *Advaita,* 309; art seen as effeminate, 308–9; the body in discourse of early, 228–29;
Chandralekha's use of, 56–58; goddess-worship (*devi-puja*), 231–32,
294, 306; Kali, 208, 308; Krishna, 2,
307; Shakti, 207–8, 230, 291, 307–8,
348n.3; Shiva, 207–8, 230, 307–8,
346n.11, 348n.3; Tantra, 238, 272,
294, 301, 307, 346n.11, 348n.12; temple sculpture, 294–95. *See also Devadasis*
Hip-hop, 41, 63, 90, 91, 103, 255
Historiography: committed historicizing, 258; cyclical notion of history,
206; of dance, 1–3, 7–8; Eurocentric,
107, 137–38; linear chronological
model, 138–39, 196; rethinking,
137–42
Home: migration, 103–4, 106, 317–18;
nation and, 324–25; in Zollar's *Shelter* and *Bitter Tongue,* 311–25
Homosexuality: Chandralekha's *Raga*
and *Sloka* read as homoerotic,
291–93; homophobia, 89, 254; lesbian women of color, 279, 280,
283–84, 288; non-normative sexualities in dance, 89; queer studies, 94,
225; same-sex partners, 134; Western
activists appropriating for their resistance, 292

Meduri, Avanthi, 150

Meera, *236, 271, 298, 298–99, 299*, 310

Meerabai, 307

Menon, Sadanand, 156, 300, 350n.3

Menstrual blood, 284

Mercer, Kobena, 102–3

Methodology of this study, 31–33

Migration, 103–4, 106, 317–18

Mill, John Stuart, 308

Miller, Bebe, 110

Miller, Joan, 164

Mind-body dualism, 74

Mitchell, Arthur, 111, 161, 336n.6

Modern dance: African American influence in, 88; African Americans in, 160, 341n.39; and artists of color, 113; Chandralekha resisting being categorized in terms of, 48; and dichotomy of high and low art, 41; monolithic construction of history of, 9; non-Western influences in, 8; postmodern dance and, 110, 122–23; radical avant-garde working with, 133; Zollar's *Batty Moves* and, 188, 189, 191–92; Zollar's integration of Africanist movements and, 51

Modernity: aesthetic modernism versus, 99–100; arriving in India, 99–101, 151–52; as category of Eurocentric historiography, 138; coalescence with the traditional, 100; disjunctions in Western formulations of, 2; historiography of dance in, 1–3; nationalism associated with, 140–41, 144, 164, 166; "others" and, 107–8; progressive-modern-to-postmodern model, 100–101; third world nations attempting to follow western standards of, 4; "tradition-bound"-ness versus Western, xi; two different readings of, 104, 105; Western disillusionment with early twentieth-century, 113. *See also* Modern dance

Monk, Meredith, 87, 110

Monsod, Trinket, 277, *283*

Monsoon Wedding (film), 118

Morris, Mark, 113, 124

Morrison, Toni, 30, 250, 257

Motherhood, 173, 229, 267–69, 273, 294, 304

Moulin Rouge (film), xii, 119

Mudras: in *angika abhinaya*, 338n.47; *anjali hasta*, 201–2, 230, 238; in Indian classical dance, 45, 46–47, 335n.1; *lingam-yoni mudra*, 227, 230, 231, 238, 239, 292, 301, 346n.10; *matsya mudra*, 302; *pataka mudra*, 227, 229, 238, 301; and the postmodern, 100; semiotic multiplicity of, 126, 201; *shikhara mudra*, 227, 229, 238, 271, 304; *varabhaya mudra*, 270, 297; *yoni mudra*, 227, 302

Muladhara chakra, 235, 346n.11

Multiculturalism, 5, 7, 17, 90, 118, 288

Multigravitational Group, 122

Munoz, Jose, 287

Murphy, Eddie, 276

Music videos, 131

Mystic Masseur (film), 118

"Naipaul fallacy," 139

Nair, Janaki, 225, 240

Namashivayam, Shangita, 58

Nandakumar, 197, 207

Nandikesvara, 194

Napier, 66, 67

Naravahana, 131, 207, 207–8

Narcissus Rising, 337n.20

Nash, Joe, 160

Nationalism: Afrocentricity, 6, 141, 163; as jingoist and dangerous, 130; modernity associated with, 140–41, 144, 164, 166; national art forms, 155; and repressive notions of sexuality, 171; tradition and, 141; women used as pawns by, 172

Nation-states, 101

Native Americans, 8, 224, 279

Nattuvanar, 45, 230

"Natural" rhythm, 25

Natyashastra, 151, 153, 194, 196, 202–3

"Nautch girls," 150, 154, 173–76, 340n.19

Navagraha, 193

"Negro Dance," 160

Negro Digest, The, 111, 337n.24

Neo-colonialism, 4, 309, 329n.7

Neon, 164, 342n.44

Ness, Sally Ann, 334n.23

Netranritya, 61

New Dance Group, 110

New Orleans, 43
Nijinsky, Vaslav, 2
Non-resident Indian (NRI) phenomenon, xi–xii
Non-Western culture: differences within, 13; irreducible differences between West and, 2–3; postmodern dance influenced by, 110, 114; tradition associated with, 8; un-freedom associated with, 9; as used in this study, 3–5; Western culture influenced by, 8–9; Western yearning for cultural forms of, 113–14, 116, 117–18. *See also* Third world
Norms, cultural specificity of, 119
Nritta, 45, 126, 203–4, 209, 338n.47
Nritya, 204, 338n.47
Nyabinghi Dreamtime, 53–55, 54, 67, 68, 67–69, 145–48

O'Connor, Cardinal, 216, 217
Odissi, 74, 152, 153, 333n.2
Offut, Treva, 53, 54, 55, *314, 317*
"Of Hummingbirds and Channel Swimmers" (Daly), 91
Okri, Ben, 345n.10
One More News (Chandralekha), 39
Oral traditions, 138
O Rangasayee, 124
Ordway Theater, 15
Organizing genres, 99
Orientalism, 1–2, 7, 154
Osumare, Halifu, 91
"Other," the: the body associated with, 28; commodification of artifacts from "other" cultures, xi; ethnicity associated with, 139; lesbian women of color, 279; modernity transformed and translated by, 107–8; third-world immigrant communities in first world, 103–4; Western conceptions of, 1–2; Western culture borrowing from, 9, 125
Oyewole, Abiodun, 246, 247, 252

Pain, 214, 221–23, 345n.16
Pakistan, 290
Pandian V., 199
Paris, Carl, 1
Parks, Rosa, 114, 142, 256, 260

Partial identifications, 279
Passing, 288
Pataka mudra, 227, 229, 238, 301
Pavlova, Anna, 338n.34
Paxton, Steve, 110, 122
Peltier, Leonard, 260
Peoples of color: as "black," 5–6; in dance of, releasing out of hip and butt, 19–20; dancers, 108; and the grotesque body, 132–33; and politics of location, 134; progressive and avant-garde borrowing from, 102–3; resistance movements of, 260; response to white Western postmodern, 106–7; struggles to keep alive or revive traditions, 108, 129–31. *See also* African Americans; Artists of color; Women of color
Performance arts: audience required for, 139; body knowledge in, 23–24; Butler on performance, 80; feminist scholars not addressing, 77–78; feminist theory on the body in, 31; visual immediacy of, 94. *See also* Dance
Phelan, Peggy, 31, 214
Philippine Islands, 279
Photography, 79, 135
Picasso, Pablo, 8
Politics: dance and, 143–44; of defiant hope, 42, 135; of disidentification, 287–88; identity politics, 16, 105–6, 119; of location, 134; of solidarity, 95
Polyphonic vocality, 94, 335n.43
Pomare, Eleo, 111, 120, 337n.20, 342n.41
Postcolonial studies, 33, 75, 76, 81
Postmodern dance: African Americans in, 1, 88, 108; artists of color in, 108–21; avant-garde practice associated with, 120–21, 163; and crisis in meaning, 121–25; and dichotomy of high and low art, 41; in Indian and African American context, 128–32; Latino, 119–20; literature on, 108; modern dance contrasted with, 110, 122–23; monolithic construction of history of, 9; non-Western influences in, 110, 114; stages in development of, 109–10
Postmodernity: African American resistance modes as postmodern, 42;

Postmodernity (*continued*)
Africanist influence on, 123, 127–28, 163; alternative postmoderns, 10, 13, 42, 72, 98, 104–6; citation as characteristic of, 123–24; continuity-yet-rupture characterizing, 168–69; cultural specificity associated with, 141; economics of, 101–3; as Euro-American cultural production, 9–10; flattening effects of, 12; gaps in postmodern movement, 42; hegemonic investments in limiting postmodernism, 139; hybridity as characteristic of, 124; migration and dislocation as persistent tropes of, 104; peoples of color's response to white Western, 106–7; progressive-modern-to-postmodern model, 100–101; radical postmodernism, 133–35; reflexive choreographers, 87–88; relationality of, 108; structural concerns of, 130; technique-less-ness of, 127; and third-world art, 100; version of universal subject of, 104; Western formulations of, 2; of Zollar and Chandralekha's work, 20–22. *See also* Postmodern dance
Pradakshina, 293
Praise House, 56, 63–67
Prentice, Beverley, *282, 312, 314, 317*
Primal Energy, 193
Primitive Mysteries, 8
Primitivism, 8, 116, 132, 138, 161, 178, 329n.6
Primus, Pearl, 113, 143, 145, 158, 159, 160
Princesse Tam Tam (film), 177
Progress: of black artists, 161; Chandralekha's *Sri* and, 265; in "civilizing mission," 101; in Duncan's view of the future, 162; Eurowestern development as, 107; third world cultures attempting to follow Western standards of, 4, 100, 329n.7; in Zollar's *Bitter Tongue,* 321
Pro-life movement, 214, 217, 219
Prostitution, 150, 174, 175, 204

Queens Museum of Art, 14, 61
Queer studies, 94, 225

Race: African Americans experiencing racism, 4; dance allowing immediate recognition of, 26; discrepant power relations and, 3; in distinguishing first and third worlds, 3; effervescent body mixing races, 132; global woman's movement hindered by racism, 172; "great distraction of Whiteness," 13; racializations in dance, 88; racial pride, 130; "reverse racisms," 5; in Zollar's *Bones and Ash,* 277, 278, 279. *See also* Peoples of color
Radha, 8
Raga, 289–310; criticisms of, 290–93; on femininity as liberatory, 56, 293; femininity associated with curvature in, 293–94; final scene in, 310; Jowitt's review of, 9; middle section of, 295; opening scenes of, 295–96; read as homoerotic, 291–93; the sexual and the spiritual intersecting in, 133; slow unfolding in, 292–93; Western influence ascribed to, 290
Rainer, Yvonne: analytical postmodern dance of, 109; on images of female body, 22–23; *India Journal,* 2, 125, 126, 127; Indian epic and drama drawn on by, 114; on Kathakali, 125, 126, 127; *The Man Who Envied Women,* 23; and performance in support of Black Panthers, 112; *Trio A,* 100, 125, 126, 163, 338n.42; on "uninterrupted surface" and "nonreferential forms," 123; and variations among Judson group, 110–11
Rainey, Ma, 251
Raised fist symbol, 253, 255, *255,* 256, 257
Rajan, Rajeswari Sunder, 78, 222, 345n.15
Ramakrishna Paramahansa, 308–9
Rao, Maya, xiii
Rape, 213, 220–21, 223, 224
Rasa, 48
Rastafarianism, 67, 146–47
Ray, Satyajit, 143
Reading: Foster paying attention to, 88; interpretive, 25–27; Martin taking on self-consciously, 89

Wild women's tradition, 40
Williams, Venus and Serena, 25
Wilson, Arthur, 342n.41
Wilson, Reggie, 162
Wilson, Robert, 109
Wimberly, Michael, 247, 252, 253
Winborne, Valerie, 146, 220, 312, *314*, *317*
Wittig, Monique, 264–65, 269
Womanism, 172
Womb Wars, 212–24; adoption in, 217, 223; chorus of women in, 216; erasure of female body in, 214; on girls valued less than boys, 216–17; layered time frame in, 213, 219; opening moments of, 212; on pain, 214, 221–23; patriarchal practices foregrounded in, 213; rape in, 213, 220–21, 223, 224; recollection of entry into the womb wars, 215; on religious opposition to abortion, 216–17; remembrance of her own birth, 215
Women: auto-eroticism in, 250, 259, 304; Chandralekha reconceptualizing female body, 47; expressive femininity foregrounded by Zollar, 56; female bodies overrepresented in dance, xii; genital mutilation, 216, 224, 345n.15; lack seen as defining, 251; mass movements of indigenous, 273; men coming from bodies of, 228, 304; menstrual blood, 284; motherhood, 173, 229, 267–69, 273, 294, 304; and politics of location, 134; prostitution, 150, 174, 175, 204; rape, 213, 220–21, 223, 224; sensation associated with, 25; as silent bearers of history, 228; wild women's tradition, 40; writing about female body, 76–80. *See also* Femininity; Feminism; Women of color
Women and Dance: Sylphs and Sirens (Adair), 95
Women of color: colonial, 80–82; as disrupting meaning and signification system, 94–95; European history of misperception of, 184–86; and feminism, 172; feminist reclaiming of black female bodies, 131; the gaze and, 22–23; Latina choreographers,

119–20; lesbian, 279, 280, 283–84, 288; and migration, 317–18; nationalism using as pawns, 172; resistive artistic production by, 12–13; in saris, xii–xiii, 131; stereotypes of, 181; and violence, 282; writing about the female body, 78–80; Zollar and Chandralekha employing women dancers, 11
Women's India Association, 173
"World Dance," 112
Wretched of the Earth, The (Fanon), 155–56
Wright, Christalyn, *282*
Writing, 29–31, 89, 95
Writing Dancing in the Age of Postmodernism (Banes), 109

Yantra, 226, 227
Yantra: Dance Diagrams, 225–40; on ancientness of female body, 228; beginning of, 226–27, 232; on circuits of energy, 227, 232, 235, 236–38; double-entendre of, 233; the erotic in, 239–40; layering of thematic material in, 238; and Lorde's view of the erotic, 239; on men coming from women's bodies, 228, 304; musical accompaniment of, 233; passion as suffusing, 226; second section of, 229–31; slow unfolding in, 292; *Soundarya Lahari* inspiring, 226; space as live medium in, 235; tradition in, 234, 239; and *varana*, 231
Yin Mei, 9
Yoga: in Chandralekha's *Angika*, 194, 196, 197–98, 200, 202; in Chandralekha's choreography, 10, 44, 47, 49, 117, 132, 293; in Chandralekha's *Yantra*, 226, 230, 232, 233, 234, 235, 237, 238; Graham and, 9; postmodern choreographers inspired by, 114; the spine in, 272; visualizations of nerve centers in, 301; in Zollar's training methodology, 51
Yoni, 266, 267, 348n.3
Yoni mudra, 227, 302
Yoruba, 219, 345n.10
Young, Iris, 77

Zamir, Batya, 24, 122
"Zip-zap-boing" game, 52
Zollar, Jawole Willa Jo, 10–11
  as academic: at Temple University
    speaker series, 18; at University of
    Florida, 11; at University of Min-
    nesota, 314
  author becomes interested in, 18
  author's working relationship with, 32
  characteristics of work of: expressive
    femininity foregrounded in, 56;
    feminism of, 11, 171; high stan-
    dards of professionalism of, 326;
    interweaving shifts in, 55–56; inter-
    weaving styles in, 50–51; process
    orientation of, 70, 72; response to
    the gaze, 23; spirituality in, 56,
    63–70; tradition in, 21
  as choreographer: collaborative work
    of, 162; in development of post-
    modern dance, 110; Dunham and
    Primus influencing, 142–48; hos-
    tility encountered while traveling,
    xiv; intervention into notions of
    technique by, 24; literature about,
    95–97; as marginal, 13–15; and
    New Epic Dance, 93; as postmod-
    ern feminist, 97; postmodernism
    of, 20–22; as radicalizing cultural
    production in her community, xiv;
    success of, 14; and technique, 44,

49–56; training methods of, 44,
    49–52, 331n.13; women dancers
    employed by, 11
  community-based work of, 15, 42–44
  as dancer: apprenticeship of, 50; as
    idiosyncratic, 73
  politics of: as cultural activist, 35; poli-
    tics of defiant hope of, 42; radical
    feminism of, 37–40
  success of, 13–14; Capezio Award for,
    13
  views of: on African American iden-
    tity, 169–70; on African and Ja-
    maican reactions to her work,
    342n.52; on dance as about people
    dancing, 41; on dance criticism, 15
  works of: *Anarchy, Wild Women, and
    Dinah*, 40; *I Don't Know, But I Been
    Told*, *If You Keep Dancin' You'll
    Never Grow Old*, 40–42, *41*; *Life
    Dance I . . . The Magician: The Re-
    turn of the She*, 98; *Nyabinghi
    Dreamtime*, 53–55, *54*, *67*, *68*,
    67–69, 145–48; *Praise House*, 56,
    63–67; *Self-Portrait*, 71–72, 129, 133;
    Transitions, 69–70, *70*. See also
    *Batty Moves; Bitter Tongue; Bones
    and Ash; Hands Singing Song; Shel-
    ter; Womb Wars*
Zou Zou (film), 177
Zuni Icosahedron, 113

ABOUT THE AUTHOR

Ananya Chatterjea is a dance scholar whose 1999 article on Chandralekha has quickly become part of the required reading for dance history students. She is Assistant Professor of Dance at the University of Minnesota and a trained classical dancer, who explores the role of women through contemporary modes of expression. She recently received an endowment from the McKnight Arts and Humanities Foundation.